KT-167-604

Sardinia

Paula Hardy

Destination Sardinia

Sardinia (Sardegna) is the maverick of the Mediterranean. It is Italy's second-largest island after Sicily, but to see it in this context is to miss the essence of a place DH Lawrence felt had 'slipped through the net of European civilisation' to retain its own instinctive passions and fiercely independent spirit.

Sardinia's unique identity and strikingly self-assured character have deep roots in a mysterious prehistoric past peopled by an ancient and unidentified populace who built the island's 7000 *nuraghi* (stone towers), *domus de janas* (literally 'fairy houses'; tombs cut into rock) and *tombe di giganti* (literally 'giants' tombs'; ancient mass graves), sacred wells and Bronze Age villages. The list reads like a location shoot for *Lord of the Rings*, and Sardinia's almost Celtic landscape of ragged hills and twisting valleys, dominated by the eerie, snow-mantled Gennargentu massif, really does have an otherworldly atmosphere.

'But what of the Costa Smeralda and the pearly white beaches?' I hear you ask. Sardinia has some of the most idyllic stretches of coast in the Mediterranean, and the English language doesn't contain sufficient adjectives to describe the varied blue, green and, in the deepest shadows, purple hues of the island's waters. The coast still represents the tourist hot spots but with a refreshingly slim choice of souvenir stalls, and many areas remain completely devoid of development.

The sea and Sardinia have always had a tricky rapport. All sorts of people have arrived from across the water, and time and again the Sardinians have fought oppression and poverty. To their credit, they have resisted cultural homogenisation to retain a mosaic of wildly different provinces and cities, each with its own flavour, from the sultry air of Cagliari to the briny taste of Catalan Alghero and resolutely rural Barbagia. This diversity combined with the warm good nature of the Sardinians makes this beautiful island one of the last great surprises of the Mediterranean.

DAMIEN SIM

Highlights

Prosperous Alghero (p153) looks out to sea from its prime location on the northwest coast

Enjoy the view from the Grotta del Bue Marino out to the Golfo di Orosei (p215)

Swimmers flock to the refreshing Spiaggia della Pelosa (p152)

PHILIP & KAREN S

The scenic tracks of the northeast coast near Santa Teresa di Gallura (p186) are a prime walking spot

Soak up the atmosphere in the former Roman settlement of Bosa (p129)

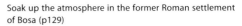

DOUG MCKINLAY

WADE EAKLE

Explore the Cattedrale di Santa Maria, at the medieval heart of Cagliari (p62)

Craggy Isola Tavolara (p174) looms across
the water from Porto San Paolo

Marvel at the stalactites and stalagmites
of the Grotta di Nettuno (p165), Capo
Caccia

The ancient Nuraghe Losa (p128), near Paulilatino, is awe-inspiring

DALLAS STRI

Dive the inviting waters off the Arcipelago di La Maddalena (p182)

The sun lights up the buildings in the
centre of Cagliari (p62)

ROCCO FASANO

DALLAS STRI

The fortress ramparts in Castelsardo (p148) are a
reminder of the town's medieval past

Tour the World Heritage site of
the Nuraghe Su Nuraxi (p113)

Laze the afternoon away in pretty Santa Teresa di
Gallura (p186).

An electrifying horse race is at the heart of Sedilo's S'Ardia festival (p128)

8

EMILY RIDDELL

Meander amid the ruins of a Roman villa at Nora (p109), near Pula

See history come alive on the walls of Orgosolo (p204)

DOUG MCKINLAY

Contents

Regional Map Contents

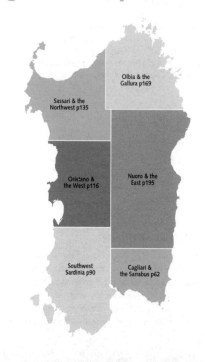

Olbia & the
Gallura p169

Sassari & the
Northwest p135

Oristano &
the West p116

Nuoro & the
East p195

Southwest
Sardinia p90

Cagliari &
the Sarrabus p62

The Author

PAULA HARDY

A peripatetic childhood between various African countries and Europe led Paula inevitably to guidebook writing and to an enduring fascination with the Mediterranean, that mini-sea from which so much culture and history have evolved. Writing projects have taken her through southern Italy, Andalucía, Morocco and Libya, and to Sardinia's closest neighbours, Sicily and Corsica. But despite repeated visits the island refuses to conform to any comfortable preconceptions and continues to surprise and delight as it matures into a very different tourist destination.

When not struggling up mountains and down canyons to work off the worst excesses of Sardinian restaurants, Paula lives in London and contributes travel articles to a variety of newspapers and travel magazines.

My Sardinia

What they say about Sardinia being an island of experiences rather than sights is true. I can't think of much that beats the experience of trekking down the Gola Su Gorruppu (p217) or to the windy heights of Tiscali (p204). My favourite diving spots are the underwater ruins of Nora (p109) and the perfect little island of San Pietro (p101); I also enjoyed diving with Diving Centre Capo Galera (p165).

You can have terrific experiences if you time your trip to coincide with village events. The villages of the Monti Ferru (p125) are great for these, and I loved the market in San Pantaleo (p178). If you can catch a festival in Barbagia (p205) you're in for a real treat, and the murals in Orgosolo (p204) are highlights. I'm a bit of a foodie, so a big enjoyment for me are the restaurants of Alghero (p153), Cagliari (p62) and Olbia (p168).

Getting Started

Sardinia may be an island, but it's a big one. Even with your own transport, you may be surprised how long it can take to get from A to B. In many places the tourist infrastructure is also very basic and it really pays to come prepared. If time is limited you should consider trying to organise trekking, climbing and diving activities before you arrive. Also be aware that changeable weather in the autumn and spring can play havoc with carefully laid plans.

Undoubtedly the most popular (and expensive) areas are the Costa Smeralda, Alghero and Cagliari, but for the independent traveller there is much to discover away from these hot spots. Although the island is well serviced by charter flights and ferries, a potential problem is Sardinia's popularity during summer. You will need to book a long way in advance if you're travelling in July and August. In general the only way to really see Sardinia is to hire your own vehicle; train and bus services are reliable but can be limited in the interior, especially outside high season.

WHEN TO GO

Sardinia is famous for its seven-month summer and in a good year you could be happily stretched out on the beaches from April till as late as October, when temperatures still hover around 20°C. Touring the interior is best between March and June, when many towns celebrate their patron saints' day (see p227). It's great fun to arrange an itinerary around one of these festivals, but book well in advance.

Average temperatures are 25°C in summer (a little hotter inland) and around 8°C to 10°C in winter (a little colder inland, naturally decreasing with altitude). Rain falls mainly in spring and autumn, and the mountainous interior receives the bulk of it, which falls as snow on the higher peaks; the plains and coastal areas in the east and south are significantly drier. The ideal time for walking in the Gennargentu is between March and June, when the wildflowers are in bloom and the countryside is at its greenest.

See Climate Charts (p225) for more information.

DON'T LEAVE HOME WITHOUT...

- Valid travel insurance (p229)
- Your ID card or passport and visa if required (p234)
- Driving licence and car documents if driving, along with appropriate car insurance (p246)
- An under-the-clothes money belt or shoulder wallet, for your money and documents
- A small Italian dictionary and/or phrasebook
- Sunglasses, a towel, a beach bag and a hat
- A universal washbasin plug and an adaptor for electrical appliances
- A small pack (with a lock) for day trips and sightseeing
- Some wet-weather gear, a warm sweater or fleece and sturdy, waterproof walking boots if you plan on trekking (p46)
- Some razzle-dazzle clothes if you plan on visiting the nightclubs and restaurants of the Costa Smeralda

From mid-July all of Italy thunders to the sound of millions hitting the holiday roads – and Sardinia is one of their primary objectives. Hundreds of thousands pour in daily until towards the end of August, when the flood starts to flow in the opposite direction. It's a bad time to join in, as accommodation can be hard to find, prices reach for the sky and the summer heat can become unbearable.

Another thing to bear in mind are varying costs between the high season – Easter and from July to August – and the rest of the year, when even the busiest resorts drop their prices. Between November and

TOP TENS

Festivals & Events

The Sardinians celebrate their festivals with fervour and passion. Elaborate costumes, profound solemnity and pagan partying are all par for the course. For a comprehensive listing of festivals throughout the island, see p227.

- Mamuthones (Mamoiada) January (p207)
- Sa Sartaglia (Oristano) February (p119)
- Pasqua (Easter; all over Sardinia) March/April
- Festa di Sant'Efisio (Cagliari) May (p72)
- S'Ardia (Sedilo) July (p128)
- Estate Musicale Internazionale di Alghero (International Summer of Music; Alghero) August (p158)

- Matrimonio Maureddino (Moorish Wedding; Santadi) August (p101)
- I Candelieri (The Candlesticks; Sassari) August (p140)
- Festa del Redentore (Nuoro) August (p200)
- Festa di San Salvatore (San Salvatore) September (p123)

Must-Have Music

Cultural isolation has made Sardinia a mecca for ethnomusicologists. For its population, it boasts the richest crop of fusion sounds anywhere in Europe; see p36 for more details on the Sardinian music scene.

- *Launeddas* (1930 and 1961) Efisio Melis and Antonio Lara
- *Musiche Sarde dalle Alture al Mare* (1985) Argia
- *Forse il Mare* (1986) Ritmia
- *Sonos* (1988) Elena Ledda
- *Meridies* (1999) Marino Derosas

- *Organittos* (1999) Totore Chessa
- *Su Banzigu* (2000) Tenore di Oniferi
- *Intonos* (2000) Tenores di Bitti
- *Alguimia* (2003) Franca Masu
- *Launeddas* (2003) Franco Melis

Best Books

Resolutely rural, Sardinia has more of an oral storytelling tradition than a written one. However, since the end of WWI some fascinating novels have started to appear. See p37 for reviews.

- *Canne al Vento* (Reeds in the Wind; 1913) Grazia Deledda
- *Cosima* (1937) Grazia Deledda
- *Sardinian Brigade* (1938) Emilio Lussu
- *Diario di una Maestrina* (Diary of a Schoolteacher; 1957) Maria Giacobbe
- *Il Disertore* (The Deserter; 1961) Giuseppe Dessi

- *Il Giorno del Giudizio* (The Day of Judgement; 1975) Salvatore Satta
- *Padre Padrone* (1975) Gavino Ledda
- *Gastronomia in Sardegna* (1988) Gian Paolo Caredda
- *Il Figlio di Bakunin* (Bakunin's Son; 1991) Sergio Atzeni
- *Diavoli di Nuraiò* (Devils of Nuraiò; 2000) Flavio Soriga

February some places close altogether (especially camp sites), so do your research first if you plan to travel during this period.

COSTS & MONEY

Sardinia sits about midway on the scale of expense in Italy, although in summer it can edge closer to the top. See the Directory's Accommodation (p221) and Food (p229) sections for detailed information on the pricing system we've used in this book.

A prudent backpacker might scrape by on €50 per day by staying in youth hostels. Realistically, a traveller wanting to stay in comfortable midrange hotels, eat two square meals per day, hire a car and not feel restricted to one museum per day should reckon on a minimum daily average of €100 to €120.

TRAVEL LITERATURE

Despite the island's striking beauty and rich, rural past, there is relatively little travel literature to recommend. Sardinia's most famous commentator was DH Lawrence, whose sharply drawn portrait of the island is the only real travel book of its kind.

The Bandit on the Billiard Table (Alan Ross) A waistcoat-straight account of Sardinia in the 1950s. Alan Ross has the tone of a schoolmaster and he takes the island to task in a masterly way, with anecdotal stories and some sensitive insights.

Grazia Deledda: A Legendary Life (Martha King) Although this is a biography of Sardinia's greatest female novelist, we glean much about Sardinia from the background of Deledda's typical Nuorese life and the boundaries she had to break in order to write.

La Civiltà dei Sardi (The Civilisation of the Sards; Giovanni Lilliu) Unfortunately only printed in Italian, Lilliu's magnum opus is the definitive book on the history, archaeology and culture of the island.

Sardinian Chronicles (Bernard Lortat-Jacob, trans Teresa Fagan) Placing the music in its cultural context, this book offers 12 vignettes which bring to life both musicians and music. A CD is also included.

Sea and Sardinia (DH Lawrence) Lawrence's ability 'to write the light' makes him a perfect, if impatient, observer of Sardinia. His empathy with the romantic, rural essence of the island tempers his often acerbic, and hilarious, tantrums at the inadequate accommodation and food.

INTERNET RESOURCES

The Lonely Planet website (www.lonelyplanet.com) has information on Sardinia, as well as travel news, updates to our guidebooks and links to other travel resources. You will also find these sites useful:

In Sardinia (www.webinsardinia.com, in Italian) A good introduction to Sardinia's history, as well as the latest news, and stories from the Sardinian diaspora.

Mare Nostrum (www.marenostrum.it, in Italian) A fantastic Sardinian portal listing events, exhibitions, festivals, restaurants and much more, as well as all the latest news.

Regione Autonoma della Sardegna (www.regione.sardegna.it, in Italian) This official site provides a wealth of information on Sardinia.

SardegnaNet (www.sardegna.net) Great for tips on outdoor activities in Sardinia, including mountain biking, sailing, diving and trekking.

Sardinia Point (www.sardiniapoint.it, in Italian) Here you will find oodles of cultural information, from what's on right now to recipes and accommodation.

Sarnow (www.sarnow.com) A magazine website with well-written features on the island and plenty of itinerary suggestions.

HOW MUCH?

City bus fare
€0.80

International newspaper
€2.50-3

Coffee and cornetto
€3

Bowl of pasta
€6-8

Packet of 20 cigarettes
€3.50

Itineraries

CLASSIC ROUTES

SEVEN ROYAL CITIES
Two weeks / Cagliari to Castelsardo

Kick off in **Cagliari** (p62), Sardinia's down-to-earth capital. Take a couple of days to explore the labyrinth of **Il Castello** (p64) and the jumble of the **Marina district** (p70). You must visit the **Museo Archeologico Nazionale** (p65), with its wonderful *bronzetti*, while kids will enjoy laid-back **Poetto** (p72) beach.

West is **Iglesias** (p91), the heart of Sardinia's mining community. Take in the enormous **Grotta di San Giovanni** (p95) on the way. Dawdle along the beautiful **Costa Verde** (p97) and see the dunes of **Piscinas** (p98) before arriving in **Oristano** (p116). Nearby are the Phoenician ruins of **Tharros** (p124).

Head inland to see the temple well of **Santa Cristina** (p127) and the **Nuraghe Losa** (p128). Detour to **Santu Lussurgiu** (p125), where you can eat well, before arriving in medieval **Bosa** (p129). Beyond is salty **Alghero** (p153) with its distinct Catalan flavour. Tackle the cliffside steps of **Capo Caccia** (p165), which descend to the enormous sea cave of the **Grotta di Nettuno** (p165).

You now reach Sardinia's second city, **Sassari** (p135). Check out the **Duomo di San Nicola** (p139) and the archaeological museum, **Museo Nazionale Sanna** (p137). Finally, you hit the north coast at scenic **Castelsardo** (p148), on its rocky bluff above the sea.

This 285km itinerary will take you through Sardinia's seven royal cities, its most famous archaeological museums and along some lovely coastline. Three weeks should allow you to savour the Costa Verde and explore the area around Oristano. Trains and buses serve all these towns.

SEA & SARDINIA
Three weeks / Cagliari to Nuoro

A wander up the eastern side of the island reveals a very different side of Sardinia. It is altogether wilder, incorporating the impressive Gennargentu massif as well as Sardinia's most secluded beaches.

The capital, **Cagliari** (p62), makes a perfect place to start. Be sure to gen up on Sardinia's prehistory at the **Museo Archeologico Nazionale** (p65). Then head north to the spectacular ancient complex of the **Nuraghe Su Nuraxi** (p113) near Barumini, and the more modest **Santuario Santa Vittoria** (p210).

With a copy of *Sea and Sardinia* in hand, head for Mandas and board the *trenino verde* as DH Lawrence did in 1921. The little steam train will whisk you through stunning high mountains to **Tortolì** (p211). If travelling by car, be sure to detour for a couple of days' hiking around **Ulassai** (p211).

Overnight in Tortolì or further north in **Cala Gonone** (p217), where you can take excursions along the **Golfo di Orosei** (p215) to fantastic beaches such as **Cala Luna** (p218) and the purple sea cave of the **Grotta del Bue Marino** (p218). After all that sun and sand, head inland for some hair-raising heights along to the Genna 'e Silana pass, where you can trek into the vast chasm of the **Gola Su Gorruppu** (p217).

For some of the most spectacular mountain scenery, head north to **Oliena** (p202) and undertake the windswept trek to the *nuraghe* (stone tower) village of **Tiscali** (p204). From Oliena you can also detour to rugged **Orgosolo** (p204) for a quick lesson in history and politics painted on the walls in larger-than-life murals.

Finish off the itinerary in **Nuoro** (p196), the heart of Barbagia and birthplace of Sardinia's most celebrated writer, Grazia Deledda.

This 305km route has many twists and turns, so a car is really the most practical way to get around. Still it's great to travel part of the way on the *trenino verde*, especially from Mandas to Tortolì. You should then be able to pick up a car in Tortolì for touring the mountains.

PAST MEETS PRESENT   One to two weeks / Alghero to the Costa Smeralda

Fancy a swim in Caribbean blue seas or a walk in an ancient cork forest? Whether you want to lie back in a VIP location or meditate on Sardinia's fine Romanesque churches, the north of the island is a smorgasbord of delights.

Start gently in picturesque **Alghero** (p153) with its cobbled lanes and honey-coloured walls. Day-trip to the dramatic cliffs of **Capo Caccia** (p165) and dine in some of the island's most stylish restaurants (p159).

Meander north to isolated **Stintino** (p151) to laze on one of the island's best beaches, **Spiaggia della Pelosa** (p152), or visit the strange **Parco Nazionale dell'Asinara** (p152). Then duck inland to gritty **Sassari** (p135) for some city atmosphere and excellent dining. Tour the Pisan Romanesque churches of the tranquil Logudoro valley – **Basilica della Santissima Trinità di Saccargia** (p145), **Chiesa di San Michele e Sant'Antonio di Salvenèro** (p145), **Chiesa di Santa Maria del Regno** (p145), **Chiesa di Sant'Antioco di Bisarcio** (p145) and the **Chiesa di Nostra Signora di Castro** (p145) on the shores of Lago di Coghinas.

Pick up the SS127 and head northeast to **Tempio Pausania** (p190) deep in verdant cork forests. Shop in **Aggius** (p192), which produces nearly 80% of Sardinia's carpets and rugs, explore the weird **Valle della Luna** (p192) and drive to the peak of **Monte Limbara** (p192).

To the northeast the country is rich with prehistoric sites, especially around **Arzachena** (p178), beyond which the bright lights of the **Porto Cervo** (p175) beckon. Armed with a fistful of dollars enjoy the high life along the Costa Smeralda before heading on to island-hop around the **Parco Nazionale dell'Arcipelago di La Maddalena** (p182).

You can expand this 265km itinerary at your leisure. To weave around the Logudoro churches and various ruins and have some time to enjoy that sun bed, you could stretch things out to a fortnight. You can visit all the main points of interest on public transport.

TAILORED TRIPS

ALFRESCO

What the island lacks in museums it more than makes up for with its alfresco attractions. Sardinia's most fantastic beaches have to be **Spiaggia della Pelosa** (p152) at Stintino and the Costa Verde's wild and woolly **Spiaggia della Piscinas** (p98). And who can complain about the dive sites in the marine parks of **Villasimius** (p87) and around **Isola Tavolara** (p174)? The waters of the **Parco Nazionale dell'Arcipelago di La Maddalena** (p182), **Isola di San Pietro** (p101) and around **Capo Caccia** (p165) are also real highlights.

Windsurfing boards line the beaches along the windy north coast at **Santa Teresa di Gallura** (p186) and **Porto Pollo** (p182). Otherwise, less energetic holidaymakers can pick up a boat trip at **Palau** (p180) or, even better, in the **Golfo di Orosei** (p215).

On dry land the mountainous terrain makes for exciting trekking and climbing. The hiking trails of the **Supramonte** (p202) are slowly developing, and serious climbers can head for **Ulassai** (p211), the spectacular **Gola Su Gorruppu** (p217) canyon or the sea cliffs of the **Golfo di Orosei** (p215). Horse riding is also becoming popular. The biggest school is **Ala Birdi** (p122), near Arborea, where you can arrange treks along the Piscinas dunes. Another good riding school is **Mandra Edera** (p128), near Abbasanta.

THE SARDINIAN TABLE

Sardinian cuisine is a weird and wonderful experience, unique to town and village. If you arrive on the island at **Cagliari** (p62) or **Alghero** (p153) you will enjoy lots of seafood treats, in particular red and grey mullet, and in Alghero rock lobster, sardines and Spanish-inspired paella. Other seafood hot spots are **Carloforte** (p102) for its tuna- and saffron-flavoured *cas-cas* (couscous); **Cabras** (p122) for mullet, *bottarga* (mullet roe) and smoked eel; and **Olbia** (p168) for stuffed squid and smoked cuttlefish, along with a whole range of unique Gallurese dishes such as *suppa cuata* (cheese and bread broth). Spanish and Genoese accents are to be found in the kitchen in **Sassari** (p135), where you can sample *panadas* (pies filled with meat and game) and *fainè* (a pizza-like snack), but Sardinia's most ancient culinary roots are in the mountains of Barbagia. For country cooking at its very best, book a meal at **Su Gologone** (p203). In mountain villages such as **Orgosolo** (p204) you can buy the island's world-class *pecorino romano*, and in towns like **Oliena** (p202) you will find some of the dozens of varieties of fragrant honey.

Other speciality products are the velvety Bue Rosso beef, the island's light, peppery olive oil – produced around **Seneghe** (p125) – and the sweet Malvasia wine of **Bosa** (p133). You can round it all off with a selection of honey-drenched treats or almond-flavoured biscuits, best sampled in **Durke** (p85) in Cagliari.

Snapshot

To historian Giovanni Lilliu (see p15 for a review of his best-known book, *La Civiltà dei Sardi*), Sardinia's past was far more than an archaeological study. For him, the age of the *nuraghe* (stone tower) builders embodied the seeds of a nation, the integrity of which has long been guarded by the shepherds of Barbagia. But Lilliu recognised that the island's lack of unity was a severe impediment to the dream of independence cherished by the *sardistas* (Sardinian separatists). He still has a point today.

In 2005, the new Centro Sinistra government of Renato Soru (see the boxed text, p29) was busy breaking the island into more administrative regions. As of May 2005 Sardinia had four new provinces – Ogliastra, Medio Campidano, Olbia-Tempio and Carbonia-Iglesias – making eight regions administered by 377 municipalities. The government argues that this is 'power to the people', but others mutter that it just means more expensive bureaucracy. These new regions are yet to be recognised by Rome, which views the dilution of central authority dimly.

Sardinia's token industrial and archaic agricultural industries continue to limp along without major investment or reform. In Cagliari, the capital, many shops have closed, and people complain that there is simply no money. Only the economy of Olbia-Tempio (Sardinia's tourist hot spot) is growing; the rest of the island is in recession.

Astonishingly, millions of euros designated by the EU for Sardinian development under Objective One (see p30) were withdrawn – not because of any shady dealings but because Sardinia failed to spend the money! For a place with unemployment hovering at 20% (rising to 50% for those under 25), few medium-sized businesses, no motorways, a dual-gauge railway system and a worryingly precarious water supply, this is unbelievable.

It's a depressing picture on a sunshine isle, and one that Sardinia's new president, Internet billionaire Renato Soru, is determined to change, although it's not clear how he proposes to do this. Soru built his global company, Tiscali, by uniting the small and fragmented telecom and Internet service providers across Europe, and the hope is that he can work the same magic in Sardinia. Already his government has set to work rewriting a new governing charter for the approval of parliament, and there is much talk of e-learning (see p33) and e-government, as many see information technology as a way out of the island's geographical isolation.

If Sardinia is going to lift itself out of its centuries-long inertia it needs outside ideas and experience. The expertise brought by a recent wave of entrepreneurs returning to the island and establishing new and varied small-scale businesses (see the boxed text, p33) should stand it in good stead. However, a delicate balance will need to be struck between modernisation and preserving Sardinia's unique native character.

FAST FACTS

Population: 1.65 million

Area: 24,090 sq km

Italy's GDP: €1355 billion

Sardinia's GDP per head: €9250

GDP growth: 0.8%

Inflation: 2.4%

Unemployment rate: 20%

Population density: 68 per sq km

Number of sheep: 3 million

Renato Soru's personal fortune: US$4 billion

History

As DH Lawrence toured Sardinia on a six-day jaunt in the early 1920s he struggled to make sense of its strange customs and unique character. When he got home to Sicily he scribbled his vivid impressions down in *Sea and Sardinia,* in which he barely spares a thought for the island's 8000 years of history. And yet the most oft-quoted line from the book – his famous description of the place as 'lost between Europe and Africa, and belonging to nowhere' – sums up the history of Sardinia perfectly. Lying 200km from any mainland, it is the most isolated island in the Mediterranean, a fact that has determined its messy and entangled history.

THE MISTS OF TIME

This strange granite isle is one of the oldest fragments of Europe. Over the years its archaeology has revealed the whole arc of human civilisation, dating from the impossibly remote Palaeolithic era (Old Stone Age). In 1979 chance findings of flint tools at Perfugas led archaeologists to mutter excitedly about primitive humans crossing from the mainland as far back as 350,000 BC. It's thought they came from the coast of Tuscany, although it is possible other waves arrived from North Africa and the Iberian Peninsula via the Balearic Islands.

Check out www.sarnow .com for a good introduction to Sardinia's prehistory, with fascinating features explaining the historical context of local arts, crafts and culture.

But it's not until a few hundred thousand years later that we really get any sense of who the Sardinians might have been. By 6000 BC the Neolithic era was in full swing. This meant cattle-raising, agriculture, mining, weaponry and busy village life. Sardinia would have been a perfect spot for the average Neolithic family – the island was covered with dense forest full of animals, there was plenty of good grazing and arable land, and above all there were veins of obsidian, a glassy black igneous stone coveted all over the Mediterranean. Used to create cutting tools and arrow tips, it was the period's most precious commodity. Shards of Sardinian obsidian have been found as far away as France.

By 3000 BC villages were dotted around the island. Archaeologists talk of the Ozieri culture, after finds made around that town (see p144). The earliest signs of complex funerary rituals also date to this period, which saw the excavation of the first *domus de janas* (literally 'fairy houses'; tombs cut into rock).

THE AGE OF THE NURAGHE

By 1800 to 1500 BC, in the early Bronze Age, things had changed radically: Sardinians had begun building the mysterious *nuraghi* (stone towers). The early *nuraghi* were simple free-standing structures and may have played a military role. The use of metals to make tools and, significantly, weapons was by now widespread.

Increasing clannishness and complexity of culture meant that the simple design of the *nuraghe* had to evolve. Those built between 1500 and 1300 BC are much bigger – some, like the Nuraghe Santu Antine (p144), reached three storeys. Walls were raised around the grand towers, and villagers began to cluster their houses within the walls' protective

TIMELINE	350,000 BC		4000–2700 BC
	Fragments of basic flint tools indicate the first traces of human culture on the island		Evidence of the island's first organised cultures at Ozieri; impressive building works result in the *domus de janus*

embrace. The most spectacular example of this is the beehive complex of the Nuraghe Su Nuraxi (p113).

Greater contact with other cultures, including the Etruscans and the Mycenaeans, as well as the peoples of southern France and Spain, made the *nuraghe*-builders more wary. There was obviously a lot of reciprocal trade, as excavated ceramics have shown, but the Sards began to feel the need for protection and more towers went up. It is thought that these marked tribal territory and frontiers, and also served as watchtowers.

Frustratingly, no written records have come down to us, leading most scholars to assume that the Sardinians never had a written language. Rich if enigmatic testimony to their social and religious life has remained. *Pozzi sacri* (well temples) like Santa Cristina (see p127) were built from around 1000 BC, and the art of the *bronzetti* (bronze figurines) was flourishing. The latter gives us the greatest insight into this watertight world; the great collection in Cagliari's Museo Archeologico (p65) shouldn't be missed.

La Civiltà dei Sardi (The Civilisation of the Sards) by Giovanni Lilliu is the definitive chronicle of Sardinia's mysterious *nuraghe* builders.

THE PHOENICIANS & CARTHAGE

Traders from Greek Mycenae are believed to have been nosing around the island as early as 1200 BC, and their influence is clear in the development of local ceramics. Far more threatening, however, was the growing interest from the Phoenicians (from modern-day Lebanon), who were fast emerging as the primary force in the Mediterranean. Brilliant sailors and traders, they set up their depots all over the place and it was natural that Sardinia would form part of that network. Semitic inscriptions suggest that Spain-based Phoenicians may have set up at Nora, on the south coast, as early as 1100 BC.

From the 9th to the 7th centuries BC the Phoenicians established and expanded their coastal settlements, adding Karalis (Cagliari), Bithia (near modern Chia), Sulci (modern Sant'Antioco), Tharros and Bosa. Their control over the lucrative lead and silver mines in the island's southwest was a big bone of contention with the native Sards, so the Phoenicians built their first inland fortress on Monte Sirai in 650 BC. This proved wise, as disgruntled Sardinians attacked several Phoenician bases in 509 BC.

Against the ropes, the Phoenicians appealed to Carthage (their sister city in North Africa) for aid. The combined Carthaginian and Phoenician forces soon had most of the island under control, except the unruly mountainous regions of the east. During this period many Sardinians chose to abandon the *nuraghi* and move to the developing coastal towns. But Carthaginian ambitions for domination of the entire western Mediterranean were soon to place them on a collision course with Rome.

ROME TAKES COMMAND

It wasn't a good idea, but Carthage thought Sardinia was the perfect place from which to raid the Roman coast. This sparked the First Punic War (264–261 BC), which eventually saw the Phoenicians run out of town in 238 BC.

The arrival of the Romans in 241 BC brought profound change to Sardinia. With characteristic efficiency they expanded the Carthaginian cities and settlements, built a network of roads to facilitate communica-

1800–500 BC	900–800 BC
The era of the *nuraghe*, during which some 30,000 fortified stone towers are built all over the island	Phoenician traders establish trading posts at Karalis (Cagliari), Nora and Tharros

tions and control of the island, and even penetrated Barbagia in the eastern mountains.

The Campidano area, an important source of grain, became, along with Sicily and occupied North Africa, the granary of the entire Roman Empire. Later on farmers diversified, producing wine, olives and fruit. Trade was active with the Italian mainland, Iberia and especially North Africa.

But controlling the island was no walkover, and the Romans found themselves frequently battling insurgents, especially in untamed Barbagia. It was the Romans who dubbed the area Barbaria after the barbarian courage of its inhabitants.

The initial campaign of conquest took seven years, and the island was only finally declared a province (with Corsica) in 227 BC. In 216 BC the Sardinians, led by Ampsicora, joined the Carthaginians in the Second Punic War and revolted against their Roman masters. The following year they were crushed in the second battle of Cornus, but rebellions remained on the menu for the next 200 years. In 177 BC around 12,000 Sardinians died and as many as 50,000 were sent to Rome as slaves.

Throughout the centuries of Roman rule an uneasy equilibrium was maintained. The more Romanised cities and inhabitants of coastal and farm country stood in opposition to the restless indigenous pastoralists of Barbagia. Although some cities and many noble families gained Roman-citizen status and came to speak Latin, the island remained an underdeveloped and overexploited subject territory.

THE VANDALS MOVE IN...

The collapse of Rome in the early 5th century AD left Sardinia in the lurch. Refugees arrived from the mainland, and invaders were not far behind. The Vandals, who had established a kingdom in North Africa, disembarked in Sardinia in 456 and in Corsica soon after.

Admittedly biased Byzantine chroniclers record the 80-odd years of Vandal rule as a time of raids and misery for the island's inhabitants. The Vandals also used the island as a place of exile for vexatious Christians, especially bishops and other notables, from North Africa. The scant reminders historians have of this time suggest that the chroniclers probably exaggerated. It appears Karalis and other port towns remained busy, especially with commerce between the island and North Africa.

...AND THE BYZANTINE EMPIRE STRIKES BACK

By the early 6th century all that remained of the Roman Empire was its eastern half, now known as Byzantium (roughly modern-day Greece and Turkey). Thoughts of the good old days of empire prompted Emperor Justinian to embark on a campaign of conquest aimed at restoring the old order. After retaking mainland Italy, his most celebrated general, Belisarios, went on to bring much of North Africa under Byzantine control. The Vandals, defeated in North Africa in 534, abandoned Sardinia, which became one of Byzantium's seven African provinces.

The Byzantines were great rubber-stampers and established the island's first formal administration. In charge was the *dux*, a military commander who controlled the garrison at Forum Traiani (Fordongianus). The island was divided into four *judex provinciae* (provinces controlled by a judge),

Log on to www.activ sardegna.com to pick up the Ichnusa webzine, which features solid articles on a range of historical topics.

241 BC–AD 400	1015
Rome takes control of the island and develops city centres at Karalis (Cagliari), Nora, Sulcis, Tharros, Olbia and Turris Libisonis (Porto Torres)	Pisan and Genoan navies help Sardinia defeat Arab forces from Mallorca and begin their long struggle for control of the island

which in turn were divided into further *partes* (municipalities). Even villages had their own *maiore* (mayor), completing a system that looks – in outline at least – remarkably like the present-day system of government.

The Byzantine period also saw the spread of Christianity all over the island. The exception was Barbagia, whose inhabitants still practised their pagan rites and continued to worship wood and stone until AD 600.

ARAB RAIDS & THE GIUDICATI

'For the first time since the Carthaginian conquest, Sardinians were running their own affairs.'

By the early 8th century the Arabs had conquered North Africa and much of Spain, and Sardinia found itself increasingly isolated. Constantinople, threatened on several fronts, could no longer protect its far-flung colony.

In the absence of any strong outside governance the Byzantine system of four ruling provincial governors (*giudici* in Sardinian) came into their own, and the *giudicati* (provinces) slowly evolved into mini-kingdoms. The territories were delineated according to the old Byzantine divisions: Cagliari in the south, Arborea in the west, Logudoro (or Torres) in the northwest and Gallura in the northeast. For the first time since the Carthaginian conquest, Sardinians were running their own affairs. The *giudici* operated as kings, although their power was circumscribed by the *corona de logu* (council of nobles).

PISA & GENOA VIE FOR CONTROL

After years of pirate raids and Arab aggression the *giudici* were fed up. When the Arabs invaded again in 1015 the territories turned to their Christian ally, the pope, for help. With Arab power weakening in the Mediterranean and Christian ambitions on the rise, the pope was only too happy to send the maritime forces of Pisa and Genoa to the Sardinians' aid.

With the Arabs out of the way the Pisans and Genoese (both ambitious trading states) saw a great business opportunity. Sardinia had rich mines and useful resources, and was strategically located on their major trade routes from northern Italy. In the late 11th century religious orders such as the Vittorini monks (with strong Pisan connections) were granted land and concessions in the Giudicato di Cagliari, beginning what was to become a 300-year tug-of-war.

Although the *giudicati* passed from Genoese to Pisan hands in a bewildering series of battles, skirmishes and intrigues, the period was on the whole a prosperous one. The island absorbed the cultural mores of medieval Europe, and powerful monasteries ensured that the islanders received the message of Roman Christianity loud and clear. The Pisan Romanesque churches of the northwest remain a striking legacy of the period (p145).

Initially the Pisans had the upper hand in the north, while the Genoese curried favour in the south, particularly around Cagliari. But Genoese influence was also strong in Porto Torres, and the *giudicato* swapped allegiances at the drop of a hat for the sake of self-preservation. The Pisans and Genoese aimed to destroy these local powerbases and by 1200 the Giudicato di Logudoro was in pieces. In 1235 the last *giudice*, Barisone III, was murdered and the land divided between the Genoese Dorias and Malaspinas. At the same time Pisan influence was growing in the Giudicato di Gallura, and the Pisans moved in to take direct control in 1297. The policy of ruling Sardinian territory direct from Pisa was extended to

1297	1392
Pope Boniface VIII declares Jaume II of Aragon King of Corsica and Sardinia	Eleonora of Arborea publishes the Carta de Logu, Sardinia's first code of common law

the Giudicato di Cagliari in the wake of Ugolino della Gherardesca's fall from grace in 1288. In the same year Nino Visconti, the last *giudice* of Gallura, was overthrown; he died the following year without heirs.

Only the Giudicato d'Arborea remained independent, but its close ties with the Crown of Aragon (in 1157 Barisone d'Arborea had married into the ruling family of Barcelona) was to be its undoing. The Catalano-Aragonese kingdom, with its heart in the thriving port city of Barcelona, was more than a little interested in the island. Some Catalan noble families already had big stakes in Sardinia's northwest. This must have motivated Pope Boniface VIII's decision in 1297 to create the theoretical Regnum Sardiniae et Corsicae (Sardinian and Corsican Kingdom) and hand it over to the Catalano-Aragonese Jaume II.

THE CROWN OF ARAGON

Jaume II never got around to making the pope's declaration a reality. Only in 1323 did Catalano-Aragonese forces, transported by 300 warships, land on the southwest coast to begin the business of conquest.

Allied with Arborea, the newcomers quickly took Cagliari and Iglesias, and established pacts of vassalage with other nobles around the island. Relations between Barcelona and Arborea soon deteriorated when the latter realised their erstwhile allies were bent on assuming complete control. By 1353 Arborea had become an adversary and a long period of insurrection began. The northwestern port town of Alghero, retaken after a brief revolt, saw its entire population expelled and replaced by Catalan colonists.

From 1356 to 1404, the rulers of Arborea (Kings Mariano IV and Ugone III and Queen Eleonora) harried the Catalano-Aragonese. The resistance lasted so long due to the steely determination and political

JUSTICE & EQUALITY FOR ALL

Throughout the island's long and sorry history one person stands head and shoulders above the rest: Eleonora of Arborea (1340–1404). Described as Sardinia's Boudicca or Joan of Arc, she was the island's most inspirational ruler, remembered for her wisdom, moderation and enlightened humanity.

She became Giudicessa of Arborea in 1383, when her venal brother, Hugo III, was murdered along with his daughter. Surrounded by enemies within and without (her husband was imprisoned in Aragon), she silenced the rebels and for the next 20 years worked to maintain Arborea's independence in an uncertain world.

Her greatest legacy was the Carta de Logu, which she published in 1392. The code was drafted by her father, Mariano, but Eleonora revised and completed it. To the delight of the islanders, it was published in Sardinian, thus forming the cornerstone of a nascent national consciousness. This progressive code, based on Roman law, was far ahead of the social legislation of the period. For the first time the big issues of land use and the right to appeal were codified, and women were granted a whole raft of rights, including the right to refuse marriage and – significantly in a rural society – property rights. Alfonso V was so impressed that he extended its laws throughout the island in 1421, and this remained so until 1871.

Eleonora never saw how influential her Carta de Logu became. She died of plague in 1404, and barely five years after her death the Aragonese took control of Arborea. She remains the most respected historical figure on the island.

1417	1400–1500
William of Narbonne, the last *giudice* of Arborea, dies and the *giudicato* system ends	Sardinia is devastated by high taxes, and famine and plagues claim 50% of the island's population

cunning of Queen Eleonora (1340–1404), who won the respect and admiration of the local people for her judicious rule and the advanced Carta de Logu (Code of Laws; see the boxed text, p25).

Five years after Eleonora's death, the Sardinians were defeated at the Battle of Sanluri. Unrest continued to simmer and resulted in a final concerted uprising in the 1470s, quickly throttled in the Battle of Macomer in 1478.

THE SPANISH MIRE

The 1479 marriage of Ferdinand and Isabella united the crowns of Castile and Aragon. Under the Spaniards the feudal structures put in place by the Catalano-Aragonese were deepened, leaving the bulk of the mostly rural population to toil for a meagre livelihood in a life of unrelenting struggle and misery. Great tracts of the country wound up as possessions of powerful Spanish nobles who never so much as visited the island. Even a century after Spanish rule ended, much of the land taken over by Iberian nobility was still in their hands.

'Great tracts of the country wound up as possessions of powerful Spanish nobles who never so much as visited the island.'

Sardinian farmers were burdened with barely sustainable taxes, and the island's economy stagnated as Spain's fortunes declined during the 16th and 17th centuries. Ironically, traders from Genoa (whose bankers had become one of Madrid's prime sources of finance) gradually came to dominate the island's international trade, replacing the Catalans.

In 1700 the death of the heirless Habsburg ruler Carlos II meant the island was up for grabs once again. In Sardinia, as in Spain, society was divided by pro-Habsburg Austrian and pro-Bourbon French factions, both of whom vied for the spoils of the enormous Habsburg empire. Carlos' death triggered the War of the Spanish Succession, a conflict that other European powers were keen to see resolved in their favour. In 1708 Austrian forces backed by English warships occupied Sardinia.

The French-backed Bourbon candidate for the Spanish throne, Felipe V, won the day, but the cost to Spain was high. Madrid lost many of its territories, including Sardinia, which was awarded to Austria under the terms of the 1713 Treaty of Utrecht. Vienna was not too keen on its new possession and did little to oppose a Spanish attempt to retake it in 1717. The rest of Europe was not amused, however, and obliged the Spaniards to pull out again a year later under the Treaty of London. This time Sardinia was assigned to the Duchy of Savoy. The dukes would have preferred the juicier morsel of Sicily to the neglected rural backwater of Sardinia, but they were satisfied to have attained a much-coveted royal crown.

HARD TIMES

The lamentable state of the island's economy came as a shock to the Piedmontese viceroys, but they were determined to make the best of a bad situation. Attributing the low farm output to underpopulation (300,000 at the time), they encouraged colonisation. The only such experiment to work was the transfer of Ligurians from Tabarqa in Tunisia to the island of San Pietro in 1738, where they founded the city of Carloforte. These fishing folk, however, did little to alter the state of farming.

Although times were rarely easy – the 18th century was marked by a series of famines – farm output generally stabilised and the population increased, reaching 436,000 in 1782. Attempts were also made to modernise the feudal system of landholding, and the moribund universities of Cagliari and Sassari were resurrected.

But rocky times were never far away. The French Revolution cast its shadow over Sardinia as over the rest of Europe. The Sardinian militia repulsed attempted landings by French forces (including some under a young Napoleon in the Maddalena islands) in 1792. In return for this demonstration of loyalty, a delegation of Sardinians went to see King Vittorio Amedeo III in Turin to demand a greater degree of self-rule, but, much to their dissatisfaction, virtually all of their requests were turned down.

It wasn't long before talk of revolution hit the streets. In 1795 senior Savoy administrators were killed by angry mobs in Cagliari. The revolutionaries were most visibly represented by a radical judge, Giovanni Maria Angioi, who attempted to march on Cagliari without success. By the time the Savoy royal family were forced to move to Cagliari in 1799, ejected from their mainland possessions by Napoleon, the revolutionary wave had been crushed.

FALTERING PROGRESS & UNIFICATION

The early decades of the 19th century brought a greater degree of calm. King Carlo Felice built the highway between Cagliari and Porto Torres, ordered the establishment of basic schooling and promoted drastic change in land ownership. The Enclosures Act of 1823, aimed at turning over common land to private ownership, may have been motivated by laudable economic thinking but it inevitably excluded poor Sardinian farmers and shepherds, who lost the use of common land. The desperate perforce turned to banditry.

The abolition of feudal privileges in 1835 was also a big step forward, but small farmers who bought land bore crushing debts to the state. In all, the painful reforms did little for the average Sardinian.

By 1847 the island's status as a separate entity ruled through a viceroy came to an end. Tempted by reforms introduced in the Savoys' mainland territories, a delegation requested the 'perfect union' of the Kingdom of Sardinia with Piedmont, in the hope of acquiring more equitable rule. The request was granted. From now on the island would be ruled directly from Turin.

At the same time events were moving quickly elsewhere on the Italian peninsula. In a series of daring military campaigns fronted by Giuseppe Garibaldi (see p185) and encouraged by King Carlo Emanuele, Sardinia managed to annexe the Italian mainland to create a united Kingdom of Italy in 1861 (a process completed in 1870).

Roman rule was not substantially different from that of Turin, but slow improvements were being made – the first railway lines opened in the 1870s, education was extended, milk and cheese products found overseas markets, and the first banks were established, allowing ordinary people access to credit. In 1913 Sardinia elected its first ever socialist MP to the Italian parliament. Still, life remained tough, and the years leading up to WWI were characterised by miners' strikes (ruthlessly put down), rampant banditry and food riots.

The miners of the Iglesiente only went on strike in September, when the wild prickly pear came into fruit. This meant their families would still have something to eat.

1823	1921
The Enclosures Act sees the sale of centuries-old communal land and the abolition of communal rights, resulting in riots	The Partito Sardo d'Azione (Sardinian Action Party) is formed, aiming to pursue regional autonomy and politicise the Sardinian public

THE WORLD WARS

Italy's decision to enter WWI in 1915 on the Allied side was motivated by a desire to grab what it considered Italian territories still in the hands of Austria. The country was utterly unprepared for conflict on such a scale and would pay a high human price.

More than most units, the 'red devils' of the Brigata Sassari (p137) distinguished themselves in the merciless slaughters of the northern Italian trenches. From the outset the men and officers of the brigade were praised in dispatches for their extraordinary valour. Per capita it is reckoned that Sardinia lost more young men on the front than any other Italian region, and the regiment was decorated with four gold medals.

When the survivors returned home after the war's end in 1918, they were changed men. They had departed as illiterate farmers and returned as a politically awakened force. Many joined the new Partito Sardo d'Azione (PSA; Sardinian Action Party), whose central policy was administrative autonomy on the island. Under the influence of thinkers such as Emilio Lussu (Sardinian Independence Movement) and Antonio Gramsci (Italian Communist Party), the flavour of Sardinian politics was heavily socialist, aiming to engage the disenfranchised factory workers and lure the peasants and shepherds out of their traditional exile from political and social life. The PSA formed the strongest opposition to Benito Mussolini's Fascists, until the Fascists took power in Rome in 1924.

In the 1940s 60% of Sardinians suffered from malaria.

The Fascist period was a strange one for Sardinia. Recognising that something had to be done to lift Sardinia out of its poverty, grand programmes were laid on but only partially or clumsily carried out. Land reclamation around the two new towns of Mussolinia (now Arborea) and Fertilia created new farming land, but only a fraction of that envisaged. Mining received a new impetus, and the extraction of lignite (the poor-quality 'Sulcis coal') was stimulated with the creation of yet another new town, Carbonia.

In all, however, Sardinia suffered from the Fascist attempts to make Italy economically self-sufficient (thus cutting it out of international trade circuits). Joining Hitler in WWII only exacerbated matters. Thankfully, Sardinia wasn't invaded, but Allied bombing raids in the first half of 1943 destroyed three-quarters of Cagliari. Perhaps worse still, war left the island virtually isolated. The ferry between the mainland and Olbia was not back in daily operation until 1947.

The end of the war brought a revolution in Italy's political structure. In a 1946 referendum the people voted to dump the monarchy and create a parliamentary republic. In 1948, along with four other regions, Sardinia was granted its own parliament and a degree of local policy-making latitude, although this fell short of many Sardinians' expectations.

MALARIA & MODERNITY

Even more significant than the creation of the Regione Autonoma della Sardegna in 1948 was the eradication of malaria. Since Roman times much of the Sardinian coast was a malarial swamp. The Sardinia Project, run by the Rockefeller Foundation, had spectacular results. Swamps were drained and the mosquitoes disappeared. In the 1920s an average of

1928–38	1952
Mussolini instigates rural regeneration with large-scale irrigation, infrastructure and land-reclamation projects	The US Army, financed by the Rockefeller Foundation, succeeds in eradicating malaria

78,000 cases of malaria were registered each year (!); the figure dropped to 40,000 in 1947. In 1950 not a single new case was reported.

Also in 1950, Sardinia was nominated as one of the main beneficiaries of the Cassa per il Mezzogiorno, a development fund intended to kick-start the pitiful economy of Italy's south. Over the decades it pumped millions into the island's economy, although poor administration meant that it was not always well spent. A good example of this is the big new factories and industrial plants that went up. Many of these were oil and petrochemical plants, such as those located at Porto Torres, Portovesme and Sarroch, which failed to provide the local jobs required and have ended up an environmental and economic headache. The collapse of the industry in the 1970s, due to the OPEC oil wars, saw much of the workforce laid off, causing an island-wide recession. Rubbing salt into the wounds, the Iglesiente mines (p91) also went into decline and finally shut down in the mid-1990s.

Agricultural and administrative reforms were also slow in coming. The net result was that, although the quality of life in Sardinia gradually rose from the 1950s to the 1980s, serious problems remained. The most eloquent expression of this was the wave of emigration that hit the island from the late 1940s. The arrival of TV (the island was the last part of Italy to be hooked up to the network in 1956) and greater awareness that life *could* be better led increasing numbers of young men to leave. In the 1960s 10% of the population left Sardinia for the Italian mainland or Western Europe.

THE FORBES MAN

Who is the richest man in Italy? No, it isn't TV-tycoon Prime Minister Silvio Berlusconi. It is Renato Soru, Internet entrepreneur and now Sardinia's president. As of September 2005 Forbes estimated that his personal fortune was worth US$4 billion, placing him around 100 on the list of the world's richest.

Like many things Sardinian, Renato Soru has a remarkable story. Born in 1957 in Sanluri, Soru was the son of Egidio, a local school caretaker, and Gigetta, who ran a grocery store. Little did they imagine that by the time he was 30 Renato would have established Europe's second-largest ISP with some 4.9 million Internet subscribers. His vision was to unite a divided Europe using the common language of the Internet, and so far he is well on his way, owning providers in the Netherlands, Germany, Switzerland, Belgium, France and the Czech Republic.

But what is the economist from Milan's Bocconi University going to do with Sardinia's lamentable economy? Can he unite his own fragmented island into a political powerhouse whose economic, social and environmental concerns Rome will consider? He seems to think he can and he has already declared that one five-year term is more than enough time to accomplish things. Coming from an Internet background, he's certainly in a unique position. The Internet doesn't rely on national boundaries, and it may just be Sardinia's ticket out of the dreadful isolationism that has plagued it over the centuries. It's also the medium of the new generation, and Soru dreams that the World Wide Web will create a new society based on youth and intellect rather than class and wealth. He's certainly already making waves: the tourism department is being restructured, regional administration has been reorganised and e-learning was the big debate in parliament at the time of writing. By the next edition of this book we should know if Soru has managed to apply his Midas touch to Sardinia's many economic woes.

1948	1950–70
Sardinia is granted autonomy and the Giunta Consultativa Sarda is recognised as the island's regional assembly	The Cassa per il Mezzogiorno and the Rinascita Plan finance developments in agriculture, education, industry, transport and banking

Tourism may yet prove to be the island's economic lifesaver. The construction of the Aga Khan's chic resort on the Costa Smeralda (p176) in the 1960s signalled a new avenue of hope for Sardinia, although it, too, has brought its own problems. Swarms of fun-seeking holidaymakers opened islanders' eyes to new and startling ways of thinking and living. Even today the more liberal coastal centres contrast remarkably with the doggedly traditional, and increasingly empty, rural heartland. This latest 'invasion' has had the effect of wrenching at least a part of the island from medieval torpor to 21st-century modernity with breakneck rapidity.

Pick up a copy of *Coast*, a fascinating photographic record of the Costa Smeralda with previously unpublished images of how the resort took shape.

SARDINIA TODAY

The 1980s brought a new force in Sardinian politics. The Partito Sardo d'Azione, dormant since its foundation in the 1920s, made a remarkable comeback as Sardinians began to reflect more profoundly on their identity. Renewed interest in Sardinian language, culture and history have outlived the party's truncated electoral successes and opened a debate on the island's political status that continues today. Though the separatists' dream of an independent Sardinia is about as likely as pigs taking to the air, the simple rediscovery of, and pride in, the islanders' *sardità* (Sardinianness) is a healthy sign for the future.

Most Sardinians would agree that the island has come a long way since the end of WWII. But much remains awry in this still comparatively isolated land. Sure, the place floods with tourists for about three months of the year, but otherwise it is left largely to its own devices. In 1999 the EU identified Sardinia as one of a handful of places in Europe in dire need of investment for 'development and structural upgrading'. To this effect the island was allocated a generous amount of money to improve basic infrastructure and invest in educational and work opportunities. Sadly, the government failed to meet its spending targets and in 2004 a large amount of the remaining money had to be returned to the EU.

Whenever a local politician makes it to a position of power in Rome, Sardinians can almost be heard to mutter prayers of intercession. The presence of Sassari's Beppe Pisanu, a key player in Silvio Berlusconi's right-wing Forza Italia-led government, and perhaps the latter's predilection for the Costa Smeralda, has directed Rome's attention to the island more than might usually be the case. Renato Soru's election to the presidency in June 2004 has also drawn attention as he takes on the island's big problems of unemployment, poor infrastructure and administration, and tourist development (see the boxed text, p43).

1985	2004
Sassari-born Francesco Cossiga is elected President of Italy	Renato Soru, entrepreneur and self-made billionaire, is elected president of Sardinia at the head of the Centro Sinistra government

The Culture

REGIONAL IDENTITY

Sardinians display none of the superficial gaiety of other Italians, none of their malleability or lightness of heart. Unlike other islanders, they don't look outwards, longing for escape and opportunity; instead they appear becalmed in the past, gripped by an inward-looking intensity. To visitors they are friendly and polite – in fact, they are famous throughout Italy for their generosity and ability to make strangers feel at ease. But dig a little deeper and you'll find them resolutely reserved.

The island's history quickly reveals that the Sards have had little opportunity to express themselves, and the fierce pride that is so characteristic of them has only been reinforced by the sense of injustice they have felt throughout centuries of colonial oppression. Geography, too, has had an impact on the island character. Straggling mountain ranges and a lack of infrastructure have created a mosaic of communities wildly distinct from one another. Such introspection has helped to preserve many of the unique aspects of the island, but it has also contributed to the lack of regional identity. There is a world of difference between the modern-minded cities of Alghero, Sassari, Olbia and Cagliari and the very traditional attitudes and lifestyle in country villages. Giovanni Lilliu, one of Sardinia's most respected historians, called it 'this incomplete nation' and longed for the Sards to unite and fulfil their real potential.

What unites the Sards is a strong sense of fraternity and tradition and a love of their island. They're also modest and serious-minded – they love to talk provincial politics – and they enjoy indulging in good food and a decent *festa*. You'll find them talented poets, writers, musicians and artists, passionate about the local scene. They may be small in numbers, but the Sardinians are big in heart.

> For a comprehensive overview of many aspects of Sardinian culture, from food to festivals and handcrafts to costumes, log on to www.sarnow.com.

Sardo

Sardo (Sardinian) is the largest minority language in Italy and is the first language of the island. It breaks down into three distinct families: Logudorese (in the northwest), Nuorese (in the east and centre) and Campidanese (in the south, with the exception of Cagliari, which has its own distinct dialect). Logudorese is considered the oldest and purest form, being the closest to the original Latin that was introduced to the island by the Romans.

Most of the grammar and vocabulary come straight from Latin, although the language is peppered with older words like *nuraghe* (stone

---

WHAT MAKES SARDINIANS DIFFERENT

- Sardinia is one of five special-status regions in Italy entitled to administer themselves autonomously
- As with the Venetians, the Italian government has recognised the Sardinians as a distinct *popolo* (people) from the Italians
- The Sardinian language, Sardo, is not a dialect of Italian but an older Romance language based on Roman Latin
- Many Sardinians still refer to Italy as *il continente* (the continent), and many islanders continue to dream of independence

tower) and *giara* (a kind of plateau), many of which describe geological features or animals. Place names heavy in vowels like Orgosolo, Ollolai and Orotelli also probably originated at the time of the *nuraghe*-builders. Spanish and Catalan have had a localised impact, having been the official languages of the island for some 400 years. Today residents of Alghero still speak a variation of Catalan, and on the island of San Pietro a 16th-century version of Genoese is spoken. The Gallura and Sassari dialects reflect the proximity of Corsica.

Sixty-seven dialects make up the island's native language, Sardo.

Sardo forms a big part of the Sardinian identity and is one of the key features that sets Sardinians apart from mainland Italy. In the 1970s calls were made for the Italian government to recognise it as the official language of the island. One of the biggest impediments to this, however, is the fragmentary nature of the dialects. So big is this problem that all of the island's great writers have chosen to write in Italian.

Although the prevalence of Italian media and the increasing use of Italian by the younger generation for business are undoubtedly having some effect, 80% of islanders still speak Sardo at home. No-one has felt the need to introduce it to the school curriculum – yet.

LIFESTYLE

Sardinian society is highly individualistic, with the family and larger community exerting ever-widening spheres of social pressure. In the past an iron code of moral conduct had the force of unwritten law. Grazia Deledda's novels (see p37) repeatedly show a traditional island torn between the church and progress, duty and desire.

Read Grazia Deledda's semiautobiographical novel *Cosima* to get a real insight into the life of a Sardinian mountain town in the late 19th to early 20th century.

The family remains of central importance in society, and Sardinians tend to guard the privacy of their personal lives. If you manage to bridge this hurdle you will find yourself warmly accepted, wined and dined way past your capacity. Even Deledda found that the kitchen hearth '[held] within itself the poetry of the house, family, domestic happiness'. Family and friends still gather on Sundays for enormous roast lunches.

Until the 1950s Sardinia was a very poor and disenfranchised part of modern Italy where 22% of the population was illiterate (that figure now stands at 4%, still double the national average). Many people still live hard lives, and there are no great extremes of wealth. Today average salaries hover around €1000 per month, and 30% of islanders are still employed in agriculture. In such a context island life is simple and unpretentious.

Given these economic realities most young Sardinians stay at home until they graduate or marry, and with the average age of graduation around 28 this represents a huge dependence on the family. Although this binds the community closer together it has also resulted in a diminishing of self-reliance and entrepreneurial ambitions, and a lack of impetus to acquire new professional skills.

Improved education, the advent of tourism and the migration of large sections of the population from the countryside to the cities (nearly half the population lives in or around Cagliari) are slowly addressing some of these social problems. But in the interior, especially in Barbagia, the old moral and social mores prevail and life remains rigidly traditional.

Men & Women

As in most rural communities, there were traditionally defined roles for men and women in Sardinia. Given the harshness of a life spent eking out an existence in an inhospitable landscape, these roles were largely about the practical division of labour. With men away from home pasturing their flocks, women were left running the house and raising the children.

WHAT SARDINIAN WOMEN SAY...

Given the traditional nature of society, surprisingly few Sardinian women appear preoccupied with gender-related issues. Instead, when we asked, most felt that men and women were in an equal position in terms of forging the future.

I hope that Sardinia begins to value its own historical, cultural and natural treasures and that it begins to develop sustainable tourism, as this would have an explosive effect on the whole of the Sardinian economy.

Valeria Pintus, marketing manager

I am proud of being Sardinian and I am proud of having my own company. Sardinia has lots to offer and I believe that, if it plays its cards right, this will increase in the future.

Sabina Morreale, marketing consultant

After 18 years in Milan, I came back to Sardinia in the hope that I would be able to realise my professional dreams on an island that until a few years ago was its own world. In many respects it still is its own little world, but technology has started to take hold even here, which means that with a virtual net geographical distances become irrelevant.

I am unable to present my own successes as true triumphs, but one thing I do know for certain: here there is a stubborn and proud workforce that is creatively inventing a way to survive the economic crisis.

Valeria Brandano, freelance photographer

Women have a lot more opportunities these days, compared to the past, although the island is still deep-rooted in tradition. Most women work and look after the children and do all the cleaning, and the idea of house husbands is unheard of. [But] I am optimistic for the future and believe the situation will continue to change.

Diletta Pia, biologist

In many ways this is why Sardinian women have few insecurities. They have always been active participants in community life. Perhaps it is this history that has allowed two women, Eleonora of Arborea (see p25) and Grazia Deledda, to become icons of Sardinia's historical and cultural landscape.

Still, without any unified organisation, women's liberation did not arrive on the island until well into the 1980s. Even now women undertake a traditional role in society. Recent initiatives such as the Progetto Marte, aimed at promoting e-learning in schools, have largely attracted the attention of boys. But it is vital that girls become more involved, as e-learning's potential to connect the next generation of Sardinians with the outside world means that it is likely to remain the most important initiative for progress and emancipation.

With the exception of rural communities, where traditional values and habits are rigidly maintained, Sardinia is no different from the rest of modern Italy. Since the 1960s education has done much to alter the roles of men and women, and plenty of women are now successful professionals. However, men continue to occupy the higher ranks of business and almost exclusively dominate the political scene.

For a stark insight into the cruelty and poverty of a shepherd's life, watch *Padre Padrone*, a film by the Taviani brothers adapted from the autobiography of Gavino Ledda.

POPULATION

The Sardinians are a hardy and proud people. There are, however, surprisingly few of them and their numbers are falling. Out of an Italian population of around 58 million, only 1,643,100 live in Sardinia. The

WEAVEAWEB

When UK-born Emma Bird moved to Cagliari from Milan in April 2003 she was in for a big surprise. Working as a journalist, she had always taken for granted her opportunities as a professional woman and assumed that as such she would easily make her way in the Sardinian workplace. Instead, she admits, it was a culture shock – her enthusiasm met a wall of resistance and she had few professional contemporaries of her own sex to confide in.

So she set up Weaveaweb, essentially an online forum supported by focus groups, where Italian-speaking women could network and develop their professional contacts and, hopefully, their businesses. From its launch in May 2004 it has proved a big success, with groups now established in Cagliari, Sassari and Alghero, and even as far afield as Rimini and Milan. Hearteningly, it has attracted all sorts of professional women, from investment bankers and stockbrokers to freelance photographers and entrepreneurs. Through the forum they have also started to offer seminars and workshops – something of a first in Sardinia – and from January 2006 they will be rolling out a mentoring programme to help graduating girls find their feet in the working world.

To find out more about their work, log on to www.weaveaweb.it.

number of Sardinians is probably much greater, since over the decades (especially 1950 to 1980) many have migrated to the mainland and abroad.

Almost half the present population is concentrated in the southern province of Cagliari (765,030), which also has the highest levels of unemployment, especially in the southwest. Next comes Sassari (460,690), followed by Nuoro (264,000) and Oristano (153,400).

Population density in Sardinia is just 69 people per sq km, compared with the Italian average of 192, and 425 in Campania, the country's most densely populated region.

With a low birth rate, little inward migration and many young people opting to move to the Italian mainland, the island's population looks doomed to drop. The national statistics institute, Istat, predicts the population could fall to 1,246,000 by 2050.

Salvatore Satta's The Day of Judgement sets the modern island in its proper cultural context – simmering family rivalries and provincial politics played out against a harsh agricultural backdrop.

RELIGION

Sardinians are fiercely Christian, but many of their traditions and festivals make reference to an older, pagan past. Like the rest of Italy, Sardinia is predominantly Roman Catholic. In the not-so-distant past, fear of retribution, both human and divine, was a constant element of rural life, where one's honour demanded that wrongs be avenged in vigorously pursued vendettas. Though church attendance has fallen across Italy since the end of WWII, churches still fill up regularly for Mass, even during the week, in many parts of Sardinia.

The Sardinian calendar is festooned with religious celebrations, and some of them reflect the long centuries of Iberian domination. This is particularly evident during several towns' Easter celebrations: Castelsardo, Iglesias and Tempio Pausania all put on solemn night processions dominated by the ominously hooded members of religious brotherhoods more readily associated with Spain.

Other customs are more particular to the island. Across Sardinia are scattered *chiese novenari*, small countryside chapels that are the object one or more times through the year of nine-day pilgrimages. These churches are generally surrounded by *cumbessias* (also known as *muristenes*), simple lodgings to house the pilgrims who come to venerate the saint honoured in the church.

Folk Roots

Although on one level the larger Sardinian festivals have an undoubted tourist appeal, it would be wrong to think that these festivities are maintained only for show. Many traditions, like Mamoiada's *mamuthones* (see p207), are so old that anthropologists believe they date to prehistoric times. No other folkloric tradition in Europe survives so completely. Unlike that of other societies, Sardinian folklore is not simply the product of a poor underclass but seen by all levels of society as a common cultural heritage. Throughout the centuries these celebrations have served as a constant reminder to Sardinians of who they are.

Each of the 370 villages and towns on the island has its own traditional costume.

For the visitor, observing a Sardinian festival holds the key to a deeper understanding of the people themselves. The striking costumes and jewellery of the women show a profound appreciation of skilled handicraft. Traditional pastimes such as horse racing and wrestling and competitive games like the Jocu de Sa Murra (see the boxed text, p214) allow men the opportunity to display their courage, nerve and skill. The contrast between the sexes is striking and clearly defined.

In all aspects these festivals express the deepest truths of Sardinian life, visually displaying the island's cultural mores and embodying its deep-rooted social values and darkest fears. The festivals may now be losing some of their currency as society moves away from its agricultural past, but they still reveal much about the character of the island.

Arts & Architecture

If you look at the Sardinian art scene from the lofty heights of the Renaissance and the grand opus of Italian arts it engendered, you will find it little more than a footnote. But Sardinia does have its own rich palette, evolved through ancient oral and craft traditions that are almost unique in their survival in 21st-century Europe. Music and poetry are the two great traditions of the island, and literature – barely begun by the 19th century – has since added its voice to the chorus of expression. You will also find a prolific contemporary-art scene, and a love of fine craftwork, constantly on display during the island's huge festivals.

THE ARTS
Music

The three-piped *launeddas* is Europe's oldest musical instrument, dating to the 9th century BC.

Shielded from outside influences, the island's musical traditions sound like nothing else on the planet and they fuel a contemporary fusion scene of vibrant beauty. Is this diluting Sardinian culture? Yes, but it also attracts new listeners, safeguarding an alien sound-world of extraordinary quality and diversity.

The two main indigenous traditions are the *launeddas* (see the boxed text, opposite), found in the south, and male-voice polyphony, found in the central and northern regions. Both reached a low ebb in the 1970s owing to a lack of interest, but the last two decades have seen a mushrooming of groups and individual artists all over the island.

To experience genuine tradition, head to one of the smaller village festivals. No procession in the Campidano region is without its *launeddas* player. If you can't attend a festival, buy the legendary recordings *Launeddas,* by Efisio Melis and Antonio Lara. Other names to look out for on the *launeddas* circuit are Franco Melis, Luigi Lai, Andria Pisu and Franco Orlando Mascia, while Furias and Sonos Isolanos are two of the best folklore groups.

Passionate about music? Learn more about the *launeddas* at http://sardinia.net/sonus.

There are two types of male-voice singing. A *tenore* is secular, and *cuncordu* is liturgical. Many towns boast good choirs, the best for *tenore* being Oniferi, Orune and Orgosolo. The most famous *a tenore* choir is the Tenores di Bitti. For *cuncordu,* head for Castelsardo, Orosei and Santu Lussurgiu. Polyphony from Gallura is smoother than *a tenore* and can be heard on Coro Gabriel's CD *Taxa* (1996).

The island has an impressive pantheon of female vocalists, most famous of whom is the 20th-century legend Maria Carta. Franca Masu is the diva of the Catalan enclave, Alghero, although the folksy tunes of Elena Ledda are probably more widely known. Solo singing was traditionally accompanied by *launeddas* in the south and by guitar in the north, and Ledda often pairs up with the accomplished Mauro Palmas on the mandolin or the laud. *Organetto* (melodeon) and *fisarmonica* (accordion) also have strong Sardinian traditions.

A superb overview of Sardinian music is the DVD *Talam Sardegna* (RTSI, 2005).

Marino Derosas is an outstanding guitar player – modern, but still very Sardinian – and Ritmia's *Forse Il Mare* is a masterpiece of Mediterranean-meets-jazz. Blending jazz improvisation with local sounds are world-class trumpeter Paolo Fresu and the superb Trio Argia.

Poetry

Among the most intriguing vocal arts are the so-called *gare poetiche* (poetry duels). At least as far back as the 19th century, villagers would gather at local festivals and face off with each other. Two verbal adver-

---

THE LAUNEDDAS *Barnaby Brown*

Although this intriguing bagpipe-like instrument appears carved on 10th-century Irish and Scottish stones, its vibrant trance-inducing music survives only in Sardinia, connecting the listener directly with the Bronze Age.

In the past, *launeddas*-playing was a profession that required superhuman determination to pursue. Teaching was wilfully ineffective, so students were forced to travel secretly from festival to festival, stealing the good music that their masters so jealously guarded. The only reason the tradition is so healthy today is thanks to recordings made by a young Dane between 1957 and 1962.

Until the 1930s each village had its own *launeddas* player, and bachelors paid handsomely to keep the best players attached to their villages. This was because the Sunday *ballu* in the piazza was how single Sardinians met, but, sadly, Mussolini's reforms put an end to all that.

Launeddas come in eight varieties, each with a distinct repertoire (*Mediana, Fiorassiu, Punt'e Organu*, etc). A player would normally have 10 to 15 instruments in his case. The two chanters have four notes, plus an invisible fifth note, which disappears into the sound of the third longer cane, 'the drone'. These two disappearing notes allow the illusion of staccato and are the source of the music's bubbliness.

Barnaby Brown is a triplepipe player

---

saries would improvise rhyming repartee that was sarcastic, ironic or simply insulting. The audience loved it and chimed in with their own improvised shooting! Little of this was ever written down, but you can find CDs featuring a classic duo from the mid-20th century, Remundo Piras and Peppe Sozu.

Bardic contests still take place in the mountain villages and there are two important poetry competitions, Ozieri's Premio di Ozieri (p144) and the Settembre dei Poeti in Seneghe (p125).

Sardinia's most famous poet is Sebastiano Satta (1867–1914), who celebrated the wild beauty of the island in his poetry *Versi Ribelli* and *Canti Barbaricini*.

In the 1930s the Fascists banned the Sardinian *cantadores* (poets), whose attacks on church and state they deemed dangerous and subversive.

Dance

Various traditional folk dances still survive in Sardinia. Many are similar and generically referred to as *ballo sardo* (Sardinia dancing) or *su ballu tundu* (dancing in the round). They have much in common with Mediterranean folk dancing elsewhere. Sometimes people dance in a circle, and on other occasions they pair off, facing the same way with one arm held around the other's waist. Various combinations of quick steps backward and forward, followed by more lively movements, typify the dancing. There has been much speculation on the connections between *ballo sardo* and the similar *sardana* (circular folk dance) of Catalonia in northeastern Spain.

Literature

Grazia Deledda (1871–1936), born in Nuoro, towers above the world of Sardinian literature and is among Italy's most important early-20th-century realist writers. Her best-known novel is probably *Canne al Vento*, which recounts the slide into poverty of the aristocratic Pintor family, but all her works share a strong local flavour. She moved to Rome in 1900 and in 1926 won the Nobel Prize.

Every traveller to the island should also pack *Il Giorno del Giudizio* (The Day of Judgement) by Salvatore Satta (1902–75). With its descriptions of family rivalry, provincial politics, agricultural struggle and landscape, the novel sets the island in its true historical perspective and is often compared to Giuseppe di Lampedusa's Sicilian classic *Il Gattopardo* (The Leopard).

Satta's contemporary Giuseppe Dessì (1909–77) is best known for his uncompromising realism. *Il Disertore* tells the story of a WWI deserter caught between a sense of duty and his own moral code. Notable contemporaries of Dessì were Salvatore Cambosu (1895–1962) and eminent politician and intellectual Emilio Lussu (1890–1975).

Post-WWII writers include Calasetta-born Paride Rombi (1921–97), whose prize-winning novel *Perdu* was also an act of solidarity with the Sulcis area's working classes, whose plight he describes in the book. Maria Giacobbe (born 1928), a journalist and writer who has lived in Denmark since 1958, is best known for her 1957 novel *Diario di una Maestrina,* about a small-town teacher.

Better known beyond Sardinia is Gavino Ledda (born 1938), who won few friends with *Padre Padrone,* a stark account of his harsh life as a shepherd. He only learned to read as an adult in the army, which was his ticket out of the cycle of poverty that still afflicted many of his age in postwar Sardinia. The book was turned into an equally heart-rending film by the Taviani brothers in 1976.

More recently Sardinia has been developing a good crop of noir writers. Although not Sardinian by birth, Massimo Carlotto (born 1956; see the boxed text, p84), the prolific crime writer, now calls Cagliari home. In his footsteps follow new Sardinian talents including Marcello Fois (born 1960) and Flavio Soriga (born 1975), who won the Premio Italo Calvino prize for his *Diavoli di Nuraiò* in 2000.

The most important Sardinian writer of recent years is Sergio Atzeni (1952–95; www.sergio-atzeni.it, in Italian). Like Deledda's, his novels suggest a society that resists the simple reductions of comfortable moral and political assumptions. His one novel in translation, *Bakunin's Son* (*Il Figlio di Bakunin*; 1991), is set in Sardinia and depicts the intractable conditions of political and social life in postwar Italy.

> 'More recently Sardinia has been developing a good crop of noir writers.'

Painting & Sculpture
THE MISTS OF TIME

Ancient Sardinia must have been a busy place, if the number of menhirs (standing stones) and *nuraghi* (stone towers) is anything to go by. The indigenous population clearly had an artistic bent even then – ceramics from the 4th millennium BC show simple engraved decorations. By the 3rd millennium BC there were etched symbols inside the rock tombs, and a millennium later the mysterious menhirs started to appear.

Over the centuries the sophistication in ceramic decoration evolved, but the really startling development made its appearance in the late Bronze Age (from about 1000 BC) with the emergence of the *bronzetti,* bronze figurines representing a whole cast of ancient characters from chieftains and warriors to wrestlers and *launeddas* players. The collection in Cagliari's Museo Archeologico Nazionale (p65) provides a tangible window onto this incredibly remote period of Mediterranean history.

PHOENICIANS, GREEKS & ROMANS

Like Sicily, Sardinia preserves a few fragments of the huge Carthaginian empire, which was wiped out by the Romans during the Punic Wars. The Carthaginians began to establish their coastal settlements in the 9th century BC and along with the Greeks and Mycenaeans brought with them some of the finer things in life, such as more sophisticated ceramics, jewellery, amulets, glassware, sculpture and coins.

But as traders they never penetrated much into the interior and accordingly not much remains, just the seaside sites of Nora and Tharros,

Cagliari's underground cisterns and tombs, and a collection of *objets d'art* that only just fills the museums of Cagliari (p65), Sassari (p137) and Oristano (p117). Although the Romans were more successful in their occupation, they too have left slender evidence that they were ever here. The broad amphitheatre in the middle of Cagliari is their only really significant lasting monument.

MAESTROS OF THE MIDDLE AGES
Spanish occupation certainly had one positive influence: an explosion of outstanding artwork in the late Middle Ages. Influenced by trends in Catalonia and Spain, local artists produced a medley of altarpieces and religious paintings, although many of these remain anonymous.

From the Catalano-Aragonese came the *retablo* or altarpiece. The idea was imported from Barcelona, as were the artists, such as Joan Mates (documented 1391–1431), whose *retablo* hangs in Cagliari's Pinacoteca Nazionale (p67), the island's most important collection of Sardinian masters.

It is unknown whether the Maestro di Castelsardo (documented at the end of the 15th and in the early 16th century) also came from Barcelona. His brooding pieces, vivid colour on backgrounds either glittering with gold or intensely dark, still hang in the cathedral in Castelsardo (p149).

Among his contemporaries were the Maestro di Sanluri (one of the earliest Sardinian artists to pick up on lessons from the Renaissance) and Maestro di Olzai, who were active towards the end of the 15th century.

THE STAMPACE SCHOOL
If Sardinian art had a golden age, it was probably the 16th century, dominated by the so-called *scuola di Stampace* (Stampace school), at whose core was the Cavaro family. The star was Pietro (documented 1508–38), schooled in Barcelona and Naples. Some of his works, among them a remarkably expressive *SS Pietro e Paolo* (Saints Peter and Paul), hang in Cagliari's Pinacoteca Nazionale (p67). His father, Lorenzo (documented 1500–18), and son Michele (documented 1538–84) are also represented in the collection, along with colleague Antioco Mainas (documented 1537–71). At a time when mainland Italy was in the final flush of its Renaissance adventure, Sardinia's isolation kept these artists apart from the ground-breaking changes in the art world and their paintings retain a rigid Gothic feel.

'If Sardinian art had a golden age, it was probably the 16th century...'

With the advent of the Maestro di Ozieri a new fluidity entered painting. Little is known about this artist other than that he worked in the latter half of the 16th century. His work is imbued with the flowing mannerism of Michelangelo and Rafael, and it shows influences from the Neapolitan and Dutch schools of art. Today one of his most important works, the *Deposizione di Cristo dalla Croce* (Deposition of Christ from the Cross), can be seen in the cathedral in Ozieri (p144). Along with Pietro Cavaro, he is considered one of the masters of Sardinian painting.

A CULTURAL DESERT
The 17th and 18th centuries were largely dominated by the work of outsiders who came and went. A couple of exceptions were the Alghero-born Francesco Pinna (documented 1591–1616) and Bartolomeo Castagnola (documented 1598–1611).

In the 18th century, Giovanni Marghinotti (1798–1865) occupied the artistic stage much as Gaetano Cima dominated the architectural scene. His work ranged from altarpieces and royal portraits to a series of romantic flights of fantasy depicting scenes of life in Roman and medieval Sardinia.

WRITING ON THE WALL

The 1970s inspired the popular art movement of *murales* (murals). Born of the students' and workers' unrest of 1968, the murals were often a political statement, although they were also a means of celebrating the island's earthy culture. On an island that gave birth to heavyweight Marxist philosopher Antonio Gramsci, it's quite apt that art has been popularised in this way. In Orgosolo (p205) there are now over 150 murals, many of them executed by the town's school students. They expound the most pressing social issues, from land reform and unemployment to the big questions of famine, warfare and terrorism. The town of San Sperate, just outside Cagliari, is another mural centre worth checking out.

THE 20TH CENTURY

Impressionism had little impact on the island – it didn't really suit the serious-minded Sards – although Antonio Ballero (1864–1932) was strongly influenced by the movement. If anything, the 20th century was dominated by the oil paintings of Giuseppe Biasi (1885–1945), who seemed to capture the Sardinian condition perfectly with his bold approach, definite brushwork and moody palette.

Landscapes and rural scenes dominated the oeuvre of some of Biasi's immediate successors, among them Stanis Dessy (1900–86), Giovanni Ciusa-Romagna (1907–58) and Cesare Cabras (1886–1965).

Sardinia's most important sculptor of the first half of the 20th century, Francesco Ciusa (1883–1949), is best known for his *Madre dell'Ucciso* (Mother of the Killed), now in Rome. It won the Venice Biennale prize in 1907.

Costantino Nivola (1911–88) took the baton from Ciusa. His bronze works and menhir-inspired statues are best admired in the Orani museum (see p207). More are on show in Nuoro, at the Museo d'Arte (p198).

A wonderful collector's item is the fully illustrated monograph Giuseppe Biasi, showcasing the work of one of Sardinia's greatest artists. It's available from www.artbooks.com.

WHAT'S HAPPENING NOW?

Since the so-called democratic Marxist movement of culture (!), Sardinian artists have launched into a period of heavy experimentation with abstractionism, modernism and multimedia, with varying degrees of success. Primo Pantoli, Cipriano Mele and Luigi Mazzarelli are the movement's greatest proponents and all have their work displayed in the Galleria Comunale d'Arte (p71) in Cagliari. Caterina Lai does something similar with her multimedia sculptures.

It's a little eclectic to say the least, but there's no denying the local demand. Stranger still is the work of younger artists such as Bob Marongiu (see his site www.bobart.it, in Italian), currently all the rage in the professional salons of Cagliari.

The Art–Culture section of www.marenostrum .it gives you the lowdown on all the up-and-coming cultural events and festivals, including art retrospectives and cinema shows.

ARCHITECTURE

Sardinia doesn't have a grand architectural tradition – most of its influences came from abroad and failed to take root in the local culture.

The Bronze Age

The few exceptions to this are the island's curious prehistoric buildings, the *domus de janas* (literally 'fairy houses'; tombs cut into rock), the menhirs and betyls, and the *tombe di giganti* (literally 'giants' tombs'; ancient mass graves), so-called because the symbolic *exedra* (entrance) was marked by an imposing central stone.

The most striking architectural testimony to the island's ancient past, however, are the *nuraghi*, some of which date back as far as 1800 BC.

Design-wise they usually comprise a tall central tower, which in some cases would have reached a height of 20m. This was fortified with further defensive towers and outside the stronghold the remains of small villages are still quite clear.

Most of the 7000 *nuraghi* on the island are little more than tumble-down ruins, but some complexes, such as the Nuraghe Su Nuraxi (p113), the Nuraghe Losa (p128) and the Nuraghe Santu Antine (p144), remain largely intact. At the latter two part of the tall central tower remains, and you can climb to the 2nd floor and look out over the countryside. The more elaborate towers have at their core what seems to have been a meeting room, from where stairs lead off to the higher floors.

Finally, from about 1100 to 1000 BC, the *nuraghe* people began constructing elaborate *pozzi sacri* (sacred wells or well temples), shaped like keyholes in the ground. The wells always face the sun and are oriented so that at the solstices the sun shines directly down the stairs to illuminate the water.

Pick up Paolo Melis' handy little book *The Nuraghic Civilization* for a thorough explanation of these mysterious structures. It's available at the ticket offices of the large sites.

Classical Sardinia

Sardinia's two most impressive classical ruins are Nora (p109) in the southwest and Tharros (p124) in the west. These ports started as Phoenician trading settlements, but what you see today are Roman roads, columns, temple remnants, public baths, theatres and patrician houses. A grander Roman theatre survives in Cagliari, too. The ruins of Porto Torres (in the north) and the hot baths of Fordongianus are further evidence of the Roman presence on the island.

Romanesque to Baroque

The only other appealing curiosities on the island's architectural landscape are the charming 12th-century Pisan Romanesque churches of the northwest.

Although the churches vary a great deal, common elements are easily traced: the simple structure, with a single nave and no transept; the square-based bell tower; and the typically Tuscan bent for two-colour banding. The biggest Romanesque church is the **Basilica di San Gavino** (p147) in Porto Torres.

The Catalano-Aragonese and subsequent Spaniards who followed the Pisans left a mix of Gothic and baroque efforts behind them, often rolled into one. Sassari's two main churches, the Duomo (p139) and the Chiesa di Santa Maria di Betlem (p139), are examples of this fusion. Sassari's Duomo is the island's only notable example of baroque.

Environment

THE LAND

At 24,000 sq km, Sardinia is the second-largest island in the Mediterranean after Sicily, but unlike Sicily it is not a tropical, or typical, Mediterranean island. Geologically speaking it is older than mainland Italy, its granite and basalt mountains predating the Apennines and the Alps. They dominate 68% of the island in a patchwork of massifs carved up by Sardinia's four mighty rivers, the Tirso, the Flumendosa, the Coghinas and the Mannu.

In the east rises the Gennargentu massif, now Sardinia's main national park. It isn't particularly high – the highest peak, Punta La Marmora, is 1834m – but it is ancient and rugged. Its ridges are broken by deep canyons, rivers and a plethora of caves, while its lower valleys are handsomely forested with holm oaks and maple, rising through the ranks of juniper, holly and yew trees towards the summit.

The forests and woodlands of the island are among its most delightful characteristics, a faint memory of an older, greener Mediterranean. Standouts are the dense cork forests that ring Tempio Pausania and the 3600-hectare forest of the Monte Arcosu reserve southwest of Cagliari, the largest forest of holm and cork oak remaining in the Mediterranean.

Sardinia's multifarious forms of terrain are sometimes bewildering, as dark forests give way to extensive plains 'running away into the distance'. The Campidano plain between Cagliari and Oristano is the most extensive and supplies much of the wheat for Sardinia's famous bread. Another, older, type of plateau is the *giara,* a large basalt tabletop constantly whipped by the *maestrale* (northwesterly wind) and home to pony-sized horses, called *achettas* in the Sardinian dialect (*cavallini* in Italian). The *giare* of Siddi, Serri and especially Gesturi are particularly noteworthy.

Lapping at the base of its rugged interior are the jewel-coloured waters of Sardinia's sea. The 1849km coastline is one of the most pristine in the Mediterranean and offers hugely varied vistas from the high cliffs of the east to the wide, wind-whipped dunes of the west. Numerous saltpans, marshes and lagoons also punctuate the coast in the south and west of the island. The largest of these are Santa Gilla, west of Cagliari, and the Stagno di Cabras and the Stagno di Sale Porcus on the Sinis Peninsula, which are home to 10,000 pink flamingos. These lagoons comprise some 30,000 acres of protected wetland, nearly half of all the wetlands in Italy.

WILDLIFE

Cut off by Sicily and Corsica from the main thoroughfares of trade and commerce, Sardinia's flora and fauna (many species of which are found only here and in neighbouring Corsica) have evolved in their own idiosyncratic way, making the island a kind of European Madagascar. Erosion and deforestation have had some impact, and hunting remains a common pastime. But these have not had the devastating effect here that they have had elsewhere in southern Italy, undoubtedly because of the obstinate terrain, which provides suitable sanctuary for the island's wildlife.

Animals

Sardinia's mountains and forests harbour a host of indigenous species, such as the swarthy *cervo sardo* (Sardinian deer) which roams the thick forests of Gennargentu, Monte Arcosu and Monte Sette Fratelli. In the

Immerse yourself in DH Lawrence's *Sea and Sardinia*. His acute observations of the changing moods of the landscape are deeply compelling.

Watch the Taviani brothers' haunting film *Padre Padrone*. Its moody shots of the island's mountainous interior are deeply atmospheric.

THE DECRETO SORU

Since the 1960s Sardinia has benefited from its reputation as an exclusive destination for the rich and famous, a clientele attracted to the island for its virgin beauty and stunning seascapes. But as Sardinia has become more accessible to tourism the risk of rampant development has begun to raise real concerns.

One of the most controversial proposals of recent years was Silvio Berlusconi's development on the protected wetlands of the Costa Turchese. The plans were to develop a huge 450-hectare site to accommodate 385 villas, 995 apartments in multistorey blocks, a golf course and a new marina.

Sardinians, luckily, are a politically proactive bunch and are all too familiar with foreigners' exploitation. Years of protests and petitions finally paid off, and in July 2004 the government suspended all development along the coast. This temporary suspension has now been passed as law, and the Decreto Soru prohibits all new building within 2km of the sea for the next two years. This bodes well for the island's future and, hopefully, signals a return to the sensitive development ideas that characterised the building of the Costa Smeralda in the 1960s.

1960s the deer came close to extinction but they have since made a healthy recovery to some 700 animals under the watchful eye of the **WWF** (www.wwf.it).

Other large mammals include the *cinghiale sardo* (Sardinian wild boar), a smaller-than-average boar that roots around the nut groves and woodlands of lower mountain slopes. Hunting has certainly reduced their numbers over the years, so a larger boar from mainland Italy has been imported to boost the population. Interbreeding is creating a newer, bigger breed, so the true Sardinian boars are becoming hard to find.

Sheep outnumber people three to one on the island.

On the high plateau of the Giara di Gesturi *achettas* run wild; weirder still are the albino donkeys of the Parco Nazionale dell'Asinara in the northwest. The Isola Asinara is also home to 500 *mouflon* (wild sheep), some of Sardinia's oldest inhabitants. Much coveted by locals for their remarkable curved horns (used to make handles for quality Sardinian knives), they were on the verge of extinction not long ago but they now scale the cliffs of less accessible parts of the interior in greater numbers.

Reptiles thrive on the island, but there are absolutely no poisonous snakes.

Marten, wildcats, foxes and hares make up the cast of smaller mammals on the island, and along the southwestern coast's arid beaches turtles come to lay their eggs.

Birds

Located on the main migration route between Europe, Asia and Africa, Sardinia is an ornithologist's paradise. Between September and March thousands of flamingos visit the island and nest in the *stagni* (lagoons) of Oristano province and around Cagliari.

The flamingos are joined by a host of other wetland birds, including herons, crane, spoonbill, cormorants, terns, dozens of waders, ducks and more. Some 200 bird species (one-third of the total number of species in Europe) make a pit stop on the island during their spring and autumn migrations.

Consult www.lipu.it (in Italian) for information on the Lega Italiana Protezione Uccelli (Italian Bird Protection League; LIPU). Its UK branch is at www.lipu-uk.org.

Inland ducks and cranes give way to an impressive crew of raptors (again, largely migratory) – Golden and Bonelli's eagles patrol the high skies in spring and autumn, as do the black vulture, the *lammergeier* (bearded vulture) and the peregrine falcon. On the Isola di San Pietro there is a semipermanent colony of the rare Eleonora falcon, named after

Queen Eleonora of Arborea, who declared the bird a protected species in 1400. The griffon vulture maintains a colony in the west of the island, along the coast between Alghero and Bosa.

Plants

To be sure of seeing the best of Sardinia's wildflowers you need to visit in spring – April tends to be a good month. If you leave it too far into May you'll miss the best as summer sets in.

In the higher woodland country of central and northeastern Sardinia, various types of oak, especially cork oak, dominate. Cork has long been an important industry on the island, and the area around Tempio Pausania is covered in cork forests. The nearby town of Calangianus is one of the main centres for processing the material and produces 90% of the corks for Italy's wine bottles.

Highland flowers such as the rare peony – also known as the 'rose of Gennargentu' – add a splash of colour to barren mountain peaks, especially around Bruncu Spina and Punta La Marmora. At lower altitudes typical Mediterranean scrub, *macchia*, predominates. The term covers a wide range of plants, including gorse, juniper, heather, broom and arbutus (also known as strawberry trees). In the grassy vegetation are many flowers, including violets, the blue of the periwinkle and lavender, the colourful mix of irises and many species of orchid. Perhaps the best known of the *macchia* plants in Sardinia is the ubiquitous *mirto* (myrtle), from whose berries and leaves two fine sweet liqueurs, bearing the same name, are extracted.

Many beaches on the western and southern coasts are backed by lovely pine stands where locals choose to picnic and lie during the hottest hours of the day. Palm trees are quite uncommon, and most are imported. An exception is the so-called dwarf palm, whose leaves are used to make wicker baskets.

NATIONAL PARKS & RESERVES

Sardinia boasts three national parks, two regional parks and a series of mostly marine reserves that cover a meagre 4% of the island's total area. This seems small given Sardinia's unique and fragile ecosystems, but so far the island has avoided the worst excesses of development and invasive tourism. However, an increasing profile combined with low-cost charter flights may have more negative effects in the future (see the boxed text, p43).

The most extensive of the national parks is the Parco Nazionale del Golfo di Orosei e del Gennargentu, which takes up a great swath of central Nuoro province, covering Barbagia (p205), the Supramonte plateau (p202) and the matchless beauty of the Golfo di Orosei (p215).

The Parco Nazionale dell'Arcipelago di La Maddalena (p182) encompasses all the islands of this northwestern archipelago, although clearly much of the main island and its port town, La Maddalena, do not quite fit the description of park. Isola di Caprera, joined to Isola Maddalena by a narrow causeway, has its own status as a natural reserve.

The most recent of the parks is the Parco Nazionale dell'Asinara (p152), a former prison island. Otherwise, one of the more important natural reserves is the Riserva Naturale Foresta di Monte Arcosu (p111), southwest of Cagliari, which is protected by the WWF.

Areas with some degree of protection owing to their status as marine reserves include Capo Carbonara in the southeast; the Sinis Peninsula and its offshore island, Isola Mal di Ventre; the Isola Tavolara and nearby Punta Coda Cavallo; and Isola Budelli, within the Parco Nazionale dell'Arcipelago di La Maddalena.

Walkers should equip themselves with specialist books such as Mediterranean Wild Flowers, by M Blamey and C Grey Wilson.

Visit www.parks.it for further information on Sardinia's parks.

For details of Sardinia's best beaches, see www.blueflag.org.

WATER, WATER EVERYWHERE

Sardinia's single biggest headache is lack of water. As demand grows in the cities and expanding tourist resorts, the problem becomes more acute. In 2002 the drought was so severe that the capital, Cagliari, was down to four hours of running water a day.

The problem is not just the drought that has afflicted the island for decades. Equally important are mismanagement and poor maintenance of water-distribution systems. In the past, estimates of water lost through leaky pipes and seepage ranged from 20% upwards. Over the last couple of years some EU funds for infrastructure projects have been used to allay the immediate crisis but longer-term solutions are needed, and in the future desalination plants could be necessary.

Thankfully, in 2004 very heavy rains hit the island. In fact, the rainfall was so extensive that money had to be allocated to deal with flood damage. Still, with 51% of the island suffering the effects of desertification, water management is clearly going to be one of the big issues of the future.

ENVIRONMENTAL ISSUES

Until the 1960s Sardinia was so poor and neglected that there simply weren't many manmade environmental issues. The only real concerns for islanders (and animals) were the perennial problems of water shortages (above), deforestation of grazing lands and the inevitable effects of wind erosion caused by the *maestrale*.

But then the Aga Khan established his consortium on the Costa Smeralda, and within a few years it seemed as if the entire world had heard of Sardinia. Suddenly booming tourism, industrialisation and the rapid transition from an agricultural to a service-based economy began to have profound effects.

The population shift from small villages to urban conurbations was driven by the establishment in the 1960s of petrochemical and other heavy industrial plants (notably at Porto Torres, Portovesme, Sarroch, Arbatax and south of Oristano) to provide employment. Ultimately, this policy of creating industrial poles of attraction in deeply depressed rural regions has contributed little to the island's economy, although it has certainly created pockets of air and water pollution. The plants still operate today, but the oil crisis of the 1970s and the end of mining in the Iglesiente have doomed them to remain ugly white elephants.

Tourism has brought its own problems. While much of the island's coast remains refreshingly wild, the spread of tourist resorts along the northeast coast from Santa Teresa di Gallura to Olbia (taking in the Costa Smeralda), and along the coast immediately southwest of Cagliari and around the Costa Rei, has forever scarred the landscape. Pockets of development elsewhere are growing, and it appears that developers could overcook the goose that laid the golden egg.

More recently Sardinians have begun to raise their voices in protest in an attempt to limit developments that run contrary to their long-term benefit (see the boxed text, p43). There is now a growing trend towards ecosensitive tourism.

Sardinia Outdoors

Sardinia lacks the suave glamour that many visitors associate with Italy. Instead the island's charms lie in its untamed natural beauty, a combination of rugged rural scenery and one of the most dramatic coastlines in the Mediterranean. Its landscapes are old and timeless, incorporating rough primeval mountains, windswept plains, sun-scorched plateaus and thick forests, all fringed by the most extraordinary Caribbean-blue seas.

Despite its island status, Sardinia embodies the great outdoors – DH Lawrence repeatedly commented on the sense of 'space', and driving through the dramatic Gennargentu one is struck by how much it feels like the American West with its mighty rocky pinnacles and swooping valleys. It soon becomes clear that the tabloid image of marinas and martinis is just a fraction of the picture, confined to a small, rich enclave in the northeast. Beyond this Sardinia is an island for doing rather than seeing, and almost any outdoor activity will form the highlight of a trip.

For tailor-made holidays to Sardinia, including a range of activities such as cycling, horse riding, windsurfing, diving, golf and fishing, check out www.justsardinia.co.uk.

Nothing can quite top descending the vertical chasm of the Gola Su Gorruppu gorge or diving in sun-split waters full of blood-red coral and barracudas. From horse riding across the salty marshes of Oristano to climbing the slate-grey faces of the Orosei, Sardinia is an outdoor wonderland. What is more, Sardinians themselves are waking up to the potential of the island's hinterland as a means of sustainable tourism. At government level more efforts are being made to protect the coast (see the boxed text, p43). But this is very much a work in progress – even in the Gennargentu, the oldest of the island's parks, infrastructure is limited and often nonexistent. Don't let this put you off, though, as the rewards far outweigh the inconveniences you may encounter.

Information

The Michelin map 1:350,000 (series 566) is a good all-round road map to the island. Other good maps that will serve cyclists well are the slightly larger-scale Touring Club Italiano and Istituto Geografico de Agostini maps (1:200,000).

Walkers will want to get hold of the Italian national survey maps (Carta d'Italia), which cover Sardinia in both 1:25,000 and 1:50,000, although some of these were published as far back as 1990. Alternatively, two useful and readily available maps are Balzano Edizioni's *Barbagia* (1:50,000) and Belletti Editore's *Parco del Gennargentu* (1:100,000), both available in bookshops in Santa Maria Navarrese and Cala Gonone.

Lonely Planet's *Walking in Italy* and *Cycling in Italy* give step-by-step coverage of a range of walking and cycling itineraries.

WALKING & CLIMBING

Landscapes of Sardinia, by Andreas Stieglitz, is a handy little pocket book full of walks and driving tours around the island.

Sardinia's varied geography makes it the perfect place for trekking, and its dramatic cliffs and gorges provide exhilarating and often challenging opportunities for serious climbers. The most popular walking destination is the rugged Parco Nazionale del Golfo di Orosei e del Gennargentu, which takes in the highest point of the island, Punta La Marmora (1834m), the limestone massif of the Supramonte and the dramatic arc of the Golfo di Orosei.

Dorgali and Oliena are both excellent trekking bases from where you can strike out and explore the remote Valle di Lanaittu (p204), the prehistoric ruins of Sa Sedda 'e Sos Carros and Tiscali (p204), and the spectacular chasm of Gola Su Gorruppu (p217). The latter, with its claustrophobic walls and deeply carved river, is a fantastic location for some serious climbing. The most challenging trek-climb on the island is the Selvaggio Blu, between Baunei and Cala Gonone.

The park incorporates the most dramatic coastline on the island as the sheer cliffs of the Gennargentu plunge to aquamarine seas. A trek along this stretch is a must, as it takes in some of Sardinia's prettiest and most private hidden coves, such as Cala Gonone, Cala Luna and Cala Goloritzè (see the boxed text, p218). Climbers can detour up the dry gorges of Codula Fuili and Codula di Luna.

The 42km Selvaggio Blu is the most difficult hiking trail in Italy.

Less demanding walking trails can be found in the northeast of the island around Monte Limbara (1076m), near Tempio Pausania (p190). Other gentler walks can be done on La Giara di Gesturi (p114), around the mining country of the Iglesiente and around Capo Caccia, west of Alghero.

Best Time of Year

Sardinia enjoys a mild Mediterranean climate with damp winters and hot summers. July and August are simply too hot for walking, with temperatures between 25°C and 30°C. Winter temperatures hover around 10°C, and rain and mist can be a real problem for walkers, especially around gorges and ravines, where there is the danger of flash floods and mud slides.

The best time for walking is undoubtedly late spring (between April and June), when the flowers are out in full force and the landscape retains a rich green flush. In addition, there are frequent patron-saint feast days in the local towns and villages (see p227). Bear in mind that the weather can be changeable and be sure to equip yourself for some rainfall.

September to October is also good for walking – with the heat of summer still in the stones, the weather is a lot more stable and it's a perfect time for swimming. Autumn walking also offers a wildly different aspect of the landscape – shades of gold and brown – and islanders are busy with the grape harvest and mushroom picking.

Prime Spots

There's a clutch of fantastic walks to be had in the Parco Nazionale del Golfo di Orosei e del Gennargentu, combining vertigo-inducing mountain views with coastal walks to the hidden coves of the Golfo di Orosei. One of the shortest and most spectacular paths is the Scala 'e Pradu (p203),

---

WHAT TO TAKE

- Comfortable walking boots are essential for walking across the jagged, potholed terrain
- Compass, whistle, torch and first-aid kit
- For trips in the Gennargentu and on the Giara di Gesturi you will need adequate waterproofs and cold-weather clothes – a wind jacket, warm headgear and gloves
- Mat, sleeping bag, fire-lighting equipment and torch if you plan on camping
- Mosquito repellent in summer
- Sun block, sunglasses, hat and small backpack
- Beach bag, towel and a tent for sun shade, as many beaches are very exposed
- Mobile phone – an excellent safety precaution, although they may not work everywhere

a tough three-hour trek along narrow switchbacks from Oliena to Punta sos Nidos (1348m), from where you have a staggering bird's-eye view of the Supramonte and the glittering Golfo di Orosei. Then there is the more straightforward ascent of Punta La Marmora, or you could opt for the fascinating trek to the prehistoric settlement of Tiscali (p204), hidden in a huge limestone cavern.

The highlight of trekking in the Supramonte is the Gola Su Gorruppu (p217), a giant cleft carved by the Flumineddu River that plunges to a depth of 400m. Walkers can only penetrate a short distance into the gorge, but experienced, well-equipped climbers can explore further.

South of the Gorruppu is the mountain village of Ulassai (p211), with its stunning amphitheatre of rock. You can combine pretty valley scenery and sunbathing by trekking from the pilgrimage site of San Pietro di Golgo to the magnificent Cala Goloritzè cove (see the boxed text, p218).

To snap some of those unforgettable coastal views you have plenty of island-wide options. In the east a path follows the coastline of the Golfo di Orosei from the cove of Cala Gonone to Cala Luna. In Gallura you can trek through the weird granite landscape of Capo Testa or around Isola Caprera (p185) in the Arcipelago di La Maddalena, while west of Alghero the headlands of Capo Caccia (p165) offer more spectacular coastal paths.

Organisations offering guided walks:

Cooperativa Ghivine (☎ /fax 0784 967 21, 338 834 16 18; www.ghivine.com; Via La Marmora 69/e, Dorgali) Excellent range of excursions covering hiking, canyoning, caving, mountain-biking and climbing.

Cooperativa Goloritzè (☎ /fax 0782 61 05 99, 368 702 89 80; goloritze@tiscalinet.it) Based 8km north of Baunei, this cooperative offers guided treks on foot, or by horse or donkey. You can spend a day exploring the Golgo plain on horseback, opt for a two-day walk from Golgo to Cala Sisine or go for a one-week walk along the Golfo di Orosei. The company also covers the Selvaggio Blu.

Cooperativa Gorropu (☎ 0782 64 92 82, 333 850 71 57; www.gorropu.com; Via Sa Preda Lada 2, Urzulei) An organisation of young, competent and environmentally friendly guides. It offers a variety of one-, five- and six-day walks, including the descent of the Codula Luna, the Gola Su Gorruppu and the strenuous Selvaggio Blu. It can also arrange caving and canyoning trips. English and German are spoken.

Servizi Turistici Corrasi (☎ 0784 28 71 44; www.corrasi.com; Piazza Santa Maria 30, Oliena) A well-established local tour operator that offers guided tours and treks in the Supramonte and Gennargentu.

WINDSURFING, KITE SURFING & SURFING

For more information on kite surfing in Sardinia, log on to www.kiteworld sardinia.com.

Given the constant winds that bluster around the island, surfing and all its derivatives are popular pastimes here. The island is well known for hosting championship events such as the Kitesurf World Cup, off the beaches between Vignola and Santa Teresa di Gallura, and the Chia Classic windsurfing competition in the southwest.

The windsurfing epicentre of the island is on the northeast coast at Porto Pollo (p182), and major schools are established on the Isola dei Gabbiani (p182). Committed surfers prefer the huge rolling waves of the west coast, in particular the Sinis Peninsula, where waves can reach 5m around the wild Capo Mannu. A popular beach is Putzu Idu at San Giovanni di Sinis (p124). Also on the west coast is the isolated beach of Spiaggia della Piscinas (see the boxed text, p98).

For those of us whose windsurfing dreams are more modest, lots of fun can be had on Stintino's beautiful beach, Spiaggia della Pelosa (p152),

TOP DIVES

With its crystal-clear waters, spectacular grottoes, granite coastlines and some of the longest, cleanest beaches in the Mediterranean, Sardinia is a diver's paradise. To get you started, here is our selection of the best island dives.

- Carloforte, Isola di San Pietro (p102) The gentle 17m Tacche Bianche dive enables you to explore the underside of this natural arc. It's dotted with little caves and gorges full of colourful fish, shellfish and coral.

- Nereo Cave, Alghero (p153) This is the biggest underwater cave in the Mediterranean. On this wonderful dive you'll see lots of Alghero's famous frilly red coral, and the water is stunningly illuminated by streaks of sunlight. The dive ranges from 11m to 30m.

- Oyster Cave, Golfo di Orosei (p215) A very pretty dive due to the rare presence of live oysters and fossils, the Oyster Cave excursion also features lots of prawns and mussels. At the top of the cave you can see submerged columns and stalactites.

- *Romagna* wreck, Cagliari (p62) The *Romagna*, a steamship built in 1899, was sunk by a mine on 2 August 1943. Located in the Golfo di Cagliari at a depth of 42m, its most interesting features are the big propeller, the pilot bridge and the kitchen. This fascinating dive is recommended for expert divers only.

- Ruins of Nora, Pula (p109) This easy but exciting 6m to 12m dive takes you close to the archaeological site of Nora, where you will see underwater ruins and amphorae on the sea bed.

- Scoglio di Tahiti, Isola Caprera, Arcipelago di La Maddalena (p185) A good dive for beginners, this excursion takes in enormous granite rocks and monoliths forming passages and small caves. It's a true labyrinth of tunnels where underwater life of any kind abounds.

- Secca di Santa Caterina, Villasimius (p87) The *secca* (underwater mountain) is about 1.2km southwest of Capo Carbonara in the Villasimius marine park. Here you can dive between 12m and 38m to see old anchors near the lighthouse, deep canyons and some big red-coral caves.

- Secca del Papa, Isola Tavolara, Costa Smeralda (p174) This is a spectacular dive spot from all points of view: morphology, colours, and quantity and variety of flora and fauna. Its medium depth is approximately 30m, although it extends to 50m. It's not suitable for open-water divers.

and Cagliari's huge Poetto beach (p72). An excellent website for booking windsurfing holidays in Sardinia is www.planetwindsurf.com.

SAILING

Never mind the little sails, Sardinia's marinas are packed full of impressive yachts and the island is a mecca for sailors. Its fabulous coasts and strong winds provide innumerable and exciting sailing itineraries and excursions further afield to Corsica, the Balearic Islands and even Tunisia. The island also hosts major sailing events such as the World Championships, held in Cagliari in September, and there is plenty of summer sailing action on the Costa Smeralda and in the Straits of Bonifacio between Sardinia and Corsica. If you don't have any sailing expertise you can get a little taste of the high life at Cala Gonone, where a group of four to eight people can hire gorgeous sailing boats like the *Dovesesto* for a long weekend (see p219).

At 15km long, the Grotta del Bue Marino, near Cala Gonone, is the largest sea cave in the Mediterranean.

The main sailing portal for the island is www.sailingsardinia.com (in Italian), which is full of information, news and events, and provides some excellent links where you can find charters and skippers for hire.

Water-skis, jet skis, motorised dinghies and other water-sports paraphernalia are a feature of all the bigger and more popular beach resorts.

HORSE RIDING

Looking at the rundown of Sardinian festivals, you won't fail to notice that horses are very much a part of Sardinian culture. Horse riding is becoming a popular activity on the island – there is something truly magical in coming upon *nuraghe* ruins on horseback, and once you're freed from the tyranny of the roads it's possible to enjoy the hidden corners of the countryside in an ecofriendly way.

Excellent equestrian centres have sprouted on the island, especially in Oristano and around Cagliari. The leading riding centre is **Ala Birdi** (www .alabirdi.com), on the coast at Arborea (p122), where you can participate in lessons, book a riding weekend or organise a week-long itinerary. In Nuoro province many trekking specialists also arrange horse-riding excursions (see p48).

A wonderful organic farm offering a range of horse-riding options, including exciting night rides, is **Mandra Edera** (☎ 0785 527 10; www.mandraedera .it, in Italian), in Oristano province (p128).

For an outdoor holiday on an authentic working farm, browse www .agriturismisardi.it (in Italian).

CYCLING

Cycling in Sardinia is not for the faint-hearted, given the largely mountainous terrain. The island does have superbly maintained and lightly trafficked roads, though, and there are spots where it isn't all uphill! The sensational and enduring panoramas and undulating open country dotted with cork oaks are certainly worth the effort.

For those more into scenery than breaking endurance records, the western coast is the place to be, especially the Riviera del Corallo around Alghero. Here you can indulge in a fantastic ride from Alghero to Bosa (see the boxed text, p162).

Another excellent area for moderate-grade cycling is the Costa Verde between Iglesias and Oristano. This coastal route passes through the old mining towns of Buggerru and Arbus and further north the lagoons around Oristano. There are plenty of more demanding off-road trails to indulge in, as well as some fabulous beaches to lie on when pedalling gets too hard.

Ambitious cyclists should head straight for the mountains of the Gennargentu, where the SS128 and SS125 will take them through an impressive landscape of towering massifs and deep gorges. The roads cling to the rugged mountainside, swoop down long, steep valleys and meander through dense green forests. This is some of Sardinia's most remote territory, so you will need to be prepared for all eventualities.

For those planning to spend more time in Sardinia, www.sardiniaby bike.cjb.net has itineraries and information on organised cycling tours.

Food & Drink

Donkey sausages, tripe sandwiches, horse *carpaccio,* black pudding and cocks' combs – the traditional Sardinian menu reads like the *Rocky Horror Show* of the food world to the antiseptic modern palate. But as Western gourmets start to rediscover their earthy roots in the kitchen, thanks to Michelin-starred chefs like Heston Blumenthal, whose menus feature a bewildering array of offal-based dishes, traditional Sardinian food is suddenly *de rigueur.*

If you don't have the stomach for the more fruity Sardinian offerings, never fear, there is plenty on the menu to savour. Highlights include spicy charcuterie made from free-range pigs, spit-roasted lamb cooked over the embers of juniper wood, red snapper simmered in Vernaccia sherry, delicate thistle honey and saffron-flavoured pasta, along with 400 types of bread and the best *pecorino* cheese in Italy. Sardinian food may be simple, but the Sardinians have long appreciated the wisdom behind strong, natural flavours. And you never need worry about the organic or free-range credentials of what is on your plate.

STAPLES & SPECIALITIES
Antipasti

Antipasti have never been a feature of the Sardinian table, but other Italian cuisines have influenced local habits. *Antipasto di terra* (antipasto of the earth) will consist of homemade bread, preserved meats, smoked sausage, cheese, olives, mushrooms and a range of cooked, raw and marinated vegetables.

Along the coast you will find seafood antipasti, which is not traditional Sardinian but an example of modern influences. Many Sardinian dishes have adapted well, such as thinly sliced *bottarga* (mullet roe) drizzled with olive oil and Cagliari's famous *burrida* (marinated dogfish). There is also *frittelle di zucchine,* an omelette stuffed with courgettes, bread-crumbs and cheese.

The Foods of Sicily & Sardinia is a highly illustrated cookery book by Giuliano Bugialli featuring some of the best traditional Sardinian recipes.

Bread

Sardinians wouldn't consider eating a meal without bread. Using durum wheat of the best quality and kneading techniques handed down through the generations, Sardinians have managed to come up with literally hundreds of types of bread, each one particular to its region and town. It would be impossible to list even half of them.

The most famous is the shepherd's bread *pane carasau,* also known as *carta da musica* (music paper). It was introduced by the Arabs in the 9th century and is vaguely reminiscent of Indian poppadoms, salty and quite addictive. Wafer-thin and long-lasting, it was ideal for shepherds out in the pasture. It predominates in the Gallura, Logudoro and Nuoro regions.

Brushed with olive oil and sprinkled with salt, *pane carasau* becomes a moreish snack known as *pane guttiau.* A fancier version often served as a first course is *pane frattau,* where *pane carasau* is topped with tomato sauce, grated *pecorino* and *uovo in camicia* (soft-boiled egg).

Originally from the Campidano region, the commonly seen *civraxiu* (siv-ra-ksyu) is a thick, circular loaf with a crispy crust and a soft white interior. The *tundu* is similar. Another common bread is the *spianata* or *spianada,* which is a little like Middle Eastern pitta. In Sassari snack bars you'll discover *fainè,* the chickpea-flour *farinata* flat bread imported centuries ago by Ligurians from northwestern Italy and used for making pizza-like snacks.

The Spaniards made a fine contribution with *panadas,* scrumptious little pies that can be filled with anything from minced lamb or pork to eel. Oschiri is especially well known for them.

Cheese

As Sardinia is an island of shepherds, it's hardly surprising that the place has got cheese-making down to a fine art. Cheese has been produced here for nearly 5000 years, and the island now makes about 80% of Italy's *pecorino romano.* Gourmands will delight in all the flavours and textures, from hard, tangy *pecorino sardo* to smoked varieties, creamy goat's cheeses (such as *ircano* and *caprino*), ricottas and speciality cheeses like *canestrati,* flavoured with peppercorns and herbs.

Fiora sarda, a centuries-old cheese recipe, is eaten fresh, smoked or roasted and packs a fair punch. It is traditionally made from ewe's milk, but varieties such as *fresa* and *peretta* are made from cow's milk. The most popular goat's cheese is *caprino,* and the soft *crema del Gerrei* is a combination of goat's milk and ricotta.

Only the bravest connoisseurs will want to sample *formaggio marcio* or *casu marzu,* quite literally a 'rotten cheese' alive with maggots!

Soups

More than any other region of Italy, Sardinia specialises in soups and meat-based broths. It is in these dishes that the island's legumes and grains are shown to their best advantage, combined with at least one defining flavour such as fennel bulbs, fava beans, chickpeas or spinach. The difference between *suppa* (or *zuppa;* soup) and *minestra* (broth) is that the latter uses short pasta instead of bread.

A *suppa* nearly always contains bread, more often than not broken pieces of *carta da musica.* Soups are often substantial meals in themselves; for example, the Herculean *pecora in cappotto,* a broth of boiled mutton, potatoes, onions and dried tomatoes made in Barbagia. In Gallura, *suppa cuata* is a favoured opener. It consists of layers of bread and cheese drowned in a meaty broth and then oven-baked to create a thin golden crust.

Minestra varieties include *gallina* (chicken), *piselli con ricotta* (peas and ricotta), *ceci* (chickpeas) and *lenticchie* (lentils). Other soups might be fennel or endive based.

La Favata for Maundy Thursday is one of the most elaborate holiday preparations in Sardinian cooking. It is based on fava beans but will also include 10 to 15 types of pork and sausage meat.

For a good selection of hearty recipes, try to pick up *Gastronomia in Sardegna,* by Gian Paolo Caredda. He covers all the basics of the Sardinian kitchen.

Pasta

Sardinia generally has an individual way of doing things, and the island's pasta is no different.

Mallodoreddus, dense seashell-shaped pasta made of semolina and flavoured with saffron, is usually served with *salsa alla Campidanese* (sausage and tomato sauce) and sometimes goes by the alternative name of *gnocchetti sardi.* Another uniquely Sardinian creation is *fregola,* a granular pasta similar to couscous. The Sardinians insist that the method for making it is nearly 2000 years old. *Fregola* is often served in soups and broths, although it is delicious when steamed and accompanied by clams.

Another popular pasta is *culurgiones* (spelt in various ways), a type of *ravioli*. Typically it has a ricotta or *pecorino* filling and is coated in a tomato and herb sauce. *Culurgiones de l'Ogliastra*, made in Nuoro province, is stuffed with potato purée and sometimes meat and onions. A little *pecorino*, olive oil, garlic and mint are added, and a tomato sauce is the usual accompaniment.

Maccarones furriaos are strips of pasta folded and topped with a sauce (often tomato-based) and melted cheese. *Maccarones de busa*, or just plain *busa*, is shaped by wrapping the pasta around knitting needles. Thus 'pierced', the pasta soaks up as much sauce as possible.

Other pastas you may come across are *pillus*, a small ribbon pasta, and *filindeu*, a thread-like noodle usually served in soups.

Meat

While it is possible to get such generic dishes as veal and entrecôte, the hearts of Sardinian carnivores beat to a quite different drum. Three particular specialities dominate the island's menu: *porceddu* (suckling pig), *agnello* (lamb) and *capretto* (kid). These dishes are flavoured with Mediterranean herbs and spit-roasted – real traditionalists will pay close heed to the type of wood being used, as this lends the meat a particular taste.

> '*Maccarones de busa*, or just plain *busa*, is shaped by wrapping the pasta around knitting needles.'

The most famous of this culinary triumvirate is the *porceddu*. It should be slow roasted until the skin crackles and then left to stand on a bed of myrtle leaves. When it's good it's very, very good, but it has to be said that in summer, when demand far outstrips the availability of good meat, it can be disappointing, so choose your restaurant with care. One place you cannot go wrong is the Hotel Su Gologone (see the boxed text, p203) in Oliena.

Agnello is particularly popular around December but can be more difficult to find at other times. A country classic is *carne a carrarglu* (literally 'meat in a hole') – the meat is compressed between two layers of hot stones, covered in myrtle and left to cook in a hole dug in the ground. Sardinians say you can still come across country folk who will prepare this, but it is a rarity.

Capretto is harder to find on menus, but it gets more common up in the mountains, where it is flavoured with thyme. Even that notorious whinger DH Lawrence waxed lyrical about Sardinian roast kid.

Sards also have a penchant for game birds, rabbit and wild boar. A wonderful local sauce for any meat dish is *al mirto* – made with red myrtle, it is a tangy addition.

WE DARE YOU TO TRY...

- *Cordula* – Lamb tripe grilled, fried or stewed with peas.
- *Granelle* – Calf's testicles sliced, covered in batter and lightly fried.
- Horsemeat or donkey sausages.
- *Tataliu* or *trattalia* – A mix of kidney, liver and intestines stewed or grilled on skewers. The dish is made with veal, lamb, kid or suckling pig.
- *Zimino russo* – A selection of roasted offal, usually from a calf, including the heart, diaphragm, liver, kidney and other red innards.
- *Zurrette* – A black pudding made of sheep's blood cooked, like haggis, in a sheep's stomach with herbs and fennel.

There is an impressive range of offal-based recipes, but few restaurants will serve them to tourists (see the boxed text, p53).

Fish & Seafood

Sardinians point out that they are by tradition *pastori, non pescatori* (shepherds, not fishermen). There is some tradition of seafood in Cagliari, Alghero and other coastal towns, but elsewhere the phenomenon has arrived from beyond Sardinia. Real Sardinians eat meat!

However, these days you will be regaled with seafood up and down the coast. Lobster (legally in season from March to August) is *the* local speciality, particularly in Alghero. It averages €10 for every 100g.

Muggine (mullet) is popular on the Oristano coast, and *tonno* (tuna) dishes abound around the Isola di San Pietro. *Cassola* is a tasty fish soup, while *zuppa alla Castellanese,* a Castelsardo speciality, is similar but with a distinct tomato edge.

Cagliari also has a long tradition of seafood recipes that run the gamut from sea bream to bass, although the most famous is based on the local *gattucio di mare* (dogfish). Clams, cockles, octopus and crab also feature, as do eels around the marshes of Cabras. You can also try *orziadas* (sea-anemone tentacles rolled in semolina and deep-fried).

Sweets & Desserts

Unlike Sicily, where sugary, creamy desserts reign supreme, Sardinia's sweet trolley has always been constrained by the natural flavours of the island. Take the simple recipe for *amarettes* (almond biscuits): there are just three ingredients – almonds, sugar and eggs – but the biscuits are delightfully fluffy and moist. In Quartu Sant'Elena the recipe is a little more complex (it includes flour and vanilla) for *mustazzolus,* a biscuit vaguely reminiscent of German *Lebkuchen.*

Other sweets and biscuits are strictly seasonal. *Ossus de mortu* (dead men's bones) are served on All Saints' Day in November, and the curd-based speciality *pardulas* (ricotta-filled biscuits flavoured with saffron) are traditionally an Easter recipe. Seasonal influences also ring the changes. After the grape harvest you'll start to see things like *papassinos de Vitzi* (an almond and sultana biscuit) and the rich *pabassinas cun saba,* little sultana patties mixed with almonds, honey and candied fruit

To discover the nuances of Sardinian cuisine, consult www.sarnow .com, which gives a great overview of the specialities of each region.

TRAVEL YOUR TASTEBUDS

To get a better picture of Sardinia's heritage as a wine producer, consider visiting some of the island's wineries for a tour and tasting. Bear in mind that these are working vineyards, so you should always phone beforehand to book a tour.

The island's largest producer is **Sella e Mosca** (☎ 079 99 77 00; www.sellaemosca.com; Località i Piani; 5.30-6.30pm Mon-Sat), near Alghero. It makes a huge variety of wine, not least the well-reviewed Marchesi di Villamarina. You can sample other award winners at the **Cantine Argiolas** (☎ 070 74 06 06; www.cantine-argiolas.it; Via Roma 56/58, Seridiano; 10am-1pm & 3-5pm Tue, Wed & Fri), near Cagliari. **Jerzu Antichi Poderi** (☎ 078 27 00 28; www.jerzuantichipoderi.it, in Italian; Via Umberto 1, Jerzu; 8am-1pm & 3-6pm Mon-Fri) has a large selection of Sardinia's most famous red, Cannonau, while the **Cantina del Vermentino** (☎ 079 94 40 12; Via San Paolo 2, Monti; 8.30am-6.30pm Mon-Fri) is the place to get your hands on the crisp Vermentino white.

Those with a penchant for dessert wines can pick up the honey-coloured Malvasia di Bosa at the **Enoteca Su Nuraghe** (☎ 0785 37 20 43; www.sunuraghe.info, in Italian; Piazza Gioberti, Bosa) and the famous Vernaccia sherry at the **Cantina Sociale della Vernaccia** (☎ 0783 3 31 55; Via Oristano 149, Località Rimedio; 10am-1pm Mon-Fri).

moulded together with grape must. One of the most delicious confections is *coffettura*, tiny baskets of finely shaved orange peel and almonds drenched in honey. They're usually served at weddings. To sample some of these specialities at their very best, visit the craft bakery **Durke** (☎ 070 66 67 82; www.durke.it, in Italian) in Cagliari (p85). The bakers there still make everything by hand according to traditional recipes.

The island's most famous national dessert, however, is the *seadas* (or *sebadas*), and deservedly so. It consists of a delightfully light pastry (vaguely like a turnover) stuffed with bran, orange peel and ricotta or sour cheese and then drenched in *miele amaro* (bitter honey). The only other widely served dessert is *crema catalana* (a local version of crème caramel), originally a speciality of Alghero from a time when the town owed its allegiance to Catalan masters.

The other way to end a meal is with a platter of Sardinian cheese and a glass of local liqueur.

DRINKS
Alcoholic Drinks
BEER
Sardinians are Italy's biggest beer drinkers. The main Italian labels are Peroni, Nastro Azzuro, Dreher (made in Sardinia) and Moretti, all very drinkable and cheaper than the imported varieties. Ichnusa (owned by Heineken) is another local drop, and you won't find it outside Sardinia. Beers come either bottled or *alla spina* (on tap).

WINE
They have been producing wine in Sardinia for millennia, certainly since the Phoenicians landed if not well before. Wine critic Hugh Johnson found the grapes 'heroically strong', and indeed this was half the problem until recently. Contemporary vintners have started to blend the powerful flavours and tame the mighty alcohol content to produce some light, dry whites and more sophisticated reds.

Among the best dry whites is the Vermentino variety, produced in much of the north of the island. The Vermentino di Gallura is the only wine type in Sardinia to have been awarded the coveted DOCG status (in 1996). Another Vermentino worth seeking out is the Canayli, which since 1998 has won several prestigious Italian wine industry awards. You'll see vineyards turning out Vermentino grapes all over the northeast of Sardinia, such as around Tempio Pausania and Berchidda.

A good bottle of 1998 Turriga will set you back around €60.

The best-known vintner on the island is the Sella e Mosca group just outside Alghero, which makes all sorts of wines. Its Torbato Terre Bianche is a nice drop of sparkling wine. Among Sella e Mosca's best reds are Tanca Farrà and the prize-winning Marchese di Villamarina.

The island's best-known reds are made from the Cannonau grape. Introduced by the Spaniards in the 13th century, it produces a rich, dark, heavy wine. To taste it in an unadulterated form, try the Nepente di Oliena, although you might find more recent blends like Dule a bit easier on the palate. The finest Cannonau blend is the award-winning Turriga, produced by the Cantine Argiolas in Serdiana. Other excellent reds produced from this winery are the silky-smooth Perdera Monica and the spicy Costera. Also worth tasting are wines using the Nebbiolo grape, introduced by the Piedmontese in the 18th century.

One of Sardinia's best-known fortified wines is Vernaccia (15% to 18% alcohol), a heavy amber drop made mostly around Oristano and taken as an aperitif or to accompany such sweets as *mustazzolus*. The

---

WHAT'S IN A LABEL?

There are four main classifications of wine – DOCG (denominazione d'origine controllata e garantita), DOC (denominazione di origine controllata), IGT (indicazione geografica typica) and vino da tavola (table wine) – which will be marked on the label. A DOC wine is produced subject to certain specifications, although the label does not certify quality. DOCG is subject to the same requirements as DOC but is also tested by government inspectors for quality. IGT is a recent term introduced to cover wines from quality regions that are of a style or use grapes that fall outside the DOC and DOCG classifications.

The Slow Food movement's annually updated Guide to Italian Wines is an excellent resource with region-by-region profiles of producers and their wines.

---

best Vernaccia is Perra from Narbiola in Oristano province. Malvasia (malmsey) is another dessert wine made mostly in the Bosa area. Sella e Mosca produces a good sweet drop, the Torbato Passito, and the Anghelu Ruiu fortified wine.

Wine is very reasonably priced in Sardinia, though (as anywhere) prices vary according to the vintage. In a restaurant a decent wine should cost between €12 and €20, with a *vino da tavola* (table wine) at around €8. Prices escalate in some restaurants on the Costa Smeralda.

LIQUEURS & HARD LIQUOR

Sardinia's national liqueur is *mirto,* distilled from the fragrant purple fruit of the myrtle bush. At its best it is a deliciously smooth drop. A less common white version is made from myrtle leaves and goes by the same name.

The island's transparent firewater is *filu e ferru.* It is made from a distillate of grape skins in much the same way as grappa and roars down your throat. Beware, as the alcohol content hovers around 40%, although some homemade brews can reach an eye-watering 60%. Zedda Piras is a reliable brand of *mirto* and *filu e ferru.*

You could also try the locally made *limoncino,* a sweet lemon-based drink that is virtually the same as the better-known *limoncello* found all over the Amalfi coast south of Naples.

> To avoid taxes Sardinians took to making their own *acquavita*. To be able to find it, they'd mark the spot with an iron wire (the *filu e ferru*) from which the drink derived its name.

Nonalcoholic Drinks

COFFEE

As in the rest of Italy, coffee drinking is taken seriously in Sardinia and you should familiarise yourself with the coffee menu if you want to get it right.

First is the espresso – a tiny cup of very strong black coffee. *Doppio espresso* is a double shot of the same. If you want the watery version, ask for a *caffè americano.*

Enter the milk. A *caffè latte* is coffee with a reasonable amount of milk. To most locals it is a breakfast or morning drink. A stronger version is the *caffè macchiato,* basically an espresso with a dash of milk. Alternatively, you can have *latte macchiato,* a glass of hot milk with a dash of coffee. The cappuccino is a frothy version of the *caffè latte.*

To warm up on those winter nights, a *corretto* might be for you – an espresso 'corrected' with a dash of grappa or some other spirit. Some locals have it as a heart starter.

After lunch and dinner it wouldn't occur to Italians to order a *caffè latte* or cappuccino – an espresso, *macchiato* or *corretto* is perfectly acceptable.

GRANITA
Mainly a summer drink, *granita* is made of crushed ice with fresh lemon or other fruit juices, or with coffee topped with whipped cream.

WATER
Although tap water is drinkable throughout the island, most locals prefer to drink bottled *acqua minerale* (mineral water). This is available *frizzante* (sparkling) or *naturale* (still), and you will be asked in restaurants and bars which you prefer. If you just want a glass of tap water, ask for *acqua dal rubinetto* or *acqua naturale*.

CELEBRATIONS
Since time immemorial Sardinians have marked the turning of the seasons with traditional festivals linked to the farming calendar. These were rare social occasions when villagers could meet up, show off their most splendid costumes and prepare their finest recipes. Throughout the year the calendar is dotted with *sagra* (festivals usually dedicated to one culinary item or theme) such as the Sagra del Pesce (Fish Festival) in the Golfo Aranci or the celebration of the chestnut harvest in Aritzo's Sagra delle Castagne. However, the biggest festivals centre on Carnevale (the period leading up to Ash Wednesday, the first day of Lent), Pasqua (Easter), Natale (Christmas) and the celebration of saints' days such as Sant'Efisio in Cagliari, Sant'Antioco on the island of the same name and San Salvatore in Cabras.

WHERE TO EAT & DRINK
Eating establishments follow the same pattern as those on the mainland. Strictly speaking, trattorias have cheap, simple, hearty menus and *ristoranti* (restaurants) have a wider selection of dishes and higher prices. The problem is that many establishments that are in fact *ristoranti* call themselves trattorias, and vice versa, usually to capture the spirit of the other establishment. So don't judge the quality of a place by its appearance.

Tavole calde, which serve street fare, are popular hang-outs, though sadly fast-food outlets have done away with many of them. In these places what you see is what you get: *brioche* (breakfast pastry), *cornetti* (croissants), *panini* (bread rolls with simple fillings) and *spuntini* (snacks). You can round off your meal with a gelato – a crowd outside the gelateria is always a good sign.

Most eating establishments have a *coperto* (cover charge) of €1 to €3 and a *servizio* (service charge) of 10% to 15%.

> Wonder where those Michelin-starred restaurants buy their gourmet ingredients? Log on to www.vallebona.co.uk. The company runs tastings and packs hampers, and can even provide you with recipe cards.

VEGETARIANS & VEGANS
Few restaurants are strictly vegetarian, although vegetables are a staple of the Sardinian table. Vegetarians will need to watch out for vegetable risottos and soups prepared with meat stock. If you're a vegan, you're in for a tough time, as the majority of dishes feature some sort of animal product, be it dairy, eggs or animal stock.

EATING WITH KIDS
At the coastal resorts children are well catered for in hotel restaurants, and in general kids are made to feel welcome. Locals eat out with their children frequently, although they tend to stick to the more popular trattorias – you'll seldom see children in an expensive restaurant. Families order a *mezzo piatto* ('half-plate'), as there's no such thing as a children's menu. Virtually all restaurants are willing to tailor a dish to suit young taste buds.

High chairs are not readily available, so bring one if you can. It's expected that kids will be well behaved and will be disciplined if they are not. Note that many restaurants are not smoke free.

For more information on travelling with children, see p251.

HABITS & CUSTOMS

Sardinians rarely eat a sit-down *colazione* (breakfast). They tend to drink a cappuccino, usually *tiepido* (warm), and eat a *cornetto* or other type of pastry while standing at a bar.

Pranzo (lunch) is traditionally the main meal of the day, and many shops and businesses close for three to four hours every afternoon to accommodate the meal and the siesta that traditionally follows. A full meal will consist of an antipasto (starter), a *primo piatto* (broth, pasta or risotto) and a *secondo piatto* of meat or fish. Italians may then follow this with an *insalata* (salad) or *contorno* (vegetable side dish), although this is less common in Sardinia.

To complete a meal *alla sarda* you should opt for cheese and a shot of grappa, although it is now common to wind up with dessert and coffee.

Cena (the evening meal) was traditionally a simpler affair, but in recent years habits have begun to change due to the inconvenience of travelling home for lunch every day.

'Sardinians rarely eat a sit-down *colazione* (breakfast).'

EAT YOUR WORDS

Want to know the difference between *cavallo* and *cavolo*? A slab of *porcetto* from *capretto*? Get behind the cuisine scene by getting to know the language. For pronunciation guidelines, see p254.

Useful Phrases

I'd like to reserve a table.
Vorrei riservare un tavolo. vo-ray ree-ser-*va*-re oon *ta*-vo-lo

I'd like the menu, please.
Vorrei il menù, per favore. vo-ray eel me-*noo* per fa-*vo*-re

Do you have a menu in English?
Avete un menù (scritto) in inglese? a-*ve*-te oon me-*noo* (*skree*-to) een een-*gle*-ze

What would you recommend?
Cosa mi consiglia? *ko*-za mee kon-*see*-lya

I'd like a local speciality.
Vorrei una specialità di questa regione. vo-ray *oo*-na spe-cha-lee-*ta* dee *kwe*-sta re-*jo*-ne

Please bring the bill.
Mi porta il conto, per favore? mee *por*-ta eel *kon*-to per fa-*vo*-re

Is service included in the bill?
Il servizio è compreso nel conto? eel ser-*vee*-tsyo e kom-*pre*-zo nel *kon*-to

I'm a vegetarian.
Sono vegetariano/a. *so*-no ve-je-ta-*rya*-no/a (m/f)

I'm a vegan.
Sono vegetaliano/a. *so*-no ve-je-ta-*lya*-no/a (m/f)

Food Glossary

acciughe	a-*choo*-ge	anchovies
aceto	a-*che*-to	vinegar
acqua	*a*-kwa	water
aglio	*a*-lyo	garlic
agnello	a-*nye*-lo	lamb
animelle	a nee-*mel*-le	sweetbreads
aragosta	a-ra-*go*-sta	lobster

arancia	a·*ran*·cha	orange
arrosto/a	a·*ro*·sto/a	roasted
asparagi	as·*pa*·ra·jee	asparagus
birra	*bee*·ra	beer
bistecca	bees·*te*·ka	steak
bollito/a	bo·*lee*·to/a	boiled
bottarga	bo·*tar*·ga	mullet roe
burrida	boo·*ree*·da	dogfish with pine nuts, parsley and garlic
burro	*boo*·ro	butter
calamari	ka·la·*ma*·ree	squid
capretto	ka·*pre*·to	kid (goat)
carciofi	kar·*cho*·fee	artichokes
carota	ka·*ro*·ta	carrot
carta di musica	*kar*·ta dee *moo*·see·ka	flat, crispy bread
cassoeula	ka·so·*we*·la	winter stew with pork
cavallo	ka·*va*·lo	horse
cavolo	*ka*·vo·lo	cabbage
ceci	*che*·chee	chickpeas
cefalo	*che*·fa·lo	grey mullet
coccoi di sautizzu	ko·*koy* dee sau·tee·*tsoo*	platter of cured meat
coniglio	ko·*nee*·lyo	rabbit
cordulas	kor·*doo*·las	tripe cooked on a skewer
cotto/a	*ko*·to/a	cooked
cozze	*ko*·tse	mussels
culurgiones (or *culorzones*)	koo·loor·*jo*·nez	ravioli filled with cheese and/or potato
fagiano	fa·*ja*·no	pheasant
fagiolini	fa·jo·*lee*·nee	green beans
fegato	*fe*·ga·to	liver
finocchio	fee·*no*·kyo	fennel
formaggio	for·*ma*·jo	cheese
fragole	*fra*·go·le	strawberries
frittata	free·*ta*·ta	omelette
fritto/a	*free*·to/a	fried
frutti di mare	*froo*·tee dee *ma*·re	seafood
funghi	*foon*·gee	mushrooms
gamberoni	gam·be·*ro*·nee	prawns
granchio	gran·kyo	crab
(*alla*) *griglia*	(a·la) *gree*·lya	grilled (broiled)
insalata	in·sa·*la*·ta	salad
latte	*la*·te	milk
lenticchie	len·*tee*·kye	lentils
limone	lee·*mo*·ne	lemon
malloredus	ma·lo·*re*·doos	semolina dumplings
manzo	*man*·dzo	beef
mela	*me*·la	apple
melanzane	me·lan·*dza*·ne	aubergine, eggplant
melone	me·*lo*·ne	melon
merluzzo	mer·*loo*·tso	cod
miele	*mye*·le	honey
mirto	*meer*·to	myrtle berries
muggine	*moo*·jee·ne	mullet
olio	*o*·lyo	oil
olive	o·*lee*·va	olive

panadas	pa·na·das	savoury pie
pane	pa·ne	bread
panna	pan·na	cream
patate	pa·ta·te	potatoes
pepe	pe·pe	pepper
peperoni	pe·pe·ro·nee	peppers, capsicum
pere	pe·ra	pears
pesca	pe·ska	peach
piselli	pee·ze·lee	peas
pollo	pol·lo	chicken
polpo	pol·po	octopus
pomodori	po·mo·do·ree	tomatoes
porcetto	por·che·to	suckling pig
prosciutto	pro·shoo·to	cured ham
riso	ree·zo	rice
rucola	roo·ko·la	rocket
sale	sa·le	salt
salsiccia	sal·see·cha	sausage
sebadas	se·ba·das	fried pastry with ricotta
sedano	se·da·no	celery
seppia	se·pya	cuttlefish
spinaci	spee·na·chee	spinach
tonno	ton·no	tuna
triglia	tree·lya	red mullet
trippa	tree·pa	tripe
uovo/uova	wo·vo/wo·va	egg/eggs
uva	oo·va	grapes
vino (rosso/bianco)	vee·no (ros·so/byan·ko)	wine (red/white)
vitello	vee·te·lo	veal
vongole	von·go·le	clams
zucchero	tsoo·ke·ro	sugar
zuppa (or suppa)	tsoo·pa	soup or broth

Cagliari & the Sarrabus

Cagliari, perched on its rocky bluff, is the great citadel of the south. Its weighty castle with boxy bastions is surrounded by a honey-coloured crinoline of houses that tumble seawards to the vast harbour. First and foremost, Cagliari is a port. More than any other city in the Mediterranean, the port seeps into one's consciousness, as if the city were merely an amphitheatre arranged around the comings and goings of ferries and tankers.

It was the port that attracted the Phoenicians, plying their trade between Lebanon and the silver mines of Tarshish in southern Spain. The Romans and Vandals followed suit, after they discovered the wealthy mines of the Iglesiente and the fertile plains of the Campidano. In and out went the local minerals; grains, salt and wool made Cagliari rich and modestly provincial. But it was the Pisans who gave the city its cloak of civilisation, its public buildings and palaces, churches and civic spaces.

However, at its heart Cagliari remains that windy city looking out to sea. It's a rocky, treeless town constantly on the move, the glint and dazzle of the southern sun bouncing off the shop windows, salt always in the breeze. Despite its sophisticated gleam in the eyes of rural Sardinians, Cagliari is a working town, struggling for economic survival. Its pleasures are incidental and incremental: a satisfying meal in a crowded trattoria, a cloudless day at the beach, a long drink on the dramatic ramparts of Il Castello (The Castle). But take some time to drive out to the salt-white beaches of Villasimius and the Costa Rei, or lose yourself in the fragrant, wooded hinterland of the Monte dei Sette Fratelli, and you'll find the hours just slipping away.

HIGHLIGHTS

- Admire the unique *bronzetti* (bronze figurines) in the island's finest museum, Cagliari's **Museo Archeologico Nazionale** (p65)
- Explore Cagliari's high-walled **Il Castello** (p64) and then sit back on the terrace of **Caffè Librarium Nostrum** (p83) and watch the sun go down over the city
- Dine on a platter of sea critters in the crowded eateries of Cagliari's **Marina quarter** (p70)
- Dive in the crystalline waters of **Villasimius** (p87) or see the port in a different light at the wreck sites in the **Golfo di Cagliari** (p72)
- Ramble in the pine-scented wilderness of the **Monte dei Sette Fratelli** (p87)
- Don't miss the colours, culture and music of Cagliari's enormous **Festa di Sant'Efisio** (p72)

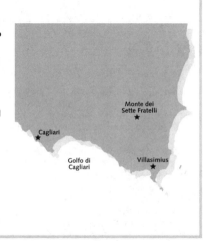

CAGLIARI & THE SARRABUS

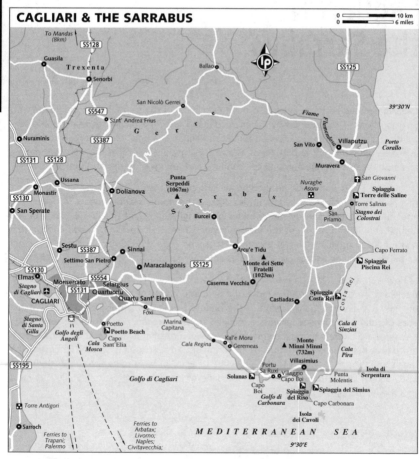

CAGLIARI

pop 162,600

Landing at Cagliari's docks is a singular experience. The proud and busy Via Roma presents the unmistakable hallmarks of a Mediterranean port city. Stately civic buildings, a grand department store and the buzz of waterfront cafés let you know you have arrived. Behind the city, alleys corkscrew north to the sand-coloured Il Castello district, its medieval walls and churches rising like the upper layers of a birthday cake.

Throughout the day the city follows its own rhythms. In the morning rush traffic sweeps up the wide Largo Carlo Felice to the shops of Via Mannu and Via Garibaldi, and to the government offices and university in Il Castello. At lunch time, drinks and snacks are sold along the arcades of Via Roma, and then the afternoon silence descends as families head home or out to Poetto beach. In the evening, the ritual is reversed; Cagliaritani out for a *passeggiata* (evening stroll) spill down the hillside to the eateries of Corso Vittorio Emanuele and the Marina district.

HISTORY

The Phoenicians established themselves around here in the 8th century BC, but it was not until the Carthaginians took control of what they called Karel or Karalis (meaning 'rocky place') around 520 BC that a town began to emerge. The Romans attached particular importance to Karalis, and Julius Caesar declared it a Roman municipality in 46 BC. For centuries it remained a prosperous port, heading the grain trade with mainland Italy, but with the eclipse of Rome's power came more turbulent times.

Vandals operating out of North Africa stormed into the city in 455, only to be unseated by the Byzantine Empire in 533. Cagliari thus became capital of one of four districts, which later became the *giudicati* (provinces). By the 11th century, weakening Byzantine influence (accentuated by repeated Arab raids) led Cagliari and the other districts to become virtually autonomous.

The emerging rival sea powers of Genoa and Pisa were soon poking around. In 1258 the Pisans took the town, fortified the Castello area and replaced the local population with Pisans. A similar fate awaited them when the Catalano-Aragonese took over in 1326. In the ensuing years of conflict around the island, the Catalano-Aragonese managed to always keep Cagliari. The Black Death swept through in 1348, with frequent repeat outbreaks in the succeeding decades.

With Spain unified at the end of the 15th century, the Catalans themselves were subordinated to the Spaniards. Cagliari fared better than most of the island under Spanish inertia and mismanagement, and in 1620 the city's university opened its doors.

The dukes of Savoy (who in 1720 became kings of Sardinia) followed the Spanish precedent in keeping Cagliari as the viceregal seat, and it endured several anxious events (such as the 1794 anti-Savoy riots). From 1799 to 1814 the royal family, forced out of Piedmont by Napoleon, spent time in Cagliari protected by the British Royal Navy.

Cagliari continued to develop slowly throughout the 19th century. Parts of the city walls were destroyed and the city expanded as the population grew. Heavily bombed in WWII, Cagliari was awarded a medal for bravery in 1948.

Reconstruction commenced shortly after the end of the war and was partly complete by the time Cagliari was declared capital of the semi-autonomous region of Sardinia in the new Italian republic in 1949. A good deal of Sardinia's modern industry, especially petrochemicals, has since developed around the lagoons and along the coast as

far as Sarroch in the southwest. For years there has been talk about a new tourist port at Su Siccu, but it's mired in controversy. City planners have, however, managed to install elevators along Viale Regina Elena to whisk you up to the castle and they're now talking about an escalator for the old town.

ORIENTATION

The part of town that will interest visitors is compact but can be a little confusing. The main port and the bus and train stations are located on or near Piazza Matteotti, where you will also find the useful city tourist office. Running through the square is the broad Via Roma, part of the principal route to Poetto and Villasimius in the east, and Pula and the south coast to the west.

The warren of lanes just inland from Via Roma is known as the Marina district. Clustered here are about a third of the city's hotels and a plethora of eateries, from cheap and cheerful trattorias to a handful of gourmet options. The area is bounded to the west by Largo Carlo Felice, which runs up to Piazza Yenne, where the island's north–south route, the SS131, officially begins.

A walk up the Scalette di Santa Chiara north of Piazza Yenne takes you high into the old medieval core of the city, the Castello district, signalled by the tall Pisan watchtowers from where you have great views. The city's main museums are up here.

Downhill to the left (west of the city) are the busy, working-class lanes of Stampace, while to the right (east) is the more modern Villanova district.

Beyond, the city spreads east to the *saline* (saltpans) and Poetto beach; in the west the housing creeps around the north shore of the immense Stagno di Santa Gilla lagoon.

INFORMATION
Bookshops
Le Librerie della Costa (☎ 070 65 02 56; Via Roma 63-5; 🕑 9am-8.30pm Mon-Sat, 10am-1.30pm & 5.30-9pm Sun) A big central bookshop with a good selection of maps and guides (mostly in Italian) and a small selection of English-language books. Also has Internet access.
Libreria Dattena (☎ 070 67 02 20; Via Garibaldi 175) Novels in a variety of languages.

Emergency
Police station (☎ 070 49 21 69; Via Amat Luigi 9) The main police station is behind the imposing law courts.

Internet Access

Intermedia Point (Via Eleonora d'Arborea 4; per hr €3.50; ☽ 10am-1pm & 4-9pm Mon-Fri, 11am-1pm & 5-9pm Sat)

Le Librerie della Costa (☎ 070 65 02 56; Via Roma 63-5; per hr €5; ☽ 9am-8.30pm Mon-Sat, 10am-1.30pm & 5.30-9pm Sun) Also has a range of English-language books.

Laundry

In the rest of Sardinia, self-service laundrettes are virtually nonexistent, but Cagliari is a soap-suds paradise for the great unwashed.

Lavanderia Ghilbi (Via Sicilia 20; ☽ 8am-10pm) A 6kg load costs €4 to wash.

Medical Services

Farmacia Centrale (☎ 070 65 82 34; Via Sardegna 10) Handy for any medicine you might need.

Guardia Medica (☎ 070 50 29 31) For a night-time emergency call-out doctor.

Ospedale Brotzu (☎ 070 54 32 66; Via Peretti 21) This hospital is northwest of the city centre. Take bus 1 from Via Roma if you need to make a non-emergency visit.

Money

Banco di San Paolo (Via Sassari) Handily located next to the main train station. There are also ATMs inside the station.

Mail Boxes Etc (☎ 070 67 37 04; Viale Trieste 65/b) You can send or receive money via Western Union here.

Post

Main post office (☎ 070 605 41 23; Piazza del Carmine; ☽ 8am-6.50pm Tue-Fri, 8am-1.15pm Sat) Has a fax service and *fermo posta* (poste restante). Closes at 4pm on the last day of the month.

Tourist Information

A private information office operates at the airport between 8am and 8pm, and another information point is located at the ferry terminal. At the time of writing all of the Cagliari tourist offices were undergoing reorganisation, which disrupted opening times (see p233).

Regional tourist office (☎ 070 66 41 95, in Italy 800 01 31 53; Via Goffredo Mameli 95; ☽ 9am-7pm Mon-Sat) Open all day, Cagliari's main tourist office can provide information on the whole province. This is also where you buy tickets for the Sant'Efisio festival (p72).

Tourist information point (☎ 070 66 92 55; Piazza Matteotti; ☽ 8.30am-1.30pm Mon-Sat) The most convenient information point in town with none-too-helpful English-speaking staff. Note that the location may change with the reorganisation.

Travel Agencies

CTS (☎ 070 48 82 60; Via Cesare Balbo 12) A branch of the national youth travel agent.

Viaggi Orrù (☎ 070 65 98 58; www.viaggiorru.it; Via Roma 95; ☽ 9am-1pm & 5-8pm Mon-Fri, 9am-1pm Sat) An efficient travel agency where you can book all manner of ferries and flights. It also arranges trips around Sardinia.

DANGERS & ANNOYANCES

At night, some spots around town are not so appealing. The steps leading up to the Bastione San Remy and the little park at the bottom of Viale Regina Margherita, for instance, attract a crowd of drunks and drug-takers. Petty theft is always a risk for tourists. Take the usual precautions, which include leaving nothing in vehicles – if you must, at least keep things hidden.

SIGHTS

The history of Sardinia is encapsulated in the geography of Cagliari. The Carthaginians settled on the plains and around the salt marshes; the necropolis of Tuxiveddu (closed for excavation) to the west delimits the edge of their influence. The Romans later sorted out the Marina district into its neat grid, and built their amphitheatre high on the hill. The remains of their city now lie buried beneath the foundations. The cityscape and all the older buildings belong to the Pisans, but the Spaniards added the more florid district of Stampace. In the 19th century Cagliari sprawled eastwards under the Piedmontese; their legacy, Villanova, is a showcase of wide roads and imposing piazzas.

A nice touch is the informative notice boards placed outside most sights. They are written, happily, in Italian and English and provide a quick insight into each location as you wander about.

Il Castello

The precipitous white stone walls of medieval Cagliari, with two of the grand Pisan towers still standing, enclose what has always been known as Il Castello. The Sardinians call it Su Casteddu, a term they also use to describe the whole city. The walls are best admired from afar – one good spot is the Roman amphitheatre across the valley to the west.

TOWERS & BATTLEMENTS

Only two of the austere white Pisan towers remain. You'll find the first, **Torre dell'Elefante**

(Via Università; admission free; 9am-1pm & 3.30-7.30pm Tue-Sun Apr-Oct, 9am-5pm Nov-Mar), right next to the university in the southwestern corner of the castle. It takes its name from a sculpted elephant at the tower's base. The Spaniards beheaded the Marchese di Cea here once the tower was built and left the severed head there for 17 years! They also liked to decorate the portcullis with the heads of executed prisoners, strung up in cages like ghoulish fairy lights. The crenellated storey was added in 1852 and used as a prison for political detainees. Climb to the top to share the view that must have made them rue their captivity.

The 14th-century **Torre di San Pancrazio** (Piazza Indipendenza; adult/concession €2/1; 9am-1pm & 3.30-7.30pm Tue-Sun Apr-Oct, 9am-4.30pm Tue-Sun Nov-Mar), standing to the right of the city gate, balances the Torre dell'Elefante in the northwestern battlement. The tower is built on the highest point in the city; if you climb to the top you can view the entire gulf spread out like a model beneath you.

Inside the battlements, the old medieval city reveals itself like Pandora's box. The university, cathedral, museums and Pisan palaces are wedged into a jigsaw of narrow high-walled alleys. Once the stately residence of officials, the old town is now strung together by lines of washing, with the shops shuttered and many of the houses in a sorry state of repair. Still, some modest restoration is taking place, and a tight-knit community of artists and students is slowly making the area fashionable again.

You can reach the citadel from various approaches. The most impressive introduction is from the busy intersection on Piazza Costituzione. After a pleasant breakfast at **Antico Caffè** (p83), you could approach the monumental stairway entrance to the **Bastione San Remy**. Once a strong point in the fortifications, the bastion is now a belvedere offering views across the city and its lagoons. For decades a flea market has set up here on Sunday, perhaps the successor to the 1948 fair, which was held as the city tried to pull itself out of the postwar mire.

GHETTO DEGLI EBREI

The area around Via Santa Croce was once the **Ghetto degli Ebrei** (Jewish Ghetto), the synagogue standing where the **Chiesa di Santa Croce** now looms (currently under restoration). Under Spanish rule the entire community was expelled in 1492 and today nothing much remains except the name, applied to a **restored former barracks** (070 640 21 15; Via Santa Croce 18; 10.30am-1pm & 6-9.30pm Tue-Sun). It's now a good place to catch temporary art and photographic exhibitions.

This is the most attractive side of the castle. You should take a wander down Via Santa Croce, where you will often catch impromptu exhibitions at venues such as **Isola** (Via Santa Croce 41-43). When such functions are on, the terrace of **Caffè Librarium Nostrum** is crowded with cultured Cagliaritani.

To find out more about the art scene, or anything going on in the castle, knock on the door of **Alberto dal Cerro** (070 65 62 17; Via Corte d'Appello 37). An artist and furniture restorer, he knows everyone in Il Castello and can help you buy some wonderful wines, olive oils and cheeses. His door is nearly always open.

CITADELLA DEI MUSEI

For many visitors, the main reason for making the arduous hike to Il Castello is this complex of museums at the highest, northern end of the citadel in the shadow of the Torre di San Pancrazio. The museums are housed in a modern complex cleverly incorporated into the remains of the old arsenal and city walls, parts of which you can see as you explore the museums. Ramps have also been installed, so getting around should present few problems.

Museo Archeologico Nazionale

Nothing is quite so impressive in Cagliari as the **Museo Archeologico Nazionale** (070 68 40 00; Piazza dell'Arsenale, Citadella dei Musei; adult/concession €4/2, with Pinacoteca Nazionale €5/2.50; 9am-8pm Tue-Sun Apr-Oct, 9am-12pm & 2-8pm Nov-Mar) with its collection of *bronzetti* (bronze figurines) glittering in their glass cases.

In the absence of any written records, these bronzes represent the 'story' of Sardinia's ancient *nuraghe* (stone tower) warriors. As they strut, pose and pray, no-one can doubt that the sculptures represent real men going about their prehistoric business on the sun-struck plains of the island. They wear rough sandals and tunics and carry aloft small circular shields. One sculpture shows a hunter returning with his game bag; others depict a flute player, an archer on the lookout and two men wrestling earnestly. Most curious of all are the pietàs,

CAGLIARI

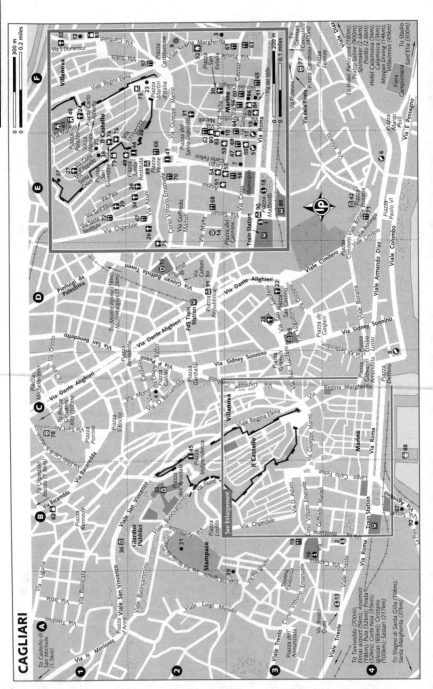

mothers cradling their fallen sons. There are even little models of the *nuraghi* themselves. Everyday details crowd to the fore: animals, tools, carts and, more elaborate, the bronze funeral barques with their distinctive stag prows.

Like a *Wallace & Gromit* animation, the *bronzetti* have a plastic accomplishment, crude but never primitive. Faces bear expression, usually stern and defiant as befits a warrior people, and the style has an effortless touch, as if the time that separates them from us is barely a moment.

Sensibly, the museum is laid out in chronological order over three floors. In a subterranean room, you move from the pre-*nuraghe* world of stone implements and obsidian tools, rudimentary ceramics and funny round fertility goddesses to the Bronze and Iron Ages and on to the *nuraghi*. Then come the Phoenicians and Romans, a model *tophet* (sacred Phoenician or Carthaginian burial ground for children and babies), and delicate debris such as terracotta vases, glass vessels, scarabs and jewellery from ancient Karalis (Cagliari), Sulcis, Tharros and Nora.

The 1st and 2nd floors contain more of the same but are divided by region and im-portant sites rather than by age. Among the highlights on the 1st floor are some Roman-era mosaics, a collection of Roman statues, busts and tombstones from Cagliari, and displays of coins. Along with the jewellery, coins and household items are some captivating Roman miniature figurines and a wonderful Punic paste necklace from Olbia, which sports a string of faces like Greek masks.

Throughout the museum, most explanations are in Italian, although some general material is in English.

Pinacoteca Nazionale

Above and behind the archaeological museum is the **Pinacoteca Nazionale** (☎ 070 68 40 00; Piazza dell'Arsenale, Citadella dei Musei; adult/ concession €2/1, with Museo Archeologico Nazionale €5/2.50; ⏱ 9am-8pm Tue-Sun Apr-Oct, 9am-12pm & 2-8pm Nov-Mar). This national art gallery exhibits a panorama of Sardinian paintings – that is to say Tuscan, Genoese, Catalan, Italian Renaissance and Spanish techniques all filtered through the Sardinian temperament.

Many of the best paintings, which date from the 15th to the 17th century, are by Catalan and Genoese artists. The collection is not particularly large and many of the works, mostly *retablos* (grand altarpieces of the kind commonly found in Spain), are robustly religious.

Of those by known Sardinian painters, the four works by Pietro Cavaro, father of the so-called Stampace school (see p39) and possibly Sardinia's most important artist, are outstanding. They include a moving *Deposizione* (Deposition) and portraits of St Peter, St Paul and St Augustine. Also represented are the painter's father, Lorenzo, and his son Michele. Another Sardinian artist of note was Francesco Pinna, whose *Pala di Sant'Orsola* hangs here. These images tend to show the influence of Spain and Italy rather than illuminating the Sardinian condition; however, there is a brief line-up of 19th- and early-20th-century Sardinian painters, such as Giovanni Marghinotti and Giuseppe Sciuti.

For a greater insight into Sardinian painting and sculpture, head to the Galleria Comunale d'Arte (p71).

Mostra di Cere Anatomiche

The oddest exhibition in town has to be the ghoulish collection at the **Mostra di Cere Anatomiche** (Piazza dell'Arsenale, Citadella dei Musei; admission €1.55; 🕑 9am-1pm & 4-7pm Tue-Sun). One wonders whether Professor Gunther von Hagen, the creator of the controversial anatomical show *Body Worlds*, found his inspiration here. The show exhibits the work of Florentine Clemente Susini, who produced a series of 23 anatomical cross-section wax models between 1802 and 1805. Unlike purist von Hagen, Susini chickened out and used wax instead of real people, but for the squeamish they're lifelike enough. The models include bisected heads and even a cutaway of a pregnant woman's torso.

Museo d'Arte Siamese

The faint-hearted can miss the anatomical show in favour of the **Museo d'Arte Siamese** (☎ 070 65 18 88; Piazza dell'Arsenale, Citadella dei Musei; admission €2; 🕑 9am-1pm & 4-8pm Tue-Sun Jun-Sep, 9am-1pm & 3.30-7.30pm Tue-Sun Oct-May). Local engineer Stefano Cardu spent many years in Thailand (formerly Siam) and, judging by this museum, had a lot of time on his hands. He collected all sorts of local arts and crafts, ranging from silk paintings to weapons and porcelain. Some of it comes from elsewhere in Asia, including China and Japan.

CATTEDRALE DI SANTA MARIA & AROUND

At the heart of the castle is the sun-drenched Piazza Palazzo, presided over by the **Cattedrale di Santa Maria** (☎ 070 66 38 37; Piazza Palazzo 4; 🕑 8am-12.30pm & 4-7pm), sporting a recently face-lifted façade from 1938. Before the 20th-century renovations, the cathedral would have looked quite different: the original 13th-century church was given a baroque remake in the 17th century. However, the city fathers had pangs of nostalgia for the cathedral's earliest incarnation, and between 1933 and 1938 they tried to turn the clock back by building a new-old neoclassical façade. Purists are horrified by this gimmick and the pouting mosaic of the Madonna and Child, but actually it's not such a displeasing imitation. The square-based bell tower is one of the few original 13th-century elements.

Inside, the once-Gothic church has all but disappeared beneath the rich icing of baroque excess. Bright frescoes adorn the ceilings, and the three narrow chapels at either side of the aisles spill over with sculptural whirls in an effect that is both impressive and appalling. The third chapel to the right is perhaps the pinnacle of the genre: a serene St Michael, who appears (in typically baroque fashion) to be in the eye of a swirling storm, casts devils into hell.

Still, there are some less gaudy bits and pieces. The two intricate stone pulpits on either side of the central door as you enter the church were sculpted by Guglielmo da Pisa and donated by the Pisans to Cagliari in 1312. The pulpits actually formed a magnificent single unit until the meddlesome Domenico Spotorno, architect in charge of the baroque remodelling, split it in two in the 16th century and removed the big stone lions that formed its base. These quite eye-catching sculptures of the lion grappling with its weaker foe now front the altar with aggressive symbolism. To the right of the altar is the worn-looking *Trittico di Clemente VII*, attributed by some to the school of Flemish painter Rogier van der Weyden.

Don't miss the **Aula Capitolare**, the crypt, beneath the altar. It's hewn out of stone tamed by the sculptor's chisel and now presents a riot of sculptural decoration – not a centimetre has been left bare.

Next door to the cathedral is archbishop's residence the **Palazzo Arcivescovile**, followed by the pale lime façade of the **Palazzo Viceregio**

(Palazzo Regio; ☎ 070 52 25 88; admission €5; Piazza Palazzo; ☺ by request only), which was once home to the Spanish and Savoy viceroys and today serves as the provincial assembly. It also hosts music concerts throughout the summer.

Stampace

Stampace is the remains of Cagliari's medieval working-class district, where Sards lived huddled in the shadow of the mighty castle. In the 14th century, when the Aragonese were in charge, Sards were forbidden to enter the castle after nightfall. Those caught were thrown off the castle walls, with the benediction *stai in pace* (rest in peace), a phrase that gave Stampace its name.

This huddle of houses abuts Piazza Yenne, which is effectively the 'centre' of the town although it's more like a traffic island. The piazza is adorned with a statue of King Carlo Felice to mark the beginnings of the Carlo Felice highway (SS131), the project for which he is best remembered. At night in summer, Piazza Yenne heaves as the city's young and restless come out to play in its various bars and cafés.

CHIESA DI SANT'EFISIO

Despite its unassuming façade and modest interior, the most important church in the quarter is the **Chiesa di Sant'Efisio** (Via Sant'Efisio; ☺ 9am-1pm & 3.30-7.30pm Tue-Sun). It's dedicated to Cagliari's patron saint, St Ephisius, a Roman soldier who converted to Christianity and later lost his head for refusing to recant his new-found faith. The church is supposedly built on the site of the martyr's prison.

He's stood the city in good stead, saving the populus from the plague in 1652 – when the church got its marble makeover – and repelling Napoleon's fleet in 1793. You can even see French cannonballs embedded in the wall beneath a picture of St Ephisius stirring up the storm that sent the fleet packing. If the church guardian is there, you may be able to see the beautifully ornate *carozza* (carriage) that is used to carry the wooden effigy of the saint in the 1 May celebrations. It's decorated with gold leaf; the golden bands around the wheels cost the municipality €20,000 when they had to be replaced.

At the side of the church is the entrance to the prison where St Ephisius was supposedly held before being executed in Nora. It's marked in stone – Carcer Sancti Ephysii

M (Prison of the Martyr St Ephisius) – and retains the column where Ephisius was tied during his incarceration. For more information on the saint's feast day, see Festivals & Events, p72.

CRIPTA DI SANTA RESTITUTA

Virtually next door is the **Cripta di Santa Restituta** (Via Sant'Efisio; admission free; ☺ 9am-1pm & 3.30-7.30pm Tue-Sun), which has been in use since pre-Christian times. It's a huge, eerie natural cavern where the echo of leaking water drip-drips. Originally a place of pagan worship, it became the home of the martyr Restituta in the 5th century and a reference point for Cagliari's early Christians. The Orthodox Christians then took it over – you can still see remnants of their frescoes – until the 13th century, when it was abandoned. In WWII it was used as an air-raid shelter, a task it wasn't up to, since many died while holed up here in February 1943. It's interesting to make out the wartime graffiti that covers the walls.

CHIESA DI SAN MICHELE

Where Via Azuni runs into the little square of the same name, you'll find the ebullient baroque façade of the **Chiesa di San Michele** (Via Ospedale 2; ☺ 7.30-11am & 7-8pm). It's unusual in that you enter via a vast colonnaded atrium that has stairs leading into the church proper on the right-hand side. Directly in front of you in the atrium is a grand pulpit named after Habsburg emperor Carlos V (who is said to have delivered a stirring speech there before setting off on a fruitless campaign against Arab corsairs in Tunisia). The majesty of the octagonal interior, with chapels radiating from the centre and topped by a grand dome, reflects the power of its Jesuit builders. The heady décor, all marble, stucco and bright frescoes, dates to the first half of the 18th century and is one of the best examples of rococo in Sardinia.

CHIESA DI SANT'ANNA

Stampace's final church is the **Chiesa di Sant'Anna** (Piazza Santa Restituta; ☺ 10am-1pm & 5-7pm), the largest but least interesting of the city's collection. It looms out at you as if from nowhere and its imposing sand-coloured façade rises high above the little square it dominates. Largely destroyed during WWII and painstakingly rebuilt afterwards, it is basically baroque, but the Ionic columns that are melded into the undulating façade give it a slightly severe neoclassical edge.

ANFITEATRO ROMANO

It's a surprise to come upon the broad arc of the 2nd-century **Anfiteatro Romano** (Viale Fra Ignazio; admission €3; ☺ 10am-1pm & 3-6pm Tue-Sun Apr-Oct, 10am-4pm Tue-Sun Nov-Mar) after the dense alleys of Stampace. Carved out of the hillside rock, much of the original theatre was cannibalised in the following centuries, but enough has survived for us to imagine a good Roman afternoon out. Crowds of up to 10,000, practically the entire population of Cagliari at the time, could watch their favourite gladiators do battle with wild beasts while the spectators munched on nuts and looked out over the Mediterranean. In summer, the amphitheatre recovers something of its vocation by hosting summer concerts – you may find it closed to visitors during concert seasons.

Marina

As you wander seawards, you finally reach the dagger-straight streets of the Marina district. The most characterful part of town, its little lanes are full of artisanal shops and good eateries.

Sequestered in its alleys is the **Chiesa di Sant'Eulalia**, interesting not so much for the church (which can't be visited) but for the adjoining **Museo del Tesoro e Area Archeologica di Sant'Eulalia** (MUTSEU; ☎ 070 66 37 24; Vico del Collegio 2; admission €3; ☺ 10am-1pm & 5-11pm Jul-Sep, 10am-1pm & 5-8pm Tue-Sun Oct-Jun). Beneath the church's altar, sections of Roman road have been uncovered. You can view the even paving stones from a raised walkway. Ongoing excavations should reveal more subterranean secrets.

Upstairs is the treasury, a particularly rich collection of religious art, ranging from exquisite priests' vestments and silverware through to medieval codices and other precious documents. Fine wooden sculptures abound, along with an Ecce Homo painting, depicting Christ front and back after his flagellation. The painting has been attributed to a 17th-century Flemish artist.

A quick stroll to the northwest is the **Chiesa di Santo Sepolcro** (☎ 070 65 51 35; Piazza del Santo Sepolcro; ☺ 10am-1pm & 5-8pm), whose most astonishing feature is an enormous 17th-century gilded wooden altarpiece housing a figure of the Virgin Mary.

Just beyond the limits of the Marina quarter stands the grand pile that is the town hall, or **Municipio** (☎ 800 01 60 58; Via Roma). A capricious neogothic affair, it was built from 1899 to 1913 and faithfully reconstructed after bombing in 1943.

Villanova

To the east of Il Castello lies Villanova, in itially an artisans' quarter that spilt out of the original city. You can wander the tight web of lanes that began the expansion; they're squashed between the eastern side of the castle and the Gothic complex of **Chiostro di San Domenico** (Piazza San Domenico). Strangely, amid the modern urban sprawl, hide some of Cagliari's oldest and most famous churches.

BASILICA DI SAN SATURNINO & CHIESA DI SAN LUCIFERO

It may look like a wreck, but the **Basilica di San Saturnino** (Piazza San Cosimo; ☺ 9am-1pm Mon-Sat) is a fascinating place. According to legend the Christian martyr Saturninus, another of those unfortunates who fell foul of Diocletian's anti-Christian campaign, was executed on this spot in 304.

Excavation has revealed that there may have been a place of Christian worship here as early as the 4th century, and certainly there was in the 6th century, making it one of Sardinia's oldest churches. You can view the necropolis (still being excavated) through the glass walls either side of the nave.

The basilica was partly demolished in 1662 to provide building material for the Cattedrale di Santa Maria. Overlying it all is the grand 11th-century remodelling undertaken by the Vittorini monks from Marseille, who transformed it into the Romanesque church it now is.

Directly across the leafy modern square is the baroque **Chiesa di San Lucifero**. Below the church is a 6th-century crypt where the tomb of the early Archbishop of Cagliari, St Lucifer, rests. In earlier times the area had been part of a Roman burial ground.

EXMA

In 1990 Cagliari's 18th-century *ex-mattatoio* (abattoir) was opened as a cultural centre called **Exma** (☎ 070 66 63 99; Via San Lucifero 71; exhibitions around €3; ☺ 10am-2pm & 5pm-midnight Tue-Sun Jun-Sep, 9am-8pm Tue-Sun Oct-May). It's run by the Centri d'Arte e Musei (CAMU), a body that

FRESH AIRS & GRACES

When the Catalano-Aragonese arrived to take Cagliari in 1323, it became clear it would be no easy task. So they sensibly set up camp on the fresh mountain slopes of Montixeddu, which came to be known as Bonaria (*buon'aria,* or 'good air'), as it was no doubt a good deal fresher here than in besieged Cagliari. In the three years of the siege, the camp became a fortress with its own church.

After ejecting the Pisans and taking the city in 1335, the Aragonese invited Mercedari monks from Barcelona to establish a monastery at the Bonaria church, where they remain to this day.

The Bonaria monks were kept well employed for centuries ransoming Christian slaves from Muslim pirates, and they are credited with saving the Genoese community of Tabarka in Tunisia and bringing them to Isola di San Pietro. But what makes this a place of international pilgrimage (Pope John Paul II came by in 1985) is a simple wooden statue of the Virgin Mary and Christ, now housed in the Santuario di Nostra Signora di Bonaria (see below).

Legend has it that the statue was washed up after being cast overboard by Spanish seamen caught in a storm in the 14th century. Monks found the Madonna not only in perfect shape on the beach in front of their sanctuary but with a candle alight in her hand. 'It's a miracle!' they cried, as one did in such circumstances, and the statue was placed in a niche behind the altar in the church.

Over the years, Christian seamen became especially devoted to Nostra Signora di Bonaria, attributing all manner of miracles on the high seas to her intervention. The Spanish conquistadors named a future capital city (Buenos Aires in Argentina) in her honour. And as a result of all the devotion, a collection of the most curious *ex voto* offerings, in the form of model ships, paintings and the like, has slowly accumulated in the church and is now held in its museum.

also coordinates the exhibitions in the Ghetto degli Ebrei and the Castello di San Michele. A permanent exhibition details the restoration of the abattoir, but it's best known for its contemporary art shows and photography exhibitions. In summer, there are frequent open-air music concerts.

SANTUARIO & BASILICA DI NOSTRA SIGNORA DI BONARIA

Little remains of the original fortress and church complex built by the Catalano-Aragonese in 1323, apart from the truncated bell tower, which originally served as a watchtower. Below it is the **Santuario di Nostra Signora di Bonaria** (☎ 070 30 17 47; Viale Bonaria; donations expected; ☺ 6.30am-noon & 4.30-7.30pm Apr-Oct, 6.30am-noon & 4-6.30pm Nov-Mar), where you will find the revered statue of the Virgin Mary and Christ (see the boxed text, above) in a niche behind the altar. In keeping with the miraculous atmosphere of the place, the tiny ivory boat hanging from the ceiling above the altar moves mysteriously to indicate the wind direction in the Golfo degli Angeli.

Among the collection of model boats and other *ex voto* offerings in the museum off the cloister is a golden crown from Carlo Emanuele I. There are also the mummified corpses of four plague-ridden Catalano-Aragonese nobles whose bodies were found

miraculously preserved in the church. If the museum isn't open, you need to approach one of the priests or volunteers.

The sanctuary is dwarfed by the **basilica** to its right, which still acts as a landmark to returning sailors. Building began in 1704, but the money ran out and the basilica wasn't finished until 1926. An Allied bomb in 1943 put paid to all its marvellous decoration shortly thereafter. The building has been meticulously repaired after a lengthy restoration that was only completed in 1998.

Beyond the Centre

GALLERIA COMUNALE D'ARTE

North of Il Castello, fronting the green Giardini Pubblici, is the **Galleria Comunale d'Arte** (☎ 070 49 07 27; Viale San Vincenzo; adult/child €3.10/1.05; ☺ 9am-1pm & 5-9pm Wed-Mon Apr-Oct, 9am-1pm & 3.30-7.30pm Nov-Mar), a grand neoclassical building housing an excellent collection of contemporary artworks. It also holds the Collezione Ingrao, which displays more than 650 works of Italian art from the mid-19th century to the late 20th century.

Most interesting, however, is the collection of work by native Sards such as Tarquinio Sinni (1891–1943). His humorous *contrasti* (contrasts), which show heavily dressed Sardinian girls standing frumpily beside glamorous, coiffed flappers, explore the social tension between traditional Sardinian ways and the perplexing freedoms of a rapidly modernising world. Another highlight is the work of Giuseppe Biasi (1885–1945), whose oils depict Sardinian life in a rich style that combines the bold brushstrokes of Gauguin with the moody atmosphere of Degas.

The museum also holds frequent temporary exhibitions of contemporary artists.

CASTELLO DI SAN MICHELE

A stout three-tower Spanish fortress, **Castello di San Michele** (Castillo de San Miguel; admission €5; 🕙 10am-1pm & 5-10pm Tue-Sun) stands in a commanding position northwest of the city centre. It was built in the 10th century to protect the capital from the province of Cagliari and it has been much added to over the years. Its location is spectacular and its grounds are a peaceful green space to get away from the city.

The castle is used for temporary exhibitions, so times and entry prices can change. To get there take city bus 5, which stops at the foot of the hill on Via Bacu Abis. From there, a paved road runs for 800m up to the castle. During the museum opening times, a shuttle bus runs from the parking lot up to the castle every 15 minutes.

PUBLIC PARKS

Established in 1858, the **Orto Botanico** (admission/guided tour €2/3; 🕙 8am-1.30pm & 3-7pm Apr-Oct, 8am-1.30pm Nov-Mar) is one of Italy's most famous botanical gardens, containing 500 species of tropical plant. Specimens from as far afield as Asia, Australia, Africa and the Americas sidle up next to the local carob trees and oaks, and the gardens are dotted with ancient ruins, an old Punic cistern, and a Roman quarry and aqueduct. It's a pleasant place for a wander; at 11am on the second and fourth Sunday of the month you can join guided visits to a greater part of the gardens.

The other public park covers the slopes of **Monte Irpinu**, which rises above Villanova in the northeast of the city and verges on the **Molentargius** salt marshes. You can drive (or take a long walk) up here for views over the city and the *saline*.

ACTIVITIES

The 6km **Poetto** (www.ilpoetto.com, in Italian) is the longest stretch of beach in Italy and forms an integral part of the life of any Cagliaritani. In summer it has a cheerful holiday atmosphere and is lined with funfairs, restaurants, bars and discos. The southern end is the most popular, with its picturesque Marina Piccola, yacht club and outdoor cinema (July and August only). You'll also find **Windsurfing Club Cagliari** (www.windsurfingclubcagliari.it) here, which offers a whole range of courses.

For bathers the beach is lined with lidos (managed sections), like the **Stabilimento Il Lido**, where you can hire umbrellas (€10) and loungers (€10). The lidos also offer useful facilities such as showers and changing cabins as well as pedalos (€10 per hour), canoes and surf-bikes. To get here catch the PF or PQ buses from the terminus in Piazza Matteotti. Both run the full length of the beach.

The **Golfo di Cagliari** is an excellent place for diving as it is littered with the wrecks of WWII ships. **Morgan Diving** (☎ 070 80 50 59; www.morgandiving.com) can arrange dives to most of these sites (€35 to €80) and is also authorised to conduct dives in the marine reserve of Villasimius (p87). It's based at the tourist port in the Marina Capitana, 14km east of Cagliari, although you can make arrangements over the phone.

TOURS

Mariposas (☎ 333 590 90 24; www.mariposas.it, in Italian) is a new initiative run by passionate Cagliaritani Giulia Fonnesu. She is full of fantastic ideas for exploring the city and can arrange anything from tours of subterranean Cagliari with archaeological guides, to city shopping trips and food and wine tastings. She can also organise tours to Nora, dives in Villasimius or a day in the Iglesiente mines. You need a group of four to six people, and prices for day tours range from €15 to €40.

FESTIVALS

The **Festa di Sant'Efisio** is a blockbuster event held from 1 May to 4 May. On 1 May Cagliaritani pour into the streets to greet the effigy of St Ephisius in his bullock-drawn carriage. As the costumed procession melts away, a hard-core retinue accompanies the statue on its 40km pilgrimage to Nora. The best place to view proceedings is from the grandstand seating arranged in and around Piazza Matteotti. Tickets (€15 to €18) go on sale at the tourist office in Via Goffredo Mameli in January and are quickly snapped up.

(Continued on page 81)

Market, Oliena (p202)

ALAN BENSON

DALLAS STRIBLEY

Sunflowers, Oristano province (p115)

Ponte Vecchio, Bosa (p129)

DOUG MCKINLAY

Boy on rocky outcrop, Isola di San
Pietro (p101)

Cala Gonone (p217), Golfo di Orosei

Spiaggia della Pelosa (p152), Capo del Falcone

DALLAS STRIBLEY

Poetto beach (p72), Cagliari

DAMIEN SIMONIS

Beach, Golfo di Orosei (p215)

Trompe l'oeil mural (p40), Fonni

Trompe l'oeil mural (p40), Fonni

Political mural, Orgosolo (p204)

Festa del Redentore (p200), Nuoro

DAMIEN SIMONIS

S'Ardia festival (p128), Sedilo

DALLAS STRIBLEY

Nuraghe Su Nuraxi (p113), near Barumini

Nuraghe Santu Antine (p144), near Torralba

ROCCO FASANO

Abandoned 19th-century mining town of Ingurtosu, Iglesiente (p95)

Castello di Acquafredda (p111), Campidano

WAYNE WALTON

Speciality bread (p51), Cavoi

ALAN BENSON

DALLAS STRIBLEY

Tempting biscuits (p54), Villasimius

Porceddu (suckling pig; p53), Sedilo

DALLAS ST

(Continued from page 72)

Cagliari also puts on a good show for **Carnevale** in February and **Holy Week** during Easter, when a hooded procession takes place between the Chiesa di Sant'Efisio and the cathedral up in Il Castello.

SLEEPING

For a capital city, Cagliari has disappointing accommodation. Travellers prepared to pay for a little style and comfort will find very few, if any, really top-end options.

However, the B&B scene is expanding rapidly and provides the most interesting and characterful accommodation at very reasonable prices. The association **Domus Karalitanae** (www.domuskaralitanae.com) lists many B&Bs on its website.

Budget

Hotel Aurora (☎ 070 65 86 25; www.hotelcagliari aurora.it, in Italian; Salita Santa Chiara 19; s/d €30/45, with bathroom €45/60; ✕) Don't be put off by the shabby exterior of this old palazzo nestled in the corner of Piazza Yenne. Inside it's bright and breezy, and although the rooms are small, the pastel colour scheme, city views and smiley service help compensate. During peak season, book your bed a month in advance. Air-conditioning costs an extra €8.

Hotel A&R Bundes Jack (☎ /fax 070 66 79 70; hotel .aerbundesjack@libero.it; Via Roma 75; s/d €43/70, with bathroom €54/82; ✕) Although it's pricey for this category, A&R is essentially a budget hotel. Agreeably showing its age, it retains a dose of character from a more elegant era – high ceilings, tiled floors and rickety furnishings that must be nearly as old as the building itself. Choose a room above the arches with the five-star views of the port. No credit cards.

Albergo La Perla (☎ 070 66 94 46; Via Sardegna 18; s/d €33/45) This simple *albergo* (hotel) is run by a stout, wheezing signora and her harried daughter. The rooms are spartan to say the least, and none has an en-suite bathroom. Still, the beds are neatly made and everything is spick-and-span. No credit cards.

Midrange

Sardinia Domus (☎ 070 65 97 83; www.sardiniadomus .it, in Italian; Largo Carlo Felice 26; s/d €45/70; ✕) This is Cagliari's best B&B, located slap-bang in the middle of town in a grand red-brick palazzo along Carlo Felice. It's beautifully finished to rustic effect – exposed stone walls and lamp-lit corridors lead to inviting bedrooms decorated with Liberty-style furnishings. Excellent value.

La Terrazza sul Porto (☎ 070 65 89 97; pierfranco .p@libero.it; Largo Carlo Felice 36; s/d €35/84; ✕) Welcome to the mad world of dog-sitters Franco and Andrea. Franco has decorated this huge top-floor flat (four flights of stairs!) with real shoestring style. The place features a Deco drawing room, a sleek stainless-steel communal kitchen, bedrooms like a Barcelona bordello and a huge communal bathroom complete with chandelier. No credit cards.

Hotel Calamosca (☎ 070 37 16 28; www.hotelcala mosca.it; Viale Calamosca 50; s/d €54/84; P ✕) This is a big, boxy beach hotel with sunny rooms and a terrace. In a fantastic location, it has lovely views over a cove near the lighthouse on Capo Sant'Elia. You can even swim off the rocks at the bottom of the hotel garden.

Hotel Italia (☎ 070 66 04 10; fax 070 65 02 40; Via Sardegna 31; s/d €66/88; ✕) Park the MG outside and don a pair of flares for the Hotel Italia. It's so '70s it's practically a museum piece, with wood-panelled ceilings, a chunky bar, orange sofas and vertical office blinds. Lucky for you, there's also 'musical transmission' in your room; we're assuming that's a radio!

Hotel Quattro Mori (☎ 070 66 85 35; www.hotel 4mori.it, in Italian; Via Angioi 27; s/d €55/75; P ✕) *Aha!* You think as you enter the vaulted lobby of the Quattro Mori, pleased at having found a hotel of character. Such hopes are rapidly dashed as you ascend the stairs to the lookalike hospital corridors and bland rooms. There's a mix of

---

SOMETHING DIFFERENT

Karel Bed & Breakfast (☎ 328 823 68 47; www.karel-bedandbreakfast.it, in Italian; Via Savoia; s/d €45/70, 2-person apt €80; ✕) Karel is the brainchild of the entrepreneurial Valentino Sanna. It's a collection of self-catering apartments as well as a four-room bed and breakfast. Accommodation is located in the Marina and Stampace districts in period buildings that Valentino has lovingly restored and furnished with comfortable modern furnishings. He speaks impeccable English, and is currently involved in expanding the remit of Karel to offer broader services such as food tastings and tours. It's a great way to experience life in the old city.

accommodation, so have a look around first. Parking in the garage costs €8.

Top End

Hotel Regina Margherita (☎ 070 67 03 42; www .hotelreginamargherita.com; Viale Regina Margherita 44; s/d €130/170; 🖵 🅿 🖭) You could be forgiven for thinking you'd chanced upon Alcatraz, such is the awful concrete exterior of Cagliari's top hotel. But leap the barbed wire and you'll find yourself in a world of slick service and business efficiency. Comfortable salmon-pink rooms with marshmallow-soft pillows are full of all the latest gizmos, and there's an impressive buffet breakfast.

Hotel Panorama (☎ 070 30 76 91; www.hotelpano rama.it; Viale Diaz 231; s/d €100/160; 🅿 🖭 🖵 🖭) Run by the same people as the Regina Margherita, the Panorama is a corporate clone. Its edges are softened by its out-of-town location, and the large pine-shaded pool is a big plus.

EATING

As a true-blue Sardinian town, Cagliari has a good range of restaurants. Cagliaritani enjoy eating out, and you'll find the stalwarts of the restaurant scene very busy. There's a certain formality to life in Sardinia, so it's always best to make a reservation. Things really get going around 9.30pm, but in summer people tend to dine later.

Beware: many of the better restaurants close for at least part of August.

Restaurants

MARINA

This area is peppered with good restaurants providing a culinary balance of traditional cheap eats and more gourmet options designed to blow minds and budgets.

Dal Corsaro (☎ 070 66 43 18; Viale Regina Margher-ita 28; menus €45-55; 🖄 Mon-Sat, closed 12-26 Aug) A classic of Cagliari's fine-dining scene, Dal Corsaro attracts the glad-rag scenesters who want to be seen. Stiff tablecloths, silver wine buckets and elegant couples murmuring over floral arrangements set the scene for some outrageously good food, while waiters provide impeccable service.

Da Lillicu (☎ 070 65 29 70; Via Sardegna 78; meals €15-25; 🖄 Mon-Sat, closed 10 Aug-1 Sep) You'll have to elbow your way into this trattoria – perhaps Cagliari's most famous eatery. The acoustics are not helped by the volume of noise arising from wine-fuelled diners. It's a great place

for a culinary adventure and certainly the place to try the *burrida* (marinated dogfish). There's a solid selection of meat mains and *antipasti*.

Antica Hostaria (☎ 070 66 58 60; Via Cavour 60; meals €35-45; 🖄 Mon-Sat, closed Aug) Pitched perfectly between Dal Corsaro and Da Lillicu is this welcoming restaurant. Antique furnishings, walls crowded with pictures and attentive service give it a cosy ambience, which is complemented by classic Italian cooking. It's popular with local VIPs.

Il Buongustaio (☎ 070 66 81 24; Via Concezione 7; lunch €25-30; 🖄 Wed-Mon) A sensory overload comes with every meal at this trattoria. The menu changes according to the season. If available, try the handmade pasta with prawns and jumbo crab meat for a real tastebud treat.

Ristorante Italia (☎ 070 65 79 87; Via Sardegna 30; meals €20-35; 🖄 Mon-Fri & dinner Sat, closed 10-20 Aug) Opposite the hotel of the same name, the Italia has the same dated atmosphere. It has two parts: the so-called bistro, which serves up cheap meals, and the 1st-floor restaurant, which has pretensions to grandeur. It's well regarded locally, especially for its superb fish dishes – try the *cassita de pisci* (fish soup).

AROUND CORSO VITTORIO EMANUELE

The *corso* (avenue) is lined with a plethora of restaurants and bars and is especially busy in winter. Good restaurants can also be found in the warren of adjoining streets.

Ristorante Flora (☎ 070 66 47 35; Via Sassari 45; meals €30-35; 🖄 Mon-Sat, closed Aug) Marble fireplaces, handsome dressers and gold-framed pictures make Flora feel like a rather grand private dining room. Dishes are strictly seasonal, and the maître d' offers excellent recommendations paired with suitable wines. This is great service in elegant surroundings.

Vineria Sant'Efisio (Via Santa Restituta 72; meals €30; 🖄 Tue-Sun Oct-Jun) This tiny, traditional *vineria* (wine bar, but not as you know it!) is tucked into the steep alleys of Stampace. It has a daily fish-only menu and on Wednesday it even offers sushi. The cosy cavelike interior provides an intimate setting and, as to be expected, there's a good selection of wine.

Crackers (☎ 070 65 39 12; Corso Vittorio Emanuele 193; meals €25; 🖄 Thu-Tue, closed 18-30 Aug) Crackers has a big cream-coloured vault beneath which you sit down to northern Italian specialities (the chef spent many years in Piedmont), including a variety of creamy risottos, mushrooms and even truffle dishes. It attracts an effortlessly stylish crowd.

Ristorante Quattro Mori (☎ 070 65 02 69; Via Angioi 93; meals €40; ☙ Tue-Sat & lunch Sun) Here you can enjoy fine Sardinian dishes in one of the city's culinary bastions. It's regularly packed to the rafters with noisy, contented diners, so reservations are essential.

La Vecchia Trattoria (☎ 070 65 25 15; Via Azuni 55; meals €30; ☙ lunch Tue-Sun) Ignore the gaudy sea-themed décor – think hanging nets and fishing paraphernalia – and enjoy a fine meal at this local favourite. It's located in a pretty spot near the Chiesa di San Michele and specialises in Cagliaritani cuisine, combining the flavours of *terra e mare* (land and sea).

OUT OF THE CENTRE

S'Apposentu (☎ 070 408 23 15; www.sapposentu.it, in Italian; Via Sant'Alenixedda; meals €40; ☙ Tue-Sat) The new restaurant at the Teatro Lirico has proved a resounding success. And as there are only 10 tables, you'll need to make a reservation. With artist-chef Roberto Petza in the kitchen you can expect plates as pretty as any picture – try Carloforte tuna, lasagne dusted with San Gavino saffron or Cabras mullet cooked in fen grass. Bravo!

Ristorante Royal (☎ 070 34 13 13; Via Bottego 24; meals €25-30; ☙ closed Sun afternoon & Mon) Tuck into a succulent Florentine steak or choose from a range of other meat and vegetable dishes from this window on Tuscany. There's not much fishy fare, but there are plenty of desserts, including an exemplary *seadas* (pastry filled with cheese and covered with honey).

POETTO

Cagliari's beach is lined with summertime bars, snack joints and restaurants. Things get really busy here between November and March (mollusc season), when shacks serving sea urchins and mussels are set up along the beach road. You're charged according to the number of shells left on your table.

Spinnaker (☎ 070 37 02 95; Località Marina Piccola; meals €30-35; ☙ Tue-Sun May-Sep) The sister restaurant of Dal Corsaro, this is one place at Poetto where you'll be guaranteed a refined dining experience. It operates on two levels: a cheap and cheerful pizzeria downstairs, and a chic 1st-floor terrace restaurant overlooking the boats bobbing in the marina. It serves up all the local favourites alongside specialities like vegetable-and-prawn couscous.

Cafés

Cagliari has some fantastic cafés, many lining the colonnaded walkway of Via Roma. They're a great alternative to a restaurant meal, especially at lunchtime, as this is where most of the Cagliaritani hang out.

Antico Caffè (☎ 070 65 82 06; www.anticocaffe1855 .it; Piazza Costituzione; salads & crêpes €5.20; ☙ 7am-2am) The city's most elegant café is a gleaming, steaming affair of copper and brass. It serves up a little bit of everything – pastries, sweets, crêpes, salads, coffee and cocktails – and is open into the early hours of the morning.

Dulcis Caffè (☎ 070 65 82 06; Viale Regina Margherita 14; executive lunch €18; ☙ Mon-Sat) Another classy café, Dulcis doubles as a wine bar in the evening. It's frequented by slick business types and sophisticates who appreciate the well-stocked wine list. Situated at the bottom of the Viale Regina, it has a decked terrace with palm-fringed views over the bay.

Caffè Svizzero (☎ 070 65 37 84; Largo Carlo Felice 6; ☙ Tue-Sun) This Liberty-style place has been part of Cagliari café society since the early 20th century. Anything from tea to cocktails is on offer in this frescoed locale, founded by a group of Swiss almost 100 years ago.

Self-catering

You can make up your own gourmet deli lunch if you pop into one of the *salumerie* (delicatessens) in the Marina quarter. A thick cut of *pecorino sardo* (a local cheese) and a slice or two of smoked ham in a freshly baked roll – what could be more satisfying? **I Sapori dell'Isola** (☎ 070 65 23 62; Via Sardegna 50) is a good place to start, or pop into **Disizos** (Via Napoli 72) for handmade pastas and delicious *seadas*.

You'll also notice the nightly crowd on Piazza Yenne, all licking furiously away at ice creams. They get them from **Isola del Gelato** (☎ 070 65 98 24; Piazza Yenne 35; ☙ 9am-2am Tue-Sun), which has an incredible 280 variations on the ice-cream theme, including several soya-based concoctions.

DRINKING

Piazza Yenne is perpetually packed with teenagers on a night out – mostly eating ice cream rather than drinking. In winter, bars along Corso Vittorio Emanuele fill up, and all the summer action takes place down at Poetto.

Caffè Librarium Nostrum (☎ 070 65 09 43; Via Santa Croce 33; ☙ Tue-Sun) Cagliari's most modish bar, Librarium Nostrum has seating against the

THE ALLIGATOR

Massimo Carlotto's life reads like the plot of one of his crime novels – hang on a minute, it *is* the plot of one of his novels, *Il Fuggiasco* (The Fugitive). It'd be hard to find a fictional equivalent quite as good.

At 19, during Italy's 'years of lead', he witnessed the murder of Margherita Magello, a 25-year-old student, who was stabbed 59 times. Covered in her blood he ran to fetch the police, who accused him of the killing. He was later sentenced to 18 years' imprisonment. On the advice of his lawyers, Carlotto went on the run in France and Mexico, where he was sheltered and fed by political activists for six years before he finally gave himself up. In 1993, after an international campaign, he was released with a full pardon from the president of Italy. It really is an incredible tale. No wonder Andrea Manni and Daniele Liotti's film version of the novel received such acclaim at its release in 2003.

When in prison, Carlotto found the true-life material for the explicit crime novels he now writes. His most famous series is the Alligator, which is developed from real legal cases Carlotto claims to have heard and read up on.

The protagonist is loosely modelled on Carlotto himself; he even drives the Skoda Carlotto once drove (the least-stopped car in Italy). The nickname comes from the character's (and Carlotto's) favourite cocktail – seven parts Calvados to three parts Drambuie, crushed ice and a slice of apple – invented by a barman in Cagliari (see Caffè Librarium Nostrum, p83), where Carlotto now lives. The cocktail's fame has since spread to bars in Rome, Milan and Naples. It's said that nobody can drink more than four.

In 2005, Massimo Carlotto signed a deal to publish five more novels in the series and his latest one, *Nordest,* was launched at Caffè Librarium Nostrum in September 2005. Two of his books, *The Columbian Mule* (2001) and *The Master of Knots* (2002), have also been translated into English. You can order his books and find out more about his fascinating life on www.massimocarlotto.it.

castle ramparts and frequent live music. Owner Danilo Argiolas created the Alligator cocktail in honour of the hero of Massimo Carlotto's novels (see the boxed text, above).

Caffè degli Spiriti (Bastione San Remy; grills €8-12, pizza €4.50-6.50) This new castle venture has the Bastione San Remy as its terrace. Sit outside under the black-and-green tented canopy or inside in the stylish modern bar. Simple plates of food are served alongside the cocktails.

Sotto La Torre (Piazza San Giuseppe 2; 8am-3am Thu-Tue) Trip through the centuries as you sip coffee, tea or grappa (grape-based liqueur). The décor is elegantly beamed 17th century. You can step back in time still further by peering into a couple of cisterns here that date back to Roman and Punic times.

Il Merlo Parlante (070 65 39 81; Via Portoscalas 69; Tue-Sun) Expect grizzled old geezers and students on the razzle at this boisterous *birreria* (brewery) shoehorned into a narrow alley off Corso Vittorio Emanuele.

ENTERTAINMENT

For information on what's going on in town, pick up a free copy of *Vivi Cagliari* from the tourist office. You can buy tickets to most shows in Cagliari (and beyond) from **Box Office Tickets** (Viale Regina Margherita 43; 10am-1pm & 5-8pm Mon-Fri, 10am-1pm Sat).

Concerts

Live-music concerts, sometimes on a big scale, occur mainly in summer. Many are staged over July and August in the **Anfiteatro Romano** (p70). Tickets, ranging from €10 to €70, are on sale at the Teatro Lirico (below).

Major rock concerts by the occasional international act and big Italian bands are staged at the **Fiera Campionaria** (Viale Diaz 221) fairgrounds in the east of the city. Tickets for good seats can easily cost around €20.

Theatre, Classical Music & Ballet

Cagliari has a lively theatrical scene, and opera performances are especially popular. Some places operate a winter-only programme (October to June), although the bigger theatres have year-round performances.

Teatro Lirico (Teatro Comunale; 070 408 22 30; www.teatroliricodicagliari.it, in Italian; Via Sant'Alenixedda; ticket office 10am-2pm & 6-8pm Mon-Sat) The main stage for classical music, ballet and opera, Teatro Lirico features a broad programme including classics like *Carmen, Nabucco* and *The Barber of Seville.*

Teatro Alfieri (070 30 13 78; Via della Pineta 29) The Alfieri hosts much of the city's grand classic theatre, from Shakespeare to Goldoni. The occasional modern piece slips through, too. Performances are in Italian only.

Exma (☎ 070 66 63 99; Via San Lucifero 71) This complex holds a year-round series of small-scale concerts. In summer it also provides an atmospheric venue for open-air jazz and classical concerts.

Teatro Saline (☎ 070 34 13 22; www.teatrodelle saline.it, in Italian; Viale La Palma) Puts on all sorts of things from children's theatre to popular modern pieces.

SHOPPING

Cagliari does not have a big shopping scene, although there are some treats tucked in the nooks and crannies of the city. The best place to have a wander is the Marina district, which has a number of artisanal shops.

Durke (☎ 070 66 79 84; www.durke.com; Via Napoli 66) At this craft bakery Maurizia Pala and her family turn out the most exquisite Sardinian sweets according to age-old recipes. The shop itself is worth seeing for its old ovens, huge mechanical mixing bowl and pasta press.

Sapori di Sardegna (☎ 070 684 87 47; Vico dei Mille 1) Franco Zola shops at this emporium when he comes to town. Staff can arrange to ship orders (such as boxes of wine) worldwide.

Antica Enoteca Cagliaritana (Salita Santa Chiara 21) Just off Piazza Yenne, this is another specialist wine shop.

Loredana Mandas (☎ 070 66 76 48; Via Sicilia 31) For something very special, seek out Loredana's workshop. You can watch her create the exquisite gold filigree for which Sardinia is so famous. Each piece is original and unique.

Isola (☎ 070 49 27 56; Via Bacaredda 176-8) Even if you don't buy any of the Sardinian crafts available here, it's useful to get an idea of products and prices.

Grand Wazoo (☎ 070 66 60 39; Via Garibaldi 143) This place is a good outlet for Sardinian music.

Sunday is market day in Cagliari, but the locations and themes move around. On the first Sunday of the month, **Piazza Giovanni XXIII** (⌚ 9am-8pm) to the northwest hosts an antiques and collectors' market. The following week the antiques move to **Piazza Carlo Alberto** (⌚ 5-11pm summer, 8.30am-2pm winter) in Il Castello. On the third Sunday **Piazza Galilei** (⌚ 6-11pm) in Villanova hosts a similar market, while on the last Sunday of the month an organic farm-produce market, with various other odds and ends on display, takes place in Piazza San Sepolcro in the Marina district. Second-hand goods markets are held every Sunday at Bastione San Remy in Il Castello.

GETTING THERE & AWAY
Air
Cagliari's Elmas **airport** (www.aeroportodicagliari .com) is 6km northwest of the city centre. It was expanded in 2003, which has greatly improved its efficiency.

The airport is served mainly by Italian carriers **Alitalia** (☎ 848 86 56 61; www.alitalia .com), **Air One** (☎ 848 84 88 80; www.flyairone.it) and **Meridiana** (☎ 070 24 01 69; www.meridiana.com). **Easyjet** (www.easyjet.com) also offers daily charter flights direct from London.

For information on tickets and routes, both international and domestic, see p236.

Boat
The Stazione Marittima ferry terminal is located in the heart of Cagliari just off Via Roma. Ferries depart regularly for Palermo and Trapani in Sicily, as well as Naples, Livorno and Civitavecchia on the mainland (see p241 for further details).

Tirrenia (☎ 199 12 31 99, 070 66 60 65; www.tirrenia .it; Via Riva di Ponente 1; ⌚ 8.30am-12.20pm & 3.30-6.50pm Mon-Sat, 4-6pm Sun) is the main company servicing Sicily and mainland Italy.

Linea dei Golfi (☎ 199 12 31 99; www.lineadeigolfi .it; Via Riva di Ponente 1; ⌚ 8.30am-12.20pm & 3.30-6.50pm Mon-Sat, 4-6pm Sun) only serves Livorno. Tickets can be purchased from local travel agents (see p64).

Bus
The main bus station is on Piazza Matteotti. Local and intercity **ARST** (Azienda Regionale Sarda Trasporti; ☎ 800 86 50 42; www.arst.sardegna.it) buses use the station. There are services to nearby Pula (€2.01, one hour, hourly) and Villasimius (€2.89, 1½ hours, 10 daily Monday to Friday, four daily Saturday and Sunday) as well as to Oristano (€5.84, one hour 35 minutes, four daily) and Nuoro (€9.50, 3½ hours, four daily). Curiously, the ticket counters are in the attached McDonald's.

FMS (☎ 800 04 45 53; www.ferroviemeridionalisarde .it, in Italian) runs services to Iglesias (€3.46, one to 1½ hours, six daily), Carbonia (€4.44, 1½ hours, six daily), Portovesme (€4.91, two hours, three daily) and the Sulcis area. Buses depart from Piazza Matteotti. Buy tickets from the café inside the station.

Car & Motorcycle
The SS131 Carlo Felice highway, first laid in 1820, links the capital with Porto Torres via

Oristano and Sassari. It is the island's main dual-carriage artery. Another, the SS130, leads east to Iglesias.

The coast roads approaching from the east and west get highly congested in peak times such as the midsummer holiday season.

Train

The main **Trenitalia** (www.trenitalia.it) station is on Piazza Matteotti. Trains serve Iglesias (€2.75, 55 minutes, eight daily) and Carbonia (€3.50, one hour, eight daily from Monday to Saturday, two on Sunday) in the southwest, while the main line proceeds north to Sassari (€12.10, 4¼ hours, five daily) and Porto Torres via Oristano (€4.75, one to two hours, hourly). A branch line from Chilivani heads for Olbia (€13, four hours, four daily) and Golfo Aranci.

The **FdS** (Ferrovie della Sardegna; ☎ 070 50 02 46; www.ferroviesardegna.it, in Italian) station for trains north to Dolianova, Mandas and Isili is on Piazza Repubblica. In summer (19 June to 11 September), the scenic **trenino verde** (www.treninoverde.com) runs between Cagliari and Mandas (€2.63, two hours, hourly) and between Mandas and Arbatax (€16.50, five hours, one daily) on the east coast. It's a slow ride on a steam locomotive through some wild country. Another similar line runs from Mandas to Sorgono (€12, 2½ hours, one daily).

GETTING AROUND

Moving around on foot, although it's tiring at times in the hilly tracts of Il Castello, is generally the best option. There are a number of lifts – one at the back of Piazza Yenne and the others on Viale Regina Margherita – that make the trip up marginally less exhausting.

To/From the Airport

Almost hourly, buses connect the city centre (ARST station in Piazza Matteotti) with Elmas airport (€0.77, 15 minutes, 24 daily) between 6.30am and 11pm.

A taxi is €15 to €20. To park in the airport's parking area you'll pay €0.80 an hour or up to €4.80 for each 24-hour period.

Bus

CTM (Consorzio Trasporti e Mobilità; ☎ 070 209 12 10) bus routes cover the city and surrounding area. You might use the buses to reach a handful of out-of-the-way sights, and they come in handy for the Calamosca and Poetto beaches.

A normal ticket costs €0.77 and is valid for 90 minutes. There are all sorts of combinations of daily, weekly and monthly passes.

The most useful lines are bus 10 from Viale Trento to Piazza Garibaldi via Corso Vittorio Emanuele, and bus 7 from Piazza Matteotti to Il Castello. Buses 30 or 31 will get you to the sanctuary at Bonaria.

Car & Motorcycle

Parking in the city centre generally means paying. Metered parking in blue zones costs €1 for the first hour and €1 for each hour thereafter.

Driving in Cagliari is a pain, although given the geography of the town (one big hill), you consider renting a scooter for a day or two. You can hire one from **Sartour** (☎ 070 65 87 65, 338 811 65 45; Via Agostino 21). Charges are €40 per day for a two-person scooter, although the rate drops to €25 for longer hire.

All the big international car-rental agencies are represented at the airport. Hertz also has an office on Piazza Matteotti. **Ruvioli Rentacar** (☎ 070 65 89 55; www.ruvioli.it; Via dei Mille 9) is a local agent located in the heart of the Marina district. Charges are €68 per day (€340 per week) for a Fiat Punto.

Taxi

There are taxi ranks at Piazza Matteotti, Piazza della Repubblica and on Largo Carlo Felice. You can call to arrange a **taxi** (☎ 070 40 01 01; ◷ 5.30am-2am). Outside those times you might have difficulty. Other numbers include ☎ 070 28 82 04, ☎ 070 65 06 20 and ☎ 070 66 79 34.

THE SARRABUS

Beyond the ragged environs of Cagliari's suburbs lies the lonely Sarrabus, one of the least-populated regions of the island and still comparatively untouched by large-scale resort-style tourism. In its centre rise the bushy green peaks of the Monte dei Sette Fratelli, a miraculously wild hinterland where some of the island's last remaining deer can wander in peace.

Along the bare, hilly coast the road rises and falls, with spectacular views of the multi-hued sea punctuated by pretty coves like Cala Regina, Kal'e Moru and **Solanas**, ending at the seaside town of Villasimius. A few kilometres short of Villasimius, a road veers south along the peninsula to Capo Carbonara, the most southeasterly point of Sardinia.

CAPO CARBONARA

Although the tip of the cape remains a military zone and is off-limits to visitors, the waters around Capo Carbonara are a **marine reserve** (www.ampcapocarbonara.it, in Italian), visitable with an authorised diving outlet. The reserve includes Isola dei Cavoli, Secca dei Berni and Isola di Serpentara just off the coast from Villasimius. **Morgan Diving** (☎ 070 80 50 59; www .morgandiving.com) at Marina Capitana is one licensed operator, as is **Air Sub** (☎ 070 79 20 33; www.airsub.com; Via Roma) in Villasimius.

On the western side of the peninsula is the new marina and what remains of a Spanish tower, signposted as the **Fortezza Vecchia**. South of the tower are a few sections of beach, although the main beach on this side of the peninsula is **Spiaggia del Riso**. The eastern side is dominated by the **Stagno Notteri** lagoon, often host to flamingos in winter. On its seaward side is the stunning **Spiaggia del Simius** beach with its Polynesian blue waters. The lagoon runs all the way to Villasimius.

VILLASIMIUS

pop 3030

Once a quiet fishing village surrounded by pines and *macchia* (Mediterranean scrub), Villasimius has grown into one of Sardin-

---

DETOUR: MONTE DEI SETTE FRATELLI

East of Cagliari, the SS125 highway proceeds north of the sawlike profile of **Monte dei Sette Fratelli** (1023m), one of only three remaining redoubts of the *cervo sardo* (Sardinian deer). The Caserma Forestale Campu Omu (forestry corps station) is about 29km further on your right-hand side, opposite the turn-off for Burcei. You can pick up a map here detailing the walks in park. They range from an easy 3.2km loop around the wooded area close to the station to a 12km trek up to **Punta Sa Ceraxa** (1016m).

Alternatively, head north to the village of **Burcei**, surrounded in springtime by cherry blossom. Beyond, a lonely road crawls a further 8km to **Punta Serpeddi** (1067m), from where you can gaze out across the whole Sarrabus to Cagliari and the sea.

---

ia's more low-key resorts. In summer it's a lively, cheerful place, although activity all but dies out in the winter months.

On the central Piazza Gramsci there's a **tourist office** (☎ 070 793 02 08; www.comune.villasimius .ca.it, in Italian; Piazza Gramsci 8; ☿ 10am-1pm & 9pm-midnight Mon-Sat mid-Jun–mid-Sep, 10am-1pm & 3.30-6.30pm Mon-Sat mid-Sep–mid-Jun). Change money at the **Banco di Sardegna** (11 Piazza Gramsci).

The tourist office has lots of information on activities in Villasimius including dive outlets. Alternatively, try **Air Sub** (☎ /fax 070 79 20 33; www.airsub.com; Via Roma). A big outfit with a second office in Cagliari, it offers all the courses and dives you could possibly want.

The **Festa della Madonna del Naufrago**, held on the second Sunday of July, is a striking seaborne procession to a spot off the coast where a statue of the Virgin Mary lies on the seabed in honour of shipwrecked sailors.

Sleeping

Stella Maris (☎ 070 79 71 00; www.stella-maris.com; Località Campulongu; half board per person €160; P ⓡ ⓧ) This gorgeous Charme e Relax hotel (see p223) is set in its own pine wood against a frosty white beach. It's crammed with tasteful crafts and furnishings. Outside, the manicured gardens slope gently to the beach and are lapped by translucent waters. Dinner on the terrace restaurant is an experience in itself.

Albergo Stella d'Oro (☎ 070 79 12 55; fax 070 79 26 32; Via Vittorio Emanuele 25; s/d €50/105, half board per person Aug €82; P ⓧ) A charming and casual small hotel, the Stello d'Oro is about 50m east of Piazza Gramsci. Rooms are of a reasonable size and all but the single have en-suite bathroom. There's a good seafood restaurant here, too, complete with pretty inner courtyard.

Spiaggia del Riso (☎ 070 79 10 52; www.villaggio spiaggiadelriso.it; camp sites per adult & tent €12, 4-person bungalows €110; ☿ May-Oct; P) This fantastic camp site has excellent facilities and attractive bungalows. Boasting a supermarket, tennis courts and a children's play area, it's right by the beach. It gets hellishly crowded in midsummer and booking is absolutely essential.

Eating

Ristorante La Lanterna (☎ 070 79 16 59; Via Roma 62; meals €30) At this quality place you enter through a garden (where you can eat in summer), which leads into the dining area. The seafood risotto is a classic. It's 150m north along a side road from Piazza Gramsci.

Ristorante Carbonara (☎ 070 79 12 70; Via Umberto I 60; meals €30; 🕑 Thu-Tue) A long-standing restaurant with a solid reputation, Carbonara has an excellent range of seafood dishes and a sunny blue-and-white colour scheme. The watery critters are on display for you to choose the subject of your main course.

Entertainment

Just before the turn-off for Capo Carbonara on the road into Villasimius from the west, Peyote and Fortesa are next to one another. They're maxi-discos in summer, and the former dishes up a little Tex-Mex cooking.

Getting There & Around

ARST buses from Cagliari (€2.89, 1½ hours) run up to nine times a day in summer. Also in summer, Autolinee Vacca runs local buses between Villasimius down to Capo Carbonara and around other nearby beaches.

COSTA REI

Take the wonderful coast road north of Villasimius to the Costa Rei and its long strip of white-sand beaches. The road runs a couple of hundred metres inland from the beaches (including Playa di Santa Giusta). Just park on the side of the road and wander down one of the dirt trails. Crystal-clear waters and the occasional snack-cum-cocktail bar await.

A few more kilometres north and you enter the Costa Rei resort proper. Uniform but not unpleasant holiday villas lead the way into the core, where you will find shops, bars, summer clubs and a few indifferent eateries. **Spiaggia Costa Rei** is, like the beaches to its south and north, a dazzling white strand lapped by remarkably clear blue-green water.

From the beaches of Costa Rei you can go on various **boat excursions** (taking up to 10 people). A **boat stand** (☎ 070 99 13 45) on the beach reached from the southern end of Via Colombo offers several trips, including one to Isola di Serpentara (€30 per person).

North of the resort scene, **Spiaggia Piscina Rei** is a continuation of the blinding white sand and turquoise water theme, with a camping ground fenced in just behind it. A couple more beaches fill the remaining length of coast up to **Capo Ferrato**, beyond which drivable dirt trails lead north.

The only hotel option is **Hotel Alba Ruja** (☎ 070 99 15 57; www.albaruja.it; Via Colombo; d €188), a set of villa-style residences at the northern

end of the core Costa Rei complex. **Camping Capo Ferrato** (☎ 070 99 10 12; www.campingcapoferrato .it; camp sites per adult/tent €9/8.60, 4-person bungalow €79; 🕑 Mar-Oct) is a good-value place at the southern entrance to the Costa Rei resort.

The same ARST buses from Cagliari to Villasimius continue around to Costa Rei, taking about half an hour.

NURAGHE ASORU

If you want to see a *nuraghe,* this is one of your best chances in southeastern Sardinia, which is virtually devoid of seriously interesting specimens. About 5km west of San Priamo, the Nuraghe Asoru stands just on the northern side of the SS125 highway. Its central *tholos* (conical-roofed) tower is in reasonable nick, but if you have already seen some of the truly important *nuraghi* this one is not likely to excite too much.

MURAVERA & TORRE SALINAS

pop 4840

On the flood plain of the Fiume Flumendosa (Flumendosa River), Muravera and surrounding villages San Vito and Villaputzu are a citrusy oasis. The river has been dammed, but these quiet towns still make their living from the orchards, and they celebrate the **Sagra degli Agrumi** (Citrus Fair), on the second Sunday before Easter Sunday, with gusto.

Within the locality are the lagoons and pristine beaches of Torre Salinas, picturesquely spread out beneath the Spanish watchtower. It's prettier than the Costa Rei, and the **Stagno dei Colostrai** is home to wintering flamingos. The few holiday homes are hidden in the greenery behind the beach, lending the place an untouched feeling. The **Spiaggia Torre delle Saline** is just the first in a line of dazzling beaches and near-perfect water that continues north up the coast to the mouth of the Fiume Flumendosa.

Stay at the inviting **Cosi in Mare…Come in Cielo** (☎ 070 99 91 23; www.hellosardinia.com; Località Torre Salinas, SS125 at km 56.7; s/d €54/115; 🖵), decorated with antiques and paintings. The B&B's wide veranda overlooks the beach, and you have the use of the kitchen and outdoor barbecue. It's popular with an artistic crowd.

Four ARST buses run from Cagliari to Muravera (€4.91, three hours, four Monday to Saturday) via Villasimius. A few others take the quicker inland route. The same buses proceed to Villaputzu and San Vito.

Southwest Sardinia

From the magnificent and little-visited beaches of the Costa Verde to the abandoned mines of the Iglesiente, the southwest of the island presents some stunning contrasts – and they aren't confined to the landscape. The history of the region has been a roller-coaster ride between great prosperity and dire poverty. Even as far back as the 13th century BC, prehistoric man has been interested in the area – just look at the enormous Nuraghe Su Nuraxi near Barumini, the biggest prehistoric site on the island grown rich on the obsidian of Monte Arci.

The Phoenicians, Carthaginians and Romans all coveted the mines of the southwest, and Mussolini survived on Carbonia's coal when the League of Nations sanctioned Italy in 1936. But, like any mines, those of the Iglesiente are inextricably linked with terrible hardships and localised poverty. After their closure in the 1990s, the region's economy collapsed, creating the majority of Sardinia's current 200,000 unemployed workers. Even the English word 'labour' comes from the Sardinian word *laore*, referring to the vast wheat fields of the Campidano plain.

However, it wasn't only the silver mountains of the interior that caught the colonists' eye; the wild coastline has long played a key role in commerce. The Phoenicians and Romans set up shop on Isola di Sant'Antioco and created one of their largest cities at picturesque Nora, where you can still see much evidence of the fine expatriate life they led. These coastal charms have not been lost on modern developers, and the southwest boasts a stretch of luxurious resorts at Santa Margherita di Pula rivalling anything on the Costa Smeralda.

HIGHLIGHTS

▣ Behold the grand pile of the **Nuraghe Su Nuraxi** (p113), Sardinia's largest *nuraghe* (stone tower) and a Unesco World Heritage site

▣ Revel in the crystal waters of some of the island's wildest and least-developed beaches on the **Costa Verde** (p98)

▣ Wander the Roman baths, theatre, temples and mosaics of the ancient port town of **Nora** (p109)

▣ Enjoy the Genoese flavours and dramatic coastline of the utterly unspoilt **Isola di San Pietro** (p101)

▣ Feel the spooky echoes of hard times gone by in the abandoned mines dotting the poignant **Iglesiente** (p95)

▣ Indulge yourself in the luxurious haven of the **Forte Village** (p108) resort at Santa Margherita di Pula

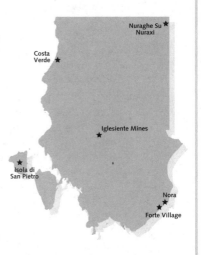

SOUTHWEST SARDINIA

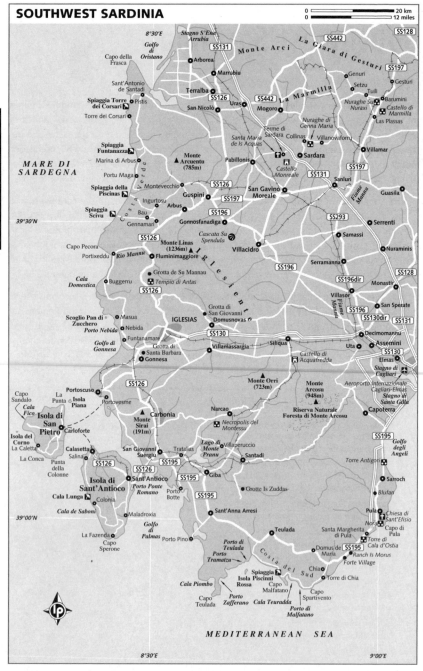

SOUTHWEST SARDINIA

0 ——————— 20 km
0 ——————— 12 miles

MARE DI SARDEGNA

MEDITERRANEAN SEA

IGLESIAS

pop 28,000
Iglesias, the capital of the southwest, was long the centre of Sardinia's mining industry; the undulating hills of Monte Linas are studded with deep mines that now lie abandoned. For a mining town it has a surprisingly urbane air, with a self-important central piazza and rows of once-grand palazzos with wrought-iron balconies. The style is Iberian, as is the town's name, which is Spanish for 'churches'. But despite the cosmetic makeover, the Aragonese were never much interested in getting their hands dirty, and Iglesias had its real heyday under the notorious Ugolino della Gherardesca in the 13th century. A Pisan count, he ran the town (then Villa di Chiesa) with great northern efficiency. He also minted the first silver coins here. Not until the 19th century would Iglesias experience such a period of prosperity, when the great era of industrialisation brought the mines to life once again.

But, as with most centres of heavy industry in Europe, modern economics have not been kind to the Iglesiente. The mines closed in the mid-1970s, laying off dozens of workers. Despite the town's fighting spirit, an air of neglect now lingers over Iglesias.

HISTORY

Mining has been big business here since classical times. The Romans called their town Metalla, after the precious metals they mined on Monte Linas. In true ruthless Roman style, slaves were condemned *ad metalla* (to the metal mines) and lived and worked in appalling conditions. But the Romans weren't the first to exploit the mines; when they were reopened in the 19th century, equipment dating back to the Carthaginians was discovered. Populated by slaves and immigrants, Iglesias grew, each group establishing a church. Their buildings gave the town one of its earlier names, Villa di Chiesa (Town of Churches).

Centuries later in 1257, the Pisans grabbed the Giudicato di Cagliari (Province of Cagliari) and granted Iglesias to Ugolino della Gherardesca, a Pisan captain and member of the pro-papal Ghibelline party. He had a good business head and quickly organised the town along the lines of a Tuscan *comune* (self-governing town) with its own laws and currency. He even instituted the statute of laws known as the Breve di Villa Chiesa, a revolutionary code that granted social benefits to the miners. You can still view it on request at the city's Archivio Stòrico (see p92).

But Ugolino was fated to make a terrible political decision when he betrayed the Ghibellines for the Milanese Guelphs. Arrested in 1288 and accused of treason, he was summarily imprisoned in the Tower of Gualandi along with two of his sons and grandsons, whom he is said to have murdered and eaten before he himself starved to death in 1289. His sons Guelfo and Lotto abandoned Villa di Chiesa and fled north. Lotto was captured and Guelfo died in the hospital of the Knights of Jerusalem in San Leonardo de Siete Fuentes in 1295.

Although they tried, the Pisans never recaptured the town. In 1323 the Catalano-Aragonese troops landed at Portovesme and took the town the following year, renaming it Iglesias. They had little interest in the mines and for the next 500 years the pits lay abandoned until private entrepreneurs, like Quintino Sella (after whom the main piazza is named), revived their fortunes. As the nascent centre of heavy industry in a resurgent and soon-to-be-united Italy, Iglesias once again became an important town until WWII and modern economics tolled its death knell in the 1970s.

ORIENTATION

The old town is bunched up in the northwestern corner of the city, bounded by Via Roma, Via Gramsci, the leafy, broad and busy Piazza Sella, Via Eleonora d'Arborea and Via Campidano. The latter is still lined by the remains of the medieval walls that are now only a memory on the other streets.

The main street in the old town is Via Matteotti, scene of the nightly *passeggiata* (traditional evening stroll). It leads to a series of squares: Piazza La Marmora, Piazza Collegio, Piazza Piscini and Piazza del Municipio.

The real fulcrum of the city hubbub in the evening is Piazza Sella, just beyond the old town at the southern end of Via Matteotti.

SOUTHWEST SARDINIA

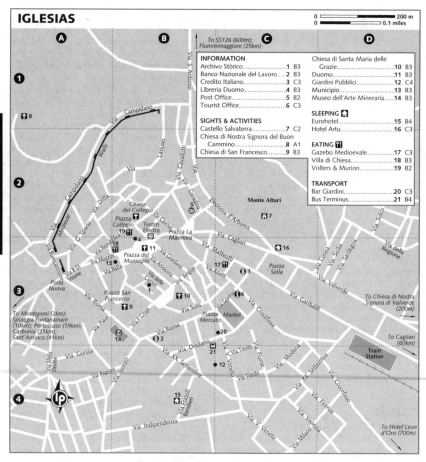

INFORMATION

Archivio Stòrico (☎ 078 12 48 50; Via delle Carceri; ☘ 9am-1pm & 4-6.30pm Mon-Fri) Iglesias' historical archive contains the whole of the town's history, including Ugolino's Breve di Villa Chiesa.

Banco Nazionale del Lavoro (Via Roma 29) You can change money at this bank, which also has an ATM.

Credito Italiano (cnr Via Matteotti & Via Gramsci) Offers the same services as Banco Nazionale.

Libreria Duomo (☎ 078 13 38 08; Vico Duomo 8; ☘ 10am-1pm & 5-9pm Mon-Sat) A small offering of guides and maps. Almost everything is in Italian.

Main post office (Via Montevecchio; ☘ 8.15am-6.15pm Mon-Fri, 8.15am-1pm Sat) Centrally located.

Tourist office (☎ 078 127 45 01, 078 13 11 70; www.prolocoiglesias.it, in Italian; Via Gramsci 11-13; ☘ 9.30am-1pm & 4-7pm Mon-Fri, 9.30am-12.30pm Sat)

Run by the local *comune*, this office has information on the whole of the Iglesiente.

SIGHTS

Most of the town today harks back to the 19th century. This was the last big boom in the city's mining fortunes, when new laws allowed a syndicate from the Italian mainland to buy up the mines and reopen them. To herald this exciting modern era, the bulk of the medieval walls were demolished and the spacious **Piazza Sella** was laid out in what had previously been a field just outside the city walls. It became the central meeting place of the town, and even today it throngs with people during the evening *passeggiata*. The statue in the centre commemorates

Quintino Sella (of Sella e Mosca wine fame), Sardinian statesman and vigorous promoter of the reborn mining industry.

Museo dell'Arte Mineraria

Inevitably, Iglesias' biggest attraction is its mining museum, the **Museo dell'Arte Mineraria** (☎ 078 135 00 37; www.museoartemineraria.it; Via Roma 17; admission free; ⊗ 7-9pm Wed, Sat & Sun Jul-Sep, 6-8pm Sat & Sun Apr-Jun). The building was constructed in 1911 as a mining school; many of the materials and displays downstairs that recreate the reality of the mines were used by the school to train senior mining workers. The tunnels downstairs were in fact dug by mining students and during WWII found an unexpected use as air-raid shelters.

Upstairs you'll find a collection of some 8000 rock and mineral specimens from around the world, including those from Sardinia, which are carefully labelled and displayed.

If you want to view the museum between October and March you'll need to ring and make an appointment. The tourist office can help you with this.

Castello Salvaterra

Just off Piazza Sella amid pleasant hillside gardens stands a stout square tower: the remains of **Castello Salvaterra**, Ugolino's mighty Pisan fortress. From up here you can appreciate fine views of the old town. To get an idea of what the city looked like before the walls came down, proceed to Via Campidano, where a stretch of the 14th-century northwestern perimeter built by the Catalano-Aragonese remains defiantly in place, complete with towers.

Churches

You'll soon notice that the compact area of old Iglesias lives up to its name as a town of churches. The **Duomo** (Piazza del Municipio) dominates the eastern flank of Piazza del Municipio and retains its lovely Pisan-flavoured façade, as does the bell tower, with its chequerboard stonework. It was begun in 1337, but Catalan architects gave it a makeover in the 16th century, which accounts for the rich internal decoration. The highlight of the interior is the gilded altarpiece that once held the relics of St Antiochus. It was removed from Isola di Sant'Antioco in the 17th century to pro-

tect it from pirate raids. And although the clerics were forced to return the relics to the cathedral in Sant'Antioco in the 19th century, they managed to hang on to the altar. The Duomo was closed for restoration at the time of research.

Directly across the square is the bishop's residence, while on the western side is the grand neoclassical **Municipio** (Town Hall).

A short walk off the square brings you to the dainty rose-red trachyte **Chiesa di San Francesco** (Piazza San Francesco; ⊗ Mass only). Although possibly older than the cathedral in origin, it now only sports its Catalan Gothic wardrobe, some of it dating to the 15th century. Inside, the single nave is flanked by chapels between the buttresses. Older still is the 13th-century **Chiesa di Santa Maria delle Grazie** (Via Manzoni), but most of the upper half of the façade dates to the 17th and 18th centuries.

There are two other churches worth seeking out in the town. The **Chiesa di Nostra Signora di Valverde**, which is about a 15-minute walk southeast from Piazza Sella, has an elegant façade similar to the Duomo's, repeating its two series of blind arches in the Pisan style. The **Chiesa di Nostra Signora del Buon Cammino**, which you reach by following a steep incline north of Via Campidano, is perched on a tall hill and commands lovely views over the city.

FESTIVALS & EVENTS

If you are in Iglesias for **Settimana Santa** (Holy Week; the week before Easter Sunday), you will think you have been transported to central Spain. From Holy Tuesday to Good Friday the town is transformed into a stage for nightly processions. Hooded members of religious brotherhoods, bearing candles and crucifixes and accompanied by a slow, deathly beating of deep drums, carry effigies of the Virgin Mary and Christ. It's all slightly sinister, but fascinating.

Much cheerier is **Estate Medioevale Iglesiente** (Iglesias' Medieval Summer). Since the mid-1990s, the town has dressed up for medieval processions and other antique antics, including markets, costume events and feasting.

SLEEPING & EATING

Iglesias is short on lodgings and not much longer on eateries.

Hotel Artu (☎ 078 12 24 92; www.hotelartuiglesias.it; Piazza Sella 15; s/d €42/72; P ⊠) The only central

SOUTHWEST SARDINIA

option, Hotel Artu has an ugly exterior that grates with the rest of the square. The rooms are faded but just about adequate. The daughter of the house speaks English and is very friendly. Ask for a view of the square, although on Saturdays this could mean sleeping with a pillow over your head.

Eurohotel (☎ 078 12 26 43; www.eurohoteliglesias.it, in Italian; Via Fratelli Bandieri 34; s/d €65/75; P ⛽) This is an unbelievably kitsch place with a grand porticoed entrance and curling balconies. The décor is heavily baroque, with faux-gilt chairs, Murano-style chandeliers and sombre oil paintings. The rooms are the best in Iglesias, and are comfortable and modern.

Hotel Leon d'Oro (☎ 078 13 35 55; fax 078 13 35 30; Corso Colombo 72; s/d €60/90; P ⛽ 🖥) Well south of the centre, the Leon d'Oro is a functional place where you might expect to bump into lonely commercial travellers. Its rooms are reminiscent of a boarding house (bare and uninviting), but it does the trick and there's even a pool.

Villa di Chiesa (☎ 078 12 31 24; Piazza del Municipio 8; meals €25; Tue-Sun) Located on the grand Piazza del Municipio, this long-standing local favourite has a tiptop position, and in summer tables are laid out in the piazza. It serves pizza in the evening, but the homemade pasta dishes are the thing to go for – the *culurgiones* (pasta stuffed with ricotta, spinach and saffron) is delicious, as is the house *sebadas* (light pastry filled with cheese and covered with honey).

Gazebo Medioevale (☎ 078 13 08 71; Via Musio 21; meals €25-30; Mon-Sat) A good winter alternative, here you can take a table beneath the long stone-and-brick arches and settle in for a mostly seafood menu. Staff prepare some fish dishes with couscous. Credit cards are not accepted.

Volters & Murion (☎ 078 13 37 88; Piazza Collegio 1; menu €12, meals €20; Wed-Mon) A cheerful eatery tucked into an elbow of lively Piazza Collegio. Enjoy lavish plates of pasta with a superb spicy tomato sauce. Mains are conventional – rather than conveyor-belt – meat and fish dishes. This place doubles as a good venue for an evening tipple in summer.

GETTING THERE & AWAY
Bus
All intercity buses arrive at and leave from the Via Oristano side of the Giardini Pubblici. You can get timetable information and

tickets from **Bar Giardini** (Via Oristano; 5.30am-2.30pm & 3.30-9pm Mon-Sat) across the road. **FMS** (☎ 800 04 45 53; www.ferroviemeridionalisarde.it, in Italian) buses run from Iglesias to Cagliari (€3.46, one to 1½ hours, six daily) and Carbonia (€1.45, 45 minutes, eight daily).

Car & Motorcycle
With the exception of the fast dual-carriageway SS130 from Cagliari (less than an hour), approaches to Iglesias by road are slow. From the south, the coast road from Cagliari joins the road from Sant'Antioco to pass via Carbonia to Iglesias. The most direct road from the north is the SS126, which drops south from Oristano province to Guspini and then heads through the mountains via Arbus and Fluminimaggiore.

Train
As many as 16 trains a day run between Iglesias and Cagliari (€3.05, 50 minutes to one hour).

AROUND IGLESIAS

MONTEPONI MINES
Barely 3km west of the town centre sprawls the enormous mining centre of Monteponi. This was the black heart of the Iglesiente mining industry, which first operated in 1324 when a certain Baron Miniato willed Monte Peone to his son. It remained in working order right up until 1992, when the operation transferred to Campo Pisano across the valley.

The galleries you see now date to the mid-19th century and penetrate the hillside to a depth of 100m. You can join tours of the main Galleria Villamarina with the **IGEA cooperative** (☎ 078 149 13 00, 348 154 95 56; www.igeaminiere.it, in Italian; adult/child under 12 €8/4.50; 9am, 10.30am & 12pm Sep-Jun, plus 3.30pm, 5pm & 6.30pm Jul & Aug by arrangement). If you drive past the complex at night along the SS126, the partially lit ruins make an eerie sight.

You can get a local Linea B FMS bus from Via Oristano in Iglesias eight times a day (€0.57, 20 minutes).

GROTTA DI SANTA BARBARA
A few kilometres further along the Carbonia road, you come across the abandoned San Giovanni mines. Back in the

1950s, the **Grotta di Santa Barbara** (☎ 078 149 13 00; www.igeaminiere.it, in Italian; adult/child €12/6; ⌚ 9am, 10.30am & 12pm by arrangement) was discovered on the mine site. The cave consists of a single enormous chamber, and its walls are entirely covered in dark-brown crystals.

FUNTANAMARE
This long stretch of fine golden sand facing the Golfo di Gonnesa is the main beach for Iglesias. It is popular but rarely gets too crowded, if only because it's so big. Behind it lies fertile farming country.

Up to 10 FMS buses run the 8km route down to the beach (€0.88, 20 minutes), and there is plenty of parking if you want to drive. Other buses head to a point known as **Plage Mesu**, which is further south along the same strand.

GROTTA DI SAN GIOVANNI
About 10km east of Iglesias on the SS130 road to Cagliari lies the unremarkable town of **Domusnovas** (there are regular FMS buses from Iglesias). Four kilometres to the north, however, lies the altogether remarkable Grotta di San Giovanni. It is a giant cave that, until 2000, you could drive your car through. Since then, the local council decided it would be better for the cave if cars went around it and they built a road to this effect; access has been left to pedestrians alone.

THE IGLESIENTE

Iglesias is picturesquely surrounded by lovely, undulating mountains cloaked in wild green scrub, almost completely devoid of any development. The landscape is poignantly dotted with abandoned houses and grand villas, which were once the homes of miners and their bourgeois overlords.

All the towns in the region were connected with mining. You can visit the old galleries on guided tours run by the **IGEA cooperative** (☎ 078 149 13 00, 348 154 95 56; www.igeaminiere.it, in Italian). In July and August you may be able to just turn up and join a tour, but it is always advisable to book ahead as getting to these places is incredibly time-consuming.

NEBIDA
Swing north from Funtanamare along the coast road to enjoy spectacular views. Even before you reach the former mining settlement of Nebida, 5.5km away, three *faraglioni* (sea stacks) and the bizarre 133m-high **Scoglio Pan di Zucchero** islet come into view against a majestic backdrop of sheer, rugged cliffs.

Nebida itself is a sprawling place that stretches for a kilometre or so along the coast road. Shortly after entering the town, stop at the **Belvedere** for mesmerising views. This fenced-off walkway around the cliff face affords prime views of the Scoglio Pan di Zucchero, and you can sit down for coffee at the **Caffè del Operaio** halfway around. From here you can also see the **Laveria Lamarmora**, ruins of a building used for washing and separating minerals back in Nebida's mining days. A dirt track winds down from the main road to the site.

About 500m further north, a side road leads down to **Portu Banda**, which has a small pebble beach.

Pan di Zucchero (☎/fax 078 14 71 14; Via Centrale 366; s/d €38/48) has neat, if spartan, rooms, some with balconies and stunning coastal views. Right next to the hotel, a narrow lane descends to a pretty sandy cove. The restaurant serves up copious helpings from a limited menu of mostly seafood pasta dishes (try the fish-stuffed *ravioli al pomodoro*).

FMS buses run between Iglesias and Masua, just north from Nebida (€1.19, 30 minutes, 11 daily).

MASUA
A few kilometres further north is another former mining centre, Masua, right by the Scoglio Pan di Zucchero. A side road leads down past a small snack-bar-cum-restaurant and the rather ugly mining complex to a reasonable beach, whose main attraction is its position facing the massive islet.

One of the most interesting tours you can take is through the original 'port'. Until the 1920s, much of the ore mined around the Iglesiente was transported to sailing vessels that were hauled up onto the beaches. The boats then sailed down to Carloforte (on Isola di San Pietro) to transfer the load to cargo vessels.

In 1924, a 600m twin tunnel was dug into the cliff here towards the open sea. An ingenious mobile 'arm' shoved the raw minerals from a conveyor belt to ships moored directly below. The tour of **Porto Flavia** (☎ 078 149 13 00, 348 154 95 56; www.igeaminiere.it, in Italian; adult/child €8/4.50; ☺ 9am, 10.30am & 12pm Sep-Jun, plus 4pm & 5.30pm Jul & Aug by arrangement), complete with yellow hard hat, takes about one hour. To find it, head down to the beach. A dirt road leads back uphill and then around the coast for 2.5km to the entrance.

The same road leads to a shady lookout point over the Scoglio Pan di Zucchero.

CALA DOMESTICA

From Masua the road rises quickly in a series of tight turns as it works its way around Monte Guardianu. After reaching the top, it drops down again towards Buggerru. Beach-lovers should take the Cala Domestica turn-off (signposted), 5km short of Buggerru. This long but thin sandy beach lies at the end of a deep natural inlet, walled on either side by craggy cliffs. The water is beautiful and sometimes curls up in decent sets of waves. A walk along the rocky path to the right of the beach brings you to a smaller, more sheltered side strand.

There is a parking area for camper vans. Parking a car close to the beach costs €2 for the morning or afternoon and €4 for the day. A snack stand behind the beach helps keep body and soul together.

BUGGERRU & PORTIXEDDU
pop 1130
Set within the natural stone walls of a steep valley, Buggerru is a quiet gem. Established in 1860 as another mining town (note the ruins of the Planu Sartu mines to the west of the road just before you reach the town), it was long accessible only by sea, making it a totally self-sufficient enclave. Production reached its peak in the early 20th century when the population swelled to more than 12,000 people. At the time Buggerru was way ahead; it had its own electricity supply (before Cagliari and Sassari), and an enlightened work ethic where miners enjoyed company-sponsored health facilities. These days the main preoccupation is trying to attract the valuable tourist dollar, although there's little evidence of crass development.

You can still visit Buggerru's mine, the **Galleria Henry** (☎ 078 149 13 00, 338 154 95 56; www .igeaminiere.it, in Italian; adult/child €8/4.50; ☺ 9am & 11am Sep-Jun, plus 4.30pm & 6.30pm Jul & Aug by ar-

rangement). The rail tunnels here allowed the transport of minerals from the rock face to filtering and washing centres. What makes this hour-long 1km tour a highlight are the views straight down the cliff to the sea.

The road out of Buggerru again climbs high along the cliff face, providing stunning views for a couple of kilometres before you hit the long sandy stretches of **Spiaggia Portixeddu**. The beach extends 3km up the coast to the Rio Mannu, the river marking the end of the Iglesiente coast. Some parking is paid (up to €4 a day), but there are plenty of free spaces, too.

There are some very basic camping facilities at **Camping Ortus de Mari** (☎ /fax 078 15 49 64; camp sites per adult/tent €7.75/10.33; ☺ Jun-Sep), a little way northeast of the beach, about 1km from the Capo Pecora turn-off.

The only other option is the big, pink **Hotel Golfo del Leone** (☎ 078 15 49 23; www.golfo delleone.it; Località Caburu de Figu; s/d €50/72), on a back trail, a few hundred metres to the right of the Capo Pecora turn-off.

FLUMINIMAGGIORE
pop 3080
A pretty but nauseatingly winding 26km stretch of road meanders north out of Iglesias to Fluminimaggiore, a sleepy place with an ethnographical museum and a couple of bars and eateries. It's a disaffected place, and like Orgosolo on Sardinia's central eastern coast, it has vented its unhappy condition in murals around the town, many of which look back to the golden days of the mines with real nostalgia.

The town itself is of little interest, but in its environs you'll find the Roman Tempio di Antas and the impressive Grotta de Su Mannau.

Up to eight FMS buses link Iglesias with Fluminimaggiore (€1.76, 45 minutes), and you can get off along the way to visit these sights.

Tempio di Antas
Even before reaching the right-hand turn-off about 15km north of Iglesias, you can spot this sand-coloured Roman **temple** (☎ 347 817 49 89; adult/child €2.60/1.30; ☺ 9am-1pm & 3-8pm May-Sep, 9am-1pm & 3-6pm Sat, Sun & holidays Oct-Apr) on the high ground across the valley.

It's an ancient site, although the temple in its present form dates to the era of Emperor

Caracalla. He dedicated it to Sardus Pater, an obscure Sardinian deity worshipped by the builders of the *nuraghi* (stone towers) and, according to one myth, founder of Sardinia. At the foot of the resurrected columns at the front of the temple are the fenced-off remains of its Carthaginian predecessor, which the Romans cannibalised to erect their version. Before you get too excited about the marvels of Roman engineering, the eight standing columns were re-erected during excavation and restoration between 1967 and 1976.

Between the ticket office and the temple, a narrow trail marked as *sentiero romano* (Roman way) leads after about five minutes to what little remains of the original *nuraghe* settlement. Following the trail for 1½ hours would theoretically take you to the Grotta de Su Mannau, but we haven't tried it out.

Another 20-minute walk (signposted) from the temple takes you to the quarries the Romans used to provide extra building material for the temple.

From the main road, it's about a half-hour walk to the main site.

Grotta de Su Mannau

From the SS126, signs indicate the turn-off for the **Grotta de Su Mannau** (☎ 078 158 01 89; adult/concession €6/3.50; ✆ 9.30am-6pm, reservations essential Oct-Apr), the largest cave of its sort so far discovered in the Iglesiente. Created by two streams, its 8km of tunnel is festooned with impressive pointy stalactites, many of them a beautiful pearly-white colour. The standard tour takes you on a 50-minute walk through a fraction of the cave's delights, passing through several lake chambers and the Archaeological Room, so called because there is archaeological evidence that it was long used as a temple for water worship. Finally you reach the Pozzo Rodriguez (Rodriguez Well), where you see an impressive 8m column, effectively a stalactite and stalagmite fused together.

More exciting tours of the cave are possible and are open to complete beginners. All the equipment is provided. These tours enable you to visit dramatic chambers like the White Room or the opalescent waters of the Pensile Lake. A six- to eight-hour tour will get you to the jewel of Su Mannau, the Virgin Room, where you can see wonderful aragonites and big snow-white slopes of solidified

calcium. The latter tour is the most difficult, and requires a wetsuit to pass through the various bottlenecks and siphons.

These excursions need to be organised in advance through the cave office. Costs vary according to duration and number of participants.

COSTA VERDE

A low rocky promontory jutting out into the Mediterranean about 4km northwest of Portixeddu, **Capo Pecora** marks the southern tip of the Costa Verde (Green Coast), named for the *macchia* (Mediterranean scrub) carpet that covers the patchy, mountainous coastline. It's a splendid mix of soaring cliffs and fine sandy beaches, some backed by towering dunes, others by soft greenery. Almost nothing impinges on the wild beauty of these beaches, which make for a magnificent detour.

MONTEVECCHIO

Northeast from Igurtosu, the dirt track will bring you over the mountains to the evocative site of the **Miniere di Montevecchio** (www.europroject.it/montevecchio, in Italian; admission €6). This vast, crumbling complex in the midst of a wooded hill peppered with mine shafts is now recognised as a Unesco World Heritage site. There is still a little town attached to the mines with a handful of inhabitants.

It's possible to join tours (usually conducted in Italian) with the **Centro Escursioni Minerarie Naturalistiche** (☎ 335 531 41 98; www.europroject.it/montevecchio, in Italian). Otherwise, inquire at the **tourist office** (☎ 070 97 03 84; www.prolocoguspini.it, in Italian; Via San Nicolò 17; ✆ 6-8pm Thu) in Guspini.

The deeply wooded country around **Monte Arcuenta** (785m), north of Montevecchio is one of the last preserves of the *cervo sardo* (Sardinian deer).

The occasional FMS bus runs from Guspini to Iglesias (one hour 20 minutes, four daily).

TORRE DEI CORSARI

Right at the northern end of the Costa Verde is scruffy **Torre dei Corsari**. This is a modest resort with a fabulous broad beach, backed by dunes and named after the ruined watchtower at its southern end. The top

---

DETOUR: BEACHES OF THE COSTA VERDE

From Capo Pecora head back via Portixeddu and northeast along the SS126 until you reach the turn-off for **Gennamari**, **Bau** and **Spiaggia Scivu**. If coming from the northeast, you'll see the signs on the right 13km from Arbus. Take this narrow mountain route into the windswept, *macchia*-covered southern heights to around 450m above sea level, when the sea comes into view. Five kilometres short of the beach, Spiaggia Scivu is signposted to the left. Going straight ahead would take you to the local penitentiary, something that has helped to keep Scivu off the developers' map for many years.

You arrive at a parking area (€4 a day in summer), where there's a kiosk and freshwater showers (€0.50) in summer only. You'll also need to bring some sort of shade (an umbrella or tent), as there are no facilities and it's very exposed. As you walk towards the beach, you find yourself atop 70m dunes from where you can view the enormous length of beach that stretches before you. Even in August few people make the effort to get here, although if developer Valtur has its way there might be a holiday village here soon.

The other famous beach of the Costa Verde is the **Spiaggia della Piscinas**, some 3.7km northeast of the Spiaggia Scivu turn-off along the SS126. Take the **Ingurtosu** exit. This is a worthwhile exercise in its own right, as the road drops down into a valley lined with the abandoned buildings, housing and machinery of a crumbling 19th-century mining settlement.

After 9km of dirt track, you'll hit a fork. Take the left branch for Spiaggia della Piscinas, and you'll reach the beach after a further 20 minutes of off-road driving. There's a designated parking area where parking costs €1 per hour (€4 per day).

Back from the broad strand of beach rise 30m-high dunes. They are ambitiously known as Sardinia's desert, but the dunes are impressive enough. In summer one or two beach bars brighten the place up and offer welcome showers, umbrellas (€5) and loungers (€5).

In summer, people park their camper vans here or stay in the stylish **Hotel Le Dune** (☎ 070 97 71 30; www.leduneingurtosu.it; half board per person low/high season €83/160), carved out of mining buildings that were once at the head of a mini-railway used to ferry ore to the coast. It's terribly chic and there are only 25 rooms so you'll need to book ahead. There's a small spa and some water sports equipment for guest use. If you can't afford to stay here, it's well worth considering the fabulous all-you-can-eat buffet lunch (€30 per person).

---

end of this beach is known as **Pistis** – a good long walk away or an 8km drive via **Sant'Antonio di Santadi**. The deep emerald-green water is incredibly limpid. There is paid parking at both ends (€2) and there are a couple of kiosks.

B&B Brezza Marina (☎ 338 367 68 86; brezzamarinatorre@tiscali.it; Viale della Torre, Torre dei Corsari; s/d €30-50) is a place where you can really get away from it all. It's run by a charming English-speaking Sardinian couple fresh from a stint in London. The accommodation has a friendly spare-room feel and there's a small garden complete with barbecue. Brezza Marina also offers cooking courses (€15 including the meal), and rents a couple of apartments with sea views.

Hotel Caletta (☎ 070 97 71 33; www.lacaletta.it; d €90, half board per person €77; Jul & Aug; P 🞄) is a big, modern option situated right on a rocky point (occupied by the hotel's boomerang-shaped swimming pool).

Rooms have all mod-cons, and the Caletta even has its own little disco.

Torre dei Corsari boasts one of Sardinia's few hostels, the **Ostello della Torre** (☎ /fax 070 97 71 55; www.costatour.it, in Italian; Viale della Torre; s/d €22/44, half board per person €37), perched up on a high point behind the southern headland.

ARBUS
pop 6900

If you are interested in Sardinian crafts, you should head for Arbus, about 6km along a winding high-country road west of Montevecchio. The town is not particularly striking, but a visit to the **Museo del Coltello Sardo** (☎ 070 975 92 20; www.museodelcoltello.it, in Italian; Via Roma 15; admission free; 9am-12.30pm & 3.30-7pm Mon-Fri) is worthwhile. The museum was founded by Paolo Pusceddu, whose *s'arburesi* (see the boxed text, p146) are among the most prized of Sardinian knives. Downstairs Signor Pusceddu has arranged his historic collection, with obsidian flint, Bronze Age blades, knives, sword blades and the like from the 14th to the 19th century. In an adjacent room is an assortment of some of Pusceddu's finest creations, true masterpieces. Behind this room, you walk into an old-style workshop, while upstairs is a collection of knives from around the island. You can also watch a 30-minute video on the making of knives. Pusceddu works in his workshop next door. This would be a good place to consider a purchase – they don't come any better. To find the museum, head down Via Roma from the central Piazza Mercato.

The **tourist office** (☎ 070 975 40 63; www.arbus .it; Piazza dell'Immacolata; ⏰ Jul & Aug) is further uphill.

Hotel Meridiana (☎ 070 975 82 83; www.wels .it/hotelmeridiana; Via della Repubblica 172; s/d €40/75; P ✿ ✉), at the eastern entrance into town, is the only hotel choice. Rooms are spotless and well equipped, and some have views out the back over the town. The restaurant serves good pizza.

Ristorante Sa Lolla (☎ 070 975 40 04; Via Libertà 225; meals €25; ⏰ Mon-Sat), on the SS126 heading out southwest towards Fluminimaggiore, is one of the town's best eating options. It dishes up good pasta and pizzas.

FMS buses stop here en route to Guspini from Iglesias. There are up to four runs a day and the trip takes about an hour.

VILLACIDRO
pop 14,700
About 9km southeast of Arbus, a minor road takes you to Gonnosfanadiga, worth popping into just to say you have been to this Tolkienesque-sounding place. Another 6km east on the SS196 brings you to the first of two turn-offs for Villacidro (which is 267m above sea level) to the south. Follow this winding country road and about 2.5km short of Villacidro you will see a signpost to the west for the **Cascata Su Spendula** waterfall. Some 500m on, you reach a parking area with a small snack bar. All around rise imposing rock walls and a thick curtain of trees. A short trail leads to the waterfall, or should do. In midsummer you could easily find it has dried up. The Italian nationalist poet Gabriele d'Annunzio, judging by his effusive verse on the subject, visited in winter!

CARBONIA & AROUND

South of Iglesias, the SS126 unfolds rapidly into flatter, less-inspiring landscapes that head straight for the second-largest city of the south, Carbonia. This grand Fascist invention was Mussolini's brainchild and, like the agricultural reclamation schemes Arborea and Fertilia, the carbon-mining town of Carbonia was going to make Italy self-sufficient. It never really worked out that way, and the city holds little of interest for visitors today, save for a couple of modest museums and an excursion into the island's ancient past, just outside on Monte Sirai.

To the west is a more successful industrial exercise, Portoscuso, which is the embarkation point for ferries to Isola di San Pietro.

CARBONIA
pop 30,620
In 1936 Mussolini invaded Ethiopia and the League of Nations promptly imposed sanctions on Italy. Feeling the squeeze, Il Duce came up with a great idea to circumvent these irritating restrictions – create a new city in the Iglesiente dedicated to mining low-grade coal. So, the unutterably depressing and unimaginatively named Carbonia (*carbone* means coal) was born. Work on the grid plan started in the same year, and in 1938 the city finally opened for business.

The whole blustering show was little more than a propaganda effort, but the second-rate coal was mined until 1972, when Carbonia, whose grid-tentacles had spread, was left out on a limb. The city has since trundled along in the doldrums but has managed to stay afloat with small business.

The focal point of town is Piazza Roma. The square is dominated by the red trachyte bell tower of the **Chiesa di San Ponziano**, modelled, we are told, on the cathedral of Aquilea in northern Italy. A plaque left over from Benito's time exhorts the workers (*O Lavoratore...!*) to give their best.

The square is also the town's bus station, which is handy because the only vague points of interest, two museums, are just down the road (signposted). If you intend to visit these and the Monte Sirai site, you should invest in the €6.50 *biglietto cumulativo* (group ticket) to all three.

SOUTHWEST SARDINIA

The **Museo Archeologico Villa Sulcis** (☎ 078 16 40 44; Via Napoli; admission €2.10; ☺ 9am-1pm & 4-8pm Tue-Sun May-Sep, 9am-1pm & 3-7pm Tue-Sun Oct-Apr) has a very modest, musty collection of archaeological finds, the bulk of them from the nearby Phoenician-Carthaginian site on Monte Sirai.

Wander behind the museum; through the gate and across the road, you arrive at the **Museo di Paleontologia e Speleologia** (☎ 078 16 43 82; Piazza Garibaldi; admission €1.60; ☺ 9am-1pm & 4-8pm Tue-Sun May-Sep, 9am-1pm & 3-7pm Tue-Sun Oct-Apr), dedicated to caves, caving and what you can occasionally turn up in caves in an ancient place like Sardinia. It was founded in 1978.

Of more interest than either of these is the site of **Monte Sirai** (admission €2.60; ☺ 9am-5pm Oct-Apr, 9am-1pm & 4-8pm May-Sep), about 4km northwest of Carbonia on the other side of the SS126 road.

The high flat-top plateau was a natural spot for a fort, commanding views over much of the mining areas of the southwest and the more recent industrial complex of Portoscuso on the coast. The Phoenicians of Sulci (modern Sant'Antioco) ventured here to build their fortress in 650 BC. Sardinian tribes prised the Phoenicians out, to be replaced a century later by the Carthaginians. Although not a great deal remains to be seen, you can make out the placement of the Carthaginian acropolis and defensive tower, a necropolis and *tophet,* a sacred Phoenician and Carthaginian burial ground for children and babies.

There's nowhere to stay and nowhere worthwhile to eat so you'll be wanting a bus out of Carbonia pretty fast. Piazza Roma is the bus terminus; for tickets go to the unnamed bar at Viale Gramsci 4, after the first set of traffic lights about 70m off Piazza Roma. Buses run to Iglesias (€1.45, 45 minutes, eight daily) and Cagliari (€4.44, 1½ hours, six daily), as well as a host of other towns like Portoscuso and Sant'Antioco.

Local buses also run from Piazza Roma to the train station to coincide with trains from Cagliari (€3.50, one hour, eight daily from Monday to Saturday, two on Sunday).

PORTOSCUSO & PORTOVESME
pop 5370
The approach roads to Portoscuso presage the worst. However, the enormous chimney stacks of the huffing, puffing thermoelectric

industrial complex of Portoscuso are a couple of kilometres east of the actual town. Once you arrive, this reveals itself as an attractive small port capped by a Spanish-era tower surrounded by a tiny warren of agreeable lanes.

It's the main jumping-off point for Isola di San Pietro although it's worth stopping over for lunch or even a night at the splendid **La Ginghetta** (☎ 078 150 81 43; fax 078 150 81 44; Via Cavour 26, Sa Caletta; s/d €120/135, half board €120-160; ☺ May-Oct). Situated above a rocky cove at the western end of town (signposted), it's one of those rare Sardinian hotels combining charm, comfort and cuisine. The ivy- and bougainvillea-covered building is a series of old fishermen's houses transformed into attractive rooms with a nautical bent. The restaurant is one of the island's best. Nonguests can eat here, too – set menus, which concentrate on seafood, start at €49 and are worth every cent.

If you just want to overnight close to the port, try **Hotel Panorama** (☎ 078 150 80 77; Via G Cesare 40/42; s/d €56/83; P ⬛), a good if characterless place with modern rooms, many with balconies overlooking the port, for which you pay an extra €6.

La Tavernetta (☎ 078 150 99 16; Lungomare Colombo 35; meals €25; ☺ 12.30-3.30pm Mon-Sat), just by the Hotel Panorama, is a good spot for fresh fish.

FMS buses run to Portoscuso and neighbouring Portovesme from Cagliari (€4.44, two hours, three daily via Iglesias). Many more run from Iglesias (€1.45, 32 minutes, 11 daily) and Carbonia (€1.19, 35 minutes, 14 daily).

Saremar (☎ 199 12 31 99, 078 150 90 65; www.saremar.it, in Italian) has up to 15 sailings from Portovesme to Carloforte (on Isola di San Pietro) between 6am and 10pm every day. The trip takes about 30 minutes and costs €2.60/7.60 per person/car. Be prepared for long queues in summer. The port is next door (east) to the industrial complex of Portoscuso.

TRATALIAS
When Sant'Antioco was abandoned in the 13th century, the archdiocese for the whole Sulcis area was transferred to this inland hamlet and the **Chiesa di Santa Maria** was built. A curious Romanesque construction, it presides over what little remains of the *vecchio borgo* (old town), abandoned

since water from the nearby artificial Lago di Monte Pranu started seeping into the subsoil in the 1950s.

At the top of the façade you'll notice a curious external stairway leading nowhere in particular. It continues on the inside of the church, which you enter by pushing open a side door. Rough hewn pillars separate the nave from the two aisles in what is otherwise a fairly bare interior.

The easiest way here is by car. Tratalias is 4km east of the SS195 and the church is right by the road.

MONTESSU

Lying 2.5km north of Villaperuccio, the **Necropolis del Montessu** (admission €5; ☺ 9am-1pm & 3-7pm) makes for some nice strolling. The site is peppered with *domus de janas* (literally 'fairy houses'). For the uninitiated, these holes in the wall are primitive tombs dating back to the age of the *nuraghe*. The Montessu tombs show some of the best relief carvings in the area, especially in the **Tomba delle Spirali**, where you can clearly make out the raised relief of spirals and symbolic bulls.

From the ticket booth it's a 500m walk up to what appears to be a natural amphitheatre. When you first arrive up the stairs from the roadway, to your immediate right is a **Tomba Santuario**, a rectangular foyer followed by three openings into a semicircular tomb area behind. Follow the trail to its right to see a cluster of tombs and then the Tomba delle Spirali. After that, you can clamber about the scenic site to your heart's content.

SANTADI

A few kilometres east of Villaperuccio, Santadi is a busy agricultural centre with the biggest winery in the southwest, the **Cantina Santadi** (☎ 078 195 00 12; Via Su Pranu 8; www.cantinadisantadi.it). You can visit the winery by calling ahead first. You could also consider visiting the curious **Museo Etnografico 'Sa Domu Antiga'** (☎ 078 195 59 55; Via Mazzini 37; admission €2.60; ☺ 9am-1pm & 4-7pm Tue-Sun Jun-Sep, 9am-1pm & 3-6pm Oct-May), which recreates a typical village house of the early 20th century.

More interesting is the town's annual festival, the **Matrimonio Maureddino** (Moorish Wedding), which takes place on the first Sunday of August. It involves the marriage

of a local couple, dressed in full rural costume, in the main square. They arrive for the event on a *traccas* (a cart drawn by red bulls), and the ceremony is followed with folk dancing, eating and drinking.

Five kilometres south of Santadi, you'll find the **Grotte Is Zuddas** (☎ 078 195 57 41; adult/child €6.50/3.62; ☺ 9.30am-noon & 2.30-6pm Apr-Sep, noon-4pm Mon-Sat, 9.30am-noon & 2.30-7pm Sun & holidays Oct-Mar), another of the island's spectacular cave systems. The limestone rock lends the stalactites and stalagmites a particularly translucent quality. A singular attraction is the helictites in the main hall. No-one really knows how these weirdly shaped formations are created, although one theory suggests wind in the cave may have acted on drops dripping off stalactites.

OFFSHORE ISLANDS

The southwest's two offshore islands, Isola di Sant'Antioco and Isola di San Pietro, are a world unto themselves. They have little if anything in common with the mainland, although Sant'Antioco's harbour at Calasetta was built to hold the fleets of mineral boats that ran between the Iglesiente and the Italian mainland. Apart from this, it's still most famous as the Phoenician city of Sulci; the island is littered with the remnants of the empire. Barely half an hour across the water lies the Genoese-influenced Isola di San Pietro, a mauve blur of pastel houses and bright bobbing fishing boats, more reminiscent of Capri or Ischia than Sardinia.

ISOLA DI SAN PIETRO

San Pietro is a mountainous trachyte island about 15km long and 11km wide. It's named after St Peter who, legend has it, was marooned there during a storm on the way to Karalis (now Cagliari). The Romans had previously called it Accipitrum after the variety of hawks that nest here, and, as on Sant'Antioco, Roman coins, amphorae and tombs are constantly being uncovered.

San Pietro's unusual character and atmosphere come from its Genoese inhabitants, ransomed from the Tunisian bey (governor) in 1736. Coral fishermen by profession, they had been sent to the island of Tabarka to harvest the precious commodity for the Lomellini family in Genoa. But they were abandoned to their fate and fell into miserable slavery until Carlo Emanuele III granted them refuge on San Pietro. Almost out of spite, North African pirates turned up in 1798 and made off with 1000 prisoners. It took five years for the Savoys to ransom them back. Even today the inhabitants of San Pietro speak *tabarkino*, a 16th-century version of Genoese.

Carloforte
pop 6500

As you approach San Pietro from Porto-scuso, the perfect, chocolate-box town of Carloforte comes into view across the silky, calm water of the port. Boats anchor along the wide waterfront, which is planted with palms and backed by a creamy curve of stately buildings that rise in a half-moon up the green hillside.

The waterfront has a spotless, scrubbed appearance and fairly bustles with activity, and a kind of old-world civility hangs in the air. Unlike most Sardinians, the islanders of San Pietro are natural fishermen and you will dine well here on fish, especially the island's prized tuna. There are no great museums or sights as such, but a slow wander through the quaint, cobbled streets makes for a pleasant prelude to a seaside apéritif and a fine meal at one of the town's good restaurants.

INFORMATION

The helpful, multilingual **tourist office** (☎ 078 185 40 09; www.prolococarloforte.it, in Italian; Piazza Carlo Emanuele III 19; ✆ 10am-12.30pm Mon-Thu, 10am-12.30pm & 5.30-7.30pm Fri & Sat) can assist with any queries. Another information service, **Isola Verde** (☎ 078 185 67 12; www.carloforte.net, in Italian), opens a booth down by the ferries in July and August. You can change money at the **Banca Comerciale Italiana** (Via Garibaldi 5) on the waterfront.

SIGHTS & ACTIVITIES

The town's modest **Museo Civico** (adult/child €2/1; ✆ 5-9pm Tue-Wed, 9am-1pm & 5-9pm Thu-Sun), housed in the little Carlo Emanuele III fort that was one of the first buildings to go up on the island, deals with the history of the town and the nearby *tonnare* (tuna processing plant), as well as a collection of Mediterranean sea shells. Follow the signs uphill (along Via Genova) from the town centre.

Aside from this one museum and the pretty distractions of the town, most of San Pietro's other pleasures are to be had at sea, and several booths along the *lungomare* (seafront road) offer **boat excursions** (€20 per person). These involve touring the island to view its dramatic coastal cliffs, grottoes and offshore sea stacks. Food is provided on board and there are plenty of swimming opportunities. **Cartur Trasporti Marittimi** (☎ 078 185 43 31) offers trips further afield including

---

MAD ABOUT THE MATTANZA

Lovers of tuna meat around the world, but especially the Japanese (the best-paying export market), watch anxiously each spring for the results of one of Sardinia's age-old fishing rituals, the *mattanza* (slaughter).

Since ancient times fishermen have awaited the arrival of schools of tuna that stream between Isola Piana and San Pietro during the annual mating season. In the past, the tuna slaughter provided the mainstay of the island's economy. Although this is no longer the case, Carloforte, along with Portoscuso on the mainland, is one of the few places left in the Mediterranean with a fully operational *tonnara* (tuna processing plant).

From around 20 May to 10 June, Carloforte's fishermen prepare for the event. This is no ordinary fishing expedition: the fishermen organise their boats and nets in a complex formation designed to channel the tuna into a series of enclosures that culminate in the *camera della morte* (chamber of death). Once enough tuna are imprisoned there, the fishermen close in and the *mattanza* begins (the word is derived from the Spanish for killing). It's a bloody affair – up to eight or more fishermen at a time will sink huge hooks into a (sometimes enormous) tuna and drag it aboard. You can see graphic photos of this in the Museo Civico.

To buy some of the locally canned produce, head to the **Consociazione Consortile delle Tonnare Sarde di Carloforte e Portoscuso** (☎ 078 185 01 26; www.tonnare.it; Località La Punta) cooperative north of Carloforte at La Punta. It also runs the restaurant Osteria della Tonnara (opposite).

a trip up the coast to the Scoglio Pan di Zucchero.

Gommoni (high-speed dinghies) are available for hire from **Carloforte Sail Charter** (☎ 347 273 32 68; www.carlofortesailcharter.it, in Italian; Via Danero 52), or try a sailing course (€120). Diving is also possible with **Isla Diving** (☎ 078 185 56 34; Corso Battellieri 21), on the main waterfront.

SLEEPING

For all its prettiness, Carloforte has few hotels that do it justice.

Hotel Riviera (☎ 078 185 40 04; www.hotelriviera-carloforte.com, in Italian; Corso Battellieri 26; d low/high season €130/200, ste €320/390; 🗷) This rust-red hotel is Carloforte's most stylish offering with a startlingly modern interior. The cool, white reception makes you think you're checking into a hotel in Milan rather than quaint old Carloforte. The rooms are similarly swanky, boasting LCD TVs, and even the classic doubles have lavish marble-tiled bathrooms. You'll pay extra, however, for sea views and a balcony.

Hotel Hieracon (☎ 078 185 40 28; fax 078 185 48 93; Corso Cavour 63; half board per person low/high season €76/94; 🗷) Carloforte's faded jewel, the Hieracon is a grey Art Nouveau mansion at the northern end of the waterfront. There's a something-for-everyone choice of rooms, including family size with up to four beds, and a pleasant internal garden.

Hotel California (☎ 078 185 44 70; fax 078 185 55 39; Via Cavallera 15; s/d €42/78) This is the cheapest deal in town and the most awkwardly placed – inland from the *saline* (saltpans).

EATING

With its annual *mattanza* (slaughter), Carloforte is *the* place to order tuna dishes of every size and style. You'll also be able to sample a fine *cuscus* (a variety of the North African couscous) alongside *zuppa di pesce* (fish soup). Genoese *farinata* (a pizza-style flatbread made from chickpea flour and olives) and pesto also make an appearance on the menu.

Da Nicolò (☎ 078 185 40 48; Via Dante 46; meals €50-60; 🕑 Tue-Sun) This is one of the island's gourmet bastions. Sardinians come from far and wide to eat in this elegant restaurant with its palm-fronted seaside terrace. The pasta dishes include such Ligurian items as *trofie* (a small, dense style of pasta) with

various tempting toppings. Fish and lobster are the house specialities.

Tonno di Corsa (☎ 078 185 51 06; Via Marconi 47; meals €35-40; 🕑 Tue-Sun) Up a few blocks from the seaside along Via Caprera (then turn right), this place is paradise for tuna lovers. Push the boat out with the delicious *ventresca di tonno*, a sublime cut of possibly the best tuna you've ever had.

Dau Bobba (☎ 078 185 40 37; Lungocanale delle Saline; meals €45-50; 🕑 Wed-Mon) Half a kilometre south of the main waterfront is another charming den of gastronomic delights. The little courtyard garden inside makes an inviting shelter to taste anything from a great pesto to the fresh catch of the day. It has an impressive local wine list, too.

Osteria della Tonnara (☎ 078 185 57 34; www.tonnare.it; Corso Battellieri 36; meals €30; 🕑 Jun-Sep) Run by the tuna cooperative (see the boxed text, opposite), this restaurant serves up a banquet of tuna delicacies including *bottarga* (mullet roe). It's a small place, so consider booking. Credit cards are not accepted

Another atmospheric place is **Niko Bistrot** (Corso Cavour 32; meals €25-30), run by the same people as Da Nicolò.

DRINKING & ENTERTAINMENT

For your evening drinks, start at one of the bars along the waterfront. A little noisier than the rest are **Barone Rosso** (Via XX Settembre 26), with a few tables in the side street, and the nameless bar across the road at Via XX Settembre 17. North of Piazza Repubblica another option in a similar vein is **L'Obló** (Via Garibaldi 23; 🕑 7.30-11pm Wed-Mon mid-May–mid-Sep), where you can also get a decent snack.

Disco Marlin (☎ 078 185 01 21; 🕑 Sat & Sun Jul, nightly Aug) In summer, this is the island's only real club, shortly before the *tonnara* (tuna processing plant) on the way to Punta.

The popular La Caletta beach is also the scene of dancing fun, with summer beach parties pounding on until dawn. In September Carloforte hosts a festival of music, theatre and film. Check with the tourist office for performances.

GETTING THERE & AWAY

There's a **Saremar** (☎ 199 12 31 99, 078 185 40 05; www.saremar.it, in Italian; Piazza Carlo Emanuele III 29) ticket office on the *lungomare*. Regular ferries depart for Portovesme on the mainland

SOUTHWEST SARDINIA

SOUTHWEST SARDINIA

(€2.60/7.60 per person/car, 30 minutes, 15 daily) and Calasetta (€2.50/6 per person/car, half-hourly) on the neighbouring island of Sant'Antioco.

Delcomar (☎ 078 185 71 23) also runs up to 11 services to and from Calasetta, mostly late-night runs into the wee hours of the morning. It operates a ticket booth just in front of where the ferries dock. The crossing costs €2.50 per person each way.

In summer, FMS buses run from Carloforte to La Punta (12 minutes, three a day), La Caletta (15 minutes, eight a day) and Capo Sandalo (18 minutes, three a day). Tickets cost €0.57.

Around the Island

Four roads radiate out of Carloforte across the island, which is sparsely inhabited and dotted only with the occasional cluster of houses.

A quick drive leads you north 5.5km to **La Punta**, a low point from where you can gaze across to the offshore islet **Isola Piana**, which rises like a marine palace in front of the billowing chimney stacks of Portoscuso. In May and June witness the frenzy of the *mattanza* in front of the old *tonnara*.

A couple of average beaches lie on San Pietro's southeast coast. At the bottom of the island two great stone *colonne* (columns) rise out of the sea, giving the point its name, **Punta delle Colonne**.

On the southwest coast is the island's most popular beach, **La Caletta** (also known as Spiaggia Spalmatore), a relatively modest arc of fine sand closed off to the south by cliffs. Further south you can detour to view the spectacular coastline of **La Conca**. Boat excursions cruising the coastline weave in and out of these sheer volcanic cliffs.

In an hour or so you can drive right across the island to **Capo Sandalo**, where you'll find a shed given over to **LIPU** (Italian Bird Protection League; www.lipu.it, in Italian), whose main concern is the nesting colony of Eleonora's falcons at nearby **Cala Fico** and on the **Isola del Corno**.

If you fancy staying outside Carloforte, there are a number of little B&Bs around the island; the tourist office can provide a list. The best of the bunch, right in the centre of the island, is **Hotel La Valle** (☎ 078 185 70 01; www.hotellavalle.com; Località Commende; s/d €60/100; 🅿 🖭), a lovely rural complex with

12 rooms, nestling amidst a swath of vineyards with a very handsome pool.

ISOLA DI SANT'ANTIOCO

Italy's fourth-largest island (after Sicily, Sardinia and Elba), Sant'Antioco really ceased to be an island when the ever-industrious Romans built a causeway across the Golfo di Palmas to link it with the Sardinian mainland. Although it may not look like it on the surface, much remains of the Roman presence here, and an old Roman galley even turned up during the construction of the harbour just before WWII.

Unlike San Pietro, it isn't picturesque at all. Rather, it has a gritty and purposeful air, the sun beating down on ugly cargo ships and busy quays.

There are two ways of approaching the island. The simplest is to follow the SS126 highway south from Iglesias and Carbonia and cross the causeway to the town of Sant'Antioco. People have been doing it this way since the Romans came along, as remnants of the abandoned Roman bridge to the right attest. Clunkier and more romantic is the car ferry between the northwestern settlement of Calasetta and Carloforte in San Pietro.

Sant'Antioco
pop 11,750

Sant'Antioco was the site of the ancient Phoenician city of Sulci (8th century BC), the industrial capital of Sardinia for centuries until the demise of the Roman Empire. It is riddled with Phoenician necropolises and one of Sardinia's biggest *tophets*. Even the town's central church is built above ancient catacombs, which the Christians took over between the 2nd and 7th centuries. The church commemorates the city's patron saint St Antiochus, whose relics are preserved inside.

These days the island is a sleepy place and exhibits none of the natural exuberance of San Pietro. Still, its atmospheric catacombs and the tiny resort of Calasetta provide pleasant interludes on any island-hopping itinerary.

ORIENTATION

Sant'Antioco is surprisingly big. On wheels, you will approach the centre from the bridge along Via Nazionale. It converges with another main road, Via Trieste, at Piazza Repubblica, which is where FMS buses stop (buy tickets at the pharmacy). Shortly afterwards, the main road enters the broad Piazza Italia (the site of a Roman spring) and becomes Corso Vittorio Emanuele, lined by trees that form a cool, leafy tunnel. This is the central boulevard and, replete with bars and eateries, it's the focus of the town's summer night-time shenanigans. It ends at Piazza Umberto I; Via Garibaldi also runs into this piazza from the waterfront. From Piazza Umberto I, Via Regina Margherita climbs to the heart of the old town.

INFORMATION

The local **tourist office** (☎ 078 18 20 31; www .santantioco.com, in Italian; Piazza Repubblica 31a; ☒ 9am-noon & 5.30-9pm Mon-Fri) can help with information. On Piazza Umberto I, you can change money at two banks, and Banca di Sassari offers the Western Union money-wiring service.

SIGHTS

You can't always judge a church by its façade, and in the case of the **Basilica di Sant'Antioco Martire** (☎ 078 18 30 44; www.basilica santantioco.com, in Italian; Piazza Parrocchia 22; admission free; ☒ 9am-12pm & 3-6pm Mon-Fri, 10-11am & 3-6pm Sat & Sun), this couldn't be more true. To all intents and purposes, the façade suggests it is a modest baroque effort, but walk inside and you're immediately transported back to the 5th century AD.

Instead of the usual baroque frippery of frescoes and marble, you find time-worn barrel vaults suggestive of the Christian hypogeum (underground burial vault) that it once was. Like many palaeo-Christian churches, it was built according to the plan of the Greek cross; in the 12th century the nave was lengthened to fit the shape of the Latin cross.

To the right of the altar stands a wooden effigy of St Antiochus, his dark complexion a sign of his North African origins. Refusing to recant his faith, Antiochus was shipped off by the Romans to work as a slave in the mines of the Iglesiente. But he escaped, hidden in a tar barrel, and was taken in by an underground Christian group who hid him in the extensive **catacombs** (admission €2.50; ☒ same times as church) beneath the church. You'll find these to the right of the

altar, although you must wait for a guide to take you around the chambers.

What you see is a succession of burial rooms used by Christians between the 2nd and 7th centuries. Even then, society was divided into rather un-Christian classes. The richest went into elaborate, frescoed family niches in the walls (up to six spaces), of which a few fragments of fresco still remain. Middle-class corpses wound up in unadorned niches and commoners in ditches in the floor. A few skeletons lying *in situ* render the idea a little more colourfully.

Since the 1970s, archaeologists have penetrated further into the underground labyrinth and revealed a series of burial chambers dating to Punic times.

A few metres down Via Regina Margherita from the church is the modest **Museo Archeologico** (☎ 078 18 35 90; adult/child €5/2; ☒ 9am-1pm & 3.30-7pm Tue-Sun Jun-Sep, to 6pm Oct-May), which holds a small selection of the artefacts that were discovered at the nearby Carthaginian acropolis, necropolis and *tophet*. The museum was closed for refurbishment at the time of writing, although previously admission was by guided tour only. The ticket covers the museum and all the sights of the archaeological zone.

Walking uphill away from the cathedral, you pass what remains of the **Forte Su Pisu**, a fort built by the Piedmontese in 1812. Just behind this lies the **Zona Archeologica**. To the left of the street are the truncated columns and rubble remaining from the **Carthaginian acropolis**. You can't enter, but all is visible from the road. Across the road and spreading down the slope of the hill are the tombs of the **necropolis** (closed at the time of writing). Another 500m downhill is the Punic **tophet**.

Lastly, get along to Via Necropoli (named because there was another Punic necropolis here) by following the signs from Via De Gasperi to the **Museo Etnografico** (Via Necropoli 24a; ☒ 9am-1pm & 3.30-7pm Tue-Sun Jun-Sep, to 6pm Oct-May). Admission is included in the Museo Archeologico ticket. For centuries, locals have recycled elaborate Punic tombs here as houses and storage rooms. Some of these have been fixed up and together are known as the **Villaggio Ipogeo**. The museum itself is housed in a typical one-time warehouse with a *lolla* (porticoed courtyard), and it contains an assortment of traditional farm and household implements.

FESTIVALS & EVENTS

Held over four days around the second Sunday after Easter, the **Festa di Sant'Antioco** celebrates the city's patron saint with processions, traditional music and dancing, fireworks and concerts. It is one of the oldest documented saint's festivities on the island, dating to 1519.

SLEEPING & EATING

Hotel del Corso (☎ 078 180 02 65; www.hoteldel corso.it; Corso Vittorio Emanuele 32; B&B s/d €54/92; ⊠) This modern hotel is the most comfortable place in town and is superbly located on the main *corso* (avenue). The rooms are well appointed, and downstairs the hotel runs the most popular café along the leafy boulevard.

Hotel Eden (☎ 078 184 07 68; Piazza Parrocchia 15; s/d €50/80; ⊠) A friendly, if shabby, option, Hotel Eden occupies a modest mansion opposite the basilica. The rooms are tiny but the homy décor gives them a welcoming feel. Driving and parking around here, however, is a real headache.

Hotel Moderno (☎ 078 18 31 05; fax 078 184 02 52; Via Nazionale 82; s/d €45/62; ⊠) This is a straightforward place to stay. The rooms are unimaginative but have all the basics. Much more impressive is the hotel restaurant, which has a good reputation for its fresh fish dishes.

Various restaurants, pizzerias and snack spots are dotted about the town but none really shines.

Outside Sant'Antioco, in Calasetta, **Ristorante Sette Nani** (☎ 078 184 09 00; Via Garibaldi 139, Calasetta; meals €25-30) is spread out over several floors, or you can mellow out with a table in the garden dining area. Sette Nani delivers the goods, with unfussy seafood dishes topped off with a selection of Sardinian sweets and a complimentary glass of *mirto* – a local liqueur made from myrtle fruit or leaves – to send you on your way.

ENTERTAINMENT

People hang around in the bars and eateries along Corso Vittorio Emanuele until well into the night.

Fox Hunter Pierre Pub (☎ 078 180 04 55; Corso Vittorio Emanuele 86) A bizarrely authentic pub with high-backed pews and stripy wallpaper. It does a lively trade in the evening and musters up a good atmosphere.

Bar Colombo (Lungomare Colombo) In summer, keep an eye out for this place. The live music can be a little kitsch, but it's fun for late-night drinkies.

Also in summer, frequent free concerts are staged in Piazza Umberto I, ranging from local pop to traditional Sardinian tunes.

GETTING THERE & AWAY

FMS buses reach Sant'Antioco from Iglesias and Carbonia regularly, while as many as four a day come in from Cagliari. Some go on to Calasetta.

Ferries run between Calasetta and Carloforte on Isola di San Pietro (p103).

Around the Island

The island's better beaches start 8km south of the town. After 5km, turn off for **Maladroxia**, a small tourist haven with a couple of hotels and a pleasant beach and port. You could do worse than stay at **Hotel Scala Longa** (☎ 078 181 72 02; s/d €45/70, half board per person €68; ☿ May-Sep), a pleasing place off the main road that leads down to the port. Rooms are simple but the all-in deal is good value.

Back on the main road, you pass inland before hitting a big roundabout. Head left (east) to reach **Spiaggia Coa Quaddus**, a wild and woolly beach about 3km short of **Capo Sperone**, the southernmost point of the island. A few houses are clustered here, among them the cheery **Hotel Capo Sperone** (☎ 078 180 90 00; www .esperia.it/caposperone.htm; s/d €59.40/92.95, half board €87.80; ☿ Apr-Sep; ☢).

A turn right (west) before you reach the Spiaggia Coa Quaddus takes you over to the southwest coast of the island and a few beaches. The best of them is **Cala Lunga**, where the road peters out. Before you reach the beach you'll pass a handy camping ground, the **Campeggio Tonnara** (☎ 078 180 90 58; tonnaracamping@tiscalinet.it; Località Cala Saboni; camp sites per adult/tent €9.70/16.50; ☿ Apr-Sep).

Calasetta, the island's second town, lies 10km northwest of Sant'Antioco. It was originally founded by Ligurian families from Tabarka in 1769, following the example of their brothers in Carloforte. The town, dominated by the late Spanish-era watchtower that originally stood here quite alone, will be your first taste of the island if you arrive by ferry from Isola di San Pietro (p103). The grid system of streets hides little else of interest, but there are several beaches a few kilometres south along the northwestern coast.

Camping Le Saline (☎ /fax 078 18 86 15; www .campinglesaline.com, in Italian; camp sites per adult/tent €8.80/10.50, 4-person bungalows up to €129) is located just back from the lovely **Spiaggia Le Saline**, 2.5km south of Calasetta. Only a few miles outside Calasetta you'll find the **Hotel Luci del Faro** (☎ 078 181 00 89; Località Mangiabarche; s/d €103/166; P ✂ ⛱), in a lovely tranquil setting barely 800m from the long sandy Spiaggia Grande, a privileged position on the southwestern exit from town. The rooms are simple enough, but some have wonderful views. It's a family-friendly place with a pool and a playground.

SOUTH COAST

If you're heading from the southwest to Cagliari, or vice versa, make every effort to follow the coastal route. Its central stretch, known as the Costa del Sud, is a wonderful 20km spectacle of twisting, turning road above rugged cliffs that plunge into the deep blue sea. It is one of the prettiest coastal drives on the island.

PORTO BOTTE TO PORTO DI TEULADA

Firmly back on the mainland after crossing the bridge from Sant'Antioco, head east (right) at San Giovanni Suergiu and follow the SS195 southeast. You could be on a beach after just 10km if you make directly for **Porto Botte**. But it's not a great beach and you're better off continuing another 13km south for the fantastically popular **Spiaggia Porto Pino**.

At the weekend this place is absolutely packed with locals, who come to take out their little pleasure boats moored in the safe creek. There's ample free parking just behind the beach, from where you cross a bridge to reach the sandy seashore. It often looks like a busy day at Brighton beach: families crowded together with picnic hampers and cool boxes, and lots of little kiddies splashing in the water and having great fun. You'll need to come prepared,

as you can't hire umbrellas on the beach. There is, however, a string of cheap and cheerful pizzerias near the parking lot and many have nice shady gardens. Just south of Porto Pino, and accessible on foot, is **Spiaggia Sabbie Bianche**. The public is only allowed here in July and August, as it is on military land.

Camping Sardegna (☎ /fax 078 196 70 13; camp sites per adult/tent €6.40/10.30, 4-person bungalows up to €64; ☾ May-Sep) is a fairly basic camping ground behind the beach. For a bit more comfort you might consider checking into the **Hotel Cala dei Pini** (☎ 078 196 70 14; www.caladeipini.com; Località Porto Pino; s/d €90/138; P ✂ ⛱), a big, modern place just 600m from the beach.

From Porto Pino you have no choice but to head inland, turning right at Sant'Anna Arresi. After 10km, branch inland (away from the signs to Teulada) towards Porto di Teulada. The hilly area between Porto Pino and Porto di Teulada is occupied by another controversial NATO base (see the boxed text, p184), making Sardinia's southernmost point, **Capo Teulada**, inaccessible.

There are several beaches along this part of the coast, including **Cala Piombo**, **Porto Zafferano** and **Portu Piratsu**. They are only accessible in July and August by boat, which could be a reason for heading down to **Porto di Teulada**. This small fishing and pleasure port is just that, but in summer you can organise a trip on a sailboat around Capo Teulada; ask around the port. The nearest beach is **Porto Tramatzu**, around on the other side of Porto di Teulada.

COSTA DEL SUD

The Costa del Sud begins east of Porto di Teulada. The first stretch is just a prelude, passing several coves and gradually rising towards the high point of Capo Malfatano. As you wind your way around towards the cape, wonderful views of the coast to the east repeatedly spring into view and just about every point is capped by a watchtower dating to Spanish times.

Along the way, **Spiaggia Piscinni** is not the greatest strand in terms of sand (you have to deal with a fair amount of sun-dried algae) but the water is an incredible colour – it's like swimming in crystal.

Stop at the lookout point high above **Capo Malfatano**. Once around the bay and the next point, you could stop at **Cala Teuradda**, to marvel at its vivid emerald-green water. It's a popular spot (you can tell in summer by all the parked cars), which happens to be right at an ARST (Azienda Regionale Sarda Trasporti) bus stop. In summer you'll find snack bars, too.

From here the road climbs inland away from the water. You can get a look at the coast here, too, if you take a narrow side road to the south at **Porto Campana** – it quickly turns to dust but does allow you to reach the lighthouse at **Capo Spartivento**. From here a series of beaches stretch north along the coast – watch out for signposted side roads leading off to **Cala Cipolla**, **Spiaggia Su Giudeu** and **Porto Campana**.

At the end of this stretch you'll find another strategic Spanish watchtower presiding over the popular summer holiday spot of **Chia**. Here you'll find the long **Spiaggia Sa Colonia** to the west of the tower and the smaller arc of **Spiaggia Su Portu** to the east. You can walk up to the tower for views up and down the coast. In summer it's open for little **exhibitions** (admission €1; ⏰ 9.30am-12.30pm & 3-7pm). The tower was a relative newcomer to these parts, as shown by the discovery of the scanty remnants of Phoenician Bythia at its foot.

Chia is a paradise for wind- and kite-surfers, and you'll often see them practising off its beaches. At Easter the Chia Classic windsurfing competition is held here. For the ultimate view, check into the **Le Meridien Chia Laguna** (☎ 070 9 23 91; www.lemeridien.com; Località Chia; half board per person €220; P ⊠ 🛒) and ask for sea-view rooms.

Otherwise you have the choice of the modest **Il Gabbiano** (☎ 070 923 01 60; www.hotel ilgabbiano.net; Località Is Tramazzeddus; s/d €90/145; P ⊠), or **Campeggio Torre Chia** (☎ 070 923 00 54; fax 070 923 00 55; www.campeggiotorrechia.it; camp sites per adult/tent €6/8, 4-person villas up to €112), a few hundred metres back from Spiaggia Su Portu and often full in August.

ARST buses to/from Chia run along the Costa del Sud a couple of times daily in summer, and others serve Cagliari (€2.69, 1¼ hours, eight daily).

CENTER PARCS SARDINIAN STYLE

'Imagine paradise…', starts the colourful publicity brochure of the extraordinary **Forte Village** (☎ 070 92 15 16; www.fortevillage.com; half board per person d/ste €400/830; Santa Margherita di Pula; P ⊠ 🖳 🛒) resort near Santa Margherita di Pula. And as we read on we raise our eyebrows at the ludicrous poetic license as poor copywriters struggle and strain to describe heaven on earth. Can it really be that good?

So much publicity is spent on the high jinks of the Costa Smeralda that barely a line gets written about Sardinia's southwest coast. It has its own little knot of luxury development between Pula and Chia, the most spectacular of which has to be the gated Forte Village.

Unlike the rocky coast of the Gallura in northeastern Sardinia, Forte Village is nestled in a veritable jungle of tropical garden, dotted with waving palms and lurid neon-coloured bougainvillea. Clever old Lord Forte bought the land in the 1970s and decided to develop the ultimate holiday village on his huge 25,000-hectare site. And you have to hand it to him, it really is an environment of pure luxury and indulgence.

How *can* one describe a holiday village of seven luxury hotels set on more than a kilometre of finely groomed sand? It's so big that electric golf carts ferry guests from pillar to post (no cars allowed, thank you!), between the shopping malls and bowling alleys, the discos and football pitches, the tennis courts and thalassotherapy spa. There are 10 swimming pools – complete with slides and underwater viewing chambers – and over a dozen top-notch restaurants. There's even a kids' club and a go-cart circuit. What's more, unlike the Costa Smeralda, where the publicity and the plebs have lowered the tone, Forte Village remains its own private fortress behind high security gates.

Where, you may ask, does this fit in with the rest of Sardinia? The answer is simple – it doesn't. Like so much on the island, Forte Village represents a self-contained world, resolutely cut off from the cultural context of island life, so huge that guests rarely venture outside its gates – and who can really blame them? But it can't be good for the island's economy, as all those thousands of euros wing their way off shore, leaving the Sards as exploited as ever.

SANTA MARGHERITA DI PULA

The next 9km of coastline between Chia and Santa Margherita di Pula is the most beautiful of the southwest: a string of magnificent beaches lapped by crystalline waters and backed by fragrant pine woods. But you won't get to see much of it, as this represents the south coast's equivalent of Costa Smeralda; luxury hotels (see the boxed text, opposite) have snapped up all the prime beach-front property, fencing it in and closing it off with unsociably big gates.

Many of the side roads leading off the highway to the beach are reserved for residents, but you may slip through one or two and get down to the white sandy beaches. You'll find one of these access roads signposted for **Camping Flumendosa** (☎ 070 920 83 64; fax 070 924 92 82; camp sites per adult/tent €7.50/13).

Opposite the camp ground is one of Santa Margherita di Pula's most reasonably priced hotels, **Hotel Mare Pineta** (☎ 070 920 83 61; www.hotelflamingo.it; s/d €104/178; ☽ mid-Apr–mid-Oct; P ☒ ☒), part of the more expensive Hotel Flamingo complex. It has a lovely setting in a vibrant tropical garden right on the edge of the beach. The whole area shuts down from about October to March.

Local orange buses serve Santa Margherita di Pula from Pula and Nora.

PULA

pop 6800

The rather busy town through which you must pass in order to reach Nora is a bustling, chaotic sort of place. Still, you will want to stop off here to look around the archaeological museum, which houses all the titbits that were dug up at the ancient site.

There is a **tourist office** (☎ 070 924 52 50; www .prolocopula.it, in Italian; Piazza del Popolo; ☽ 10am-1pm & 7-11pm Jul-Sep, 9am-1pm & 4-7.30pm Mon-Sat Oct-Jun), but far more useful is the private **Agenzia Le Torri** (☎ 070 920 83 73; www.agenziale-torri.com; Via Corinaldi; ☽ 9am-1pm & 5-8pm Mon-Sat Jun-Sep), which has tons of information on Pula, Nora and around. It also hires out bicycles from €10 a day and scooters from €25 a day.

Sights

PULA

The **Museo Archeologico** (☎ 070 920 96 10; Corso Vittorio Emanuele 67; adult/child incl Nora site €5.50/2.50; ☽ 9am-8pm Sep-Jul, 9am-midnight Aug), near the central Piazza Municipio, consists of one room of carefully selected finds from Nora, mostly ceramics found in Punic and Roman tombs, some gold and bone jewellery, and Roman glassware. There is also a model of the site to help you put the ruins in context when you visit, and there are helpful explanations in both English and Italian.

In AD 303 the disgraced Roman commander Ephisius was hauled down to the beach behind the port city of Nora, condemned for his conversion to Christianity and executed. On the way from Pula to Nora you will see the little **Chiesa di Sant'Efisio**, which marks his martyrdom and where the pilgrims of Cagliari's Festa di Sant'Efisio bring his effigy every 1 May (see p72).

NORA

In the days of Ephisius, **Nora** (adult/child incl Museo Archeologico in Pula €5.50/2.50; ☽ 9am-7pm) was one of the most important urban settlements on the island and the seat of the Roman government, linked to Karalis (now Cagliari) in the east and Bythia in the west. However, the site dates way back to the 11th century BC, when Phoenicians from Spain first founded a trading depot here. But the town's position was exposed and by the Middle Ages it had been abandoned, the temples looted by Arab pirates and the marble columns broken.

These days only a fraction of the original site remains; it is only when you reach the rocky outline of the promontory that you see any remnants of the once-great imperial city.

Upon entry, you pass a single melancholy **column** from the former temple of Tanit, the Carthaginian Venus, who was once the centre of a great cult here. Much of the glass in Pula's museum was found around here, giving rise to theories that the whole temple may have been decorated with it. Beyond this is a small but beautifully preserved Roman **theatre** facing the sea, which is now used for summer concerts. Towards the west are the substantial remains of the **Terme al Mare** (Baths by the Sea). Four columns (a tetrastyle) stand at the heart of what was a patrician villa; the surrounding rooms retain their mosaic floor decoration. More remnants of mosaics can be seen at a temple complex towards the tip of the promontory.

SOUTHWEST SARDINIA

Most of the ruins are now submerged beneath the wind-whipped waves and make for spectacular dives. Contact **Conan Diving** (☎ 338 610 82 34; www.conandiving.com, in Italian; SS195 km 25) for further details. You'll find this outfit on the main road between Pula and Santa Margherita di Pula.

Up to 16 local shuttle buses circulate between Pula and Nora.

LAGUNA DI NORA

Just before the entrance to the ancient site of Nora are the pleasant **Spiaggia di Nora** and, a little further around, the bigger **Spiaggia Su Guventeddu**. Note that you won't be permitted into the site in your bathing costume.

On the western side of the Nora promontory stretches the **Laguna di Nora** (☎ 070 920 95 44; www.lagunadinora.it, in Italian), where a didactic centre organises activities, many of them aimed at kids. Apart from the aquarium, the centre offers guided snorkelling and canoe excursions in the lagoon. A visit to the aquarium costs €7/5 per adult/child, or you can combine this with canoeing (adult/child €20/12; 10am and 5pm from June to August, 10am and 4pm in September) or snorkelling (adult/child €25/12; 10am from June to September).

Festivals & Events

Every year **La Notte dei Poeti** (Night of Poetry; www.lanottedeipoeti.it, in Italian) is held during July and August, and is responsible for the concerts, theatre and poetry readings that take place in the theatre. Tickets cost between €16 and €20 and can be bought at the gate. Otherwise, inquire in Pula at **Agenzia Le Torri** (☎ 070 920 83 73; www.agenzialetorri.com; Via Corinaldi; ☯ 9am-1pm & 5-8pm Mon-Sat Jun-Sep).

Sleeping & Eating

Although there is accommodation in Pula, it's far preferable to stay in the more attractive hotels that cluster around Nora.

Hotel Baia di Nora (☎ 070 924 56 00; www.hotelbaiadinora.com; Località Su Guventeddu; half board per person low/high season €90/185; ☯ Apr-Oct; P ⊠ ☲) This absolutely gorgeous hotel is barely a kilometre from Nora. Rooms nestle amid a profusely flowering garden, while guests take drinks on bar stools in the enormous spiral pool. There's also a huge swath of private beach, as well as tennis courts and courtesy bikes.

Nora Club Hotel (☎ 070 92 44 22; www.noraclubhotel.it; Viale Nora; s/d €125/155; P ⊠ ☲) Much more modest in scale but no less lovely, the Nora Club clusters around its palm-fringed pool. It has a tranquil atmosphere with only 25 rooms elegantly decked out in a modern rustic style. It's also open year-round.

If you're staying in Pula itself, there are a couple of unexciting hotels, including **Hotel Sandalyon** (☎ 070 920 91 51; Via Cagliari 30; s/d €50/75).

Zio Dino (☎ 070 920 91 59; Viale Segni 14; meals €30; ☯ Mon-Sat) This is one of central Pula's best eateries, with a tempting mix of seafood and meat dishes on the menu. Meals are best begun with the *spaghetti alla Zio Dino*, a seafood special.

CAMPIDANO

Heading north out of Cagliari along the SS131, you enter a broad, flat corridor known as the Campidano. While it represents a capital source of agricultural wealth for the island, it can be a little dispiriting for the visitor. On high summer days, when temperatures soar and the southern half of the island is often enveloped in a thick, grey heat haze, it all just looks so damn dusty and yellow. The dual-carriage highway means you can hurry northward through the plains, but a few spots are worth a detour for those with time.

Uta, Castello di Acquafredda & San Sperate

Barely 20km northwest of Cagliari, at the eastern edge of the sprawling farm town of **Uta**, is one of the finer examples of Romanesque church-building in Sardinia and one of the few in the south of the island.

The **Chiesa di Santa Maria** (follow the brown signs for the Santuario di Santa Maria), built around 1140 by Vittorini monks from Marseille, is remarkable above all for the variegated statuary that runs around the top of its exterior. Busts of people and various animals (real and imaginary) mix in with floral and geometric patterns.

The church, for lovers of Romanesque architecture at any rate, is worth the effort of getting here from Cagliari. But if you come by bus, the journey will try your patience as it's a good half-hour walk from central Uta, a town that offers precious little else in the way of entertainment.

If you head west from here (a dual-carriage road roars across the plains to Iglesias), consider a quick southward diversion at the Siliqua crossroads, 14km west of Uta. About 5km to the south you can see the fairy-tale image of castle ruins atop an extraordinary craggy mount that bursts forth from the plains. As you get closer, you come to realise that little more than the crumbling walls of **Castello di Acquafredda** remain. The castle served as a temporary hiding place for Guelfo della Gherardesca when his father Ugolino was imprisoned in Pisa and the family banished.

Another minor diversion is **San Sperate**, situated 19km northwest of Cagliari. Like Orgosolo (p204), it's famous for the murals that dot its walls. Unlike those in Orgosolo, however, the 22 murals of San Sperate don't represent keenly felt injustices. Instead, they present a Daliesque tableau of traditional country life, like the hanging laundry on Via Monastir or the epic country scene *Storia di San Sperate* (Story of San Sperate) on Via Sassari. The work was begun by Pinuccio Sciola (born 1942), a local sculptor who was inspired by the Mexican artist Diego Rivera.

ARST buses from Cagliari (€1.19, 40 minutes, 10 daily from Monday to Friday, one on Sunday) make day trips possible to Uta and San Sperate. For Castello di Acquafredda, you need your own car.

Sanluri
pop 8560

A busy rural centre some 45km north of Cagliari on the SS131, Sanluri has ancient roots, of which it displays virtually nothing. Just nearby the Catalano-Aragonese

defeated the Sardinian forces in the Battle of Sanluri in 1409, thus extinguishing what was left of Sardinian independence.

As you penetrate the town's centre from the south you cannot help but run into the largely 18th-century **Chiesa della Madonna delle Grazie**. Little of the Gothic original remains, and what stands out from afar is the rococo bell tower.

Further up the main road, Via Carlo Felice, you emerge in Piazza Castello, which takes its name from a squat, brooding 14th-century bastion. Nowadays the building houses the private **Museo Risorgimentale Duca d'Aosta** (☎ 070 930 71 05; admission €5 incl guided tour; ⏰ 4.30-9pm Tue-Fri Jul-Sep, 9.45am-1pm & 3pm-sunset Sun year-round). Modern artillery pieces greet you in the garden, and once inside you can see an extraordinary array of objects, from period furniture to military mementos. The latter, which includes photos, maps, arms and other oddments, covers conflicts ranging from Garibaldi's battles against the Austrians to WWI and Fascist Italy's escapades, particularly in Ethiopia (then known as Abyssinia).

Cross Via Carlo Felice and follow Via San Rocco a few hundred metres east, then take a left towards the Franciscan monastery at the top of the rise. Here you'll find the rather bizarre and eclectic collection of the **Museo Etnografico Cappuccino** (☎ 070 930 79 19; www.museocappuccini.it; admission €3; ⏰ 9am-noon & 3.30-7pm), the result of the limitless curiosity of one of the friars, Fra Fedele. Entry times (and fee) are completely hit and miss. If you turn up and Fra Fedele is around, you may find yourself being led around for a good hour or two. One room contains ancient artefacts such as obsidian arrowheads and Roman-era coins. Another

---

DETOUR: RISERVA NATURALE FORESTA DI MONTE ARCOSU

From Uta, you can pick up brown signs for the Riserva Naturale Foresta di Monte Arcosu, a natural reserve run by the WWF that's dedicated to preserving a small handkerchief of the original habitat of the rare *cervo Sardo*. The park rings the peak of Monte Arcosu (948m) and shelters a growing number of deer, wild boar, martens, wildcats, weasels and plenty of birds of prey, including golden eagles.

Visits to the park are with a guide only, who takes you on a rambling walk through the dense woods along various natural trails pointing out interesting flora and fauna (in Italian). There are also two visitor centres with displays on the wildlife.

The **Cooperativa Il Caprifoglio** (☎ 070 96 87 14; admission €3) runs the park, which is open all day on Saturday and Sunday and during holidays.

is devoted to farm tools, with all sorts of objects on display, including ploughshares and horseshoes.

A plethora of buses and trains reach Sanluri from Cagliari. The train station is 5km out of town and linked to the centre by local buses.

Sardara
pop 4300

An 8km sprint northwest of Sanluri along the SS131 brings you to Sardara. The centre of the village is dominated by the Gothic **Chiesa di San Gregorio**, a nice example of transitional architecture from Romanesque to Gothic. Hints of the latter are the soaring façade, rose window and Gothic window in the apse.

Further uphill is the fine **Civico Museo Archeologico Villa Abbas** (☎ 070 938 61 83; Piazza Libertà 7; admission €4.13; ⏰ 9am-1pm & 5-8pm Tue-Sun). Several tombs from the Terr'e Cresia necropolis excavations have been recreated, with skeletons and all.

Among the finest pieces on display are two bronze statuettes of archers with strong Assyrian features, found on the edge of Sardara in 1913 and dating to the 8th century BC. Outside, excavations have been carried out on the Sa Costa site that forms the museum's back yard.

A few hundred metres away is the **Chiesa di Sant'Anastasia** (Piazza Sant'Anastasia; admission free; ⏰ 9am-1pm & 5-8pm Tue-Sun), a little Gothic church planted right in the middle of what is now an archaeological dig, the site of a *nuraghe* well temple. You can wander into the simple church and downstairs into the well temple; enter to your left as you face the church entrance.

A few kilometres west of the town (on the other side of the SS131) is **Santa Maria de Is Acquas**, the site of thermal baths since Roman times and nowadays home to a couple of thermal spa hotels. The low, speckled walls of the late-Gothic **Chiesa di Santa Maria** give the area its name. About 4km to the south, a dirt road leads to the empty walls of the **Castello Monreale**, built by the governor of Arborea and used as a temporary refuge by the defeated troops of Brancaleone Doria after the Battle of Sanluri. The Catalano-Aragonese garrisoned it for a time in 1478, but thereafter it soon fell into disuse. You can see some of

the colourful medieval ceramics and other material dug up in the castle in Sardara's museum.

Hotel Sardara (☎ 070 938 78 11; Via Cedrino 5; s/d €35/50) is a no-nonsense eight-room hotel in the new part of town. Those in need of thermal water treatment could try their luck at the two hotels in Santa Maria de Is Acquas.

LA MARMILLA

The land directly north of Sardara changes aspect radically from the flat plains of the Campidano, which continue to accompany the SS131 on its northwestern route towards Oristano.

La Marmilla has an oddly bumpy landscape, although it too is interspersed with tracts of broad plains, especially in the shadows of La Giara di Gesturi, a high plateau that closes off the northern limits of Cagliari province.

VILLANOVAFORRU & GENNA MARIA
pop 700

Villanovaforru could win a tidy-town award, although apart from its museum it has little to hold your interest. Just outside to the west is the important *nuraghe* settlement of Genna Maria, which, with the Nuraghe Su Nuraxi (opposite), is a must on the ancient-history buff's travels through this part of the island.

The **Museo Archeologico** (☎ 070 930 00 50; Piazza Costituzione; admission €2.50; ⏰ 9.30am-1pm & 3.30-7pm Tue-Sun) displays a broad collection of material found mostly in the Marmilla region, including items from Su Nuraxi and Genna Maria. Exhibits include enormous amphorae and other pots, oil lamps, jewellery, and coins from the *nuraghe* era to Roman times.

The **Sala delle Mostre** (☎ 070 930 00 50; admission €1.50; ⏰ 9.30am-1pm & 3.30-7pm Tue-Sun) is adjacent to the archaeological museum and often hosts temporary exhibitions on local life and history.

To visit the complex of **Nuraghe Genna Maria** (☎ 070 930 00 50; admission €2; ⏰ 9.30am-1pm & 3.30-6pm Tue-Sun), drive 1km out on the road west to Collinas; turn south at the sign. The *nuraghe* is a tumbledown site but, archaeologically speaking, one of the most important on the island. It consists of a central tower, around which was later raised the three-cornered bastion. Much later an encircling wall was also raised to protect an Iron Age village, but little of it remains today.

Residence Funtana Noa (☎ /fax 070 933 10 19; www.residencefuntananoa.it; Via Vittorio Emanuele III 66-68; s/d €40/62; 🔀) is the nicest option here. It's a tasteful hotel with 30 rooms, all decorated with timber furniture in a crisp, unfussy style. Rooms are gathered around a courtyard, and most have views over the surrounding countryside.

ARST buses run here from Cagliari on weekdays (€3.72, 1½ hours, three daily from Monday to Friday). Up to four a day run to and from Sardara (€0.67, 15 minutes) and Sanluri (€1.19, 25 minutes).

LAS PLASSAS

Zigzagging northeast from Villanovaforru, you find yourself heading in the direction of Barumini. Long before you hit this town, you will see the ruined walls of the 12th-century **Castello di Marmilla** atop an impossibly conical hill beside the hamlet of Las Plassas. The castle was part of the defensive line built on the frontier with Cagliari province by the rulers of Arborea.

To get there, take the left fork (for Tuili) at the beginning of Las Plassas and you will see on your left a winding footpath to the top of this hill. If approaching from Barumini, make for the yellow **Chiesa di Maria Maddalena**, cross the Las Plassas–Tuili road and start hiking.

BARUMINI & NURAGHE SU NURAXI

pop 1390

From Las Plassas, you speed up the road through lumpy hillocks to Barumini. The tiny **Chiesa di Santa Tecla** marks the crossroads in the centre of town. Make a pit stop here to admire the curvaceous rose window of the church, and enter for a small multimedia show and a visit to the **museum** (admission €1.03; 🕙 10am-1pm & 3.30-7pm Thu-Sun) dedicated to the Nuraghe Su Nuraxi.

A kilometre west of the village is **Parco Sardegna in Miniatura** (☎ 070 936 10 04; www.sardegnainminiatura.it, in Italian; admission €5; 🕙 9am-6pm Apr-Sep, 9am-6pm Sat & Sun Oct-Mar), a miniature park of the whole island, which younger children will thoroughly enjoy. Boat trips

float you around the most important island sights, such as the Pisan church of Saccargia or Su Nuraxi itself. There's a play area and plenty of picnic tables.

Albergo Sa Lolla (☎ 070 936 84 19; www.wels.it /salolla/; Via Cavour 49, Barumini; s/d €47/67; 🅿 🖭) is a nicely renovated mansion with just seven rooms. It also has an excellent restaurant (closed Wed). To find it head east from the Chiesa di Santa Tecla in Barumini and follow the signs – it's only a few hundred metres from the church. You will need to book in July and August.

The Unesco World Heritage site of the **Nuraghe Su Nuraxi** (adult/concession €4.20/3.10; 🕙 9am-8pm) is barely half a kilometre west of Barumini on the road to Tuili. The ruined hulk of the central tower makes a prominent landmark.

Right at the summit of the hill the Nuraxi tower once stood a majestic 10m high, rising over three storeys. It was built – wait for it – in the 13th century BC. Now all that remains are the mighty basalt blocks of its wide circular base. But what makes the site so amazing is the extent of the village ruins around it, a veritable beehive of circular interlocking buildings that tumble down the hillside. As the village grew, a more complex defensive wall was built around the core, consisting of nine towers pierced by arrow slits. Weapons in the form of massive stone balls were also found during the dig. In the 7th century BC the site was partly destroyed but not abandoned. In fact it grew and was still inhabited in Roman times. Elements of basic sewerage and canalisation have even been identified. Given the dates, this is incredible.

The site was rediscovered by Giovanni Lilliu (Sardinia's most famous archaeologist; see p20) in 1949, after torrential rains eroded the compact earth that had covered the *nuraghe* and made it look like just another Marmilla hillock. Little could he have imagined that the excavation of the site would take him six years to complete.

Entry is by guided tour only. These run nearly every half-hour and consist of no more than 20 people. This arrangement does cause queues in summer, so be prepared for a bit of a wait. Still, this is the island's most impressive *nuraghe* site, so persevere.

SOUTHWEST SARDINIA

SOUTHWEST SARDINIA

LA GIARA DI GESTURI

Five kilometres west of Barumini is the town of Tuili, which borders the strange **Giara di Gesturi**, a high basalt plateau that looms above the surrounding country. This remarkable 45-sq-km plain, splashed with *macchia* and small cork oaks, is home to the red long-horned bulls peculiar to Sardinia, and the unique wild *cavallini* (literally 'minihorses'); at last count, as many as 500 of them were living here.

The best places to find the horses, in the early morning or late afternoon, are the seasonal lakes, called *paulis* (such as Pauli Maiori). In winter the lakes usually have a shallow patina of surface water, but in the warmer months most of it evaporates. At some, such as Pauli S'Ala de Mengianu, the water trapped in underground basalt sources bubbles to the surface around the *paulis*, and that is where the horses will be slaking their thirst.

The plateau also has its own microclimate, which fosters an array of unusual flora, best seen in spring, when the ground is covered in heather and the 15 species of orchid are in bloom. It's an interesting place to go walking; paths crisscross the plateau, and there are a few dirt tracks that make it possible to get around in a vehicle. You can still see the occasional *pinedda* (old-style thatched shepherd's hut), such as the one on the left if you start following the trail from the Setzu approach road.

One place to find guides for the plateau is **Sa Jara Manna** (☎ 070 936 81 70; www.sajaramanna .it; SS197 km 44) outside Barumini. It offers a number of guided excursions either on foot (prices depend on the size of the group) or by 4WD (€115 for a half day). It also hires out mountain bikes (€9 for a half day). A half-day or day's excursion will include a shepherd's lunch on the plateau in one of the old *pinedda*.

Another organisation that runs similar excursions from Tuili is **Centro Servizi Giara** (☎ 070 936 42 77, 348 292 49 83; www.jara.it, in Italian; Via GB Tuveri 16).

If you're coming from **Setzu**, turn right just north of the town. The road winds up 3km above the stark plains; at the 2km mark you'll see the Sa Domu de S'Orcu *tomba di gigante* (literally 'giant's tomb'; ancient mass grave) to the left. The asphalt peters out at the entrance to Parco della Giara, but you can follow the rough dirt track (slowly) in a normal car east to the Gesturi exit.

There is another approach road from **Tuili**, from which locals set out in August for the annual round-up and branding of the *cavallini*. In the town's **Chiesa di San Pietro** are some fine works of art, including a grand *retablo* (altarpiece) done in 1500 by the Maestro di Castelsardo.

Finally, you can also enter the Giara at its eastern end from **Gesturi**. The town is dominated by the big 17th-century baroque **Chiesa di Santa Teresa d'Ávila** and is a centre of pilgrimage for the faithful, who flock here to celebrate Gesturi's greatest son, Fra Nicola 'Silenzio' (1882–1958), a Franciscan friar known for his religious devotion, wisdom and simplicity of life. His beatification in 1999 was a source of great pride to the good citizens of Gesturi, who have decorated the town with murals and grand portraits of the man they knew as Brother Silence.

One or two ARST buses run from Cagliari to Tuili between Monday and Friday, from where you can pick up tours with Centro Servizi Giara (see above). Otherwise you will need your own transport.

Oristano & the West

Fields of prickly, pale wheat blowing in the salty air, small market towns going about their daily business, hunters with game bags, and hoary-haired fishermen – Oristano is an endearing tableau of typical Sardinian scenes. To the west the province is fringed by silvery lagoons, and the landscape, a jigsaw of stone-walled smallholdings, is the flattest on the island.

In its centre sits Oristano, the great cattle market of the island, and from its rooftops you can just about espy the gun-metal grey lagoons running away to Cabras and Tharros, that evocative Roman ruin on the windy San Giovanni peninsula. To the north the red mountain of Monti Ferru rises, a patchwork of market towns. You'll eat the island's finest Bue Rosso steak here and taste its best olive oil. Milis is famous for its citrus crop, and the marshside town of Cabras has a unique gastronomy – mullet, eels, *bottarga* (mullet roe) and clams.

This big-horse country is more Wild West than southern Italy. The races of Oristano's Sa Sartiglia and Sedilo's S'Ardia are breathtaking for their recklessness and daredevil antics. Stables such as Ala Birdi and Mandra Edera provide an excellent way of seeing the countryside.

One of the island's least-explored provinces, Oristano is often overlooked by visitors. It's a shame, as the region certainly rewards a little effort.

ORISTANO & THE WEST

HIGHLIGHTS

- Marvel at the colours of Carnival at Oristano's **Sa Sartiglia** (p119) and the thundering madness of Sedilo's **S'Ardia** (p128) horse race
- Enjoy a bucket-and-spade day at **Marina di Torregrande's** (p121) impressive stretch of beach
- Go west on one of **Mandra Edera's** (p128) horse-riding excursions or sleep easy in the gorgeous **Hotel Lucrezia** (p120) in Riola Sardo
- Shop at a village market in **Monti Ferru** (p125)
- See if Asterix is at home in the carefully maintained site of **Nuraghe Losa** (p128)
- Discover lonely **Tharros** (p124) on its windy peninsula

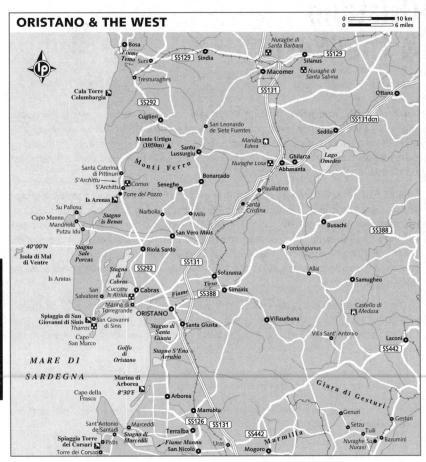

ORISTANO & THE WEST

0 ——— 10 km
0 ——— 6 miles

ORISTANO

pop 32,200

Oristano lives in the shadow of its legendary past. In the 14th century, when the Aragonese overran Sardinia and crushed the three other independent provinces – Cagliari, Gallura and Logudoro – Arborea, with Oristano as its capital, retained its independence and territories.

The largest market town of the west, it is home to a handful of churches, a good archaeological museum and some worthwhile restaurants where you'll undoubtedly be eating with the locals. Oristano makes a handy base for the surrounding area.

HISTORY

Around the 8th century BC, the Phoenicians built the city of Tharros. Later occupied by the Romans, Tharros was the urban centre of the west for hundreds of years.

During the Middle Ages the site was abandoned in favour of a more easily defended spot further inland, and so Aristiane came to be. By the 11th century it was the capital of the Giudicato d'Arborea, one of four independent provinces. Giudicessa Eleonora of Arborea (c1340–1404) organised the 14th-century war against the Spanish and concluded Arborea's famous diplomatic victories. She also published the Carta di Logu (Code of Laws; see p25) before dying of plague. Alfonso V was so impressed by the code that he decided to apply it to the whole island in 1421.

Trade collapsed under the Catalano-Aragonese and the city suffered beneath appalling administration, plague and famine. The 18th century was marked by repeated riots and rebellions.

The creation of the Cagliari–Porto Torres highway in the 1820s and, a century later, Mussolini's programmes to drain swamps and establish model farms gave Oristano a much-needed boost.

INFORMATION
Bookshops
Libreria Pergomena (☎ /fax 0783 7 50 58; Via V Emanuele II 24) An excellent range of books on all aspects of Sardinia, plus a handful of novels in English, French and German.

Internet Access
Tharros Net (Via San Francesco d'Assisi 6; per hr €5; ☽ 9.30am-1pm & 3.30-7.30pm Mon-Fri)

Medical Services
Guardia Medica (☎ 0783 7 43 33; Via Carducci) For medical assistance.

Hospital (Viale Fondazione Rockefeller) South of the town centre.

Farmacia San Carlo (Piazza Eleonora d'Arborea 10/11) Well-supplied central pharmacy.

Money
There are a few banks around Piazza Roma, including Banca Nazionale di Lavoro.

Post
Post office (Via Mariano IV d'Arborea; ☽ 8.15am-6.15pm Mon-Fri, 8.15am-noon Sat)

Tourist Information
Information booth (Piazza Roma; ☽ 9am-1pm & 4-9pm, to 10pm Sun & public holidays Jul–mid-Sep) In town during summer.

Main tourist office (☎ 0783 3 68 31; www.inforis tano.it, in Italian; Piazza Eleonora d'Arborea 19; ☽ 8am-2pm & 4-7pm Mon-Fri, varied hr Sat) The most helpful tourist office. Has regional information as well.

Tourist office (☎ 0783 7 06 21; Via Ciutadella di Menorca 14; ☽ 9am-noon & 4.30-7.30pm Mon-Fri) For city information.

Travel Agencies
CTS (☎ 0783 77 20 33; www.cts.it; Via Grazia Deledda 9) A branch of the national youth travel agent.

SIGHTS
Oristano's tidy historic centre a whiff of its former glory, with rows of solid stone houses with shuttered windows and lofty internal courtyards. It's almost circular in plan and was once surrounded by a fortified wall whose only remnants are the **Torre di Mariano II** on Piazza Roma, and the **Portixedda** (admission free; ☽ 10am-12.30pm & 4-6.30pm Tue-Sun) just off Via Giuseppe Mazzini to the east. The latter contains an exhibition showing what the city's defences would have looked like before they were pulled down in the late 19th century.

Duomo & the Chiesa di San Francesco
The onion-domed bell tower of the **cathedral** (Piazza Duomo; admission free; ☽ 7am-noon & 4-7pm Mon-Sat, 8am-1pm Sun) dominates the Oristano skyline.

The majority of what you see today is a baroque makeover, although some elements, including the apses and a chapel, survive from a Gothic predecessor. The 14th-century wooden sculpture *Annunziata* or *Madonna del Rimedio*, in the first chapel on the right as you enter, is believed to have been carved by Nino Pisano, a Tuscan sculptor whose late-Gothic works stand on the cusp of the Renaissance. Two marble panels that once fronted the statue bear 11th- to 12th-century sculptural reliefs on one side depicting Daniel in the lion's den. The other side, carved about 300 years later by an unknown Catalan artist, depicts a host of prophets, saints and apostles, the Annunciation, and Christ in judgement.

The fine but gory 14th-century wooden sculpture *Crocifisso di Nicodemo* is in the **Chiesa di San Francesco** (Via Sant'Antonio; admission free; ☽ 8am-noon & 5-7pm Mon-Sat, 8am-noon Sun).

Antiquarium Arborense
Oristano's neat little archaeological **museum** (☎ 0783 79 12 62; Piazzetta Corrias; adult/child €3/1; ☽ 9am-1.30pm & 3-8pm), in the old Palazzo Parpaglia, houses one of the island's most important archaeological collections, which the mayor of Oristano purchased from Efisio Pischedda in 1938.

On the ground floor things kick off with prehistoric finds from the Sinis, obsidian and flint spearheads and axes, bones and a smattering of jewellery. More interesting

ORISTANO & THE WEST

is the stash of finds from Carthaginian and Roman Tharros. Ceramics predominate, such as the lovely figurines and the unusual terracotta mask from the 5th century BC, but also on show are glassware, oil lamps and amphorae, and a range of pots, plates and cups. Upstairs is a model of the classical city of Tharros as it might have appeared around the 4th century AD. Texts in Italian explain the city layout while glass cases exhibit more finds from Tharros and Cabras.

Next door to the main room is the museum's **pinacoteca** (art gallery), which hosts a small collection of *retabli* (painted altar pieces). One series of panels, *Retablo del Santo Cristo* (1533), by the workshop of Pietro Cavaro, depicts a group of apparently beatific saints. But take a closer look at the composition and you'll see they all sport the instruments of their gory tortures slicing through their heads, necks and hearts.

Piazza Eleonora d'Arborea & Around

Piazza Eleonora d'Arborea became the city's central square through 19th-century urban reforms. Today it is a quiet spot where you can sit beneath the benign gaze of Queen Eleonora's **statue**. She holds the ground-breaking Carta di Logu and raises a finger as if she were about to launch into a political speech. Also on the square is the neoclassical **Municipio** (Town Hall).

FESTIVALS & EVENTS

Oristano's carnival, the **Sa Sartiglia**, is the biggest festival of the province and the most colourful carnival on the island. It is attended in February by hundreds of costumed participants and involves a medieval joust, horse racing and incredible acrobatic riding. See the boxed text, below.

SLEEPING

If you are looking to stay in a private house rather than a hotel, check out **Sardinian Way** (☎ 0783 7 51 72; www.sardinianway.it; Via Carmine 14). Another possibility is **La Mia Casa** (☎ /fax 0783 41 16 60; www.lamiacasa.sardegna.it; Posidonia Tourist Services, Via Umberto I 64, 09070 Riola Sardo), with more than 20 B&Bs in seven villages in the province.

Eleonora B&B (☎ 0783 7 04 35; www.eleonora-bed-and-breakfast.com; Piazza Eleonora d'Arborea 12; s/d €35/60) Situated on the main piazza, this rambling house has parts dating to medieval times. It's the home of young couple Paola and Andrea, who have converted three en-suite rooms into guest rooms. It has loads of character and a laid-back atmosphere.

Duomo Albergo (☎ 0783 77 80 61; www.hotelduomo.net; Via Vittorio Emanuele 34; s/d €70/140; 🖳 🖳) Opened in late 2004, this is a real charmer, with the best rooms set around a central courtyard. Decorations are traditional, with wall hangings of local embroidery in the rooms. The same owner runs Ristorante Craf (p120).

Hotel Mistral 2 (☎ 0783 21 03 89; fax 0783 21 10 00; Via XX Settembre; s/d €66/98; 🅿 🖳) A big, modern hotel on the western edge of the city centre, the Mistral has a dated, corporate feel. It's popular with big groups, as it has the only pool in town.

Villa delle Rose (☎ 0783 31 01 01; fax 0783 36 01 01; Piazza Italia 5; s/d €44/80) Discreetly tucked away on a nondescript square, this family-run place has a cosy feel. The rooms are nothing fancy, but they're large, neat and clean.

EATING

Oristano looks more to the sea than is generally the case in Sardinia. Mullet (*muggine*), fished from the Stagno di Cabras lagoon and the Golfo di Oristano, is so common that it is also known as *pesce di Oristano* (Oristano fish). A local speciality is *mrecca*, mullet that is boiled, wrapped in pond grass and then dried and salted. Grilled eel is popular, as are *patelle*, limpet-like dark clams.

Antica Trattoria del Teatro (☎ 0783 7 16 72; Via Parpaglia 11; meals €28-35; ⌚ Thu-Tue) Located on a quiet elbow in the pedestrian area, opposite the theatre, the interior of this trattoria exudes subtle elegance. The menu includes vegetarian options such as *tempura di*

ORISTANO & THE WEST

MARDI GRAS

Sa Sartiglia is undoubtedly Sardinia's most colourful and carefully choreographed festival. Its origins are unknown and its godlike central figure, the Su Cumpoidori, smacks of pagan ritual and theatre. The jousts and costumes are undoubtedly Spanish, probably introduced to the island by the *giudicati* (provincial governors), who were trained at the Court of Aragon. The word Sartiglia comes from the Castilian Sortija, which means ring, and the central event of the festival is a medieval joust in which the Su Cumpoidori, the King of the Sartiglia, must pierce a star (ring) suspended overhead. The virgin brides who dress the Su Cumpoidori, his effeminate, godlike status and the throwing of grain all suggest older fertility rites heralding spring.

The event is held over two days, Sunday and *martedí grasso* (Fat Tuesday or Mardi Gras). At noon the Su Cumpoidori is 'born'. He sits on a table (the altar) and is reverently clothed and masked by the *sas massaieddas* (young virgins). From this point on he cannot touch the ground and is carried to his horse, which is almost as elaborately dressed as he. The Su Cumpoidori's white mask is framed by a stiff mantilla on top of which he wears a black top hat. In his hand he carries a sceptre decorated with violets and periwinkles with which he blesses the crowd. It is his task to start the Sartiglia, the race to the star, which he does with two other knights, his *segundu* (second) and *terzu* (third), who all try to pierce the star. The more times they strike it, the more luck they bring to the coming year. The last ritual the Su Cumpoidori performs is the Sa Remada, where he gallops along the course lying on his back. Then the games are open to acrobatic riders who perform feats that draw gasps from the crowd.

pesce all'oriental (vegetable tempura) and a hearty minestrone.

Ristorante Craf (☎ 0783 37 06 89; Via de Castro 34; meals €30; ☽ Mon-Sat) Craf is housed in a former 17th-century granary with vaulted dining rooms and folksy clutter. The menu includes a delicious *panne frattau* (Sardinian bread soup), fish dishes and, if you're game, *asinello in padella al funghi* (donkey with mushrooms).

Da Gino (☎ 0783 7 14 28; Via Tirso 13; meals €25-30; ☽ Mon-Sat Sep-Jul) This place has been around in one form or another since the 1930s. Seafood dishes, using fish from the nearby lagoons, stand out. *Aragosta* (lobster) is one of the house specialities. It also has an enticing *antipasti* trolley and does great risottos prepared in various ways.

Cocco Dessì (☎ 0783 30 07 35; Via Tirso 31; meals €40-45; ☽ lunch Tue-Sun) A grand turn-of-the-century façade gives way to a surprisingly modern interior with a huge curved bar. It's popular for its excellent food, including some non-Sardinian dishes, which you can enjoy either in the restaurant or under the gazebo.

La Grotta (Via Diego Contini 3-7; pizza €6-8; ☽ 7.30-11pm daily) Every day you'll see the little truck arrive to deliver logs for La Grotta's wood-burning stove – the sign of a good pizzeria. It's only open in the evenings, when the cosy wooden interior fills with a laid-back clientele.

Gelateria Pinna (☎ 0783 7 00 32; Piazza Mariano 38; ☽ Mon-Sat) A great gelateria. Alongside all your favourite flavours are some lesser-known concoctions. Wine gelato is becoming a hit in Italy and here you can try the Passito di Sardegna Duchessa ice cream, an intoxicating cone.

DRINKING

Lola Mundo (Piazzetta Corrias 14; snacks €1.50-2.50; ☽ 8am-9pm Mon-Thu, 8am-1am Fri & Sat) A stylish, modern bar with sleepy jazz tunes playing in the background. By day people hang out here reading the paper and at lunchtime take a glass of wine with crudités at the marble-topped bar. There are also a few tables outside to take advantage of those warm summer evenings.

For anything busier you need to head down to Marina di Torregrande.

SHOPPING

Specialità Sarde (☎ 0783 7 27 25; Via Figoli 41; ☽ closed Sun) A one-stop showroom for all the gourmet Sardinian goodies, including cheese and all kinds of fancy fare in jars. Basketry is also on sale.

Cantina Sociale della Vernaccia (☎ 0783 3 31 55; Via Oristano 149, Rimedio) Most of Oristano's local Vernaccia producers bring their grapes here to be crushed. You can also buy wine from the cantina's shop.

GETTING THERE & AWAY
Bus

The main intercity bus station is on Via Cagliari. ARST (Azienda Regionale Sarda Trasporti) buses leave for destinations all over the province as well as to Sassari (four daily) and Cagliari (three daily). Buses leave once every half-hour for the 10- to 15-minute trip to Santa Giusta.

Car & Motorcycle

Oristano is on the SS131 highway between Cagliari, Sassari and Porto Torres. Branch highways head off to the northeast for Nuoro and Olbia.

AUTHOR'S CHOICE

Hotel Lucrezia (☎ 0783 41 20 78; www.hotellucrezia.it; Via Roma 14/a, Riola Sardo; s/d €80/120; ☒ ▯) This ancient *cortile* (courtyard house) has been in David Loy's family since the 17th century. It's named after his great-great-grandmother, who would have used all the traditional elements that David has restored – the well in the courtyard, the wine cellar, the olive press and the old bread oven. Fronting the main house is a loggia supported by Roman columns, and across the main door there's a pergola weighed down by wisteria. The inside is no less enchanting. The lounge with its enormous stone fireplace leads to a billiard room and the three largest rooms, Mentha, Lavanda and Salvia. They're gorgeously furnished with 18th-century antique beds and mighty wooden wardrobes. Bikes are provided, and occasionally wine tastings and cookery courses are on offer. David and the manageress, Francesca, are delightful company and full of local titbits that make for a perfect holiday. You'll find Lucrezia 9km north of Oristano in the village of Riola Sardo.

Train
The main Trenitalia train station is in Piazza Ungheria, east of the town centre. Six or seven trains run between Oristano and Abbasanta and Paulilatino to the northeast.

As many as 20 trains, sometimes involving a change en route, run between Oristano and Cagliari (€4.75, one to two hours). Only a handful make the run from Oristano to Sassari (€7.75, 2½ hours, four daily). For Olbia there are only two through trains (€9.25, three hours); otherwise you have to change at Chilivani.

GETTING AROUND
Bus
The town centre is easily done on foot, although you will probably want to use buses to get in from the train station. The *rossa* (red) and *verde* (green) lines stop at the station and terminate in Piazza Mariano.

Oristano city buses on the *azzurra* (blue) line run from Via Cagliari to Marina di Torregrande (€0.57, 15 minutes).

Car & Motorcycle
Parking is fairly easy if you leave your car a little out of the centre (such as in the streets south of Via Cagliari). **Parking** (per hr €0.60; 8.30am-1pm & 4-7.30pm Mon-Sat) is available in the blue spaces in the centre.

Taxi
You'll find that taxis tend to congregate at the train station and around Piazza Roma. You can also call a **taxi** (☎ 0783 7 02 80, 0783 7 43 28).

AROUND ORISTANO

Oristano's main beach, the **Marina di Torregrande**, lies 7km west and is named after its stout Aragonese watchtower. The real focus, however, is the impressive broad beach that stretches over 1km long, shelving gently into the waves. It's perfect for a family day out.

Behind the sand is an esplanade with cheerful restaurants and bars that comes to life during the evening *passeggiata*. It's a very Italian scene, with suntanned locals promenading, kids running about and some awful but jaunty local pop tunes emanating from the terrace bars. You can hire loungers (€10) and umbrellas (€10) on the beach, and in summer **Eolo** (☎ 335 38 44 40; www.eolowindsurf.com, in Italian) hires out windsurfing equipment (€10 to €15 per hour).

Out of season you'll find the holiday homes shuttered and most of the restaurants closed.

At the southern end of town, **Spinnaker** (☎ 0783 2 20 74; www.spinnakervacanze.com, in Italian; Marina di Torregrande; camp sites per adult & tent €14, bungalows €90; 🏊 🐕) is a very well run camp site with a pool and its own private stretch of beach. There are plenty of activities on offer as well as bikes for hire. The site is also nice and shady, but beware of the mosquitoes.

Da Giovanni (☎ 0783 2 20 51; Via Colombo 8; meals €35; Tue-Sun) is one of those Italian restaurants with a frighteningly bland exterior serving up sublime food. The interior is lit like a stage, but the décor is immaterial beside the succulent lobster and shrimp ravioli, followed by the exquisite *capone* (rockfish) stewed in Vernaccia.

The pick of the culinary crop fronting the palm-flanked promenade, **Maestrale** (☎ 0783 2 21 21; Lungomare Torregrande; meals €35; Tue-Sun) puts the emphasis firmly on fishy fare, including a recommended seafood risotto.

The beach strip is lined with summertime drinkeries. A few kilometres inland on the road to Cabras is **Banana Disco** (☎ 338 235 75 40; Strada Torregrande-Cabras; Thu-Sun), which does everything from eurotrance to mainstream Italian and international disco pop.

Oristano city buses on the *azzurra* line run from Via Cagliari to Marina di Torregrande (€0.57, 20 minutes).

SOUTH OF ORISTANO

The fertile plains south of Santa Giusta were once carpeted by thick cork woods but are now long gone, replaced by wide open farmland, the result of Mussolini's drainage and reclamation policies of 1919.

At the heart of it all a new town, Mussolinia, was established. Most of the colonists encouraged to come here were from the northern Italian Romagna and Veneto regions. After the war Mussolinia was rebaptised Arborea and the land was gradually distributed to independent farmers, again mostly northern Italians. Among the fruits

ORISTANO & THE WEST

of all this effort are the light Terralba red wines and occasional rosés.

SANTA GIUSTA
pop 4540

Santa Giusta grew on the site of ancient Othoca, a Punic foundation later expanded by the Romans. Today it's virtually a satellite of Oristano.

Dominating the centre of town is the proud **Basilica di Santa Giusta**, which rises like a galleon aground in the lagoon. Built between 1135 and 1145, the basilica was one of the first Pisan-Romanesque churches built on the island. Up close it is long and low, with blind arcades and a simple Lombard façade. The interior is supported by columns and decorated with marble and granite from Tharros. Its austere beauty perfectly suits the sparse landscape.

The church is the centre of four days of celebrations around 14 May, the **Festa di Santa Giusta**.

Six kilometres to the south shimmers the **Stagno S'Ena Arrubia**, a flamingo hot spot. If you are taken with the place, you can stay in the quiet and basic **Camping S'Ena Arrubia** (☎ /fax 0783 80 20 11; camp sites per adult/tent €6.50/7; ☼ Jul & Aug). It's on the southwest side of the lagoon (follow the signs from the main Santa Giusta–Arborea road).

Buses from Oristano's main bus station leave once every half-hour to Santa Giusta (€0.57, 10 to 15 minutes).

ARBOREA
pop 3990

At the very heart of Mussolini's grand land-reclamation scheme lies this odd town. A quiet place, its focus is the immaculate **Piazza Maria Ausiliatrice**, a patiently tended and flourishing garden. It is flanked by architectural whimsy of the 1920s and '30s. The neo-Gothic **Chiesa del Cristo Redentore**, delightfully decorated inside, vies for attention with the Art Nouveau **Municipio**.

Inside the latter, on the 1st floor, six glass cases contain a **collection** (admission free; ☼ 10am-1pm & 3.30-5.30pm Mon & Tue, 10am-1pm Wed-Fri, 9-10.30am Sat) of Roman ceramics and other artefacts dug up in the area.

Hotel Gallo Blanco (☎ /fax 0783 80 02 41; Piazza Maria Ausiliatrice 10; s/d €22/39) has nine pleasant rooms, some overlooking the square. You can also get a good meal in its restaurant.

Marina di Arborea
The turn-off for this pleasant and often ignored beach, fronted by a couple of houses, a seaside hotel and pine stands further back, is 2km north of Arborea.

The large **Ala Birdi** (☎ 0783 8 05 00; www.alabirdi .com; Strada a Mare; half board per person €77-99; ☐ ☒ ☒) complex consists of two hotels and a scattering of bungalows catering to various budgets. It's the biggest equestrian centre on the island and one of the most important in Italy, with a stable of Arabian, Andalucian and Sardinian horses. Staff can arrange day excursions to Marceddi, Tharros and the Costa Verde, lessons and courses.

MARCEDDI
This dusty fishing settlement couldn't be much further off the tourist trail. People fishing paddle about in the shallows and a cheerful congregation of passers-by stop to lunch on what they have caught at **Da Lucio** (☎ 0783 86 71 30; Via Lungomare 40; meals €25-30; ☼ lunch Fri-Wed Sep-Jun, lunch & dinner daily Jul & Aug).

Across the **Stagno di Marceddi** rise the hills of the Costa Verde (p97). If you have your own vehicle it will be hard to resist the temptation to cross the narrow causeway and explore this wild and beautiful stretch of Sardinian coast.

You could disappear for a couple of days at the **B&B Brezza Marina** (☎ 338 367 68 86; Viale della Torre; s/d €30-50), just 7km south at Torre dei Corsari (p97).

SINIS PENINSULA

Heading west from Oristano you enter the watery world of Sardinia's largest lagoons – the Stagno di Cabras, Stagno Sale Porcus and Stagno Is Benas – which Punic fishermen navigated with their reed-built *fassoi*. In winter (October to March) the shallow waters fill with migrating birds, the queen of the show being the gorgeous pink flamingo. Otherwise tourists gather for one of Sardinia's finest Punic-Roman sites, and windsurfers let rip off the western beaches.

CABRAS
pop 8700

Cabras is a dusty fishing town of battered-looking houses, where you half expect to hear the theme tune from *High Noon* blaring at you in the empty square. Still this place is the centre of the island's mullet fishing and where Italians flock to buy the golden *bottarga* (mullet roe). The place may not look like much, but you'll certainly eat well here.

Sights

Cabras has a small, dusty **Museo Civico** (☎ 0783 29 06 36; www.penisoladelsinis.it, not in English; Via Tharros 121; admission incl Tharros €4; ⊗ 9am-1pm & 4-8pm Tue-Sun Jun-Sep, 9am-1pm & 3-7pm Tue-Sun Oct-May) at the southern end of town. It houses finds from the prehistoric site of **Cuccuru Is Arrius**, 3km to the southwest, and Tharros.

Festivals & Events

On the first Sunday of September, the Festa di San Salvatore, several hundred young fellows clothed in white mantles set off on the **Corsa degli Scalzi** (Barefoot Race) – an 8km dash to the sanctuary of San Salvatore (right). They bear with them a figure of the Saviour to commemorate an episode in 1506, when townspeople raced to San Salvatore to collect the figure and save it from Moorish sea raiders. They race back to Oristano in similar fashion the following day.

Sleeping

Sa Pedrera (☎ 0783 37 00 40; www.sapedrera.it; Strada Provincial Cabras; s/d €70/97; 🅿 ⊗) You'll find this hacienda-style hotel 7.5km out of town on the way to San Giovanni di Sinis. The low stone buildings are hidden by a lovely lush garden – a real feature in this baking landscape. The rooms are simple but cool and comfortable.

Eating

Sa Funtá (☎ 0783 29 06 85; Via Garibaldi 25; meals €30; ⊗ Wed-Sun) A centuries-old house with its own stone well (you are invited to take a look) in central Cabras. It's an excellent place to try *mrecca* (boiled mullet in pond grass). Then finish with the house dessert, *mustazzolus* (cinnamon biscuits), and a glass of Vernaccia.

Il Caminetto (☎ 0783 39 11 39; Via Cesare Battisti 8; meals €30-35; ⊗ Tue-Sun) Barely 100m away is this bigger place with a classier feel. It's generally packed and again fishy delights are the main melody.

L'Oliveto (☎ 0783 39 26 16; Via Tirso 23; meals €30-35; ⊗ Wed-Mon) Hard to find (head for the

northern end of town and ask) but worth the effort. Set in gardens, it is another centre of seafood excellence with a menu featuring *carpaccio* of salmon, octopus, mussels and *bottarga*.

Getting There & Away

ARST buses run every 20 minutes or so from Oristano (€0.88, 15 minutes).

SAN SALVATORE

Like Cabras, San Salvatore feels like a still from a spaghetti western. In fact it was the location for a number of films back in the 1960s, and the little tiled *cumbessias* (pilgrims' houses) piled up next to each other play the part of a dusty Mexican village rather well.

The place has a much longer and less frivolous history. The unobtrusive 16th-century **Chiesa di San Salvatore** is a *chiesa novenara*, open for nine days in late August to celebrate the feast of San Salvatore, the saint after whom it is named. Pilgrims take up lodgings in the *cumbessias*.

The church was built atop a site of ancient pagan worship. If you are lucky enough to find it open, you will be able to head downstairs to the 4th-century rendition of the site, with faded frescoes and intriguing black-ink drawings and graffiti.

The September **Corsa degli Scalzi** (Barefoot Race) that starts in Cabras ends here, before turning around to return to Cabras (opposite) the next day.

SAN GIOVANNI DI SINIS

Five kilometres further on you'll come to another important pilgrimage site, San Giovanni di Sinis. On the left as you enter the row of pilgrim accommodation you might spot the low, crouching form of Sardinia's oldest Christian church, the sandstone **Chiesa di San Giovanni di Sinis**. It dates to the 11th century, but incorporates its 6th-century predecessor, a domed, square-based Byzantine church.

The church was abandoned in the 18th century and by the early 1800s was being used as a shepherds' refuge. It was partly restored in 1838 and again in the 1960s and 1990s. In summer you will almost certainly find it open.

It was long-surrounded by a makeshift fishing village, most of whose thatched *domus de cruccuri* (reed huts) have long been demolished.

THARROS

Right at the tip of the promontory where the land snakes into the sea sits the impeccably sited Phoenician city of **Tharros** (☎ 0783 37 00 19; admission incl Museo Civico in Cabras €4; ☉ 9am-sunset). It was among the Phoenicians' most important ports on the long sea voyage west from their home in Lebanon, and now its disarranged ruins are nearly all that remain of Sardinia's imperial legacy, along with Nora in the southwest (see p109). Be sure to visit early in the morning or just before sunset, when the site is at its quietest and most atmospheric.

History

The original town was raised on the site of a *nuraghe* (stone tower) settlement and subsequently absorbed by the Carthaginian empire, which expanded its field of commerce to Italy, Cyprus and even Egypt. But, as it was an important naval base with a tactical position, it was always vulnerable and Rome quickly snatched it after the First Punic War (238 BC).

Tharros remained a key naval town, but once the main road from Cagliari to Porto Torres was finalised it was pretty much sidelined. Nevertheless, the city got a thorough overhaul under the Roman Empire, particularly in the 2nd and 3rd centuries AD. Basalt streets were laid, baths were built, and the aqueduct and other major monuments were raised. Increasingly aggressive raids from the Vandals and later from the North African Muslims led to the decision to abandon the site in the 11th century. Much of the ancient city was subsequently stripped to build a new capital at Oristano.

Sights & Activities

It is impossible to see even a glimmer of the ruins until you enter the site, such is its position on the sloping seaward side of the promontory.

From the entrance you follow a brief stretch of the wide *cardo* (typically the main street in Roman settlements) and reach, on the left, the *castellum aquae* (the city's water reserve). Two lines of pillars can be made out within the square structure. Turn left towards the sea and you pass the remains of

a **Punic temple** before arriving at the seaside. Here was one set of **thermal baths**, and to the north are the remains of a **palaeo-Christian baptistry**. At the southernmost point of the settlement along the coast is another set of baths, dating to the 3rd century AD. On the bare rise north of the ticket office was the *nuraghe* village and, later, the Phoenician and Punic *tophet* (sacred burial ground for children and babies).

You may visit the nearby late-16th-century **Torre di San Giovanni** (admission €2; ☉ 9am-sunset) watchtower, which is occasionally used for photo and art exhibitions and commands magnificent views north along the coast and south to Capo San Marco. There is nothing to stop you wandering down the dirt tracks to Capo San Marco and the lighthouse.

On summer weekend evenings, music and theatre bring the ruins of Tharros to new life. Tickets cost around €15 (available at the site's ticket office) and shows begin at 10pm. Bars and pizzerias line the approach road.

Close to the site is the golden strand of **Spiaggia di San Giovanni di Sinis**, so bring a towel if you fancy a swim after rooting around the ruins. Unlike most of the more northern beaches, San Giovanni is relatively free of rocks and algae. On the other hand, it gets busy.

Getting There & Away

Four ARST buses per day travel here from Oristano in summer (€1.45, 20 to 30 minutes). Parking is free around the Chiesa di San Giovanni di Sinis, but near the site you pay €2 for two hours.

BEACHES

Seventeen kilometres north of Tharros is the popular surfing centre of **Putzu Idu** with its long, sandy beach. It's a basic place backed by beach bars and wind- and kite-surfing outlets such as **Capo Mannu Kite School** (☎ 347 007 70 35; info@capomannukiteschool.it). From here, and next-door Mandriola, you can also take boat excursions to **Capo Mannu** (€6 per person) or the colourfully named **Isola di Mal di Ventre** (Stomachache Island), 10km off the coast to the southwest. It takes about 15 minutes to get there and depending on the tour you'll get to circumnavigate the uninhabited isle before being dropped off on one of the little beaches. One such tour is run by

Mare Mania (☎ 347 191 94 80; www.mare-mania.it, in Italian) in Putzu Idu. It costs €20/15 per adult/child and the boat departs at 10am.

Behind Putzu Idu is the **Stagno Sale Porcus**, a wide, flat lagoon that hosts flamingos in winter and is baked to a shimmering white crust in summer.

A trio of hotels (one each in Putzu Idu, Mandriola and Su Pallosu) offer the option of staying here and a handful of restaurant-pizzerias keep hunger at bay.

MONTI FERRU

The thickly wooded highland of Monti Ferru, culminating in the 1050m peak of Monte Urtigu, formed a naturally protective barrier for the medieval Giudicato d'Arborea. Its slopes are dotted with market towns well worth exploring. Seneghe produces the island's finest olive oil, and you can sample the famous Bue Rosso beef at a number of local restaurants. Poetry competitions and wine fairs are also on the cards if you time your visit right.

MILIS
pop 1700
Surrounded by the citrus gardens that enchanted French poet Paul Valéry and made it prosperous, Milis is a quiet and happy place. People from surrounding villages such as Seneghe will tell you the people of Milis are a little smug, too. Centuries-old rivalries have not abated, and while only a few kilometres separate Milis from other towns, a gulf divides them. Even now, they say, Milis lads wouldn't dare go looking for girls in neighbouring towns, nor vice versa!

The **Chiesa di San Paolo**, a Romanesque church at the entrance to town, is Tuscan in style and contains several interesting paintings executed by Catalan masters in the 16th century. Closer to the centre is the 14th-century **Chiesa di San Sebastiano** with its basalt bell tower and, opposite, the crimson **Villa Boyle**, an 18th-century residence now used as a cultural centre.

In early November (around the 10th to the 12th), Milis holds the **Rassegna del Vino Novello** (Festival of Young Wine), an occasion when Sardinia's wine producers gather to show off their best products. You can do the rounds sampling the wines and grazing the food stalls that line the streets.

SENEGHE
pop 1970
Five kilometres north of Milis lies Seneghe, its narrow streets lined with dark stone houses. Sartos, the local olive oil, is a winner of Italy's most prestigious award, the Ercole. Seneghe is also in the heart of cattle-raising country. The russet-red Bue Rosso cows are bred only here and in Mòdica in Sicily, and gourmets consider their beef to be some of the finest in Italy.

A useful point of reference for hikers who want to get to know Monti Ferru is the Seneghe-based **Benthos** (☎ /fax 0783 5 45 62; Via Lamarmora 15), run by Raimondo Cossa.

You can fill your bags with local goodies from **Enogastronomia del Montiferru** (☎ 0783 5 44 50; www.enogastronomiamontiferru.com, in Italian; Corso Umberto 141/b; ⏱ 8.30am-1pm & 3.30-7pm Mon-Fri).

Don't leave without eating at the **Osteria Al Bue Rosso** (☎ 0783 5 43 84; Piazzale Montiferru 3/4; meals around €25), housed in a 1920s dairy. Here you can try an impressive array of dishes based on Bue Rosso beef. The organically produced house wine is good, and you are welcome to just sit back and enjoy the views of the surrounding hills. You'll find it near the town's Narbolia exit. Management can also advise on a number of characterful B&Bs in the area.

BONARCADO
pop 1665
From Milis or Seneghe you can make for the village of Bonarcado (no great friend of the Milesi either!), at whose northern exit stands the modest Romanesque **Chiesa di Santa Maria** (once part of a medieval monastery) and, a short walk away, the curious **Santuario della Madonna di Bonacattu**, a rudimentary chapel built on a Greek cross plan and topped by a simple dome. Although expanded in the 13th century, the original structure dates to about the 7th century.

The main pilgrimage to the site is from 18 to 20 September.

SANTU LUSSURGIU
pop 2620 / elev 503m
Eight kilometres north of Bonarcado, Santu Lussurgiu lies inside an ancient volcanic crater on the eastern edge of Monti Ferru.

Whichever way you approach it you will end up on the main road that follows the crater's rim and affords panoramic views of the town. Some 18th-century houses huddle with a trio of churches in the heart of the old town. Long known for its crafts (less so nowadays), Santu Lussurgiu is a centre for carpet weaving, woodwork and leatherwork.

Clever Gabriela Belloni has converted her historic courtyard house into a hotel, **Antica Dimora del Gruccione** (☎ 0783 55 20 35; www.anti cadimora.com, in Italian; Via Michele Obinu 31; incl break-fast/half board per person €38/60). The place oozes character with its double-flanked staircase, giant wooden floorboards and silk wallpaper. The rooms in the main house on the 1st floor are the best, and the ground-floor apartment (sleeps four) is huge. Breakfast is served in an impressive barrel-vaulted dining room.

Just off the central piazza is the gorgeous restaurant **Sas Benas** (☎ 0783 55 08 70; Piazza San Giovanni; meals €35), run by a group of musicians. The mouth-watering food is a symphony of local flavours – Bue Rosso with chicory and flakes of *casitzolu* cheese; Santa Lussurgiu sausages; *culurgiones* (a kind of pasta) stuffed with almond paste and fennel, mushrooms and wild boar – all cooked with Seneghe olive oil. Soft classical music and low lighting set a romantic tone. The restaurant can also arrange rooms dotted throughout the historic centre.

SAN LEONARDO DE SIETE FUENTES

The Santu Lussurgiu–Cuglieri road is a refreshing mountain route that leads north and then west towards the coast. Just 4km out of Santu Lussurgiu, a branch road runs north for Macomer, but you only need to follow it for 2km, admiring the panorama across the eastern plains, to arrive in this oasis.

To those accustomed to the dry Sardinian landscape, this cool retreat comes as a shock. Wander up through the shady park, full of oaks and elms, to the seven taps from which pours abundant fresh water. Even in the heat of midsummer you can almost feel chilly here.

The charming 12th-century **Chiesa di San Leonardo**, now a mix of Romanesque and Gothic styles, was the property of the Knights of St John of Jerusalem, and in the past a hospital flanked the church.

CUGLIERI
pop 3030 / elev 483m

Instead of proceeding north to Macomer, turn back south and head west for Cuglieri. The road passes through the hill country of Monti Ferru and snakes down through dense forest towards Cuglieri. Long before you reach the town, you'll see the silvery dome of the **Basilica di Santa Maria della Neve**.

Cuglieri (which you pass through on your way to Bosa) is another good place to buy the region's olive oil. The **Azienda Agricola Peddio** (☎ 0785 36 92 54; Corso Umberto 95; ⏰ 8.30am-1pm & 3-8pm Mon-Fri) is on the main road. A litre of oil costs between €5.50 and €7.50.

Albergo Desogos (☎ /fax 0785 3 96 60; Via Cugia 6; s/d €20/36), Cuglieri's only hotel, is tucked away in the middle of the old town. Rooms are basic but OK, and the restaurant is known all over the area. Try the Spanish-style *panadas* (pies filled with meat and game).

SANTA CATERINA DI PITTINURI & AROUND

A low-key resort, Santa Caterina offers a reasonable beach, closed off at the southern end by dramatic cliffs.

A few kilometres south are the very scanty remains of the ancient town of **Cornus** and an adjacent early-Christian site (closed to the public). A yellow sign to Cornus 1km south of Santa Caterina points to a dirt road leading to the site.

The next bay, **S'Archittu**, has little sand but the enticing water is a deep emerald green. Around the following bend, **Torre del Pozzo** (also known as Torre Su Putzu) has a small, sheltered beach.

From here the SS292 curves gently away from the coast. About 3km south of Torre del Pozzo you'll see signs for the first of three camping grounds. A couple of hundred metres on are the other two – turn off here (if you have a car) to access the northern end of the long Is Arenas strand.

La Capanna is a classic summer club in Torre del Pozzo. It has been going since the early 1980s and still attracts clubbers from all over the province on Friday and Saturday nights.

Buses between Oristano and Bosa stop at Santa Caterina, S'Archittu (from Oristano €1.76, 30 minutes) and Cuglieri (€3.58, one hour). They will stop on request at the camping grounds.

DETOUR: FORDONGIANUS

Southwest of Lago Omedeo, almost at the confluence of the Tirso and Mannu Rivers, sits the spa town of Fordongianus, most easily reached along the SS388 from Oristano, although country roads weave down from Abbasanta and Lago Omedeo.

The spa waters here were known to Ptolemy, and the Romans took little time setting up a health spa here, renaming it Forum Traiani. Their 1st century AD baths, the **Terme Romane** (☎ 0783 6 01 57; www.forumtraiani.it, in Italian; admission incl Casa Aragonese €4; ☒ 9am-1pm & 3-7pm summer, 9am-1pm & 2.30-5pm winter), are still in operation today. The centre of the complex is a rectangular pool that was once surrounded by a portico (of which only one side now stands). Around it were other pools and service rooms.

Outside the perimeter are two 'baths' into which steaming-hot water pours. In one locals are allowed to wash clothes, as they have done for centuries, and in the other they may clean containers of milk and other nontoxic materials. In winter the steam floating off the Rio Tirso as the thermal water gushes in is an eerie sight. If you arrive when the centre is closed you can take a dip in the river – but be careful as it is really hot (48°C)! In town, don't be tempted to drink from the many water fountains – the water is far from potable.

The red trachyte stone of which everything is built lends the village a rosy glow. As red as the rest is the lovely late-16th-century **Casa Aragonese** (admission incl Terme Romane €4; ☒ 9.30am-1pm & 3-7.30pm Tue-Sun, to 5.30pm Oct-Mar). Although there isn't a great deal to see inside, it's worth a quick look just to see how a noble Catalan family lived. The strange statues outside, also in the ubiquitous trachyte, are the result of an annual sculpture competition held here.

A few buses run from Oristano (€1.76, 40 minutes).

LAGO OMEDEO CIRCUIT

Although it is possible to reach some of these places by public transport, it is frequently difficult and time consuming. Your own vehicle is infinitely preferable, especially for the prehistoric sites of Santa Cristina and Nuraghe Losa.

SANTA CRISTINA

For thousands of years men and women have practised their faith here. *Nuraghe* people gathered around the temple well in the remote past, and Christian pilgrims still visit the Chiesa di Santa Cristina today.

The **site** (admission incl Museo Archeologico -Etnografico in Paulilatino €3.50; ☒ 9am-1hr before sunset) is just east off the SS131, a few kilometres south of Paulilatino. Buy tickets in the bar and wander out through the garden to the **Chiesa di Santa Cristina** (built around 1200) and its surrounding *muristenes* (pilgrims' huts originally for Camaldolesi monks). The church and huts open for nine days to celebrate the feast days of Santa Cristina, around the second Sunday in May, and San Raffaele Arcangelo, on the fourth Sunday in October.

Beyond lies the outline of a huge *nuraghe* village (1500 to 1200 BC), set in a peaceful grove of olives. The site was inhabited not only by ancient Sards but right up to the early Middle Ages. Its centrepiece (about 150m east of the church) is the extraordinary temple well, which dates to the late Bronze Age (11th to 9th century BC) and was excavated in the 1960s.

Its granite blocks are perfectly cut to form a keyhole shape in the earth, through which you descend a flight of stairs to the well at the bottom. From here you can gaze up at the perfectly constructed *tholos* (conical ceiling) above. A hole in the *tholos* allows light into the dark well shaft, and every 18 years, one month and two days the full moon shines directly through the aperture into the well. This is next due to happen in December 2007, and pilgrims are already preparing for what will be an extraordinary pilgrimage.

Otherwise you can catch the yearly equinoxes in March and September, when the sun lights up the stairway down to the well.

PAULILATINO

pop 2460

Finds from the Santa Cristina site are displayed in the small **Museo Archeologico-Etnografico** (admission incl Santa Cristina €3.50; ☒ 9am-1pm & 4.30-7.30pm Tue-Sun May-Sep, 9am-1pm

ORISTANO & THE WEST

& 3.30-5.30pm Tue-Sun Oct-Apr), set in a proud village mansion in Paulilatino. The museum also contains a few items typical of ethnographical museums, including farm and domestic implements from tougher rural days. The Santa Cristina ticket allows you to visit the museum on a separate day.

NURAGHE LOSA

A few kilometres north of Paulilatino and barely a few hundred metres west off the SS131 highway stands one of the most impressive **nuraghe** (☎ 0785 5 48 23; www .nuraghelosa.net, in Italian; admission €3.50; ☼ 9am-1pm & 3-7pm) on the island.

The area around the *nuraghe* is a neatly kept garden, making the building appear even more dinosaur-like against the landscape. Although its central tower has been lopped off, the sturdy basalt structure, which dates to the Middle Bronze Age (1500 BC), is still an impressive sight. It's triangular in shape and you enter the backlit interior via one of the side towers. A narrow corridor leads into the main tower. The keystones at the top of the conical structure could be

moved to let in more light. Passages lead left and right off the corridor to two towers, one fully enclosed, the other open. A tiny entrance on the north corner of the triangle leads into a small tower.

There's a museum on site where the helpful guardian can show you what the *nuraghe* may originally have looked like. Otherwise the on-site shop sells an excellent selection of literature and serves a nice cup of coffee.

Two kilometres north of Nuraghe Losa along the SS131 is the turn-off for Abbasanta. Take this exit and turn left over the bridge to find the sign for **Mandra Edera** (☎ 0785 56 23 00; www.mandraedera.it, in Italian; d/ste €60/75; Ⓟ ✖ ☎) on your right. Originally famous for its restaurant cooking, the place now offers accommodation in a handful of tastefully decorated bungalows dotted around the farm. The big draw, however, is the stables. You can choose from several horse-riding activities (€15 per hour), ranging from beginners' lessons to exciting night rides. In the evening everyone comes together in the convivial atmosphere of the dining room.

THE ARDENT GUARD

On 6 and 7 July Sedilo hosts Oristano's most exciting festival, **S'Ardia**, when nearly 50,000 people pack themselves into the tiny village to see Sardinia's most reckless and dangerous horse race, which makes Sienna's Palio look positively pedestrian.

It celebrates the courage and daring of the Roman Emperor Constantine, who defeated the vastly superior forces of Maxentius at Rome's Ponte Milvio in AD 312. Since then, however, the festival has received a Christian gloss. Tales say Constantine received a vision before the battle, in which he saw a cross inscribed with the words 'In Hoc Signo Vinces' ('in this sign you will conquer'). He took the sign as the insignia for his forces and the following year he passed an edict granting the Christians religious freedom. So, locally, although not officially, he was promoted to St Constantine (Santu Antine in the local dialect).

The race circles his sanctuary and the stone cross bearing his insignia. One man – the Prima Pandela (First Flag) – is chosen to bear Constantine's yellow-brocade standard. He selects two of the best horsemen to ride with him, and they choose three cohorts each. These men will be the Prima Pandela's guard and, armed with huge sticks, they will strive to prevent the hundred other horsemen from passing him. To be chosen as the Prima Pandela is the highest honour of the village. Only a man who has proven his courage and horsemanship and substantiated his faith can carry the flag.

On 6 July the procession prays in front of the stone cross and the riders are blessed by the parish priest. In theory the priest should start the race, but in practice it is the Prima Pandela who chooses his moment and flies off at a gallop down the hill. In seconds the other horsemen are after him, aiming to pass him before he reaches the victory arch. Hundreds of riflemen shoot off blanks, exciting the horses. The stampede towards the narrow entrance of the victory arch is the most dangerous moment, as any mistake would mean running into the stone columns at top speed. In 2002 one rider died. If all goes well, the Prima Pandela passes through the arch and races on to circle the sanctuary, to deafening cheers from the crowd.

NORTH OF ORISTANO

North of the pretty Monti Ferru region the land flattens out towards Macomer. Originally a big dairy-farming town, nowadays Macomer is primarily a railway centre and transport hub for the western side of the island. Directly west, however, you'll find the pretty medieval town of Bosa.

MACOMER

pop 11,050

Macomer is an untidy place with no discernible centre, but you may find yourself travelling through here, as it is the main rail and bus junction for Alghero in the northwest and Nuoro in the east.

In town you can pass some time at the modest **Museo Etnografico** (☎ 0785 7 04 75; Corso Umberto 225), which displays typical furnishings and utensils from the small-town world. Those with a car can visit the **Nuraghe di Santa Barbara**, just north of the SS131 about 2km north of Macomer. On the other side of the highway is the more ruined **Nuraghe Ruiu**. Finally the **Nuraghe di Santa Sabina** is south of Silanus and 15km east of Macomer. It has a cute neighbour in the form of a Byzantine chapel.

Hotel Su Talleri (☎ /fax 0785 7 14 91; Via Cavour; s/d €30/45; ✕) is probably the best of the town's three hotels. Its homy en-suite rooms are reached by an odd external staircase. It's just off Corso Umberto and a stone's throw from the museum.

Ristorante Su Talleri (☎ 0785 7 16 99; Corso Umberto I 228; meals €30; ✕ Mon-Sat) does a great version of *ravioli di ricotta* and some fine grilled meats. It has the feel of an anonymous roadside diner, but you'll have no complaints about the grub.

As many as 12 Trenitalia trains make the journey to Macomer from Oristano (€3.05, 45 minutes); six of them originate from Cagliari (€8.15, two to 2½ hours). Five leave from Sassari (€5.90, 1½ to 1¾ hours). A handful of FdS (Ferrovie della Sardegna) trains and up to four buses make the journey between Macomer and Nuoro (€2.63, 1¼ hours).

The Trenitalia and FdS train stations, along with the bus station, are located together at the western edge of town along Corso Umberto.

BOSA

pop 7970

Lying along the narrow banks of the Fiume Temo (Temo River), the town of Bosa presents a pretty picture, its rust-red roofs and lemon-yellow walls offset by the tall green reeds of the river. The Temo is Sardinia's only navigable river, and the Romans established a thriving settlement here. By the early 12th century the Malaspina family (a branch of the Tuscan clan of the same name) had moved in and built their huge castle.

Like Alghero, Bosa made a name for itself with its coral and gold filigree jewellery, but these days Alghero gets the best of the crop. Later, the Savoys established lucrative tanneries here, but these too have since fallen by the wayside. The only things that remain are Bosa's golden Malvasia wine and the hope that tourism will bring this medieval town to life.

Orientation

Sa Costa, Bosa's old town, is like a tight plaster web stretched around the western face of the hill. Below it, Corso Vittorio Emanuele, the main boulevard, runs east to west, taking in the cathedral and Piazza Costituzione before running into the straggly grid of the modern town.

The charming Ponte Vecchio spans the river, on whose southern bank are lined up the former tanneries. Via Nazionale runs west 3km to Bosa Marina, the town's seaside satellite.

Information

Banco di Sardegna (Piazza IV Novembre) You can change money here. Has an ATM.

Farmacia Sardu (Corso Vittorio Emanuele 51) A handy pharmacy.

Hospital (☎ 0785 37 31 07; Via Salvatore Parpaglia)

Information Point (☎ 0785 37 71 08; ✕ 10am-1pm & 7-10pm Mon-Fri Jun-Sep) In Bosa Marina train station.

Post office (Via Pischedda; ✕ 8.15am-1.15pm Mon-Sat)

Tourist medical service (☎ 0785 37 46 15; Viale Italia) Just off the beach at Bosa Marina.

Tourist office (☎ 0785 37 61 07; www.infobosa.it, in Italian; Via Alberto Azuni 5; ✕ 9am-1pm Mon-Fri & 6-8pm Tue & Thu, 9.30am-1.30pm Sat) The main tourist office; has some good brochures.

Web Copy (☎ 0785 37 20 49; fax 0785 37 21 91; Via Vincenzo Gioberti 12; per hr €6; ✕ 9am-1pm & 5-8.30pm Mon-Sat) Has six fast computers.

BOSA

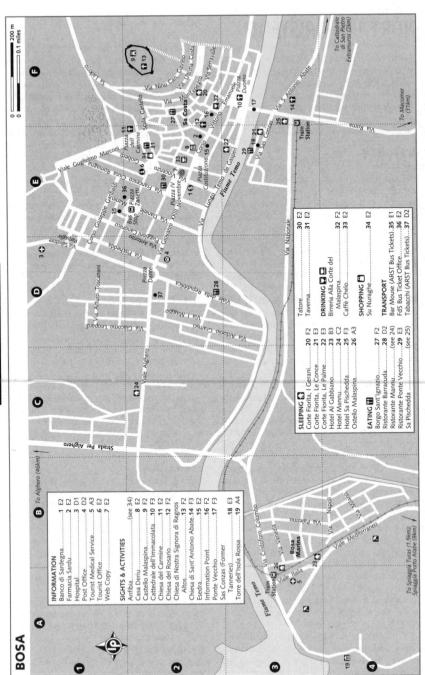

INFORMATION
Banco di Sardegna........................1	E2
Farmacia Sardu............................2	E2
Hospital......................................3	D1
Post Office...................................4	D2
Tourist Medical Service................5	A3
Tourist Office..............................6	E2
Web Copy....................................7	E2

SIGHTS & ACTIVITIES
Anfibia................................(see 34)	
Casa Deriu..................................8	E2
Castello Malaspina......................9	F2
Cattedrale dell'Immacolata.......10	F3
Chiesa del Carmine...................11	E2
Chiesa del Rosario....................12	F2
Chiesa di Nostra Signora di Regnos	
Altos.......................................13	F2
Chiesa di Sant'Antonio Abate..14	F3
Esedra.....................................15	E2
Information Point.....................16	F2
Ponte Vecchio.........................17	F3
Sas Conzas (Former	
Tanneries)...............................18	E3
Torre dell'Isola Rossa...............19	A4

SLEEPING
Corte Fiorita, I Gerani..............20	F2
Corte Fiorita, Le Conce............21	E3
Corte Fiorita, Le Palme............22	E3
Hotel Al Gabbiano...................23	B3
Hotel Mannu...........................24	C2
Hotel Sa Pischedda..................25	F3
Ostello Malaspina....................26	A3

EATING
Borgo Sant'Ignazio..................27	F2
Ristorante Barracuda................28	D2
Ristorante Mannu..............(see 24)	
Ristorante Ponte Vecchio.........29	E3
Sa Pischedda....................(see 25)	
Tatore......................................30	E2
Taverna...................................31	E2

DRINKING
Birreria Alla Corte del	
Malaspina...............................32	F2
Caffè Chelo.............................33	E2

SHOPPING
Su Nuraghe.............................34	E2

TRANSPORT
Bar Mouse (ARST Bus Tickets)...35	E1
FdS Bus Ticket Office................36	E2
Tabacchi (ARST Bus Tickets)....37	D2

To Cattedrale
di San Pietro
Extramuros (2km)

To Macomer
(31km)

To Alghero (46km)

Strada Per Alghero

To Spiaggia Turas (1.5km);
Spiaggia Porto Alabe (8km)

ORISTANO & THE WEST

Sights

The mighty walls and towers of the **Castello Malaspina** (☎ 0785 37 32 86; adult/concession €2/1; ⏰ 10am-12.30pm & 5-8pm Jul-Sep), also known as the Castello di Serravalle, still dominate the town despite having seen much better days. The castle was closed for renovation at the time of writing. Inside is the humble-looking chapel, the **Chiesa di Nostra Signora di Regnos Altos**, which houses an extraordinary and anonymous 14th-century fresco cycle, a veritable who's who of famous saints ranging from a giant St Christopher through a party of Franciscans to St Lawrence in the middle of his martyrdom on the grill.

You can get here by virtually any route climbing up through the maze of lanes in Sa Costa. It is an atmospheric warren, and you'll notice that most of the houses have an opening onto two streets, one much steeper than the other.

At the bottom of the hill, the **Cattedrale dell'Immacolata** (Piazza Duomo) is a rare if not overly riveting example of rococo (officially called Piedmontese baroque). From here the main boulevard, Corso Vittorio Emanuele, leads west past elegant 17th-century houses lent a certain *je ne sais quoi* by their airy wrought-iron balconies.

On the same street, the **Chiesa del Rosario** is known above all for the unsightly clock that juts out into the street from its white-washed façade.

Casa Deriu (Corso Vittorio Emanuele 59; adult/concession €3/1.50; ⏰ 11am-1pm & 7.30-11pm Tue-Sun) is a grand mansion that today doubles as a museum with a mixed vocation. The 2nd floor is a remake of a 19th-century interior. On the 1st floor you can see a display on the old tanning business as well as typical products from the surrounding region. The top floor is dedicated to Melkiorre Melis (1889–1982), an important exponent of the applied arts in Italy.

At the northern end of the old town, the **Chiesa del Carmine**, located on the square of the same name, is from the same period as the cathedral.

Across the **Ponte Vecchio** line up the former 18th-century tanneries known as **Sas Conzas**, which were still in business shortly after WWII and are now a heritage site. One or two restaurants operate in them in summer.

East of the Ponte Vecchio is the little **Chiesa di Sant'Antonio Abate**, focus of a town festival dedicated to the saint on 16 and 17 January and again at Carnevale time.

Two kilometres upstream is the isolated former **Cattedrale di San Pietro Extramuros** (☎ 0785 37 32 86; admission €1; ⏰ 10am-12.30pm & 5-8pm Tue-Sun), with its Gothic façade (look at the detail above the central doorway) and largely Romanesque interior.

Activities

The countryside around Bosa is a pretty crisscross of vineyards and rivers. To get out and explore it, contact Marcello at **Anfibia** (☎ 328 831 51 17; www.anfibia.it; Via Marghine 8), who can arrange some wonderful ecotours including activities such as kayaking, cycling and visiting local vineyards. The organisation aims to put travellers in touch with local people in an effort to create a more happy and sustainable form of tourism. Tours cost around €42 per person and require a group of six. Anfibia also hires out bikes (€2/12 per hour/day) and kayaks (€6.50/20 per hour/day) so you can do your own thing.

Esedra (☎ 0785 37 42 56; www.esedrasardegna.it; Corso Vittorio Emanuele 64), located on the *corso*, arranges treks and sells Isola handicrafts.

For information on the Strada della Malvasia di Bosa (a wine trail around Bosa's vineyards), pop in to the **information point** (Via Giovanni XXIII; ⏰ 11am-1.30pm Mon-Sat). Staff can give you a list of the producers.

Less than 1km away is Bosa Marina's sandy beach. It's a busy family spot and is popular with windsurfers. You can hire boards on the beach. A couple of **diving** outfits operate here, too.

The squat Catalano-Aragonese **Torre dell'Isola Rossa** (watchtower) stands guard at the end of the beach. Occasionally temporary exhibitions are held here.

Festivals & Events

Bosa's **Carnevale** kicks off with a burning pyre outside the Chiesa di Sant'Antonio Abate and follows with all sorts of parades in the succeeding days. The last day, *martedì grasso*, is the most intriguing. The morning funereal lament for the end of the Carnevale is followed in the evening by a search for the *giolzi*, symbol of carnival and sex, by groups of boisterous locals dressed in white. It's not clear what happens if they find it, or indeed just what it is!

For four days around the first Sunday of August Bosa celebrates the **Festa di Santa Maria del Mare**. Fishers form a colourful procession of boats to accompany a figure of the Virgin Mary along the river from Bosa Marina to the cathedral.

In the second week of September folk celebrate the **Festa di Nostra Signora di Regnos Altos**. The old-town streets are bedecked with huge palm fronds, flowers and *altarittos* (votive altars).

Sleeping

A handful of hotels in Bosa are complemented by a few others down the track at Bosa Marina. They are open year-round.

BOSA

Corte Fiorita (☎ 0785 37 70 58; www.albergo-diffuso.it; Via Lungo Temo de Gasperi 45; s/d €54/90; 🍴 🖳) At last someone has started to restore Bosa's charming houses. This is a winning collection of three properties – Le Palme, I Gerani and Le Conce – dotted around Bosa's historic centre. The restoration has been carried out sensitively, and the views over the river and the old town are magical. Check-in for all three properties is at Le Palme.

Hotel Sa Pischedda (☎ 0785 37 30 65; fax 0785 37 70 54; www.hotelsapischedda.it; Via Roma 2; s/d €70/86; 🅿 🍴) The apricot façade of this restored house greets you on the southern side of the Ponte Vecchio. Several rooms have original frescoed ceilings, some are split-level, and there are terraces overlooking the river. This place is a real gem, and the restaurant is exceptional (see right).

Hotel Mannu (☎ 0785 37 53 06; fax 0785 37 53 08; Viale Alghero; s/d €50/79; 🍴) A big, modern yellow villa with comfortable, if bland, rooms. The real feature is the shaded restaurant, which has a solid local reputation (see right).

BOSA MARINA

Hotel Al Gabbiano (☎ 0785 37 41 23; fax 0785 37 41 09; Viale Mediterraneo; s/d €56/78; 🍴) Barely a Frisbee throw from the beach, the Gabbiano is the best option in the marina. The rooms don't exactly sparkle but are spacious and comfy. Guests have their own sun-bed space on the beach, and sea-view rooms with balconies cost the same.

Ostello Malaspina (☎ /fax 0785 37 50 09; Via Sardegna 1; per person incl breakfast €12) This cheap hostel has 48 beds in dormitories of six to eight. It's very convenient for the beach, but the service could do with a bit of a shake-up. Lockout is between 11am and 4pm. Meals cost €8.

Eating

Sa Pischedda (☎ 0785 37 30 65; Via Roma 2; meals €25-30; 🕑 Wed-Mon, daily summer) Recognised by the Slow Food movement and the Michelin guide, this kitchen is run with passion. The delicious dishes have plenty of aesthetic wow factor. Try the *anguleddas porcini e bottarga* (homemade pasta with mushrooms and mullet roe).

Ristorante Mannu (☎ 0785 37 53 06; Viale Alghero; meals €30-35) This is a great place in summer, when you can eat under the shady bamboo terrace. Despite appearances, this place has a reputation as one of Bosa's best and serves a range of Sardinian and Italian dishes, including spaghetti with lobster.

Ristorante Ponte Vecchio (☎ 0785 37 52 18; Lungo Temo Emilio Scherer; meals €30-35; 🕑 daily Jun-Sep) Has a delightful seating arrangement right on the river with views across to northern Bosa and the Ponte Vecchio. The pasta is good, as are some of the fresh fish options. Other seafood mains are not so great.

Borgo Sant'Ignazio (☎ 0785 37 46 62; Via Sant'Ignazio 33; meals €24; 🕑 Tue-Sun) Hidden amid the web of lanes in the heart of the old town, Sant'Ignazio has a tastefully decorated dining area that's an enticing setting for typical Sardinian dishes. This is a good place to indulge in the earthy flavours of aubergines, mushrooms, ricotta and rich meat sauces.

Tatore (☎ 0785 37 31 04; Via Giuseppe Mannu 13; meals €25-30; 🕑 Thu-Tue, daily summer) This place dishes up whatever its owners find in the fish markets that day. Hardly surprisingly the seafood pasta is good, as is the *zuppa di pesce* (fish soup).

Ristorante Barracuda (☎ 0785 37 45 10; Viale della Repubblica; meals €25-30) Seeming like a suburban house, Barracuda is indeed a family operation. The emphasis is on seafood.

Taverna (Piazza del Carmine; sandwiches €3.50-4; 🕑 Wed-Mon Oct-Apr, daily summer) Stop here for a *panino* in the shade.

Drinking

Like everyone else in Bosa you'll find yourself settling into a routine that includes long bouts sitting in cafés along the *corso* just watching the world go by. The best place to do this is **Caffè Chelo** (☎ 0785 37 30 92; Corso Vittorio Emanuele 71; ☽ 8am-10pm, later in summer), an original Liberty-style café overlooking Piazza Costituzione.

In the evening things go on pretty much the same, but you might want to swap location to the cosy drinking den **Birreria Alla Corte del Malaspina** (Corso Vittorio Emanuele 39; ☽ Mon-Sat).

Shopping

While in Bosa you'll undoubtedly try the local sweet dessert wine, Malvasia. If you want to take a bottle home you'll find a good selection at **Su Nuraghe** (☎ 0785 34 20 43; www.sunuraghe.info, in Italian; Piazza Gioberti). It also stocks *torrone* (nougat), Sardinian sweets, olive oils, cheeses and salami.

Getting There & Away

BUS

All buses terminate at Piazza Zanetti. Most services are run by FdS, which has a ticket office on the square. Up to four buses run to/from Alghero. The quicker ones take the scenic coastal route (€2.89, 55 minutes). Other services connect with Macomer (€2.01, 50 minutes, seven daily) and Sassari (€5.84, 2¼ hours, two daily). Some ARST buses also run to/from Bosa, with services to Oristano (€4.44, two hours, five daily Monday to Saturday). Buy tickets at **Bar Mouse** (Piazza Zanetti) or at the *tabacchi* on Viale Alghero.

CAR & MOTORCYCLE

Parking on the beachfront can cost €0.50 an hour or €3 a day, although you can probably find a space in a side street. In central Bosa it is generally easy to find a parking spot in the streets of the modern town west of Sa Costa.

TRAIN

In July and August a **trenino verde** (www.treninoverde.com, in Italian) service connects Bosa Marina with Macomer (€9, two hours, one Saturday and Sunday). The train leaves Macomer at 9.30am, but the return trip departing at 11.20am from Bosa only goes as far as Tresnuraghes, where you connect with an FdS bus for Macomer.

Macomer is in turn connected by a year-round train service to Nuoro.

Getting Around

Up to 21 daily FdS buses run from central Bosa (Piazza Zanetti) to Bosa Marina (€0.67, 10 minutes).

AROUND BOSA

Stretching south are the beaches of **Spiaggia Turas**, **Spiaggia Porto Alabe** and **Cala Torre Columbargia**. The first two are respectively a 1.5km and 8km drive from Bosa Marina and can get busy in high season. The last of the beaches is reached from Tresnuraghes and involves some dusty trail driving. It's about 18km from Bosa Marina.

ORISTANO & THE WEST

Sassari & the Northwest

The northwestern corner of Sardinia is different in spirit from the rest of the island – less rural and less 'Sardinian' in many ways. This is because the Genoese made Sassari their city of choice, fortifying it with mighty walls and imbuing its inhabitants with a cosmopolitan attitude that still sets them apart today. Picturesque Castelsardo, with its medieval historic centre, is another Genoese town – the private fiefdom of the Dorias for many years. The Dorias also founded seaside Alghero, although it is more famous for its Catalan character.

The humid African plains of Oristano and the dramatic granite formations of the Gallura give way to the straggling mountains of Anglona. It is bare, stony countryside more reminiscent of Provence than Italy. A string of Pisan-Romanesque churches dot the landscape and add to the northern atmosphere.

Yet this was one of the first corners of the island to be settled by the ancient Sards, and a wealth of tumbledown prehistoric ruins attests to their presence here. The country around the Nuraghe Santu Antine is littered with the enormous building blocks of other long-gone *nuraghi* (stone towers). Other significant ruins include the weird ziggurat of Monte d'Accoddi – the only example in the Mediterranean – and the necropoli at Anghelu Ruiu.

The province is at once self-contained and open-minded, and tourism has had little impact on the area's character. The food and wine are also particular. You'll eat some of your best meals in Sassari and Alghero.

HIGHLIGHTS

- Meander through the cobbled lanes and along the sea walls of the medieval Catalan town of **Alghero** (p153)

- Explore the charming Romanesque churches scattered about the **Logudoro** (p145)

- Submerge yourself in the shimmering turquoise waters of **Spiaggia della Pelosa** (p152)

- Drive or cycle the spectacular coast road from **Alghero to Bosa** (p162)

- Marvel at the perfectly preserved medieval town of **Castelsardo** (p148)

- Don't miss the gorgeous windswept headland of **Capo Caccia** (p165) and the fairy-tale cave of **Grotta di Nettuno** (p165)

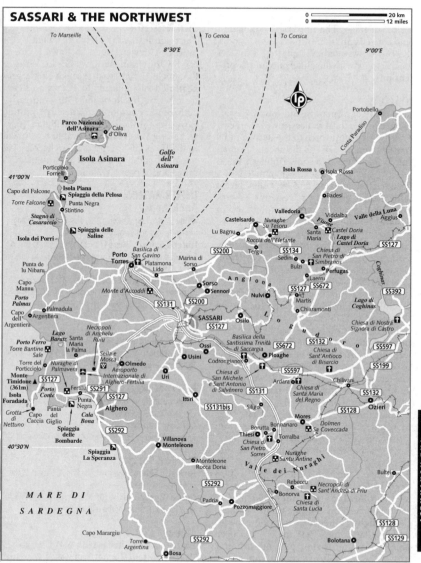

SASSARI & THE NORTHWEST

SASSARI

pop 121,850

Sardinia's second city and rival to the capital, Cagliari, Sassari has a proud history as a centre of culture (its university opened in the 16th century) and as a hotbed of rebellion and politics. It is a cool, inland town, unaffected by beach life, which makes the Sassaresi appear more formal, suited and booted in a serious city way.

It may be less open than Cagliari, but physically it feels more like a capital city. For a start it's not overwhelmed by a commercial port, and the central squares and boulevards create busy arteries and pools of activity that culminate in the grandeur of Piazza Italia. The university population lends the city an interesting tension, as does the run-down medieval quarter, a hive of local activity with absolutely no tourist pretensions.

HISTORY

Like many Sardinian inland towns, Sassari (Tatari in the local dialect) owes its medieval rise to prominence to the decline of its coastal counterparts. As the ancient Roman colony of Turris Libisonis (modern Porto Torres) succumbed to the hammer blows inflicted by malaria and repeated pirate raids, people gradually retreated to Sassari. Porto Torres (and at one point the town of Ardara) remained capital of the Giudicato di Torres (or Logudoro), but Sassari's increasing importance led it to break away from the province and, with support from Genoa, declare itself an autonomous city state in 1294.

But the Sassaresi soon tired of Genoese meddling and in 1321 called on the Crown of Aragon to help rid them of the northern Italians. The Catalano-Aragonese arrived in 1323, but Sassari soon discovered it had leapt from the frying pan into the fire. The first of many revolts against the city's new masters came two years later. It would take another century for the Iberian interlopers to fully control Sassari.

For a time the city prospered, but waves of plague and the growing menace from Ottoman Turkey sidelined Sardinia, leaving Sassari to slide into decline in the 16th century.

It wasn't until the middle of the 19th century that Sassari began to take off again following the modernisation of Porto Torres and the laying of the Carlo Felice highway between the port, Sassari and Cagliari. Since 1945 the city has been able to maintain a slow pace of economic growth. It has also been an industrious producer of national politicians. The biggest names are former presidents Antonio Segni (1891–1972) and Francesco Cossiga (born 1928), and the charismatic communist leader Enrico Berlinguer (1922–84). Segni's son, Mario (born 1939), is an active left-of-centre leader in Rome, and another local, Beppe Pisanu, became Prime Minister Berlusconi's interior minister in mid-2002.

ORIENTATION

The main lines of the city run roughly east to west. The western end of town is closed off by the train station. Corso Vittorio Emanuele II runs east through the largely neglected old quarter to Piazza Castello, from where much of the 19th- and early-20th-century additions to the city continue eastward through the grand Piazza Italia and along Via Roma. Around here you will find offices of interest, the archaeological museum, some hotels and a fistful of mid-range and top-end restaurants.

INFORMATION
Bookshops
Koinè (Map p138; Via Roma 137) The only place selling foreign-language newspapers.
Libreria Gulliver (Map p141; ☎ 079 23 44 75; Portici Bargone e Crispo 8) A big, central bookshop. Being refitted at the time of research.
Libreria Messaggeri e Sarde (Map p141; Piazza Castello 11) Best for Sardinian literature (mainly in Italian). Also has maps and guides.

Emergency
Medical emergency (☎ 118)
Police station (Map p141; ☎ 079 283 55 00; Via Angioi 16) The main police headquarters.

Internet Access
Dream Bar (Map p141; Via Cavour 15; per 30 min €3.50; ☿ 7am-1pm & 5-8pm Mon-Sat)
Net Gate Internet (Map p141; ☎ 079 23 78 94; Piazza Università 4; per hr €3; ☿ 9am-9pm Mon-Fri, 9am-1pm Sat)

Medical Services
Farmacia Simon (Map p141; Via Brigata Sassari 2) The only pharmacy that does a night shift.
Nuovo Ospedale Civile (Off Map p138; ☎ 079 206 10 00; Viale Italia) South of the centre.

Money
Banca Comerciale Italiana (Map p141; Piazza Italia 23)
Banca di Sassari (Map p141; Piazza Castello 8) Western Union representative.

Post
Main post office (Map p141; Via Brigata di Sassari; ☿ 8.15am-6.15pm Mon-Fri, 8.15am-1pm Sat) Centrally located.

Tourist Information
Tourist office (Map p138; ☎ 079 23 17 77; aastss@tiscali.it; Via Roma 62; ☿ 9am-1.30pm & 4-6pm

Mon-Thu, 9am-1.30pm Fri) Very helpful multilingual staff. Lots of information on Sassari and the surrounding area.

Travel Agencies
CTS (Map p141; ☎ 079 20 04 00; Via Manno 35) A branch of the national youth travel agent.

DANGERS & ANNOYANCES
Sassari is a fairly orderly provincial town. You should take the normal precautions in the old centre, especially in the more run-down streets towards the station.

SIGHTS
Sadly, little of the medieval city remains. Rather than spreading beyond its 13th-century walls, the town slowly regenerated itself over the centuries, eliminating the old so as to make way for the new. Some jewels remain intact, and Sassari's two grand churches, the Duomo and Chiesa di Santa Maria di Betlem, are impressive. The archaeological collection in the Museo Nazionale Sanna is the second most important on the island.

Museo Nazionale Sanna
Tucked away in a Palladian villa is the national **museum** (Map p138; ☎ 079 27 22 03; Via Roma 64; adult/under 25 yr €2/1; ☺ 9am-8pm Tue-Sun). It's home to the art collection of Giovanni Sanna, a mining engineer whose family built the museum. Only some of these paintings are on public display in the *pinacoteca* (art gallery), which is to the left as you enter the museum. The works are mostly ponderous 18th-century portraits and paintings, although the fine 14th-century Pisan triptych, *Madonna con Bambino* (1473), by Bartolomeo Vivarini, is worth seeking out.

The room to the right of the entrance is the Sala Preistorica, covering the very earliest Stone Age and Neolithic finds on the island. Staff have even built a rudimentary Neolithic hut in papier-mâché and arranged it with props – just in case you can't envisage the typical Bronze Age dwelling. A glass cabinet showcases a charming *bronzetto* (bronze figurine) holding a plate in extended arms. With his pleading expression he looks for all the world like Oliver Twist.

Beyond these two rooms the museum opens up in a series of chronological displays from megalithic tombs and *domus de janas* (literally 'fairy houses'; tombs cut into rock) to Phoenician and Carthaginian finds. It's not on the same scale as the museum in Cagliari, but there's plenty of interest. Among the ceramics (pots, pans, stoves and so on), it is the bronze ware that stands out. They include axe heads and similar tools, weapons, bracelets, votive boats and *bronzetti*.

Back downstairs, room X is dedicated to Phoenician and Carthaginian objects. Some exquisite pottery is mixed in with gold jewellery (window case Nos 41 and 43) and masks (No 42). Rooms XI and XII contain Roman finds, mostly ceramics and oil burners but also some statuary and a sprinkling of coins, jewellery and objects like bronze belt buckles. Off to one side lies a stash of heavy Roman anchors.

There is also a good collection of Sardinian folk art in the separate ethnographic section. Carpets and saddlebags, rich embroidered skirts and waistcoats, and curious terracotta hot-water bottles.

Piazza Italia
The grand dust-brown **Piazza Italia** sits right at the heart of town, surrounded by imposing 19th-century buildings, including the neoclassical **Palazzo della Provincia** (Map p141), the seat of the regional government. Across the square a rather different note is struck by the neo-Gothic **Palazzo Giordano** (Map p141), the Banco di Napoli's ornate HQ. A statue of King Vittorio Emanuele II presides over it all. The monument's inauguration in 1899 was the occasion for the first Cavalcata Sarda, and the piazza also marks the starting point for Sassari's other big festival, I Candelieri (see p140).

Museo della Brigata Sassari
Sassari is rightly proud of its military heritage, especially the well-decorated Sassari Brigade, which fought with great gallantry during WWI. You can glean something of the terrible conditions they endured in this tiny **museum** (Map p141; Piazza Castello; admission free; ☺ 9am-12.30pm & 2.30-4.30pm Mon-Fri, 9am-12.30pm Sat) in the military barracks. Uniforms, photos, documents and other memorabilia evoke the ghastly conditions and ferocious bravery of the brigade, who were thrown into the thick of the trench

SASSARI

INFORMATION	
Koine.......................................1	E4
Tourist Office........................2	D3

SIGHTS & ACTIVITIES	
Chiesa di Santa Maria di Betlem...3	A2
Chiesa di Sant'Antonio Abate.....4	B1
Fontana di Rosello...................5	C1
Medieval Walls........................6	C1
Museo Nazionale Sanna.............7	E3
Palazzo della Giustizia..............8	D3

SLEEPING	
Frank Hotel............................9	E4
Hotel Leonardo da Vinci.........10	E4

EATING	
Trattoria Da Peppina..............11	B1

DRINKING	
Caffè Italiano........................12	D3

ENTERTAINMENT	
Sergeant Pepper Disco Bar......13	D4
Teatro Il Ferroviario..............14	B1

TRANSPORT	
Avis.....................................15	D3
Bus Station...........................16	A2
Euronet...............................17	D3

See Central Sassari Map (p141)

To SS331 Highway (1km);
Il Gatto e La Volpe (7km);
Porto Torres (19km);
Airport (28km);
Alghero (36km)

fighting against the Austrians in northern Italy. You can even read the letter in which the Austro-Hungarian commander first gave the brigade their epithet 'the red devils'. There are old guns and grenades on show, and a re-creation of a modern trench. Most touching, however, are the proud poses of the men in the old black-and-white photographs. As this is still an operational barracks you may often find the museum closed.

Corso Vittorio Emanuele II & Around

From Piazza Castello an arrow-straight road leads into the heart of the old town. It is the original Roman road that ran from Porto Torres to Cagliari and was once the top address for city notables. Now it's slowly crumbling, although here and there a few of its finest buildings are finally being renovated. Hopefully the newly opened Hotel Vittorio Emanuele (see p140) will bring renewed interest – and investment – to the quarter.

Casa Farris (Map p141; Corso Vittorio Emanuele II 25) remains in a lamentable state, but its Gothic windows are a clear indication that the building has managed, barely, to survive down the centuries. More interesting is **Casa di Re Enzo** (Map p141; Corso Vittorio Emanuele II 42), a remarkable 15th-century Catalan Gothic setting for what is now a stocking store. It is fronted by thick-set double arches and heavy hanging lamps. Wander inside to get a closer look at the vibrant frescoes and ceiling paintwork.

The Liberty-style **Teatro Civico** (Map p141), opposite Casa di Re Enzo, was built in 1826 and modelled on Turin's Teatro Carignano. It's currently being completely renovated, and once it's complete it will host a programme of plays and concerts.

North of Corso Vittorio Emanuele II, Via Cesare Battisti leads into the leafy Piazza Tola. It used to be the centre and main market of the medieval town, and you'll still find a market here on weekday mornings. When the Spaniards were in charge they burnt heretics here, looking on from fine palazzos such as the 1577 **Palazzo d'Usini** (Map p141). It's a rare example of 16th-century civil architecture in Sardinia and now houses the public library.

Following Via Lamarmora west off the square, make for the Porta Rossello and then west along Corso Trinità, where you can admire the only substantial remnant of the city's **medieval walls**. Nearby you'll find the Renaissance **Fontana di Rosello** (Map p138), where water-carriers once drew water from the eight lion-head spouts that ring the base. It is an elegant affair – a pale white marble box topped by two fine marble arches that protect the figure of San Gavino.

Duomo di San Nicola & Around

In the heart of the medieval quarter the extraordinary baroque façade of Sassari's **cathedral** (Map p141; Piazza Duomo; ☺ 9am-noon & 4-7pm) seems to emanate its own radiant light. Busy with bulging sculptural caprice, it bears an uncanny resemblance to the ebullient baroque style of Apulia, in southeastern Italy.

The 18th-century façade was added to a 15th-century Catalan Gothic body, which itself replaced a Romanesque church. The bare interior is a little disappointing after the frills and spills outside. Worth looking out for are the frescoes in the left transept and the Gothic fresco in the first chapel on the right as you enter. In the second chapel is a fine painting of the *Martirio dei SS Cosma e Damiano* (Martyrdom of Saints Cosimo and Damien). A small **museum** (admission free) of valuable religious bits and bobs is out the back in the sacristy.

The narrow streets around here are much neglected but full of life – a tableau that takes you far from the suntan-lotion-soaked tourist spots on the coast! You will no doubt arrive in the huge Piazza Mazzotti, locally dubbed the Piazza di Demolizione (Demolitian Piazza). It was once a warren of old streets like the rest of the quarter, but hard-to-control prostitution plagued its narrow lanes, so the authorities decided to knock it all down and create a civic-minded car park instead!

Chiesa di Santa Maria di Betlem

Just beyond what were the city walls stands the proud Romanesque façade of this eclectic **church** (Map p138; Piazza di Santa Maria). The exterior betrays Gothic and even vaguely Oriental admixtures. Inside, the Catalan Gothic vaulting has been preserved, but much baroque silliness has crept in to obscure the original lines of the building. Lining each aisle in the chapels stand some of the giant 'candles' that the city guilds parade about town for the 14 August festivities.

The church is not always open, but your best bet is the morning.

FESTIVALS & EVENTS

On the second-last Sunday of May hundreds of people from villages and towns around the island gather for the **Cavalcata Sarda**, or Sardinian Procession, a costume parade that was inaugurated in the 1950s. It is similar to the parade held in Nuoro for the Festa del Redentore in August.

Sassari's big traditional festival is **I Candelieri** (14 August), where teams wearing medieval costume and representing various guilds from the 16th century bear huge wooden columns (the 'candlesticks') through the town. The celebrations are held to honour a vow made in 1652 for deliverance from a plague but are also connected with the **Feast of the Assumption** (15 August).

SLEEPING

Sassari has a handful of good hotels aimed at the business crowd. More recently a number of B&Bs have started to open in the old town. The tourist office can provide a list.

Hotel Vittorio Emanuele (Map p141; ☎ 079 23 55 38; www.hotelvittorioemanuele.ss.it, in Italian; Corso Vittorio Emanuele II 100/102; s/d €60/89; ☒ ⌨) At last someone has restored an old-town palazzo into some characterful accommodation. The Vittorio Emanuele stands proudly right on the *corso*. The management has gone for modern elegance, which is slightly disappointing, but the stone wine cellar and refined restaurant are anything but.

Hotel Leonardo da Vinci (Map p138; ☎ 079 28 07 44; www.leonardodavincihotel.it; Via Roma 79; s/d €80/110; ⓟ ☒ ⌨) This conveniently located place is the most popular business hotel. The service is courteous and efficient, and the rooms have been revamped with shiny modern bathrooms, half of which have actual baths. There's Internet access in the lobby.

Casa Chiara (Map p141; ☎ 079 200 50 52; www.casachiara.net; Vicolo Bertolinis 7; s/d €30/60; ⌨) This 2nd-floor B&B near the buzzing streets around the university is an excellent choice. The three rooms are decorated in bold, bright colours and share two bathrooms. Guests also have use of the cute retro kitchen.

Frank Hotel (Map p138; ☎ 079 27 64 56; Piazza Sant'Antonio 21; s/d €50/75; ⓟ ☒) A solid no-surprises hotel with the real bonus of private parking. The rooms are in better nick than the tired-looking lobby, and have plenty of space, colourful rugs, minibars and balconies. The view is pretty pedestrian, so satellite TV is a plus.

Also recommended is the friendly **Il Gatto e La Volpe** (☎ 079 318 00 12; www.ilgattoelavolpe bandb.com; Monti di Jesgia 23, Caniga; s/d €22/44), located in a country house in Caniga.

EATING

Eating out in Sassari is a real pleasure. A local curiosity is *fainè*, a cross between a crepe and a pizza with a base made from chickpea flour. It was introduced by the Genoese and is similar to their *farinata*.

Budget

Trattoria L'Assassino (Map p141; ☎ 079 23 50 41; Via Ospizio Cappuccini 1/a; set lunch €8; ☺ Mon-Sat) This trattoria is hidden away in a back alley off Piazza Tola. The more adventurous will step beyond the set meal and try a selection of 10 starters (€18). These can include classics such as *funghi arrosto* (roasted mushrooms) and *lumaconi* (big snails). If you get really lucky you may find calf's testicles on the menu as well.

Fainè alla Genovese Sassu (Map p141; Via Usai 17; meals €3.50-6; ☺ dinner Mon-Sat) This is Sassari's original purveyor of fine *fainè*. Toppings vary from onions to sausage, and with prices starting at €3.50 they are a filling option if you're suffering from wallet stress.

Zia Forica (Map p141; Corso Margherita Savoia 39; meals €15-20; ☺ closed evenings Aug) Here's another good spot for a lunchtime helping of donkey. Students treat it almost as a fast-food place.

Da Bruno (Map p141; ☎ 079 23 55 73; Piazza Mazzotti 12; pizza up to €5; ☺ Thu-Tue) On offer here is cheap pizza in a very ugly location. Da Bruno is also one of the few places to open on Sunday night.

Midrange

Il Castello (Map p141; ☎ 079 23 20 41; Piazza Cavallino de Honestis 6; meals €20-25; ☺ Mon-Sat) This wildly popular place serves monstrous portions of pasta and some justifiably famous meat platters. The most mind-blowing is the Chateaubriand steak (€30 for two people),

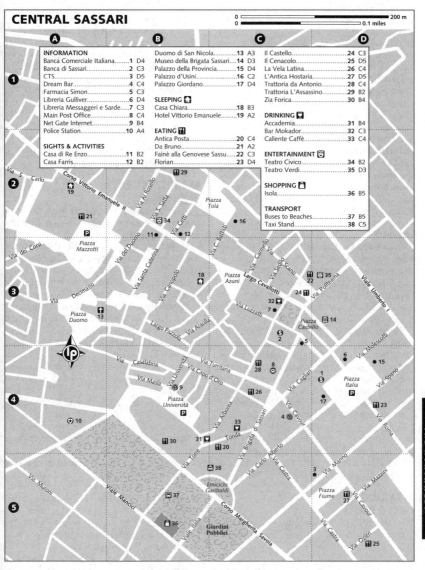

CENTRAL SASSARI

0 ————————————— 200 m
0 ————————————— 0.1 miles

INFORMATION		Duomo di San Nicola	13 A3	Il Castello	24 C3
Banca Comerciale Italiana	1 D4	Museo della Brigata Sassari	14 D3	Il Cenacolo	25 D5
Banca di Sassari	2 C3	Palazzo della Provincia	15 D4	La Vela Latina	26 C4
CTS	3 D5	Palazzo d'Usini	16 C2	L'Antica Hostaria	27 D5
Dream Bar	4 C4	Palazzo Giordano	17 D4	Trattoria da Antonio	28 C4
Farmacia Simon	5 C3			Trattoria L'Assassino	29 B2
Libreria Gulliver	6 D4	SLEEPING		Zia Forica	30 B4
Libreria Messaggeri e Sarde	7 C3	Casa Chiara	18 B3		
Main Post Office	8 C4	Hotel Vittorio Emanuele	19 A2	DRINKING	
Net Gate Internet	9 B4			Accademia	31 B4
Police Station	10 A4	EATING		Bar Mokador	32 C3
		Antica Posta	20 C4	Caliente Caffè	33 C4
SIGHTS & ACTIVITIES		Da Bruno	21 A2		
Casa di Re Enzo	11 B2	Fainè alla Genovese Sassu	22 C3	ENTERTAINMENT	
Casa Farris	12 B2	Florian	23 D4	Teatro Civico	34 B2
				Teatro Verdi	35 D3
				SHOPPING	
				Isola	36 B5
				TRANSPORT	
				Buses to Beaches	37 B5
				Taxi Stand	38 C5

SASSARI &
THE NORTHWEST

which arrives on its own trolley accompanied by a mountain of chips and grilled vegetables.

Antica Posta (Map p141; ☎ 079 200 61 21; Via Torre Tonda 26; meals €20, menu €18; ☼ Mon-Sat) A new venture on one of the busiest streets in the old town, this is a wine bar–cum–grill room of the 'industrial architecture' type. Unlike

many places in Sassari, it serves modern Sardinian food such as grilled steaks and fillet of fresh fish, as well as some interesting pastas like *fregola con funghi* (pasta with mushrooms).

La Vela Latina (Map p141; ☎ 079 23 37 37; Largo Sisini 8; meals €30; ☼ Mon-Sat) This restaurant has a handful of tables in a nicely restored building and on the pleasant veranda. The menu changes with the seasons: there's lots of seafood (including good swordfish) in summer, and meats and mushrooms from autumn into winter.

Trattoria da Antonio (Map p141; ☎ 079 23 42 97; Via Arborea 2/b; meals €20; ☷ Mon-Sat) Affectionately known as Lu Panzone (the Big Belly), this is a boisterous, no-nonsense establishment for trad Sardinian fare.

Trattoria Da Peppina (Map p138; ☎ 079 23 61 46; Vicolo Pigozzi 1; meals €22; ☷ Mon-Sat) This scary local option is only for the adventurous. It specialises in Sassaresi cuisine – snails and (asinello) donkey meat. It's tucked into a messy side alley off the lower end of Corso Vittorio Emanuele II.

Top End
L'Antica Hostaria (Map p141; ☎ 079 20 00 60; Via Mazzini 27; meals €40-45; ☷ Mon-Sat) L'Antica is one of Sassari's top addresses. In intimate surroundings you are treated to inventive cuisine rooted in local tradition. Meat lovers should try the tagliata di manzo con rucola (thinly sliced beef with rocket).

Florian (Map p141; ☎ 079 200 80 56; Via Capitano Bellieni 27; meals €35-40; ☷ Mon-Sat) This classic place has an unwaveringly authentic menu and an elegant dining area flanked by mirrors and stained glass. The adjacent café is similarly swanky, with Toulouse-Lautrec–style murals and girth-expanding cakes.

Il Cenacolo (Map p141; ☎ 079 23 62 51; Via Ozieri 2; meals €35; ☷ Mon-Sat) Behind Il Cenacolo's modest entrance lies an opulent interior perhaps more in keeping with its previous life as a luxury gym. The emphasis here is on fish and seafood.

DRINKING
Cafés & Bars
With its big student population and busy business community, Sassari has a vibrant café culture. The cafés that line Via Roma and cluster around Piazza Castello, as well as the student hub, Via Torre Tonda, are perpetually full. In the evening they undergo an imperceptible transformation as coffee is shunted aside for cocktails.

Along Via Roma a popular spot with the business crowds and lunching couples is **Caffè Italiano** (Map p138; Via Roma 38/40), as is **Bar Mokador** (Map p141; Largo Cavallotti 2), which you'll find just off Piazza Castello.

Otherwise, head down towards the university to **Accademia** (Map p141; Via Torre Tonda 11; snacks €6-10). Its outdoor veranda is packed at lunchtime. It's also an agreeable spot for a drink at night, and you may be treated to a little live music. Along the same road is the **Caliente Caffè** (Map p141; Via Torre Tonda 1/b), a good wine bar with tables and chairs set out beneath a stretch of the 13th-century city wall. Try a glass of the fragrant Vermentino, Frinas.

Several bars are secreted in the nearby lanes around Via Arborea.

ENTERTAINMENT
Nightclubs
The dance options in Sassari are not overly inspiring, and young Sassaresi say that the scene in Alghero is better.

If you're in town outside the summer you could try **Sergeant Pepper Disco Bar** (Map p138; ☎ 079 282 80 55; Via Asproni 20; ☷ 9pm-6am Fri-Sun). Otherwise, what action there is takes place well beyond the city centre – you'll need your own wheels or a taxi. **Meccano** (Off Map p138; ☎ 079 27 04 05; Via Carlo Felice 33; ☷ 10pm-6am Wed, Fri & Sat) is probably the most popular. Another option is **Club Milano** (Off Map p138; Via Milano 26; admission €10-20), a sports centre with a pizzeria. It has a Latin night on Wednesday.

Theatre
The town's theatres don't tend to move into gear until September or October, after the sting has gone out of the summer heat.

Teatro Civico (Map p141; Corso Vittorio Emanuele II 39) This beautiful Liberty-style theatre is currently undergoing refurbishment. When in action it showcases plays and concerts.

The Sassaresi, however, prefer the opera, usually staged at **Teatro Verdi** (Map p141; ☎ 079 23 94 79; Via Politeama) between October and January. The rest of the year this theatre is used as a cinema. A much smaller place is the **Teatro Il Ferroviario** (Map p138; ☎ 079 63 30 49; Corso Vico 14), which has a permanent company specialising in more experimental pieces.

SHOPPING
Isola (Map p141; ☎ 079 23 01 01; ☷ 9am-1pm & 4.30-8pm Mon-Sat) Set in the town's central green lung, the leafy Giardini Pubblici, the Padiglione dell'Artigianato is a good showcase for handicrafts.

SASSARI &
THE NORTHWEST

GETTING THERE & AWAY

Air

Sassari shares **Fertilia airport** (Off Map p138; ☎ 079 93 50 39) with Alghero. It is about 28km west of the city centre. There are money-changing and car-hire facilities at the airport.

For information on flights in and out of Fertilia, see p162.

Bus

The *autostazione* (bus station) is on Via XXV Aprile near the train station. ARST (Azienda Regionale Sarda Trasporti), FdS (Ferrovie della Sardegna) and some ATP local buses travelling beyond the city leave from here, and you can buy tickets at the station. For smaller companies (such as Nuragica Tour to Olbia airport) buy tickets on the bus.

ARST (☎ 079 263 92 03) buses service Oristano (€7.59, 2¼ hours, seven daily), Porto Torres (€1.45, 35 minutes, hourly) and Castelsardo (€2.01, one hour, 11 Monday to Saturday, six Sunday).

FdS (☎ 079 24 13 01) buses run to Alghero (€2.32 to €2.58, 50 to 60 minutes, hourly) and other destinations in the locale.

Turmo Travel (☎ 079 2 14 87; www.turmotravel .it) runs a direct service to Olbia (€5.84, 1½ hours, one daily). It terminates at the port.

Car & Motorcycle

Sassari is on the SS131 highway linking Porto Torres in the north and Cagliari in the south. From Alghero, take the road north towards Porto Torres and then the SS291 east to Sassari (follow the signs for the new four-lane *corsie,* or highway). You take the same route from Fertilia airport.

A host of car-hire outlets are based at Fertilia airport. In Sassari itself **Avis** (Map p138; ☎ 079 23 55 47; Via Mazzini 2) is handy, as is **Eurorent** (Map p138; ☎ 079 23 23 35; www.rent.it; Via Roma 56), where you can also rent scooters (€45 per day).

Train

The main **Trenitalia** (Map p138; ☎ 8488 8 80 88; www.trenitalia.it) station is just beyond the western end of the old town on Piazza Stazione. Three direct trains link the city with Cagliari (€12.10, 4¼ hours). Otherwise you have to change along the way, say in Oristano (€7.75, 2½ hours). There are also services to Olbia (€5.90, one hour 50 minutes, six Monday to Saturday, three Sunday).

Several daily **FdS** (☎ 079 24 13 01) trains connect with Nulvi, 35km to the northeast. From there you can link up with the **trenino verde** (☎ 079 24 57 40; www.treninoverde.com, in Italian) for the slow panoramic ride to Tempio Pausania (€12, two hours 40 minutes, one daily). The train runs from 22 June to 7 September. FdS also runs a line to Alghero (€1.85, 35 minutes, hourly).

GETTING AROUND

In 2005 Sassari completed the first phase of its tram system. Ultimately the system should connect the train station with the top of town.

To/From the Airport

Up to 11 ARST buses run daily from the main bus depot off Via XXV Aprile to Fertilia airport (€1.45, 30 minutes). A taxi to the airport costs €20.

For Olbia airport you need to catch the train to Olbia and then the city bus to the airport.

Bus

ATP local (orange) buses run along most city routes, but you probably won't need one. ATP buses also run to the beaches north of Sassari.

Car & Motorcycle

Parking is free in some of the streets southeast of Via Asproni and around the train station. Around busy Piazza Italia you must pay an attendant to park in blue zones – up to €2 for the first two hours and €1 for each hour thereafter.

Taxi

You can catch a **taxi** (☎ 079 25 39 39) from ranks on Emiciclo Garibaldi (Map p141) or along Viale Italia and Via Matteotti. You can also arrange excursions with them to some of the sights around Sassari.

AROUND SASSARI

The most scenic route from Sassari to the coast is the SS200, lined with umbrella pines standing sentry. The road passes through two market towns, **Sennori** and **Sorso**.

It is worth factoring in a visit to the well-known local restaurant **Da Vito** (☎ 079 36 02

45; Via Napoli 14; meals €30-40) in Sennori, which lays on an impressive spread of fish and antipasti. It does a great *zuppa di faggiole e cozze* (mussels and bean soup). The owners will try to tempt you with all manner of delicious items. Trust them.

At the weekends the Sassaresi abandon the city for the long sandy beaches at **Marinella** and **Platamona Lido**. The latter is a cheerful and, on summer weekends, crowded local beach known optimistically as the Sassari Riviera.

Regular summer buses run up to a point just east of Platamona and then the length of coast as far as Marina di Sorso. Look for the Buddi Buddi bus (line MP) from Via Eugenio Tavolara.

THE LOGUDORO & MONTE ACUTO

If you have a car it's definitely worth touring the fertile countryside of the Logudoro, south of Sassari. The original name meant 'place of Torres', but that has come to mean 'place of gold' after the golden summer plains of wheat.

Further west, right in the heart of the island, is the *comune* of Monte Acuto, a collection of village communities sharing a common mountain heritage. You'll find www.monteacuto.it (in Italian) a useful website.

OZIERI

pop 11,300

Ozieri is a substantial town, its tight web of lanes and houses cut into the slopes like farming terraces. Follow the signs for the *centro* and you will wind up in Via Vittoria Veneto, where intercity buses gather (adjacent to Piazza Garibaldi).

Behind and above this square, the **Museo Archeologico** (Piazza San Francesco; admission with Grotta di San Michele €4; 9am-1pm & 3.30-7.30pm Tue-Sun), housed in the former convent of the Chiesa di San Francesco, contains ancient finds, especially ceramic fragments, left behind by the Ozieri people in the Grotta di San Michele. The *grotta* is signposted from the top of town.

From Piazza Garibaldi take Via Umberto I, which climbs to Piazza Carlo Alberto, a noble semicircular space fronted by sober 19th-century mansions. From there Via Vittorio Emanuele III leads up to a little square capped by the **Fonte Grixoni**, a marble caprice erected by a noble on the site of what for centuries had been the town's main fountain. From there, swing around to the left and follow Via Grixoni up to the **Cattedrale dell'Immacolata** (Piazza Duomo), which displays more bombast than the modest square before it can fairly contain. Inside is an important *Deposizione di Cristo dalla Croce* (Deposition of Christ from the Cross) by the enigmatic Maestro di Ozieri.

During December Ozieri hosts one of the island's major poetry competitions, the **Premio di Ozieri**. It started in 1956, inspired by the *gare poetiche* (poetry wars) that took place informally at local festivals, and now showcases the poetry of an impressive list of Italian and Sardinian poets.

The only hotel in town is **Hotel Il Mastino** (079 78 70 41; fax 079 78 70 59; Via Vittorio Veneto 13; s/d €45/65), a fairly characterless no-nonsense affair with clean, tidy rooms.

Buses from Sassari (€2.50, 50 minutes, eight Monday to Saturday) stop just off Piazza Garibaldi. Three or four FAB buses head west to Olbia (€4.44, up to 1½ hours). Regular buses run to Chilivani station, 7km northwest, to meet trains and return to town.

TORRALBA & NURAGHE SANTU ANTINE

Heading west from Ozieri, you pass through **Mores**, to the south of which lies the majestic **Dolmen Sa Coveccada**. Take the exit just before you enter Mores from the east and it's a couple of kilometres down the road. The dolmen, raised at the end of the 3rd millennium BC, consists of three massive slabs of stone roofed by a fourth. They were cut and chiselled to measure, although erosion has masked that fact.

From Mores proceed to Torralba, the village at the head of the so-called Valle dei Nuraghi (Valley of the Nuraghi). Driving around here you will see several of the ancient structures, but top priority goes to the **Nuraghe Santu Antine** (079 84 72 96; admission €3; 8.30am-sunset), 4km south of the town. The site of Santu Antine is a unique blast from the past – at least 1600 BC! Set in fields and surrounded in the distance by the distinct-

DETOUR: THE CHURCHES OF THE LOGUDORO

The **Basilica della Santissima Trinità di Saccargia** (Comune di Codrongianus; admission €1.50; 9am-12.30pm & 3.30-7pm) lies in the centre of a fertile valley, just 15km southeast of Sassari along the SS597 to Olbia. You can't miss its stripy limestone and basalt campanile, which dominates the horizon as you approach. Legend has it that it was built by the Giudice Constantino di Mariano in 1116, after he and his wife camped the night here and received a revelation that they were to have their first longed-for child. The delighted Giudice built the church and a neighbouring monastery, which the pope gave to the Camaldolite monks. Little remains of the monastery, although the dramatically simple church with its blind basalt walls is still in use.

A further 3km beyond the Santissima Trinità you'll see the abandoned **Chiesa di San Michele e Sant'Antonio di Salvènero** at the road junctions to Ploaghe, but continue to Ardara, 10km further on. It was once the capital of the Giudicato di Torres, and a quick turn to the left as you enter the town will bring you face to face with the brooding mass of the **Chiesa di Santa Maria del Regno**, made of deep rust-red basalt. One of its oddest features is the squat bell tower, finished in rough-and-ready manner after the church was completed and not at all typical of the style.

Further east along the SS597 you'll see a turn-off for the majestically ruined 11th- to 12th-century **Chiesa di Sant'Antioco di Bisarcio** (admission €1.50; 9am-1pm & 4-7pm), 2km north of the highway. The bell tower was decapitated by a burst of lightning, and much of the façade's decoration has been lost, but the uniquely French-inspired porch and interior convey the impression of its one-time grandeur; perhaps even more so in its forlorn state of abandonment in the middle of the countryside.

From here you can either continue along the SS597 and hunt out the tiny **Chiesa di Nostra Signora di Castro** on the banks of the Lago di Coghinas, or head north along the winding SS132 towards **Chiesa di San Pietro di Simbranos** (or delle Immagini) at Bulzi and the **Chiesa di San Giorgio** at Perfugas.

If you're planning this route you may also want to consider staying in the lovely manor house **Funtanarena** (079 43 50 48; www.funtanarena.it; Via S'Istradoneddu 8/10; half board per person €84; P) in Codrongianos. It is an artistic place sometimes hosting classical music in the orchards, and organising archaeological, ethnographic and naturalistic itineraries. The nine rooms are furnished with unusual period beds and lots of books, and the restaurant terrace overlooks undisturbed countryside. It's the first house as you enter the village.

ive conical forms of ancient volcanoes, it is a bizarre sight.

You enter the compound from the southern side and can walk through the three towers, connected by rough parabolic archways. Stairs lead to the top of these towers and the upper perimeter. The enormous basalt boulders are 1.8m long and 1.2m wide. How were they carried here and from where? The entrance to the main tower is separate. Inside, four openings lead into the chamber from an internal hall. Stairs lead up from the hall to the next floor, where a similar but smaller pattern is reproduced. Apart from tiny vents there is no light, and the presence of the dark stone is overwhelming. You ascend another set of steps to reach the floor of what was the final, third chamber, now open to the elements.

Back in Torralba is the **Museo Archeologico** (Via Carlo Felice 143; admission incl Nuraghe Santu Antine €3; 9am-8pm May-Oct, 9am-5pm Oct-May). The first item is a scale model of the Nuraghe Santu Antine, followed by a modest archaeological display from the Santu Antine site.

Up to 10 buses from Sassari run to Torralba (€2.32). To get to the *nuraghe* from there you will have to walk (about an hour).

BORUTTA

As the crow flies, the hamlet of Borutta is only a few kilometres from Torralba, but the circular road will make it about a 10km trip. The object, the fine Romanesque **Chiesa di San Pietro Sorres** (admission free; 8.30-11.45am & 3.30-6.45pm) lies on a lane just southwest of the town.

Long abandoned, the church and neighbouring abbey had life breathed into them

---

SARDINIA'S CUTTING EDGE

Of all the fine knives made in Sardinia, the most prized is *sa pattadesa* (the Pattada knife) and these days they are only made by a handful of artisans. The classic Pattada knife, first made in the mid-19th century, is the *resolza*, with its so-called myrtle-leaf–shaped blade that folds into a horn handle. Only the finest knives have their blades protected in such a way. To a Sardinian a *sa pattadesa* is the ultimate in Sardinian craftsmanship, more impressive than any valuable piece of jewellery.

Most of the best craftsmen only work to order and take at least two days to fashion such a knife, folding and tempering the steel for strength and sharpness. The handle is then carved from a single piece of mouflon horn. If you're looking at a handle that is two parts screwed together, you're not looking at a quality piece. A good knife will cost at least €10 a centimetre.

In the past such knives were made all over the island, but now only a few towns follow the traditional methods. Pattada is the most famous, although quality knives are also made in Arbus, Santu Lussurgiu and Tempio Pausania. The classic *s'arburesa* (from Arbus) has a fat, rounded blade and is used for skinning animals, while the *lametta* of Tempio Pausania is a rectangular job good for stripping the bark from cork oaks. Of the *pattadesa* knives the best known is the *fogarizzu*. The best *s'arburesa* to look for is the *pusceddu*.

Note that it is illegal in Italy to carry a blade longer than 4cm. Getting the knife home may prove another headache, due to increased levels of security.

---

by a small Benedictine community invited to install themselves there in 1955. The abbey had to be rebuilt from scratch, but the church was in better shape and has been much improved over the years. The white-and-grey banded façade with three levels of blind arches and patterned decoration hark to its Pisan origins. Inside is an intriguing stone Gothic pulpit that rests on four legs.

BONORVA & AROUND

About 14km south of Torralba along the SS131 highway (exit to the east), this ridgetop farming town is home to yet another **Museo Archeologico** (☎ 079 86 78 94; admission €2, with Necropoli di Sant'Andrea di Priu €4; ☾ 4-7pm Tue-Sat, 10am-1pm & 4-7pm Sun Jun-Sep, by appointment other months), just off Piazza Sant'Antonio. Housed in former convent buildings adjacent to the Chiesa di Sant'Antonio, the display starts in the Middle Ages and proceeds back in time through vaulted rooms to the Neolithic era.

More interesting is the excursion east of the town to the **Necropoli di Sant'Andrea di Priu** (☎ 079 86 78 94; admission €3.50; ☾ 9.30am-7.30pm Jun-Sep, call ahead other months). The road drops from the heights that cradle Bonorva into farming country, and the way is signposted. Before reaching the necropolis, take the turn-off for **Rebeccu**, a windswept and largely abandoned medieval hamlet with tiny lanes and tinier houses.

Back on the main road, you push on a couple of kilometres eastward and take the turn-off for the rustic **Chiesa di Santa Lucia**, which retains some Romanesque traces and attracts jolly groups of pilgrims on the first days of May. The necropolis, virtually across the road, is made up of around 20 small grottoes carved into the trachyte and dating as far back as 4000 BC. The **Tomba del Capo** is by far the most interesting. In the early-Christian period three of the main rooms were transformed into a place of worship, and partly restored frescoes from the 5th century survive in two of them. Most striking is the fresco of a woman in the *aula* (hall) where the faithful heard Mass.

Getting around this area without your own transport is well-nigh impossible, although a few ARST bus services run from Sassari to Bonorva (€3.15, 40 to 50 minutes). Two come from Alghero (€4.03, 1½ hours).

THE NORTH COAST

Northwest of Sassari the land flattens out towards the sea. It's hotter and drier up here, a flat landscape of cactus and junipers. Porto Torres is the north coast's most important port, but it's a dusty, dead-end place fringed by petrochemical plants. This is a shame, as the coast is lovely. If you head further west to Stintino you'll find one of the island's most beautiful beaches.

PORTO TORRES
pop 21,700

Porto Torres had its heyday under the Romans, who first founded the town as their principal port along Sardinia's north coast. It remained one of the island's key ports until well into the Middle Ages and was long the capital of the Guidicato di Torres. Little is left of this former glory – pirate raids and debilitating malaria reduced the town to little more than a backwater, and today it has a hang-dog appearance. The port, however, is still busy with ferries to and from Corsica, and it's certainly worth making the effort to see the lovely Pisan Basilica di San Gavino.

Orientation

From the main port and Piazza Colombo you enter the heart of town, crossing the adjacent square, Piazza XX Settembre, from where the main boulevard, Corso Vittorio Emanuele, pushes south.

Information

Banca Nazionale del Lavoro (Corso Vittorio Emanuele 20) One of several banks with ATMs along the main drag.
Post office (8.15am-1.15pm Mon-Fri, 8.15am-12.15pm Sat) At Via Ponte Romano, it's three blocks right of Corso Vittorio Emanuele, close in from the port.
Tourist office (079 51 50 00; Via Roma 3; 8.30am-1pm & 6-8pm Mon-Sat) A couple of streets back from the port just off the *corso*. If you want to embark on a tour of Isola Asinara from Porto Torres, inquire about tickets here.

Sights

BASILICA DI SAN GAVINO

The limestone **Basilica di San Gavino** (admission €1.50; 8.30am-1pm & 3-7pm) is Sardinia's largest Romanesque church, and it must have been an impressive sight before the urban sprawl crept up and surrounded it. The Pisans made a good job of pilfering its two dozen marble columns from the nearby Roman site. More unusual still, each end of the church is rounded off by an apse – there is no façade.

The church is built on the site of an ancient pagan burial ground and takes its name from one of the great Sardinian saints, the Roman soldier Gavino, who commanded the garrison at Torres in Diocletian's reign. Ordered to put to death two Christian priests, Protus and Januarius, he was converted by them and himself shared their martyrdom. All three were beheaded on 25 October 304. Evidence for these events is scanty, but the legend of the *martiri turritani* (martyrs of Torres) flourishes.

To get here follow the signs down Corso Vittorio Emanuele south from the port for about 1.5km. The basilica is one block west of the street.

PARCO ARCHEOLOGICO & ANTIQUARIUM

Most of Roman Turris Libisonis lies beneath the modern port, but some vestiges have been uncovered. Known collectively as the 'archaeological park', it is made up of the remains of public baths, an overgrown Roman bridge and the so-called Palazzo del Re Barbaro. The latter is the centrepiece and constitutes the main public bathing complex of the Roman city. Parts of the town's main roads, some *tabernae* (shops) and some good floor mosaics can also be seen on the site, which is entered via the **Antiquarium** (admission €2; 9am-8pm Tue-Sat). Almost all the items in this museum were found in Roman Turris, and they include a range of ceramics, busts, oil lamps and glassware. The site is on the road between the main port and the Grimaldi line's docks, about a five-minute walk.

Sleeping

Porto Torres is not the kind of place you really want to hang around in long, but if you get stuck there are three hotels.

Hotel Elisa (079 51 32 60; fax 079 51 37 68; Via Mare 2; s/d with breakfast €50/73;) You can almost drop anchor here as this small but neat hotel is only a block back from the port. The rooms are painted blue and have all mod cons, including TV, phone and minibar. Most rooms have sea views.

Eating

Cristallo (079 51 49 09; Piazza XX Settembre 11; meals €35; closed Mon) This is a sprawling modern restaurant with a terrace on the town's main shopping street. Exercise your tastebuds with good seafood and a selection of Sardinian favourites, such as lamb. Sweet treats include *pan a spagila con crema*, a decadent cream-cake affair.

DETOUR: MONTE D'ACCODDI

Midway between Porto Torres and Sassari, 11km along the SS131, you'll find a signpost for the temple of **Monte d'Accoddi** (☎ 079 201 60 99; admission €2.07, with guide in Italian €3.10; ⏰ 9am-6pm Apr-Jun, 9am-8pm Jul-Sep, 8am-5pm Oct-Mar), built in the 3rd millennium BC.

Nowhere else in the Mediterranean has such a structure been unearthed. The closest comparable buildings are the fabled ziggurats of the Euphrates and Tigris River valleys in the Middle East, and so the temple is often referred to as a ziggurat. Excavations have revealed there was a Neolithic village here as early as 4500 BC. The temple went through several phases and appears to have been abandoned around 1800 BC. Soon after, the first *nuraghe,* perhaps the architectural signature of another race, began to be raised.

Before you get too excited, you won't actually see anything like the Mayan temple you might be imagining. Instead you will just make out a rectangular-based structure (30m by 38m), tapering to a platform and preceded by a long ramp. On either side of the ramp are a menhir and a stone altar believed to be for sacrifices. The altar belongs to a temple that predates the ziggurat. Images in Sassari's Museo Nazionale Sanna (p137) will help you to visualise the temple as it was.

Crossing's Café (Corso Vittorio Emanuele 53) This place does good *panini* (filled rolls) for €3.

Getting There & Away

Tirrenia (☎ 199 12 31 99; www.tirrenia.it) and **Grandi Navi Veloci** (☎ 079 51 60 31; www.gnv.it) run ferries from Porto Torres to Genoa (€82, 11 hours). Between the two lines there are at least two sailings daily.

The French line **SNCM** (www.sncm.fr) also runs summer-only ferries to Marseille (€70, four weekly June to September). In high season you'll need to book well in advance. You can purchase tickets from **Agenzia Paglietti** (☎ 079 51 44 77; fax 079 51 40 63; Corso Vittorio Emanuele 19).

Most buses leave from Piazza Colombo, virtually at the port. Plenty go to Sassari (€1.45, 30 to 40 minutes). Others head for Alghero (€3, 50 minutes, six daily) and to Stintino (€2.01, 30 minutes, six daily). You can get tickets at **Bar Acciaro** (Corso Vittorio Emanuele 38) or at newsstands along the same street.

Trains run regularly to Sassari (€1.20, 15 minutes). There are a couple of direct trains to Cagliari (€13.60, 4½ hours, two daily), but otherwise you have to make connections along the way and it can be painfully slow going.

EAST OF PORTO TORRES

The coast east of Porto Torres gradually gains height. The flat-topped tablelands of the Anglona, a struggling farm district, lie sandwiched between the Gallura to the east, Logudoro to the south and the small Ro-

mangia district to the west. Those arriving from the Gallura (see p167) will notice the switch from the grey granite that predominates the northeast to the russet tones of trachyte used commonly for building here.

Castelsardo

pop 5550

Huddled around the high cone of a promontory that juts northward into the Mediterranean, Castelsardo is one of those Genoese cliff cities whose beauty has survived their function. It was founded in the 12th century by the Dorias, who in a flash of inspiration called it Castel Genoese. The Spaniards came to town in 1326 and changed its name to Castel Aragonese, and it only became Castel Sardo (Sardinian Castle) in 1767 under the Piedmontese. By then this rocky outpost, once an independent *città demaniali* (royal city) with its own statutes and government, had already lost its point. Now the fortress is a museum, and locals linger on as reluctant custodians.

ORIENTATION

Buses pull up in Piazza Pianedda, where the coast road (undergoing several name changes as it passes through town) meets Via Nazionale, the main street that winds up to the top of the old town. You can drive all the way to the end of this road, but finding a parking spot is frequently impossible. A more dramatic approach on foot is to follow a path above the sea that cuts around from Via Nazionale beneath the city walls and around to a set of steps leading up to the cathedral.

INFORMATION

Tourist office (☎ 079 47 15 06; www.castelsardo .net, in Italian; Piazzetta del Popolo; 10am-12.30pm & 5-7.30pm) Note that it sometimes doesn't open.

SIGHTS

The best thing to do in Castelsardo is to just wander through the tight web of lanes as you gradually make your way to the top of the town.

The crowning piece is the medieval **Castello** built by the Doria family, or rather what remains of it (it's currently under renovation). You can see as far as Corsica on a clear day. Inside the castle, the **Museo dell'Intreccio** (admission free; ⏱ 9am-midnight Jul & Aug, 9am-1pm & 3-9pm Sep) provides an instructive lesson on traditional basket-weaving.

Just below the castle is the **Chiesa di Santa Maria**, largely a 16th-century structure. Its main interest lies in its 13th-century crucifix, known as the Critu Nieddu (Black Christ).

You will no doubt have already noticed the bell tower of the **Cattedrale di Sant'Antonio Abate**, a slender dark finger pointing to the heavens and topped by a brightly tiled cupola. In a setting worthy of northern European fairy tales, the church almost appears suspended in mid-air atop the craggy cliffs. A small terrace just nearby and slightly above the church affords views of it and along the northwestern coast of the island.

Inside, the main altar is dominated by the *Madonna con gli Angeli*, by the mysterious Maestro di Castelsardo. More of his works can be viewed in the **crypts** (admission €2; ⏱ 10am-8pm Jul & Aug, 10.30am-1pm & 3.30-8pm Jun) below the church. A series of small rooms chiselled out of the living rock are what remain of the Romanesque church that once stood here. You can admire several more works by the Maestro here, the best of them his *San Michele Arcangelo*.

The crypt exit takes you past neat lawns that separate you from the Spanish-era seaward battlements.

A couple of small **beaches** flank the promontory.

FESTIVALS & EVENTS

On the Monday of Holy Week, the people of Castelsardo celebrate a series of Masses and processions as part of **Lunissanti**, ending with a solemn evening torchlight parade

through the old town that culminates at the Chiesa di Santa Maria.

SLEEPING

It's definitely worth staying overnight in Castelsardo, especially now that a number of B&Bs are opening up in the historic centre.

Hotel Riviera (☎ 079 47 01 43; www.hotelriviera.net; Lungomare Anglona 1; d low/high season €78/160; 🅿 🐾) Below the castle on the sweeping bay, Hotel Riviera is recently renovated and offers comfortable modern rooms. It's also just across the road from the town beach and at night you have fantastic views of the magically lit old town. Its restaurant, Fofo, is one of Castelsardo's best.

Casa Doria (☎ 349 355 78 82; Via Garibaldi 10; s/d €34/70; 🐾) This B&B is located right in the heart of the old town. Three double rooms make up the accommodation and all are furnished with period beds. The 3rd-floor breakfast room has a fantastic view of the Gulf of Asinara.

A few kilometres west of Castelsardo, just outside the average beach resort of Lu Bagnu, is one of the island's three youth hostels.

Ostello Golfo dell'Asinara (☎ 079 47 40 31; ostello .asinara@tiscalinet.it; Via Sardegna 1; per person incl breakfast €12; ⏱ Easter & mid-Jun–mid-Sep) Set in a leafy location, this hostel makes a cheap alternative. You can eat on the big veranda. A bed in a family room costs €14. The hostel hires out bikes, canoes and the like.

EATING

La Trattoria (☎ 079 47 06 61; Via Nazionale 20; meals €20-25; ⏱ Tue-Sun Oct-May) This is a refreshingly modest eating option. Inside, try for the table by the window overlooking the port. The pasta is the trattoria's strong point, especially the *pasta mazzafrissa*, made with ewe's milk.

La Guardiola (☎ 079 47 07 55; Piazza Bastione 4; meals €35; ⏱ Tue-Sun Oct-May) One of Castelsardo's most expensive restaurants, this place serves up quality seafood but its main selling point is the wonderful views from its unbeatable position at the top of the old town.

Cormorano (☎ 079 47 06 28; Via Colombo 5; meals up to €50; ⏱ Wed-Mon Oct-May) Another good seafood restaurant, Cormorano serves a recommended *linguine con sarde* (thin pasta with sardines) and all sorts of things from tuna to sea anemones.

SASSARI & THE NORTHWEST

Da Ugo (☎ 079 474124; Corso Italia 7/c; meals €40-45; ☺ closed Thu Oct-May) At the eastern entrance of Lu Bagnu (about 2km from Piazza Pianedda) is another local star. The main courses are Ugo's strong point, with classics such as *capretto al forno* (oven-baked kid meat) and some fine seafood.

Il Piccolo Borgo (☎ 079 47 05 16; Via Seminario 4; plates €10) This handy snack bar is in the historic centre. It serves delicious plates of cured hams and cheeses, and there's a small seating area upstairs.

SHOPPING
You won't fail to notice the handicrafts shopping emporia on the way into Castelsardo. This all started with the basket-weaving for which the town is best known. As you wander through the old town you'll still see women settled on their doorsteps, creating intricate baskets and other objects of all shapes and sizes.

GETTING THERE & AWAY
ARST and other buses stop just off Piazza Pianedda. They run each way between Sassari (€2.01, one hour, five daily) and Santa Teresa di Gallura (€4.44, 1½ hours, five daily). Some buses run to/from Porto Torres too (€2.01, 50 minutes). You can buy tickets for ARST buses from the nameless *edicola* (newsstand) on Piazza Pianedda.

Local orange minibuses run regularly from Piazza Pianedda to Lu Bagnu.

Around Castelsardo
With your own vehicle you could comfortably take in the following places in a one-day circuit from Castelsardo. If you're relying on public transport it becomes substantially more difficult.

TERGU
Barely 10km south of Castelsardo lies a fine Romanesque church, the **Nostra Signora di Tergu**. A series of modern statues representing the Stations of the Cross (the episodes of Christ's punishment and death) lead the way into town. The church is set in a pleasant garden, partly made up of the few visible remains of a one-time Benedictine monastery. Built in the 13th century of dark wine-red trachyte and white limestone, the façade is a particularly pretty arrangement

of arches, columns, geometric patterns and a simple rose window.

NURAGHE SU TESORU & VALLEDORIA
On the left-hand side of the SS200 road, 5km east of Castelsardo, you'll see the **Nuraghe Su Tesoru**, built towards the end of the era of *nuraghe* construction. There's nowhere convenient to stop here, so blink and you could miss it.

Seven kilometres on you arrive at the sprawling settlement of Valledoria, fronted by beaches that stretch more than 10km east to Isola Rossa. West of the settlement shady pine stands provide a thick buffer between the sea and the inland roads. Campers will be happy at **Camping La Foce** (☎ 079 58 21 09; fax 079 58 21 91; www.foce.it; camp sites per adult €12, d bungalows €100; Ⓟ ⚲), which has great facilities (including a pool) and backs onto a lagoon. There's a free boat across the lagoon to the beach.

ARST buses running between Santa Teresa di Gallura and Castelsardo stop in the town itself. If you can't convince the bus driver to stop at the camping ground turn-off, you'll have to hitch or walk.

SEDINI
With some of its houses built into the living rock, Sedini makes a worthwhile excursion from Castelsardo.

Before you get there, stop at the so-called **Roccia dell'Elefante** (Elephant Rock), a bizarre trachyte rock formation right on the Sedini road at the highway interchange with the SS200. Inside are some pre-*nuraghe* tombs, or *domus de janas*. Across the road a cluster of likely lads hang about trying to sell Sardinian souvenirs – anything from cork-covered bottles to Pattada knives.

Eleven kilometres south is Sedini, where you will soon see the *domus de janas* on the main road (Via Nazionale) through town. By the Middle Ages farmers had made their home in this series of ancient tombs. The *domus* was then used as a prison until the 19th century, when it was again converted into a house. It now contains a small **display** (☺ 9am-8pm Jun-Sep) of traditional farming and household implements. Contact the **Cooperative Setin** (☎ 079 58 85 81; web.tiscali .it/sedini).

ARST buses run from Castelsardo (€1.19, 22 minutes, three daily).

WEST OF PORTO TORRES

The headland west of Porto Torres is a flat, dry plain more in keeping with the semi-deserts of Africa than with Italy. Frequently whipped by the *maestrale* (northwesterly wind), the undulating countryside has a desolate feel. But follow the road around to the northwestern tip of the headland and you'll find laid-back Stintino, approached via its shimmering *saline* (saltpans) and culminating in Spiaggia della Pelosa, a beach of adjective-defying beauty.

Stintino

Once a small coterie of fishing families dedicated to tuna fishing, Stintino has since become a tiny tourist resort with a sunny disposition, its rows of cubist houses reminiscent of southern Spain or North Africa. The pastel-painted town has real charm, wedged between its two ports – one full of bobbing blue fishing boats (Porto Mannu), the other given over to yachts (Porto Minori). Then there are the beautiful Caribbean-blue beaches of Spiaggia delle Saline and Spiaggia della Pelosa.

A tight community of about 1000 lives in Stintino. Many are descended from the 45 families forcibly removed from Isola Asinara in the 1880s, when the state decided to turn the island into a prison and quarantine station. Stintino developed a reputation for its tuna hunt, a bloody annual event known as the *mattanza* (slaughter).

The private tourist office **Mare e Natura** (☎ 079 52 00 97; info@marenatura.it; Via Sassari 77; ☯ 9.30am-1pm & 5-8pm Mon-Sun Jun-Sep, 9.30am-1pm Mon-Sat Oct-May) has information on accommodation, boat hire and excursions to the Parco Nazionale dell'Asinara (p152).

You can also book cruises around the island, including lunch on board, with **Stintours** (☎ 079 52 31 60; www.stintours.com; Lungomare C Colombo 39). The most exciting is the cruise on an old-fashioned boat with a *vela latina* (triangular sail). It costs €57 per person (minimum of six).

SIGHTS

The bloody scenes of the *mattanza* are captured on film in the **Museo della Tonnara** (adult/child €2/1; ☯ 10am-1pm & 6-9pm Mon-Sun Jun-Sep) at Porto Mannu. The six rooms are ordered as the six chambers of the *tonnara* (the net in which the fish are caught), and documents,

seafaring memorabilia, photos and film recall this centuries-old trade. The *tonnara* here was shut down in 1974, although locals attempted to revive it briefly in the late 1990s for scientific purposes. The *mattanza* still takes place in Carloforte and Portoscuso, in the south, as well as a couple of spots in Sicily. For more on the tuna hunt, see the boxed text, p102).

Just south of Stintino a signpost left will direct you to the abandoned *tonnara* and the **Spiaggia delle Saline**, once the site of a busy saltworks. The marshes extend inland to form the **Stagno Casaraccio**, a big lagoon where you might just see flamingos at rest.

ACTIVITIES

Aside from excursions to the Parco Nazionale dell'Asinara you can indulge in all sorts of water activities, such as **windsurfing** and **diving**. You'll find most of these operators at Spiaggia della Pelosa (p152).

In late August you can also catch Stintino's **regatta**, a race of 'Latin' sailing boats whose triangular sails fill the narrow causeway between Stintino and the Isola Asinara like a flock of big, white birds.

SLEEPING

There are three hotels in Stintino; the bigger resorts are further up at Capo del Falcone (p152). Inquire at Mare e Natura (left) or Stintours (left) about villa and apartment rentals.

Albergo Silvestrino (☎ 079 52 34 73; www.silves trino.it, in Italian; Via XXI Aprile 4; s/d €56/98; ☯) This tastefully spruced-up hotel near the port has good-sized if slightly sparse rooms. Go for the top floor if you can, as the spacious terraces are well worth the stairs. The restaurant is the best in Stintino, serving dishes such as *riso al tonno mantecato* (tuna risotto).

Albergo Lina (☎ 079 52 30 71; www.linahotel.it, in Italian; Via Lepanto 38; d €72) A neat little hotel right in front of Porto Minori, Lina has 10 simple rooms. The only drawback is the lack of air-con in summer.

EATING

Ristorante L'Ancora (☎ 079 527 90 09; meals €35; ☯ Jun-Sep) Featuring a charming veranda with magnificent sea views, L'Ancora offers good seafood. It's north of Stintino on the way to Spiaggia della Pelosa; turn right into the Ancora residential complex and follow the signs.

Skipper (Lungomare C Colombo 57; salads & meals €6.50, burgers €4.50; ⊗ daily Jun-Sep) This popular, casual bar has chairs set out overlooking Porto Mannu. The food is freshly made and quite delicious. Salads, hamburgers and hot plates from lasagne to *melanzane* (aubergines layered with cheese and tomato) are on offer. It's well worth saving some room for the homemade *seadas* (pastry turnovers with ricotta and honey).

Ristorante Da Antonio (☎ 079 53 70 77; Via Marco Polo 16; meals €30-35) This bright family-run place is just off Porto Minori. The strong points are fish and local vegetables.

GETTING THERE & AWAY
Up to eight buses run from Sassari to Stintino and Spiaggia della Pelosa in summer (€3.15, one hour 10 minutes). Up to six run from Porto Torres (€2.01, 30 minutes).

Capo del Falcone

Holiday complexes, residences and restaurants fill in the gaps between the town and the northern tip of the peninsula, **Capo del Falcone**. Some lucky folk have built their holiday homes on the craggy reaches of the northern tip. You can walk around to the cliffs, where the sunsets are awesome.

People stream up here to the **Spiaggia della Pelosa**, a salt-white strip of sand lapped by turquoise waters. Overlooked by a craggy Catalano-Aragonese watchtower on a lonely offshore islet, it presents a dream-like picture.

Two kilometres north of Stintino, just before Pelosa beach, you'll find the **Asinara Diving Centre** (☎ 079 52 70 00; www.asinaradiving center.it; Porto dell'Ancora) at the Ancora hotel. It offers a range of dives around Capo del Falcone and the Asinara park. Further north, on Pelosa beach, is the **Windsurfing Centre Stintino** (☎ 079 52 70 06; www.windsurfingcenter.it), which offers windsurfing lessons (€30 per lesson) and full courses (€140), including courses for children aged over eight.

Right at the northern tip of the beach is the gorgeously sited **La Pelosetta Residence Hotel** (☎ 079 52 71 88; www.lapelosetta.it; half board per person low/high season €49/98, 4-bed apt per week low/high season €266/1015; ⊗ Apr-Oct). It's a mixture of hotel rooms and self-catering apartments, all with uninterrupted views of the stunning beach. The half-board option is not such a restriction when you consider that this is one of the finest restaurants on the cape.

An hourly summer bus service runs from Spiaggia delle Saline via Stintino to Spiaggia della Pelosa and Capo del Falcone. If driving you must pay an attendant (up to €4.50 for half a day) to park around Spiaggia della Pelosa.

Parco Nazionale dell'Asinara

Across the shimmering waters from Spiaggia della Pelosa lies the Isola Asinara (Donkey Island), which was designated a national park in 1997.

The name comes from the island's unique population of miniature albino donkeys, which along with mouflon (silky-haired wild sheep) and pigs are its only inhabitants. It wasn't always so. The Ligurians who settled on this coast lived here until the state evicted them in the 1880s, forcing them to settle in Stintino. The island then became a maximum-security prison and a quarantine station for cholera victims.

In recent years the park has been the subject of much controversy. The justice ministry has still not ceded all its land to the regional government, and competing private interests want to build villas and even tourist complexes despite the area's national-park status. Much remains to be done before the park will be properly up and running.

Tours of the island are only possible with licensed operators setting out from Stintino. Regular bus boats are run from Stintino (€22) at 9.30am and 3.30pm, and from Porto Torres (€29) at 9am between Easter and September.

Once debarked at the southern end of the island at Porticciolo Fornelli you can take a bus (€6.60) to **Cala d'Oliva** beach in the northeast. From there you can hire bicycles (€5.80) or join a 4WD tour (€27). However, much of the island remains off-limits to visitors, in an attempt to protect the unusual fauna. This includes the beach of **Cala Sant'Andrea**, which is a breeding ground for turtles. You will need to bring your own lunch and drinks, as there is nowhere on the island to buy anything.

If you opt for the afternoon trip from Stintino, you will be taken on a guided

SASSARI &
THE NORTHWEST

hike about one quarter of the way up the island via a ruined castle (the Castellaccio) and back. Other walking, biking, nature-watching and 4WD excursions can be arranged with a couple of agencies in Stintino (see p151).

Tickets are available at **Agenzia La Nassa** (☎ 079 52 00 60; www.stintinoincoming.com; Via Sassari 6) in Stintino and the tourist office in Porto Torres (p147), or you can book by calling ☎ 800 56 11 66 (toll free in Italy).

ALGHERO

pop 40,000

Alghero is Sardinia's most picturesque medieval city. Its sand-coloured historic centre is a medley of moulded cornices, domes and turrets, basking in a warm apricot glow, and most of its alleys slope down to the port, set in a wide bay. Sandy beaches curve away under the slope of green headlands to the north. It remains a prosperous fishing port, and is justifiably famous for its blood-red coral, lobsters and sardines. Many fisherfolk still speak a pure form of Catalan, and Alghero is unique in Sardinia for having retained its Spanish linguistic heritage. Even today, Catalan nationalists in Barcelona think of Alghero as Barceloneta (little Barcelona).

In recent years the city seems to have woken up to its own attractiveness, and its popularity is such that in summer the population swells to more than 100,000. It is the least Sardinian of the island's cities, open to the sea and outside visitors, and the Algheresi seem to have inherited something of the Catalan business sense, sedulously promoting local tourism.

HISTORY

Alghero doesn't appear on history's radar until around the 13th century, by which time it was a small fortress port founded by the Genoese. Theories of an earlier Arab or even Roman settlement abound but enjoy no proof. Little is known of the Genoese settlement except that it was briefly taken by their rivals, the Pisans, in the 1280s.

Alghero remained a focus of resistance to the Catalano-Aragonese invasion of the island in 1323 and was only subdued 30 years later. The local population, part Gen-

oese and part Sardinian, rebelled but in 1354 King Pere the Ceremonious led another force and this time held on to the city. Catalan colonists were encouraged to settle here, and after another revolt in 1372 the remaining Sardinians were expelled and relocated inland. From then on Alghero (apparently named after algae that washed up on the coast) became resolutely Catalan and called itself Alguer.

The settlement remained a principal port of call in Sardinia for its Catalano-Aragonese and subsequently Spanish masters. Raised to the status of city in 1501, Alghero experienced a frisson of excitement when Holy Roman Emperor (and king of Spain) Charles V arrived in 1541 to lead a campaign against North African corsairs. Unhappily, the discovery of the Americas was bad news for Alghero, whose importance as a trading port quickly ebbed.

In 1720 the town passed to the House of Savoy. By the 1920s the population was scarcely more than 10,000. Bombardment of the historic centre in 1943 left scars that have never healed, but only since WWII has the frenetic process of expansion beyond the old centre taken place.

ORIENTATION

The old town's seaward walls encircle land jutting west into the Mediterranean. On its northern side is the modern port, and the new town radiates inland to the north, east and south. Several of the classier hotels and some lively summer bars spread out along the coastal road south, while Alghero's beaches stretch to the north, backed by residential blocks, hotels and a camping ground. The train station is also here, but buses terminate just outside the old town on Via Catalogna.

INFORMATION
Bookshops

Il Labrinto (Map p156; ☎ 079 98 04 96; Via Carlo Alberto 119) Has a good range of books (mostly in Italian) on all things Sardinian. Stocks English novels.

Libreria Ex Libris (Map p156; Via Carlo Alberto 2) Has a nice selection of art books. Stocks English novels.

Emergency

Municipal police (Map p154; ☎ 800 31 61 77; Via Vittorio Emanuele 113)

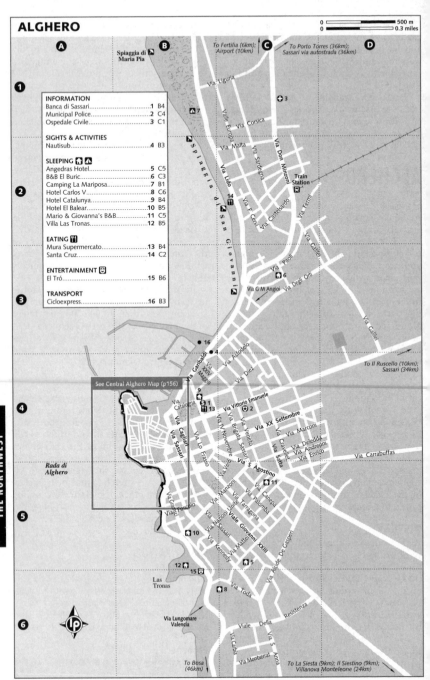

ALGHERO

0 — 500 m
0 — 0.3 miles

INFORMATION
Banca di Sassari...........................1 B4
Municipal Police...........................2 C4
Ospedale Civile...........................3 C1

SIGHTS & ACTIVITIES
Nautisub...........................4 B3

SLEEPING
Angedras Hotel...........................5 C5
B&B El Buric...........................6 C3
Camping La Mariposa...........................7 B1
Hotel Carlos V...........................8 C6
Hotel Catalunya...........................9 B4
Hotel El Balear...........................10 B5
Mario & Giovanna's B&B...........................11 C5
Villa Las Tronas...........................12 B5

EATING
Mura Supermercato...........................13 B4
Santa Cruz...........................14 C2

ENTERTAINMENT
El Tró...........................15 B6

TRANSPORT
Cicloexpress...........................16 B3

See Central Alghero Map (p156)

Spiaggia di Maria Pia

To Fertilia (6km);
Airport (10km)

To Porto Torres (36km);
Sassari via autostrada (36km)

Via Liguria

Viale Europa

Via Corsica

Via Malta

Via Lido

Via Don Minzoni

Train Station

Via Sardegna

Via Ferni

Via F Cervi

Via Castelsardo

Via Caller

Via Paoli

Via Degli Orti

Via G M Angioi

To Il Ruscello (10km);
Sassari (34km)

Via Garibaldi

Via XXIV Maggio

Via Astoddo

Via Diez

Via Vittorio Emanuele

Via Catalogna

Via Cagliari

Via Lp Frasso

Via Brigata Sassari

Via Venezio

Via V Novembre

Via S Agostino

Via XX Settembre

Via Marcom

Via Deledda

Via Andreoni

Via Enrico

Via Carrabuffas

Via Carlo
Felice

Via Cavedet

Via Sata

Via Cenina

Via Palomba

Via Tarragona

Via Manzoni

Via Kennedy

Via Nazioni Unite

Viale Giovanni XXIII

Via Matteotti

Via Alcide De Gasperi

Rada di Alghero

Via Gian Pascolo

Las Tronas

Via Toda

Via Lungomare Valencia

Viale Della Resistenza

Via Cuba

Via Montserrat

Via S Anna

To Bosa (46km)

To La Siesta (9km); Il Siestino (9km);
Villanova Monteleone (24km)

Spiaggia di San Giovanni

Internet Access

Bar Miramare (Map p156; ☎ 079 973 10 27; Via Gramsci 2; per hr €5; ⏰ 8.30am-1am & 4.30pm-2am) Surf your way through a cappuccino while checking your emails at this gruff, old-fashioned bar.

Poco Loco (Map p156; Via Gramsci 8; per hr €5; ⏰ 7.30pm-1am daily) Live-music spot Poco Loco has three computer terminals.

Medical Services

Farmacia Bulla (Map p156; Via Garibaldi 13)
Farmacia Cabras (Lungomare Dante 20) English-speaking service.
Ospedale Civile (Map p154; ☎ 079 99 62 00; Via Don Minzoni) The town's main hospital.

Money

You'll find banks with ATMs and change facilities all over the old town.
Banca Carige (Map p156; Via Sassari 13) Has an ATM.
Banca di Sassari (Map p154; Via La Marmora) A Western Union agent.

Post

Main post office (Map p156; Via Carducci 35; ⏰ 8.15am-6.15pm Mon-Fri, 8.15am-1pm Sat)

Tourist Information

Tourist office (Map p156; ☎ 079 97 90 54; www .comune.alghero.ss, in Italian; Piazza Porta Terra 9; ⏰ 8am-8pm Mon-Sat, 9am-1pm Sun Apr-Oct, 8am-2pm Mon-Sat Nov-Mar). Has to be the best-organised tourist office in Sardinia.
Tourist office (☎ 079 93 51 24; ⏰ 8.30am-2.30pm & 5-10pm) At the airport.

Travel Agencies

CTS (Map p156; ☎ 079 98 00 98; Via XX Settembre 30) A branch of the national youth travel agent. It operates out of Shardana Tours.

SIGHTS

Alghero's *centro storico* (historic centre) is a compact mesh of narrow cobbled alleyways, hemmed in by Spanish Gothic palazzos gently mouldering away.

The landward city walls were largely torn down in the 19th century and partly replaced by the **Giardini Pubblici**, a green space that now effectively separates the old town from the new.

All that remains of the main entrance to the city is the **Torre Porta a Terra** (Map p156; ☎ 079 973 40 45; ⏰ 10am-1pm & 6pm-midnight Mon-Sat, 6pm-midnight Sun May-Sep, reduced hr Oct-Apr), a single

tower that once formed part of the original Porta a Terra (Land Gate). It now does duty as an information office and bookshop.

To the south, another tower, **Torre di San Giovanni** (Map p156; ☎ 079 973 16 05; admission €2; ⏰ 10am-1pm & 6.30-10pm Tue-Sat, 6.30-10pm Sun-Mon Jul-Aug, 10am-1pm & 5-8pm Tue-Sun Apr-Jun), has been turned into a multimedia history display on Alghero (closed at the time of writing).

The **Torre Sulis** (Map p156; also known as the Torre dello Sperone) closes off the defensive line of towers to the south of the old town, while to the north the **Bastione della Maddalena** (Map p156), with its like-named tower, forms the only extant remnant of the city's former land battlements.

Just west of that bastion is the **Porta a Mare** (Map p156), by which you can enter Piazza Civica. Steps by the gate lead up to the portside bastions, which stretch around to what remains of the northern **Torre della Polveriera** (Map p156). The Mediterranean crashes up against the seaward walls of the **Bastioni di San Marco** (Map p156) and **Bastioni di Cristoforo Colombo** (the southern wall of the city), and the views out towards Capo Caccia are wonderful. It's a great place to come in the early evening as the promenade is lined with some delightful eateries and bars – great for a summer sunset and a romantic spot for dinner.

Cattedrale di Santa Maria

The bombastic, bright, neoclassical façade of the city's **cathedral** (Map p156; ☎ 079 97 92 22; Piazza Duomo; ⏰ 7am-noon & 5-7.30pm), with its fat Doric columns out of all proportion to the square at their feet, is an unfortunate 19th-century addition to what was a bit of a hybrid anyway. Built along Catalan Gothic lines in the 16th century, the cathedral preserves some original elements. Inside, the style is largely Renaissance, with some late-baroque baubles added under the Savoy family in the 18th century.

Of greater interest is the Catalan **campanile** (€1.50; ⏰ 7-9.30pm Jul-Sep) around the back in Via Principe Umberto. This tall octagonal tower displays an Isabelline flourish in the gracious lines of its doorway.

Museo Diocesano d'Arte Sacra

In the grand spaces that were once the Oratorio del Rosario is the cathedral **museum** (Map p156; ☎ 079 973 30 41; www.algheromuseo.it; Via

Maiorca; adult/concession €2.50/1.50; 🕙 10am-12.30pm Thu-Tue year-round & 5-8pm Mar-May & Oct-Dec, 6-9pm Jun & Sep, 7-11pm Jul & Aug). It houses a good collection of religious art including silverware, statuary, paintings and wood carving. A ghoulish touch is the reliquary of what is claimed to be one of the *innocenti* (newborn babies slaughtered by Herod in

his search for the Christ child). The tiny skull is chilling, but apparently it appealed to Alghero artist Francesco Pinna, who received it from a Roman cardinal in the 16th century.

The low, flat arch of the former chapel is clearly inspired by the Catalan Gothic style.

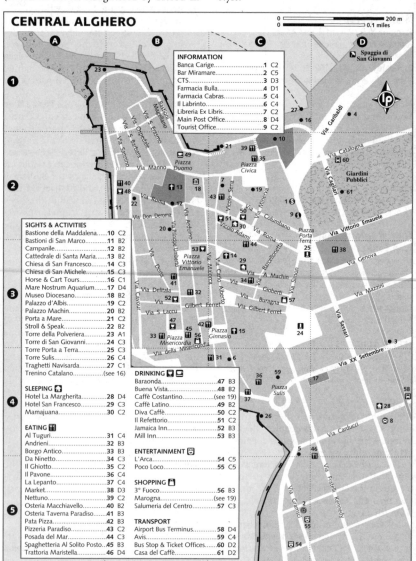

CENTRAL ALGHERO

0   200 m
0   0.1 miles

INFORMATION
Banca Carige	1 C2
Bar Miramare	2 C5
CTS	3 D3
Farmacia Bulla	4 D1
Farmacia Cabras	5 C4
Il Labrinto	6 C4
Libreria Ex Libris	7 C2
Main Post Office	8 D4
Tourist Office	9 C2

Spaggia di San Giovanni

Giardini Pubblici

SIGHTS & ACTIVITIES
Bastione della Maddalena	10 C2
Bastioni di San Marco	11 B2
Campanile	12 B2
Cattedrale di Santa Maria	13 B2
Chiesa di San Francesco	14 C3
Chiesa di San Michele	15 C3
Horse & Cart Tours	16 C1
Mare Nostrum Aquarium	17 D4
Museo Diocesano	18 B2
Palazzo d'Albis	19 C2
Palazzo Machin	20 B2
Porta a Mare	21 C2
Stroll & Speak	22 B2
Torre della Polveriera	23 A1
Torre di San Giovanni	24 C3
Torre a Porta a Terra	25 C3
Torre Sulis	26 C4
Traghetti Navisarda	27 C1
Trenino Catalano	(see 16)

SLEEPING
Hotel La Margherita	28 D4
Hotel San Francesco	29 C3
Mamajuana	30 C2

EATING
Al Tuguri	31 C4
Andrieni	32 B3
Borgo Antico	33 B3
Da Ninetto	34 C3
Il Ghiotto	35 C2
Il Pavone	36 C4
La Lepanto	37 C4
Market	38 D3
Nettuno	39 C2
Osteria Macchiavello	40 B2
Osteria Taverna Paradiso	41 B3
Pata Pizza	42 B3
Pizzeria Paradiso	43 C2
Posada del Mar	44 C3
Spaghetteria Al Solito Posto	45 B3
Trattoria Maristella	46 D4

DRINKING
Baraonda	47 B3
Buena Vista	48 B2
Caffè Costantino	(see 19)
Caffè Latino	49 B2
Diva Caffè	50 C2
Il Refettorio	51 C2
Jamaica Inn	52 B3
Mill Inn	53 B3

ENTERTAINMENT
L'Arca	54 C5
Poco Loco	55 C5

SHOPPING
3° Fuoco	56 B3
Marogna	(see 19)
Salumeria del Centro	57 C3

TRANSPORT
Airport Bus Terminus	58 D4
Avis	59 C4
Bus Stop & Ticket Offices	60 D2
Casa del Caffè	61 D2

Piazza Sulis

SASSARI & THE NORTHWEST

Piazza Civica

Just inside the Port a Mare (Sea Gate) and once the administrative heart of Alghero, this busy, uneven square is still faced by reminders of Alghero's late-medieval splendour. It was from the window of the Gothic mansion **Palazzo d'Albis** (Map p156) that Charles V leaned out during his 1541 stay to declare in generous mood, 'You are all knights.'

Chiesa di San Francesco

Along Via Carlo Alberto, the Carrer Major (Main St) of old, now lined with shops and awash with their customers, is the restored **Chiesa di San Francesco** (Map p156; Via Carlo Alberto; ☺ 9.30am–noon & 5–7.30pm Mon-Sat, 5–7.30pm Sun), a combination of Romanesque and Gothic with an austere stone façade. Inside, most of what you see is a late-Renaissance remake of the church, which partly collapsed in 1593. The tranquil cloister's lower level dates to the 13th century. The buttery sandstone used in the arcades and columns lends it special warmth and makes it a wonderful setting for summer concerts.

Chiesa di San Michele

Further along Via Carlo Alberto is a **church** (Map p156; ☺ Mass) whose main feature is its majolica dome, typical of churches in Valencia, another former Catalan territory. The present tiles were laid in the 1960s, but this doesn't detract from the visual pleasure.

Just before you reach the church you cross Via Gilbert Ferret. The intersection is known as the *quatre cantonades* (four sides), and for centuries day-labourers would gather here in the hope of finding work.

ACTIVITIES

There are few activities within the huddle of Alghero proper, but you can visit **Mare Nostrum Aquarium** (Map p156; ☎ 079 97 83 33; Via XX Settembre 1; adult/child €5/3; ☺ 10am-1pm, varied afternoon hr Apr-Oct, 3-8pm Sat, Sun & holidays Nov-May), Sardinia's only aquarium. It's a good diversion for kids, with quite a variety of fishy elements from piranhas and leopard sharks to seahorses and reptiles.

Head to the port to join an excursion to the Grotta di Nettuno, an enormous sea cave at the foot of the Capo Caccia headland (p165). A couple of operators make the 2½-hour return trip but the main company is **Traghetti Navisarda** (Map p156; ☎ 079 95 06 03).

It runs several boats a day from April to October that allow you a fish-eye view of the coast from Alghero to Capo Caccia before depositing you at the grotto (adult/child €12/6 excluding admission to the grotto).

You can organise dives with a handful of outlets in Alghero, but they can't compare with **Diving Centre Capo Galera** (see p165), just outside Alghero at Capo Galera. **Nautisub** (Map p154; ☎ 079 95 24 33; Via Garibaldi 45) hires out gear for underwater fun.

North of Alghero's port, Via Garibaldi sweeps quickly up to the town's beaches, **Spiaggia di San Giovanni** (Map p154) and the adjacent **Spiaggia di Maria Pia**. Indeed, the line of beaches continues pretty much uninterrupted around the coast to Fertilia. The sand is fine and white, and the waters are a shade of clear turquoise, but the beaches get crowded in high summer and are sometimes inundated with seaweed.

TOURS

In summer, **horse and cart tours** (Map p156; adult/child €6/3) trot around the old town. The one-hour tour is a pleasant enough excursion and is particularly good with children. You will find the carriages drawn up on the port side of the Bastione della Maddalena.

For tiny tots you could pick up the **Trenino Catalano** (Map p156; adult/under 8 yr €5/3; ☺ Apr-Oct), a miniature train that tours the old town. Kids love it even if their parents wear those long-suffering expressions! Again, you'll find it down at the port. Buy tickets on board.

COURSES

If you fancy a course in Sardinian cuisine (or to brush up your Italian), **Stroll & Speak** (Map p156; ☎ 328 765 54 77; www.strollandspeak.com; Via Cavour 4; ☺ 9am-1pm & 2.30-8pm Mon-Sat) organises year-round culinary courses. A one-week, 13-hour session costs €200. Shorter courses are also available.

FESTIVALS & EVENTS

Alghero has a full calendar of festivals and events that preserve more than a whiff of the centuries of Catalan occupation.

February

Carnevale Celebrated with great vim and vigour. On *martedì grasso* (fat Tuesday or Shrove Tuesday) the effigy of a French soldier (the *pupazzo*) is tried and condemned to burn at the stake, followed by much merry-making.

March/April

Easter Holy Week Spanish-influenced processions carry figures of Christ and the Virgin through the old town enacting the *Misteri* (Passion of Christ) and *Incontru* (Meeting of the Virgin with Christ).

July/August

Estate Musicale Internazionale di Alghero (International Summer of Music) Runs throughout July and August, and features classical-music concerts in the contemplative setting of the Chiesa di San Francesco as well as impromptu outdoor performances around town.

Ferragosto (Feast of the Assumption) Celebrated all over Italy on 15 August. Alghero puts on a good show with fireworks, boat competitions, music and folkloric events.

September

Sagra dei Pescatori (Fisherman's Fair) Big food festival celebrating Alghero's long fishing tradition. There's lots of food and seaborne events. Dates vary, so check with the tourist office.

SLEEPING

Alghero is an increasingly popular destination in Sardinia and you'll need to book well in advance for accommodation in summer (July and August). For private parking you'll usually have to pay an additional €8 to €12.

Budget

There are no large budget options in Alghero. Your best bet is to check out the town's B&Bs and self-catering apartments, which offer a high standard of accommodation. The tourist office can give you a list. However, most of these places don't accept credit cards.

B&B El Buric (Map p154; ☎ /fax 079 989 20 19; www .bed-and-breakfast-sardinia.com; Via Enrico Costa 26; d low/ high season €55/75; P) El Buric has a top spot on the 6th floor of a modern apartment block (don't worry, it has a lift!). Simple, neat and summery, it's full of books and has a fabulous shaded veranda. It's also just a few steps from the beach, and Mario and Fiorella will lend you all the kit you need. They also have bikes on hand and can help arrange well-priced sailing trips.

Mamajuana (Map p156; ☎ 339 136 97 91; www .mamajuana.it; Vicolo Adami 12; s/d €60/80) This tiny B&B is in the old town overlooking Piazza Municipio. Three doubles and a single have been shoehorned in, but it's decorated with some style and the wooden ceilings lend it character. Breakfast is served in the nearby

café. The owners can also suggest other apartments for rent if they're booked up.

Mario & Giovanna's B&B (Map p154; ☎ 339 890 35 63; www.marioandgiovanna.com; Via E Porrino 17; s/d €30/50, d with bathroom €55) Run by an affable couple, this B&B has lovingly furnished, homy rooms. Mario worked as a chef in England and guests are welcomed with a glass of wine and titbits. Located in the blander modern part of town, it's around a 10-minute stroll to the historic centre.

Camping La Mariposa (Map p154; ☎ 079 95 03 60; www.lamariposa.it; Via Lido 22; camp sites per adult/tent €10.50/8, 4-person bungalow €75; ☀ Apr-Oct) About 2km north of the centre, this camp site is on the beach and has plenty of mature shady trees. We've had good feedback about this place, which isn't surprising given the switched-on reception and host of facilities, including a windsurfing school.

Midrange

Most of Alghero's midrange hotels flank the seafronts to the north and south of the centre. Those fronting the beaches to the north tend to be fairly big and characterless, although there are one or two worth considering. The finer hotels line the Lungomare Dante to the south of town.

Angedras Hotel (Map p154; ☎ 079 973 50 34; www .angedras.it; Via Frank 2; s/d €62/105; ☒ ☐) A cubist vision in white in a quiet residential street, the Angedras brings a touch of style to the hotel scene. The rooms are light and airy, with big French doors opening on to flowery patios. The breakfast is a delightful buffet of homemade pastries and sweets, and the wide terrace dotted with white umbrellas is a chic place to hang out in the evenings.

Hotel San Francesco (Map p156; ☎ /fax 079 98 03 30; www.sanfrancescohotel.com; Via Ambrogio Machin 2; s/d €55/90; ☒) This is the only place in the old town, and it's alone in exuding historic charm. Housed in the former convent of the Chiesa di San Francesco, the rooms are five star in monastic terms but still nothing fancy – aside from the satellite TV. Go for a room overlooking the lovely medieval cloisters.

Hotel Carlos V (Map p154; ☎ 079 97 95 01; www.hotel carlosv.it; Via Lungomare Valencia 24; d €95; P ☒ ☐ ☒) In a fine seafront position, this big low-rise hotel has recently benefited from a revamp. The exec-style rooms are slickly furnished with dark-blue fabrics and plenty of shiny wood. The best have views of the palm-fringed pool with the ocean beyond. There are large terraces and tennis courts.

Hotel El Balear (Map p154; ☎ 079 97 52 29; www .hotelelbalear.it; Lungomare Dante 32; s/d €70/103; ☿ Mar-Oct; ☒) The most modest waterfront option on the southern *lungomare*, the family-run Balear has a cheerful, lived-in feel even if its big, boxy furnishings scream '70s summer holidays.

Hotel Catalunya (Map p154; ☎ 079 95 31 72; www .hotelcatalunya.it; Via Catalogna 20; s/d €135/170; ℗ ☒) Boasting the red and yellow of the Catalan flag and situated opposite the Giardini Pubblici, the Catalunya has comfortable rooms. The top ones benefit from the building's height and have great views, which are equally enticing from the penthouse restaurant.

Hotel La Margherita (Map p156; ☎ 079 97 90 06; hotel.margherita@tiscalinet.it; Via Sassari 70; s/d incl breakfast €62/99; ℗ ☒) It's certainly not pretty, but the Margherita's got a helluva location, which allows it to charge midrange prices for somewhat worn accommodation. Still, it is an endearing place with energy-saving light bulbs in old chandeliers and big airy rooms above a noisy street.

Top End

Villa Las Tronas (Map p154; ☎ 079 98 18 18; www.hotel villalastronas.it; Via Lungomare Valencia 1; s/d €180/210; ℗ ☒ ▣ ▨) Splash out and stay at this palatial 19th-century hotel, situated on a promontory with balconies overlooking the waves. The rooms are pure *fin de siècle* plush with acres of brocade, elegant antiques and moody old oil paintings. A beauty centre, complete with indoor pool, hammam-massage facility and gymnasium, opened in late 2005.

EATING

Alghero has some fine restaurants offering varied menus for all budgets. Seafood predominates, and the town is famous for its sardines and rock lobsters. The latter is the most expensive item on the bill and is charged per gram, so get it weighed first.

Budget

Il Ghiotto (Map p156; ☎ 079 97 48 20; Piazza Civica 23; meals €10-15; ☿ Tue-Sun) This deli-cum– wine bar is a great place for an informal lunch. You need to get here early (around 12.30pm) before the ravening hordes descend. There are about five daily lunch options at the counter inside (once they're

gone, that's it!), and there are also freshly made sandwiches. The wine list is excellent, and this is one of the few places where you can try a glass (€8) of the famous Turriga.

Spaghetteria Al Solito Posto (Map p156; ☎ 328 913 37 45; Piazza Misericordia; meals €15-20; ☿ Fri-Wed) The corner TV and plastic tablecloths provide an underwhelming ambience, but the freebie plate of smoked ricotta and olives and toothsome choices equal excellent dining. The *seadas con miele* (fried Sardinian cheese pastry with honey) will make a soul-satisfying finale to your meal.

Santa Cruz (Map p154; Via Lido 2; pizza €6.50-8) This beach shack is a good place for an evening pizza after a strenuous day's tanning. Its wide terrace is also a nice spot for sundowners in summer.

A good stop for the impecunious but hungry is **Pizzeria Paradiso** (Map p156; Via Carlo Alberto 8). A big wedge of pizza won't cost more than €4 to take away. **Pata Pizza** (Map p156; Via Maiorca 89) is in much the same vein.

Other good alternatives to a full-blown restaurant meal are the menus of Alghero's stylish cafés. Diva Caffè, Caffè Latino and Caffè Costantino all serve excellent snacks and light meals (see p160).

Midrange

Osteria Taverna Paradiso (Map p156; ☎ 079 97 80 07; www.cheeseland.it, in Italian; Via Principe Umberto 29; meals €25; ☒) This unpretentious trattoria is presided over by Pasquale Nocella, the artistic-looking guy with the wild hair. The food here is excellent: hearty plates of grilled steak, mountains of steaming pasta, and lots and lots of cheese. The osteria has even won awards for its cheese. The pasta with aubergines and smoked ricotta packs a flavourful punch.

Nettuno (Map p156; ☎ 079 97 97 74; Bastione della Maddalena; meals €25-35; ☿ Thu-Tue) In a great location with a 3rd-floor terrace overlooking the port, Nettuno's atmosphere is positively boisterous and the boating décor jollies the whole thing along. The pasta with clams is *the* thing to eat here – the delicious aroma pervades the restaurant. Follow it with a plate of barbequed king prawns.

Osteria Macchiavello (Map p156; ☎ 079 98 06 28; Bastioni Marco Polo 57; meals €20-25; ☿ Wed-Mon) This is a restaurant for those who want full-on meaty flavours. Grilled meats include horse, beef and (sorry about this) – donkey.

Alternatively, there's a tasty wild-boar ragù and a few fishy dishes, including *zuppa di polpi e patate* (octopus and potato soup) as a whet-your-appetite starter.

Posada del Mar (Map p156; ☎ 079 97 95 79; Vicolo Adami 29; meals €30-35; ☽ Mon-Sat) A formal little place, Posada del Mar has tables covered in flowery tablecloths intimately arranged beneath its big barrel vaults. In summer the French doors are opened to the piazzetta outside. The house speciality is the *ricci* (sea urchins), although pizza is also served in the evenings.

Borgo Antico (Map p156; ☎ 079 98 26 49; Via Zaccaria 12; meals €30-35; ☽ Mon-Sat & lunch Sun) This place has the same formal air as Posada del Mar, but there is outdoor seating on the square. The cooking is Mediterranean and the *spaghetti all'aragosta* (lobster spaghetti; €26) is a price-savvy way to try some of that famous lobster.

Trattoria Maristella (Map p156; ☎ 079 97 81 72; Via Fratelli Kennedy 9; meals €22-25; ☽ lunch Mon-Sun) This is one of the best deals in town. The sunny yellow décor is classic modern Mediterranean, and in summer you can sit out in the street. There are plenty of vegetarian choices, including our favourite: pasta shells with tomatoes, rocket and ricotta.

Da Ninetto (Map p156; ☎ 079 97 80 62; Via Gioberti 4; meals €30; ☽ Wed-Mon) A bright hole-in-the-wall arrangement, Da Ninetto is the best place in town for reasonably priced lobster dishes.

Top End

Andrieni (Map p156; ☎ 079 98 20 98; Via Arduino 45; meals €50; ☽ Tue-Sun) This is Alghero's restaurant of the moment. In summer tables are set outdoors beneath the huge fig tree, where you dine on innovative dishes mixing cured meats and fruit, delicately cooked fish with seasonal vegetables and herbs, and some excellent grilled and roasted meats. The wine list is a weighty tome, and you need a menu for the cheese trolley. Unfortunately, the maître d' is a little on the haughty side.

Il Pavone (Map p156; ☎ 079 97 95 84; Piazza Sulis 3/4; meals €40-50; ☽ Mon-Sat) A classic of the Alghero dining scene, Il Pavone isn't as grand as Andrieni or La Lepanto, but the service is a lot more palatable. Tables overlook the lively Piazza Sulis and the food is seasonal, a mixture of Mediterranean and innovative Sardinian dishes.

Al Tuguri (Map p156; ☎ 079 97 67 72; Via Maiorca 113; meals €35-40; ☽ Mon-Sat) This cosy Catalan house serves dishes based on the fresh fish of the day, tuna, squid, rock lobster and the very best *bottarga* (mullet roe). It also has a range of speciality pastas, such as the *maltagliati con carciofi e fave* (pasta with artichokes and fava beans).

La Lepanto (Map p156; ☎ 079 97 91 16; Via Carlo Alberto 135; meals €40; ☽ closed Mon) This has long been Alghero's top fish restaurant: check out the grand tank of fish as you enter, the packed tables and the waiters run off their feet. But the service and food are not what they used to be – the increase in tourist trade has dulled Lepanto's innovative edge.

Self-Catering

If you want to put your own meals together you can stock up on fresh produce at the market (Map p156) between Via Sassari and Via Cagliari. Pick up anything missing at the **Mura Supermercato** (Map p154; Via La Marmora 28; ☽ 8.30am-10pm Mon-Sat).

DRINKING

Several bars along or near Spiaggia di San Giovanni can be fun for a drink or two earlier in the evening. Most of these places are open until 2am.

Baraonda (Map p156; Via P Umberto 75) This moody wine bar for swooning couples has burgundy walls and just a few tables; there's outside seating as well. It's quieter than a lot of the other places, so you should be able to find a seat here.

Il Refettorio (Map p156; ☎ 079 973 11 26; Vicolo Adami 47) A trendy wine bar crowded with a fashionable clientele, this is a great spot for a classy aperitif accompanied by plenty of gourmet nibbles. Food is served, but the main action is around the bar.

Diva Caffè (Map p156; Via Roma 40; cocktails €6.50; ☽ 10am-midnight Mon-Sat) This daytime café turns into a showy evening hub, where the suntanned come to take a cocktail in the square. It stays open until about 3am on Friday and Saturday in summer.

Caffè Latino (Map p156; Bastioni Magellano 10; cocktails €6.50, sandwiches €4.50; ☽ 9am-11pm Wed-Mon) This elegant cocktail (or coffee) spot is in a prime waterfront location with harbour views. Kick back in comfort in the stone-vaulted interior or outside on the promenade among the strollers.

Caffè Costantino (Map p156; Piazza Civica 31) The classiest coffee stop in town is located on the ground floor of the late-Gothic Palazzo d'Albis. It has an elegant terrace on the square.

Buena Vista (Map p156; Bastioni di San Marco 47) Buena Vista is the prime drinking spot for taking in the sunset over an early-evening aperitif…or two. If it gets too chilly, retire to the cavernous tavern below decks.

Mill Inn (Map p156; Via Maiorca 37; ☾ Thu-Tue) One of the busiest and cosiest bars in the old town, here the punters crowd in below the stone vaults for a Guinness. There's live music at weekends in summer.

Jamaica Inn (Map p156; Via Principe Umberto; snack €2.50-4.50; ☾ Tue-Sun) Drop in to this cheerful place for a beer and *bruschetta* (a rather un-Sardinian snack of toasted bread that can be covered in all manner of toppings).

ENTERTAINMENT

As the bars fade from about 1am on, the centre of pleasurable gravity shifts to the chi-chi waterfront area south of the old city.

In summer especially, the crowds head here for their drinks until about 4am.

Live Music

Poco Loco (Map p156; ☎ 079 973 10 34; Via Gramsci 8; ☾ 7pm-2am) With its cavernous atmosphere, good service and regular programme of live music, Poco Loco gets the thumbs up from readers. There's frothy draught beer, pizza (€6 to €8) to help stave off the midnight munchies and a bowling alley upstairs (closed Monday).

L'Arca (Map p156; Lungomare Dante 6) This big, open bar has masses of seating along the street (closed to traffic). Markets across the road add to the festival atmosphere and there's live music at weekends.

Nightclubs

Those who still haven't had enough can make for the summer (June to September) discos outside town. Entry to these places is generally €10 to €20. Drinks cost €5 to €10.

El Tró (Map p154; Via Lungomare Valencia 3; ☾ Tue-Sun) This beach bar is on a rocky outcrop just

---

BLOOD-RED GOLD

Since ancient times the red coral of the Mediterranean has beguiled and bewitched people. Many believed it to be the petrified blood of the Medusa, attributing to it aphrodisiac and other secret qualities, and fashioning amulets out of it.

Alghero's coast south of Capo Caccia is justifiably called the Riviera del Corallo (Coral Riviera). The coral fished here is of the highest quality and glows a dark orangey-red. The strong currents around the headland mean the little coral polyps have to work super hard to build their small coral trees, making them short and very dense to withstand the drag of the sea. Technically speaking, this is great news for Alghero's jewellers, as it means the coral trees have few air pockets – the sign of top-quality coral.

The coral is a precious commodity and nowadays fishing is strictly controlled. Only 10 boats are licensed to fish around Alghero, the season running from 15 May to 15 November. It's difficult work, requiring sophisticated equipment and decompression chambers, as the coral is fished at a depth of 135m. It's then sold to Alghero's jewellers in chunks, prices varying according to colour, quality and size.

Agostino Marogna has been working in the business for years and now owns the finest coral shop in Alghero, where his daughter, Sara, and son-in-law, Giuseppe, also work. The display is staggering and includes showcases of antiques and rare pieces notable for their style and quality. Their signature necklaces composed of big, round coral beads often take years to create. To make one smooth red ball results in nearly 60% wastage. As there is only a certain amount of coral for sale each year, they often have to put these necklaces aside until the new season, when they have to hunt for exactly the same shade and quality of coral. One such necklace with beads measuring 11mm in diameter will set you back a cool €11,000, rising to €30,000 for beads measuring 13mm.

Not everything in the shop is this expensive, and it's certainly worth a visit to see the sheer artistry of some of the work. You'll find **Marogna** (Map p156; ☎ 079 98 48 14; Piazza Civica 34) at Palazzo d'Albis.

below Villa Las Tronas. On Friday and Saturday it's a steamy dance pit until dawn.

Il Ruscello (Off Map p154; ☎ 079 95 31 68; ☯ 11pm-5am Jun-Sep) A big open-air disco about 10km northeast of Alghero on the Olmedo road, Il Ruscello has two dance areas. Mostly mainstream international and local music is played.

La Siesta (Off Map p154; ☎ 079 98 01 37; Scala Piccada; ☯ midnight-5am Fri & Sat Jun, Jul & Sep, nightly Aug) La Siesta is another big place, mostly open air, for summertime dancing. Music ranges from Latin to house, but nothing too heavy. Virtually next door is a companion disco, Il Siestino. They are about 10km out of town on the SS292 road to Villanova Monteleone.

SHOPPING

You can barely shoulder past the meandering crowds along Via Carlo Alberto, Alghero's main shopping strip. The streets are lined with jewellery shops full of Alghero's famous coral (see the boxed text, p161), and there are lots of chic boutiques and delis.

Salumeria del Centro (Map p156; ☎ 079 97 58 14; Via Simon 2) This place is a veritable treasure chest of Sardinian goodies, ranging from typical foods through to a selection of wines and handicrafts.

3° Fuoco (Map p156; ☎ 338 964 44 98; Via della Misericordia 20) A broad range of pottery and ceramics is available here.

GETTING THERE & AWAY
Air
Fertilia airport (Off Map p154; ☎ 079 93 50 39; www .aeroportodialghero.it) is about 10km north of Alghero. All the major car-rental companies are represented, and there's an ATM.

The airport is served by a host of domestic carriers that service Italian mainland hubs, notably Milan and Rome. The main charter airline is **Ryanair** (www.ryanair.com), which serves London, Frankfurt and Girona (Barcelona). For more information on flights, see p236.

Bus
Intercity buses terminate in and leave from Via Catalogna, by the Giardini Pubblici. You can buy tickets for **ARST** (☎ 079 95 01 79) and **FdS** (☎ 079 95 04 58) in a booth in the gardens (Map p156).

SASSARI & THE NORTHWEST

MARE E MONTE

One of Sardinia's great scenic roads unfurls along the coast south of Alghero to Bosa, 46km away. The corniche dips and curves through the coastal cliffs, offering sensational panoramas and taking in the best of *il mare* (the sea) and *il monte* (the mountains). It can be done as either a full-day road trip or a two-day cycling tour (detailed in the following paragraphs). It's best to travel south via the inland road (SS292) through Villanova Monteleone and return via the coastal corniche to enjoy the spectacular views of the Riviera dei Corallo and Capo Caccia.

For the cyclist day one (62km) is the hardest, a classic up-and-over day gaining ground to 600m. The road winds up into the hills, revealing views across the water to Capo Caccia, before dipping over a ridge into deep woods that take you out of sight of the coast. After 23km you reach **Villanova Monteleone** (567m), perched like a natural balcony on the slopes of the Colle di Santa Maria. The centre of town is just off the main route and every morning except Sunday you'll find a produce market here (follow the signs to *mercato*).

On the high road beyond Villanova you will enjoy some great coastal views as the road bobs and weaves through shady woods. The final 5km climb is far outweighed by the sizzling 10km descent to Bosa.

The return journey via the corniche road takes you along a truly spectacular stretch of deserted coastline (bring sandwiches and water). There's only one significant climb of 6.2km to 350m, but the effort is offset by the commanding views. The brilliant white cliffs of Capo Caccia (after 16km) can often be seen on the northern horizon. Other than the jangle of goats' bells from the rugged, high slopes or a bird of prey winging on the thermals, there's little to disturb you.

There are two swimming spots along the way: a path to the beach after about 5.4km (look for cars parked by the roadside) just south of Torre Argentina, and **Spiaggia La Speranza** at 35.4km. At Spiaggia La Speranza there's also a bar and the very good **Ristorante La Speranza** (☎ 079 91 70 10; meals €30; ☯ Thu-Tue, daily summer). It's a nice place to break the ride before the final 10.8km run into Alghero.

A plethora of buses (ARST and FdS) run to/from Sassari (€2.32 to €2.58, one hour). ARST also runs buses to Porto Torres (€2.58, 55 minutes, eight daily) and Bosa (€2.90, 55 minutes, two daily).

There are no direct links with Olbia. Instead you have to travel to Sassari, from where you can pick up the Turmo Travel link (see p143).

Car & Motorcycle

The quickest route into Alghero from Sassari is via the new four-lane highway that connects with the north–south SS131 highway west of the provincial capital. From Porto Torres a similarly new route from the western side of the port town links up with this road. Otherwise you can take the slower but direct SS291.

Train

The train station (Map p154) is situated 1.5km north of the old town on Via Don Minzoni. Up to 11 trains a day run to/from Sassari (€1.85, 35 minutes).

GETTING AROUND

Your own feet will be enough to get you around the old town and most other places, but you may want to jump on a bus to get to the beaches.

To/From the Airport

FdS buses run to Alghero (€0.57, 20 minutes, eight daily) between 5.30am and 10pm, arriving at Piazza della Mercede in Alghero.

A **taxi** (☎ 079 93 50 35; ◔ 24hr) from the airport to central Alghero will cost around €24.

Bus

Line AO runs from Via Cagliari (by the Giardini Pubblici) to the beaches. Urban buses also operate to Fertilia and several places beyond. You can pick up these buses at stops around the Giardini Pubblici. Tickets (€0.57) are available at Casa del Caffè (Map p156) and most *tabacchi* outlets.

Car & Motorcycle

Although summer can get hectic, it is generally possible to find parking not too far from the old centre. In the streets around the Giardini Pubblici you'll have to pay parking attendants around €0.50 an hour.

Local and international car-hire companies (such as Avis, Hertz and the big Italian company Maggiore) have booths at Fertilia airport. **Avis** (Map p156; Piazza Sulis 9) also has a handy office in town.

Cicloexpress (Map p154; ☎ 079 98 69 50; www .cicloexpress.com; Via Garibaldi), on the port side of the road, has bicycles and mountain bikes from €8 to €13 a day, and scooters for up to €35 a day.

Taxi

You can find **taxis** (☎ 079 97 53 96) along Via Vittorio Emanuele.

AROUND ALGHERO

The countryside immediately north and west of Alghero is dotted with minor archaeological sites and some good *agriturismi*. You could make a day of it, potter around a couple of ruins, enjoy a big farmhouse lunch and maybe even stop at the huge Sella e Mosca vineyards for the evening tour of the winery.

NURAGHE DI PALMAVERA & NECROPOLI DI ANGHELU RUIU

About 10km west of Alghero on the road to Porto Conte is the **Nuraghe di Palmavera** (admission €3, with Necropoli di Anghelu Ruiu €5; ◔ 9am-7pm Apr-Oct, 9.30am-4pm Nov-Mar), a 3500-year-old *nuraghe* village. At its centre stands a limestone tower and an elliptical building with a secondary sandstone tower that was added later. The ruins of smaller towers and bastion walls surround the central edifice, and beyond the walls are the packed remnants of circular dwellings, of which there may have been about 50 originally.

The circular **Capanna delle Riunioni** (Meeting Hut) is the subject of considerable speculation. Its foundation wall is lined by a low stone bench, perhaps for a council of elders, and encloses a pedestal topped by a model *nuraghe*. One theory suggests there was actually a cult to the *nuraghi* themselves.

About 7km north of Alghero, just west of the road to Porto Torres, lie scattered the ancient burial chambers of the **Necropoli di Anghelu Ruiu** (admission €2, with Nuraghe di Palmavera €5; ◔ 9am-7pm Apr-Oct, 9.30am-4pm Nov-Mar). The 38 tombs date to between 2700 BC and 3300

BC. A torch might be handy for peering into the nooks and crannies. In some of the chambers are lightly sculpted bull's horns, perhaps the symbol of a funeral deity.

You'll need your own transport to get to both of these sights. An AF bus to Porto Conte passes the Nuraghe di Palmavera but returns via the inland road, leaving you stranded.

TENUTE SELLA E MOSCA

Prestige wine producer Sella e Mosca is the best known on the island. You can visit the immaculately maintained property and its **wine cellars** (☎ 079 99 77 00; admission free; ☾ tours 5.30pm Mon-Sat mid-Jun–mid-Oct), just 2km up the road from Anghelu Ruiu. Around the low buildings and exquisite gardens spread 600 hectares of vineyards that have been going since 1899. The cellar tour gives you some insights into old and modern production methods. You can visit the **enoteca** (wine shop; ☾ 8.30am-1pm & 3-7.30pm daily) afterwards and sample some of the wares.

SLEEPING & EATING

Along the inland road between the main north–south P42 and Porto Conte you'll find two notable *agriturismi*, where you can reserve a table for a traditional lunch. Both places are signposted from Fertilia.

Sa Mandra (☎ 079 99 91 50; Regione Sa Segada, Podere 21; meals €30-35) This amazing place has a justifiably good local reputation. The fixed menu gives you more than you could possibly eat of a classic Sardinian banquet, including succulent hunks of roast lamb and suckling pig, all home produced. It's 2km north of the airport. You'll need to book well in advance.

Barbagia (☎ 079 93 51 41; Regione Fighera, Podere 26; meals around €40) Another wonderful place offering traditional fare, Barbagia has a shaded terrace overlooking the lawns.

RIVIERA DEL CORALLO

The long curve of the bay between Alghero and Capo Caccia makes for a scenic drive north, through the seaside towns of Fertilia and Porto Conte. At Capo Caccia you can descend an incredible staircase into the Grotto del Nettuno at the base of the cliffs.

FERTILIA

Alghero's sandy beaches extend almost all the way to Fertilia across the bay. This bizarre town, with its ruler-straight roads and rationalist architecture, was a brainchild of Mussolini. It was originally intended as the centre of an agricultural reclamation project in the dusty wastes of the Nurra. Mussolini brought farmers from Ferrara in Italy's northeast, and after the war refugees arrived from Friuli-Venezia Giulia, bringing with them the lion of St Mark, symbol of Venice, which adorns the statue at the waterfront.

Fertilia is spookily quiet after Alghero, but you may want to seek out the charming **Spiaggia delle Bombarde** a few kilometres to the west. When coming from Alghero take the turn-off south for Hotel dei Pini (before you reach the Nuraghe di Palmavera). A favourite with locals, the beach is set amid lots of green, with a play area for kids back from the beach and views across to Alghero. If it's too crowded you could try the next one along, **Spiaggia del Lazzaretto**. You'll find parking and bar-cafés at both.

Sleeping & Eating

Hotel Punta Negra (☎ 079 93 02 22; www.hotel puntanegra.it; Strada Fertilia-Porto Conte; s/d €175/460; ☾ Mar-Oct; P ☒ ☒) A big, fancy beach hotel with its own private beach, the Punta Negra is set in a pine grove and decorated in typical Mediterranean style. All rooms have balconies facing the sea. The place is very popular with families. You'll find it 1km west of Fertilia.

Hostal de l'Alguer (☎ /fax 079 93 20 39; hostal alguer@tiscalinet.it; Via Parenzo; r incl breakfast €16, d €50; P ☒) One of Sardinia's three youth hostels, this place is set at the western end of town. Rooms are spread over a series of modern houses in a dusty compound. Evening meals cost €9.

Da Bruno (☎ 079 93 00 98; Strada Santa Maria la Palma; meals €40; ☾ Wed-Mon, daily summer) Da Bruno offers seasonal cooking including boar, lamb and pork as well as mushrooms in autumn. There's also some great seafood. Try the *gnocchetti alla Bruno*.

Acquario (☎ 079 93 02 39; Via Pola 34; meals €35; ☾ Tue-Sun, daily summer) This popular seafood eatery is right in Fertilia, just off the waterfront road about 50m east of Hotel Bellavista.

AUTHOR'S CHOICE

Diving Centre Capo Galera (☎ 079 94 21 10; www.capogalera.com; Località Capo Galera; s/d €55/70) The diving centre at Capo Galera is really something else. Stranded on the promontory right at the sea edge, it is a world unto itself. Days pass in a blur of sun, sea and rocks as you discover a magical underwater environment. As they will modestly tell you, the instructors have more experience in diving than a Top Gun pilot in flying, and there are more courses on offer than fish in the sea (single dive/beginners' course €35/90). But it's so much more than a dive centre. The big white villa sits right on the edge of a cliff, and all the rooms have splendid balconies. Dinner is usually a barbeque where guests gather to share the day's excitement and listen to the stories Gaddo, the host, has to tell. Children and nondivers are warmly welcomed, and there's no shortage of things to do as Alghero is just a few minutes' drive away. It's a magical place, and one you won't forget any time soon.

Getting There & Away

The local AF bus from Alghero (€0.57, 15 minutes) runs every 40 minutes from 7.50am to 9.50pm. Up to 10 of these go on to Porto Conte and stop at the turn-off for Spiaggia delle Bombarde.

PORTO CONTE

The signs to Porto Conte lead you along the southern flank of this broad bay past bobbing yachts, spruce gardens and discreet residences. The road ends at a Catalano-Aragonese tower and lighthouse, where you'll find the gorgeous **Hotel El Faro** (079 94 20 30; www.elfarohotel.it; Porto Conte; d low/high season €272/364; P X ⬚ ⬚), with its two pools, private jetty and coolly stylish rooms overlooking the Baia di Ninfe.

The road to Capo Caccia leads you west through a nature reserve characterised by myrtle, lentisk and agave plants, and around the bay, along which there are several beaches. On your right-hand side rises Monte Timidone (561m), surrounded by the **Foresta Demaniale Porto Conte** (⬚ 8am-4pm Mon-Sat, 9am-5pm Sun & holidays), also known as the Arca di Noé (Noah's Ark) because of the variety of animals introduced here since the 1970s. They include deer, unique white donkeys from the Isola Asinara, little horses from the Giara region and wild boar. Griffon vultures and falcons fly its skies.

You can drive into the 12,000-hectare park from the main road just south of the Hotel Baia di Conte and follow a restricted route. Walkers and cyclists have greater liberty.

The AF bus runs between Alghero and Porto Conte (€0.88, 30 minutes, at least 10 daily).

CAPO CACCIA

The road down the eastern flank of the nature reserve skirts the waters of Porto Conte on its way to this impressive headland, where cliffs rise like huge waves – you have an easy green slope on the eastern side and a sheer rock wall to the west. Stop at the marked lookout point, from where you have a dramatic view of the cape and the wave-buffeted offshore island of Isola Foradada.

The end of the road is marked by the entrance to the **Escala del Cabirol**, a vertiginous staircase of 656 steps that descends 110m to the **Grotta di Nettuno** (☎ 079 94 65 40; adult/child €10/5; ⬚ hourly tours 9am-7pm Apr-Sep, 9am-6pm Oct, 9am-2pm Nov-Mar), an underground fairyland of stalactites and stalagmites. The tour takes you along a 200m walk around the grotto. It has taken several million years for the stalactites and stalagmites to develop into all sorts of curious shapes, such as the organ, the church dome (or warrior's head) and so on. Another longer path, closed to tourists, leads to seven little freshwater lakes deep inside the cave system. In bad weather the grotto is closed.

If you don't fancy the climb down the spectacular staircase – or suffer vertigo – then you can visit the cave via boat trips from Alghero (see p157). The 27km from Alghero to Capo Caccia makes a very scenic and relatively easy-going bike ride.

One FdS bus from Via Catalogna in Alghero (€3.25 return, 50 minutes) leaves daily at 9.15am (returning at midday). It runs right to the cape and stops in the car park, where you'll find the staircase down to the grotto. A couple of extra services are put on from June to September.

SASSARI & THE NORTHWEST

NORTH OF CAPO CACCIA

The road north of Porto Conte leads to a couple of lovely getaways. The first turn-off takes you to the coast at **Torre del Porticciolo**. A tower stands atop the northern promontory that protects this tiny natural harbour, backed by a small arc of beach. High cliffs mount guard on the southern side and you can explore adjacent coves along narrow walking trails.

Six kilometres north of Torre del Porticciolo is one of the island's longest stretches of wild sandy beach, **Porto Ferro**. Waves often crash in from the west, attracting the occasional surfer. In summer a snack bar sets up just back from the beach. To get there, take the Porto Ferro turn-off and, before reaching the end of the road (which is where the bus from Alghero stops), take a right (follow the Bar Porto Ferro signs). The summer bus from Alghero (€1.45, 35 to 65 minutes depending on route and traffic) runs three times a day.

From Porto Ferro a series of back roads lead about 6km around to **Lago Baratz**, Sardinia's only natural lake. You can walk down to the lake's marshy edge from the road that sidles up against its southwestern flank. Surrounded by low hills, the lake attracts some bird life, although the winged fellows tend to hang about the less accessible northern side. A 3km dirt track connects the lake with the northern tip of Porto Ferro beach.

A few kilometres further east tipplers might visit the **Cantina Sociale di Santa Maria la Palma** (☎ 079 99 90 44; ☉ 8am-1pm & 3.30-8pm daily Jun-Sep, 7.30am-1pm & 2.30-5.30pm Mon-Fri Oct-May) in the eponymous village. It is the Nurra's second winery after the grand Sella e Mosca spread. You can mosey around the *enoteca* and may be taken on a tour of the winery.

There are a couple of accommodation options along this section of coast, including the shady **Campeggio Torre del Porticciolo** (☎ 079 91 90 07; www.torredelporticciolo.it; camp sites per adult/tent €14/10, 2-person bungalows €95; P 🐾), located a few steps back from the beach. You could also stay at **Agriturismo Porticciolo** (☎ 079 91 80 00; www.agriturismoporticciolo.it, Italian only; apt day/week €42/725; P 🐾), about 1km back towards the main road, which offers accommodation in little apartments. Between June and September they are usually rented out on a weekly basis. You should try to eat in the grand dining area, made welcoming with its heavy timber ceiling and huge fireplace.

In Santa Maria la Palma, 2km west on the SS291, you can eat well at **Da Gino** (☎ 079 99 91 38; meals €30). Call ahead.

Olbia & the Gallura

At first glance, the Gallura's harsh yet fantastical granite landscape seems an unlikely location for one of Europe's trendiest and most exclusive resorts – the famous Costa Smeralda. But it's a clever combination of beauty and brains, a ragged coastline of emerald-green inlets married to a cushioned world of uniform luxury, glitz and glamour. Glossy magazines never tire of reporting the high jinks of the film stars, royals and tycoons who load the multitude of marinas with their massive boats in July and August.

Yet up until the 1960s this was a wild, waterless and remote part of the island without so much as a paved road to ease the way for high-living Europeans. The Fiume Coghinas (Coghinas River) to the west and Monte Limbara to the south contributed further to the region's isolation. As a result the Gallura does things rather differently from the rest of the island and has a distinct local character.

For many visitors the ravishing beaches of the Costa Smeralda *are* Sardinia. But while they are undeniably beautiful, they represent just a fraction of the Gallura's charms. The wilder, windswept beaches of the north are also a big draw for wind- and kite-surfing enthusiasts, while inland the rolling green vineyards and cork forests are dotted with stone *stazzi* (farmhouses) and a number of curious reminders of Sardinia's prehistoric past. Likewise the Parco Nazionale dell'Arcipelago di La Maddalena, the American base of choice in the Mediterranean, provides another excellent diversion and is a great spot for diving, sailing and walking.

HIGHLIGHTS

- Splash out on a mind-boggling feast of Gallurese specialities prepared by Rita Denza at Olbia's **Hotel Ristorante Gallura** (p171)

- Island-hop around the **Parco Nazionale dell'Arcipelago di La Maddalena** (p182)

- Eschew the glitz and the glamour of the Costa Smeralda to stay in one of Arzachena's charming **agriturismi** (p179) and explore its **prehistoric sites** (p179)

- Clamber all over the granite seascapes of **Capo Testa** (p189) and search out the fine coves of the **Costa Smeralda** (p175)

- Join the windsurfing and sailing fiends at chilled-out **Porto Pollo** (p182)

- Check into hip hotel **La Coluccia** (p189) for that ultimate slice of pampered paradise

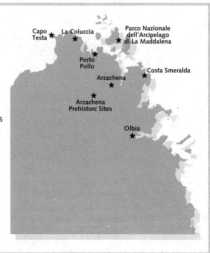

Capo Testa ★
La Coluccia ★
Parco Nazionale dell'Arcipelago di La Maddalena ★
Porto Pollo ★
Costa Smeralda ★
Arzachena ★
Arzachena Prehistoric Sites ★
Olbia ★

OLBIA

pop 46,250

Olbia is one of the oldest towns in Sardinia, but you wouldn't guess it gazing upon the modern sprawl that spreads across the bay. The climate is largely to blame, as this low-lying bay, bogged down in marshes, was plagued with malaria right up until the 1950s. When fusty Alan Ross visited Olbia in 1954 he said it gave him the same feeling as the transit camps of the war, 'as though [the] inhabitants only keep it going for the people passing through'.

It's maybe not quite that bad, but Olbia is hard to love, not least because of the infuriating roadworks that send you into a spin the minute you enter town. Still, once you've settled yourself in the heart of the old town, things start to look up as you contemplate the evening's dining opportunities, for Olbia has some very good restaurants. With planes, trains, buses and boats all converging on the town, you will undoubtedly find yourself overnighting here, so put your time to good use in sampling some of the better food on the island.

HISTORY

Little light has been shed on Olbia's past, but the town was almost certainly founded by the Carthaginians. The natural port set inside the deep Golfo di Olbia was important in Roman times – a dozen or so relics of Roman vessels were unearthed in the 1990s. Known as Terranova, the town seems to have muddled along in the Middle Ages, but it declined under Catalano-Aragonese and later Spanish rule. Not until the arrival of the highways and railway in the 19th century did the town show signs of life again. The surrounding area was slowly drained and turned over to agriculture and even some light industry. The port cranked back into operation and since the 1960s Olbia has boomed.

With a main airport, port facilities and a big chunk of the island's tourist industry only a jaunt up the coast on the Costa Smeralda, Olbia has long been pushing to have a new province created around it. Under the Soru government this has become a reality with the creation of Olbia-Tempio.

ORIENTATION

The waters of the Golfo di Olbia carve a deep wound into the northeastern Sardinian coast, creating an ideal location for a port. The heart of the town stretches west from that port. Boats dock at the Stazione Marittima, at the end of a narrow lick of land jutting 2km into the gulf.

The town's main thoroughfare, Corso Umberto, runs up from the waterfront and inland about 1km to the train and bus stations. On its way it passes the central interlocking squares of Piazza Margherita and Piazza Matteotti. The town fathers have seen fit to pipe relentlessly jaunty pop music through loudspeakers up and down the street and in the squares all day long. One wonders if this is supposed to put locals and visitors into a summer-holiday mood, although the inescapable dulcet tones of Laura Pausini and Eros Ramazzotti might have the opposite effect on some.

The web of narrow streets to either side of Corso Umberto constitute what might be called the 'old town', although nothing much dates to more than a century ago. The bulk of the hotels, restaurants and bars are crowded into this small area.

INFORMATION
Bookshop

Libreria dell'Isola (Corso Umberto 54) The usual maps and guides, along with a good selection of art books and the hard-to-come-by *Coast,* a photographic history of the Costa Smeralda.

Emergency

Ambulance (☎ 0789 55 22 01)

Internet Access

Inter Smeraldo (☎ 0789 2 53 66; www.intersmeraldo.com; Via Porto Romano 8/b; per 30 min €1.80; ☿ 10am-11pm Mon-Sat, 5-11pm Sun) A busy Internet café full of students in the early evening.

Medical Services

Hospital (☎ 0789 55 22 00; Viale Aldo Moro) In town.
Night Doctor (☎ 0789 55 24 41)

Money

Banca di Sassari (Corso Umberto 3) Change money at this Western Union representative.
Banco di Sardegna (Corso Umberto 142) You can also change money here.

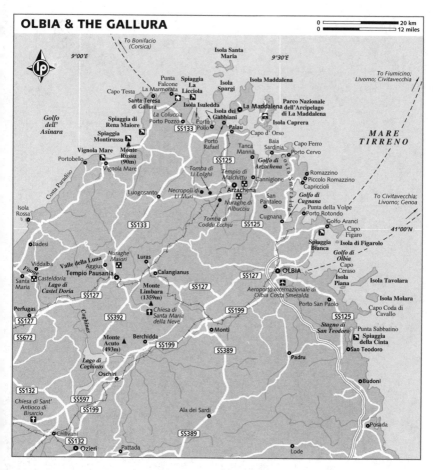

OLBIA & THE GALLURA

Post

Post office (Viale Aldo Moro; ⏰ 8am-1pm Mon-Fri, 8am-12.30pm Sat) The nearest post office to central Olbia is on the corner of Via Amedeo, north of the hospital.

Tourist Information

Tourist office (☎ 0789 2 14 53; www.olbia.it, in Italian; Via Catello Piro 1; ⏰ 9.30am-12.30pm & 3.30-6.30pm Mon-Sat) Helpful English-speaking staff. Run by the *comune*, this office will be subject to the changes when they come into effect (see p233).

Travel Agent

Unimare (☎ 070 2 35 24; www.unimare.it; Via Principe Umberto 1; ⏰ 9am-1pm & 5-8pm Mon-Fri, 9am-1pm Sat) A central travel agent where you can book ferries and flights.

SIGHTS

The tightly packed warren of streets that represent the original fishing village have a certain charm, and in the evening they come to life with bustling locals out on a spending spree.

A stroll along the *corso* at this time, culminating in a drink on Piazza Margherita, is an agreeable way to spend the evening. You may notice the occasional vaguely Liberty-style (or Art Nouveau–style) building from the early 20th century.

To leap centuries back into the city's history, head past the train station and track down the **Chiesa di San Simplicio** (Via San Simplicio; ⏰ 9am-1pm & 4-7pm), a Romanesque jewel set aside from the town hubbub. Built entirely

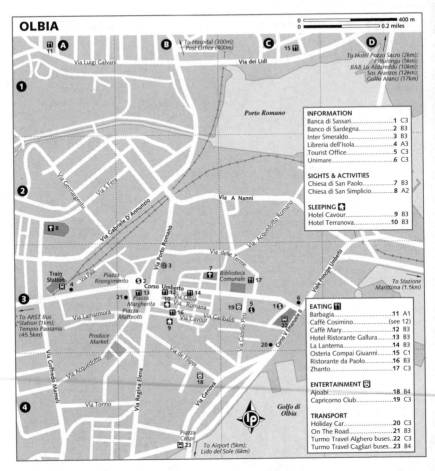

OLBIA

0 _____ 400 m
0 _____ 0.2 miles

To Hospital (300m);
Post Office (400m)

15

To Hotel Pozzo Sacro (2km);
Pittulongu (5km);
B&B Lu Aldareddu (10km);
Sos Aranzos (12km);
Golfe Aranci (17km)

Via Luigi Galvani

Via dei Lidi

Porto Romano

INFORMATION
Banca di Sassari	1 C3
Banco di Sardegna	2 B3
Inter Smeraldo	3 B3
Libreria dell'Isola	4 A3
Tourist Office	5 C3
Unimare	6 C3

SIGHTS & ACTIVITIES
Chiesa di San Paolo	7 B3
Chiesa di San Simplicio	8 A2

SLEEPING
Hotel Cavour	9 B3
Hotel Terranova	10 B3

EATING
Barbagia	11 A1
Caffè Cosimino	(see 12)
Caffè Mary	12 B3
Hotel Ristorante Gallura	13 B3
La Lanterna	14 B3
Osteria Compai Giuanni	15 C1
Ristorante da Paolo	16 B3
Zhanto	17 C3

ENTERTAINMENT
Ajoabi	18 B4
Capricorno Club	19 C3

TRANSPORT
Holiday Car	20 C3
On The Road	21 B3
Turmo Travel Alghero buses	22 C3
Turmo Travel Cagliari buses	23 B4

Via A Nanni

Via delle Terme

Biblioteca Comunale

Train Station

Piazza Risorgimento

Corso Umberto

Piazza Margherita

Via Olbia

Via Romana

Piazza Matteotti

Via Cavour

Via Garibaldi

To ARST Bus Station (1km); Tempio Pausania (45.5km)

Via Lamarmora

Produce Market

Via de Filippi

Via Acquedotto

Via Regina Elena

Via Genova

Via Torino

Golfo di Olbia

To Stazione Marittima (1.5km)

Piazza Crispi

To Airport (5km); Lido del Sole (6km)

of granite, it is a curious mix of Tuscan and Lombard styles.

Another granite church worth a look is the **Chiesa di San Paolo**, with its pretty Valencian-style tiled dome (added after WWII).

SLEEPING

Olbia has a good selection of reasonably priced hotels.

Hotel Pozzo Sacro (☎ 0789 5 78 55; www.hotel pozzosacro.com; Località Pozzo Sacro, Strada Panoramica Olbia; s/d €80/160; P 🐕 🖳 🖭) If you have a car, consider this tasteful complex 2km east of Olbia. The terraced stone villas housing some 40 rooms afford fantastic views of the bay. The rooms are huge and decorated

with fine furnishings, and all have a balcony over the curvaceous pool.

Hotel Cavour (☎ 0789 20 40 33; www.cavourhotel .it; Via Cavour 22; s/d €65/90; P 🐕) This attractive, medium-scale hotel is in the heart of Olbia's old town. It's been well renovated with soft-focus pastel colours, which give it a breezy, beachside feel. The double-glazed windows are a godsend on a Saturday night.

Hotel Terranova (☎ 0789 2 23 95; www.hotelter ranova.it; Via Garibaldi 6; s/d €65/110; P 🐕) In the middle of town, the Terranova has small, plush rooms with classy, dusky-pink–marble bathrooms. Most have balconies overlooking the cobbled lane below.

B&B Lu Aldareddu (☎ 0789 6 85 79; www.lu aldareddu.com; Località Monte Plebi; d low/high season

OLBIA & THE GALLURA

€75/100; ☺ May-Sep) This relaxing alternative is about 10km north of the town centre on a low olive-tree–covered hill. The 18th-century house has been nicely restored, and the proprietors put on courses of anything from cooking to pottery. From here you are within reasonable cycling distance of the Costa Smeralda's finest beaches.

EATING

Gallurese cooking has its quirks, including *suppa cuata*, a casserole made of layers of bread, cheese and meat ragù drenched in broth and baked to a crispy crust. Look out for some fine Vermentino white wines, too.

Barbagia (☎ 0789 5 1 64 02; Via Luigi Galvani; meals €30) Out of the centre, Barbagia is one of the best spots in Olbia to get a taste of the traditional Sardinian cuisine of the interior. All sorts of odd names in Sardinian, which no amount of Italian will help you recognise, pop out of the menu at you.

La Lanterna (☎ 0789 2 30 82; Via Olbia 13; meals €15-25; ☺ Thu-Tue winter, daily summer) The Lanterna distinguishes itself with its cosy subterranean setting and beautifully fresh food. A fine antipasti buffet, succulent pizzas and steaks the size of a doorjamb are rounded off with homemade desserts. Try the strudel, or perhaps the chocolate and almond torte, or maybe the *panna cotta* – you can beat the problem.

Zhanto (☎ 0789 2 26 45; Via delle Terme 1/b; meals €25-30; ☺ Mon-Sat) Like a welcoming family home, Zhanto has good food and the bonus of a garden. There's an excellent choice of antipasti and some speciality pasta dishes – try the *ravioli di mazzancolle* (ravioli stuffed with king prawns).

Ristorante da Paolo (☎ 0789 2 16 75; Via Cavour 22; meals €25-30; ☺ lunch Mon-Sun) This place offers several variations on that favourite Sardinian theme, horse meat, alongside other more

palatable Gallurese dishes. Gobble your choice up in the cosy atmosphere created by the exposed stone walls and timber ceilings.

Osteria Compai Giuanni (☎ 0789 5 85 84; Via dei Lidi 15; meals €25; ☺ Mon-Fri) Also a hike from the centre, this unlikely looking spot is the place to come if you want to try splendid fish and seafood soups or the Gallurese speciality, *suppa cuata*.

The best spot for breakfast is Piazza Margherita. Caffè Mary and Caffè Cosimino, next door to one another, are both good for a cappuccino, although Caffè Cosimino is the more fashionable bar in the evenings and also serves cocktails.

ENTERTAINMENT

Not too many people hang about in Olbia for fun, especially not in summer, when anyone who is anyone heads directly up the coast to the Costa Smeralda and beyond.

Still, Corso Umberto, cut off to traffic from 7pm, becomes an ebullient scene for the *passeggiata* (evening stroll). At the lower port end, marketers add a little more colour with their stands of knick-knacks.

At the weekend, night owls can head for **Ajoabi** (Via Filippi 34; ☺ 8pm-2am Fri-Sun) for live music and steak, or for something more up-market you can try the central **Capricorno Club** (☎ 0789 2 31 09; Via Catello Piro 4; ☺ Fri-Sun 9pm-2am).

FESTIVALS & EVENTS

From July onwards Olbia hosts the **L'Estate Olbiense**, a cultural festival that includes lots of concerts and outdoor performances on Piazza Margherita.

GETTING THERE & AWAY
Air

Olbia's swanky new airport, **Aeroporto Internazionale di Olbia Costa Smeralda** (☎ 0789 6 90 00; www.geasar.com), is about 5km southeast of

---

AUTHOR'S CHOICE

Hotel Ristorante Gallura (☎ 0789 2 46 48; fax 0789 2 46 29; Corso Umberto 145; meals €30-45; ☺ Tue-Sun) Unlike the hotel (singles/doubles including breakfast €75/150), the restaurant of the Gallura is absolutely top-notch. The menu reads like a dictionary of Gallurese dishes, and the waiters dash back and forth carrying intriguing platters of exotic food such as smoked cuttlefish with wild beetroot, fish cooked in a paste of courgette and ricotta, and rabbit in saffron. Go with the recommendations – it's all good. Lovely Rita Denza, the maestro behind it all, flits from table to table in her apron making sure her customers can navigate the multitude of choices. Reservations are essential.

the centre. It's so close that you might even consider popping in for a spot of shopping, especially at the outlet Kara, which stocks a selection of very good souvenirs and food products. Consult the website for an excellent source of information on the island.

The airport now handles flights from Rome, Milan and Verona, as well as international and charter flights from London, Paris and Frankfurt. Both Easyjet and Hapag-Lloyd Flug run regular flights here. For more information, see p236.

Boat

Olbia's Stazione Marittima is an impressive affair, more like an airport.

All the big companies – **Tirrenia** (www.tirrenia.it), **Moby Lines** (www.moby.it) and **Grandi Navi Veloci** (www.gnv.it) – run regular services to Olbia from Civitavecchia (€29, eight hours), Livorno (€49, 10 hours) and Genoa (€82, 11 hours). You can book tickets at any travel agent in town, or at the port, where they all have a counter.

For more information on times and fares, see p241.

Bus

The intercity *autostazione* (bus station) is on Corso Vittorio Veneto where you can also buy tickets.

ARST (Azienda Regionale Sarda Trasporti; ☎ 0789 55 30 00) has buses from the *autostazione* to destinations all over the island, including Arzachena (€1.76, 45 minutes, 11 daily), Golfo Aranci (€1.19, 25 minutes, eight daily, summer only) and Porto Cervo (€2.58, one hour, up to five Monday to Saturday). Further afield you can get to Dorgali (€6.30, two hours, three daily), Nuoro (€6.30, 2½ hours, up to seven a day), Santa Teresa di Gallura (€3.72, 1½ hours, six daily) and Sassari (€5.84, 1½ hours, two Monday to Saturday) via Tempio Pausania (€2.89).

Turmo Travel (☎ 0789 2 14 87; www.turmotravel.it) runs a bus from Cagliari (€15, four hours 15 minutes, one daily Monday to Saturday). It arrives in Piazza Crispi. Another daily bus operates to/from Alghero (€7.64, two hours) – it arrives in Corso Umberto in front of the Municipio building. You can purchase tickets at the Stazione Marittima or on the bus.

Car & Motorcycle

All the big international hire outfits are represented at the airport. Some local ones are also dotted about town. **Holiday Car** (☎ 0789 2 84 96; Via Genova 71) will rent you a Fiat Panda from €40 a day in high season, or a Fiat Punto for €45.

To rent scooters up to 150cc (€35 per day) or mountain bikes (€13 to €23 per day), try **On The Road** (☎ 0789 20 60 42; www.ontheroadrent.com; Via Sassari 8).

Train

The train station lies parallel to Via Gabriele D'Annunzio.

One direct train a day runs to Cagliari (€13, four hours). Otherwise you have to change at Chilivani (and sometimes Macomer as well). Up to three trains run to Sassari (€5.90, one hour 50 minutes) and up to seven to Golfo Aranci (€1.85, 25 minutes).

GETTING AROUND

You are unlikely to need local buses, except for getting to the airport and the Stazione Marittima. Buy tickets at tobacconists and some bars.

To/From the Airport

Bus 2 (€0.57) runs every half-hour from 7.30am to 8pm from the airport to the town centre (Corso Umberto). A **taxi** (☎ 0789 6 91 50) will cost about €12.

Several buses for destinations around the island leave directly from the airport. Among them is a service for Nuoro run by **Deplano** (☎ 0784 29 50 30), which operates five times a day from June to September.

Bus

Bus 3 (€0.57) can be picked up in Via Genova and Viale Principe Umberto for the short trip to the Stazione Marittima.

Car & Motorcycle

It's forbidden to enter the heart of town (Corso Umberto and around) from 7pm to 2am. Metered parking (€0.60 per hour) is available around Olbia. Near the station is a good place to look.

Taxi

You can sometimes find **taxis** (☎ 0789 2 27 18) at the rank on Corso Umberto near Piazza Margherita.

AROUND OLBIA

Olbia's main beach is the busy **Lido del Sole** (catch bus 5). It's fine for a swim, but far preferable is the swath of white sand at **Pittulongu** or **Sos Aranzos** on the northern side of the gulf.

GOLFO ARANCI

pop 1950

North of Olbia unfolds the ravishing coastline of the Costa Smeralda, with its yacht-filled marinas and iridescent waters. But before you reach this pampered playground you'll find the more reasonable resort of Golfo Aranci, located on the tip of Capo Figaro, 18km northeast of Olbia.

Golfo Aranci has been growing steadily since the 1880s, when the railway was extended to connect with its little port, which now runs numerous summer services to the mainland. It is blessed with sandy white beaches – **Spiaggia Primo**, **Secondo** and **Terzo** (the best) – and surrounded by a fragrant belt of ilex and olive trees.

It also has a decidedly family feel to it – the public parks are full of well-maintained playgrounds – and behind the port rise the craggy heights of **Capo Figaro** (340m), now converted into a minor nature reserve. The cape stands in counterpoint to the sheer cliffs of Isola Tavolara, eminently visible across the gulf to the south. Coquettishly placed just off the coast is the **Isola di Figarolo** islet, a popular spot for snorkelling and spear-gun fishing.

Sleeping & Eating

Hotel Gabbiano Azzurro (☎ 0789 4 69 29; www .hotelgabbianoazzurro.com; Via dei Gabbiani; half board per person low/high season €72/110; ☒ mid-May–mid-Oct; ℗ ☒ ☒) In a stunning location overlooking the aquamarine waters of the Spiaggia Terzo, the Gabbiano Azzurro is a great family choice. The majority of the rooms have the same impressive views as the sweeping terrace. A section of this perfect beach is for the exclusive use of hotel guests, or you can just lounge by one of the two hotel pools.

La Lampara (☎ /fax 0789 61 51 40; www.albergola lampara.it; Via Magellano; d €98) Just off Via della Libertà, this is one of the more economical of the town's half-dozen hotels. Rooms are

simple and don't have air-con, but other than that La Lampara is a comfortable, friendly place.

A string of restaurants on or near Via della Libertà keep hunger at bay. Those closer to the port have a grittier look but can be quite good for seafood. Try **Ristorante Miramare** (☎ 0789 4 60 85; Piazzetta del Porto 2; meals €25).

Getting There & Away

Regular ARST buses (€1.19, 30 minutes, up to eight a day in summer) and trains (€1.85, 25 minutes, seven daily) link Golfo Aranci with Olbia.

Tirrenia (www.tirrenia.it) runs a summer-only ferry to Fiumicino (€41 to €49, 4½ hours, one daily) from mid-June to September. **Sardinia Ferries** (also called Corsica Ferries; www .corsicaferries.com) serves Civitavecchia (€42, 6¾ hours, one weekly) and Livorno (€63, six hours, eight weekly).

For information on boats between Golfo Aranci and other points on mainland Italy, see p241.

SOUTH COAST

The coast south of Olbia is a busy stretch, with a handful of beaches that attract locals and a sprinkling of Italian holidaymakers. Resort developments pepper the coast until you reach lively San Teodoro, about 25km south. All the action takes place here during July and August, but outside high season the coast is strangely bereft of life. Looming offshore is Isola Tavolara.

PORTO SAN PAOLO

The resort of Porto San Paolo lies 14km south of Olbia. It's a quiet cluster of modest, bougainvillea-clad holiday homes, all neatly laid out along the seaside. It's grown big around its excursions to Isola Tavolara, which you can join at the port, and it's now the most lively resort along the coast after San Teodoro.

At Easter and between June and September **boat excursions** depart from the port to Isola Tavolara (see p174). Outward-bound boats leave on the hour between 9am and 1pm, and return trips start at 12.30pm and depart every hour (on the half-hour) until 6.30pm. The return trip (25 minutes each way) costs €10 per person, but longer

OLBIA & THE GALLURA

cruises taking in the smaller Isola Molara and Piana cost between €20 and €30.

The rocky coves of Tavolara present some wonderful diving opportunities, such as the underwater mountain Secca del Papa (see the boxed text, p49). You can arrange these with **Centro Sub Tavolara** (☎ 0789 4 03 60; www.centrosubtavolara.com; Via Molara 4/a).

There's not much to hold you in San Paolo, but you might like to indulge in an excellent lunch in the shady courtyard of **Cala di Junco** (☎ 0789 4 02 60; Via Nenni 8/10; meals €30; ☺ Wed-Mon). The menu includes specialities such as *mazzamurro* – layers of bread soaked in a tomato and pecorino sauce.

SAN TEODORO
pop 3500
Young Italians have taken San Teodoro by storm, and in 2005 it won the coveted tourism trophy. It's a pleasant town with model piazzas and pretty, pastel-coloured houses surrounded by some good beaches. Given its youthful crowd there are lots of activities on offer, from horse riding around the lagoons to innumerable boat excursions.

You'll find plenty of good information at the helpful multilingual **tourist office** (☎ 0784 86 57 67; www.santeodoroturismo.com, in Italian; Piazza Mediterraneo 1; ☺ 9am-1pm & 4pm-midnight Jul & Aug, 9am-1pm & 4-8pm Sep-Jun). Another useful website is www.visitsanteodoro.com (in Italian).

San Teodoro has its own beach, **Cala d'Ambra**, about half a kilometre downhill from the centre. A little further on, however, at the end of the village, is the unfeasibly long and broad strand of **Spiaggia della Cinta**. Northwards, too, is the **Stagno San Teodoro**, a big lagoon home to lots of bird life.

Sleeping & Eating
There are plenty of hotels in San Teodoro, although many of them are set back from the beach and most of them close out of season. You can find a list of them on www.visitsanteodoro.com and the tourist office website.

Hotel L'Esagono (☎ 0784 86 57 83; www.hotel esagono.com; Via Cala d'Ambra; half board per person low/high season €48/100; ☺ Apr-Oct) Set on a stretch of sandy white beach in an attractive tropical garden, Hotel L'Esagono has a perfect setting. The single-storey buildings nestle prettily in the greenery, and the rooms are nicely decorated. The only drawback is the nearby disco, which can make shuteye problematic on some summer nights.

Camping San Teodoro (☎ 0784 86 57 77; www.campingsanteodoro.com; Via del Tirreno; camp sites per adult/tent €9.60/9.50, 4-person bungalow €97; ☺ May-mid-Oct) Set in a huge tree-filled plot right on the southern end of La Cinta beach, this is the main camp site. It's well organised and very popular.

Il Covo (☎ 0784 86 30 43; meals €35-40; ☺ Apr-Sep) At Puntaldia, a tiny spot on the Punta Sabbatino promontory just north of the Stagno San Teodoro (and about 8km from San Teodoro itself), this is a fine feeding choice for fresh seafood. Try the *insalata di aragoste* (lobster salad).

DETOUR: ISOLA TAVOLARA

The excursion to Isola Tavolara makes for a great day trip. The place used to be known as the Island of Hermes, perhaps because you need wings to reach the plateau (565m), which is inhabited only by sea birds and falcons, as well as a few nimble-footed wild goats. The few people who live here reside on the western side on the **Spalmatore di Terra**, where the boats land.

Aside from snacking at a couple of beachside eateries, there is nothing much to do but splash about in the translucent water of the **Spiaggia Spalmatore**, and admire the incredible views of Tavolara's heights and mainland Sardinia. You could wander down to the little cemetery to see the graves of Tavolara's kings (the title was bestowed by Carlo Alberto in 1848 after a successful goat-hunting trip), each marked with a crown. The present 'king', Tonino Bertoeoni, runs one of the island's two restaurants, **Ristorante da Tonino** (☎ 0789 5 85 70; Via Tavolara 14; meals €25-35).

Since 1991 the island has hosted an occasional summer cinema festival, usually between 20 July and 25 July. Special boats ferry ticket holders from Porto San Paolo out to the island in the evening for screenings at 9.30pm. Even if your grasp of Italian isn't that good the festival is wonderfully atmospheric, the huge, bright screen set against the rocky peaks. For details log on to www.cinematavolara.it (in Italian).

Gallo Blu (☎ 0784 86 60 41; Via degli Afodeli; pizza €6-10, meals €25-30) This popular hang-out serves pizza in the evening and an abundance of seafood.

Entertainment

Apart from lying about on the beaches, the main activity in San Teodoro is nocturnal. On and around the main street, Largo E Lussu, you will find a series of pizzerias that double as music bars, including Birreria In Bocca al Luppolo.

These start closing around 2am, at which point a couple of clubs kick in. The most convenient disco-club, opposite Hotel L'Esagono, is **L'Ambra Night** (Via Cala d'Ambra). Otherwise, try the self-consciously stylish **Luna Glam Club** (www.lalunadisco.com; Località Stirritoggiu), south of the town centre just off the exit road from the SS125.

Getting There & Away

ARST buses make the run up the coast to Olbia (€2.58, 40 minutes, six daily) and inland to Nuoro (€6.30, one hour, four daily).

COSTA SMERALDA

Back in 1961 the Aga Khan and some pals bought a strip of beautiful Sardinian coast from struggling farmers and created the Costa Smeralda – a 10km strip of coast between the Golfo di Cugnana and the Golfo di Arzachena that covers some 8000 hectares. The 'capital' is the yachtie haven of **Porto Cervo**, distinctive for its troglodyte-style architecture, favoured back then (and looking a tad dated today). Visit out of season and this is a surreal, deserted place with more seagulls than celebs. During July and August, however, the resort throbs with footballers' wives and Italian sophisticates.

For all the latest news on what's happening on the Costa Smeralda, log on to www.costasmeraldaresort.com.

PORTO CERVO

Some of the villas facing the hushed port of Porto Cervo seem based on sets for a *Star Wars* desert-town scene. The oddly rounded, pseudo-Moroccan fantasy they exude clearly owes more to imagination than local reality. It was all part of a very grand architectural plan to borrow the best

of the rest – Greek, North African, Spanish and Italian architecture – and create the ideal Mediterranean village. But the trouble with borrowing is that it lacks any distinctive flair – there's no discernible Sardinian character, and nothing in particular to catch the eye and intrigue, so it's all a bit bland.

Sights & Activities

As nearly everyone in Porto Cervo has a boat (it has the best marine facilities on the island, with 650 berths), most of the action takes place elsewhere during the day – a hard day spent pottering about the paradisal inlets and developing that perfect port-side tan. If you're not one of the lucky owners of a 15m yacht it's best to visit during the early evening, when the playboys and girls come out to cavort in the bars and eateries.

The heart of 'town' is the **Piazzetta**, graced by a couple of restaurants and surrounded by discreet shopping alleys. It's the place to see and be seen in the evenings, preferably with cocktail in hand. From here stairs lead down to the **Sottoportico della Piazzetta**, where you can tempt fate in a string of fancy boutiques. Above it all stands Michele Busiri Vici's **Chiesa di Stella Maris**, which hosts classical-music concerts in the summer. Unsurprisingly, it's also done rather well in the donations department, receiving El Greco's impressive *Mater Dolorosa* as a Dutch aristocrat's bequest.

Sleeping & Eating

Hotel Le Ginestre (☎ 0789 9 20 30; www.leginestre-hotel.com; Località Porto Cervo; half board per person low/high season €110/170; ⊙ May-Sep; 🅿 ⊠ 🔊) This lovely hotel 1km south of Porto Cervo is set in refreshingly tropical gardens. It has the Charme e Relax seal of approval (see p223) and all the requisite comforts you expect on this coast – private beach, boating décor, tennis courts and a big pool.

Da Gianni Pedrinelli (☎ 0789 9 24 36; Località Porto Cervo; meals €50; ⊙ Mar-Oct) Near Le Ginestre on the road south to Capriccioli is one of the Costa Smeralda's most notable restaurants, which has its own garden for summer dining. It's rustic-chic and specialises in elegantly prepared Sardinian dishes.

Mama Latina (☎ 0789 913 12; Porto Cervo Marina; meals €25-35) A rare open-all-year choice with an elegant dining room and a café in front where you can chomp on a pizza for as little as €8 – a rarity in these parts.

OLBIA & THE GALLURA

THE AGA KHAN'S DREAM WORLD

In 1958 one of the world's most flamboyant playboy millionaires, Karim Aga Khan (born 1937), attended a business lunch in London. During the meeting one of the bankers mentioned his latest holiday in Sardinia, waxing lyrical about how beautiful and unspoilt it was. So they cooked up a plan to buy a huge swath of the coast where they would all build holiday homes. It would cost each investor just US$25,000. So in 1962 the Consorzio della Costa Smeralda (www.consorziocostasmeralda.com) was established. The idea of holiday homes was quickly dropped and a more ambitious plan for an exclusive luxury resort came into being.

Beautiful people were soon flocking to Sardinia, dividing their time between Porto Cervo, Porto Raphael and Porto Rotondo. Later, Baia Sardinia, the Piccolo Romazzino villas, Porto Cervo Marina, and the Golf and Pantogia villas sprang up. All of them were governed by strict rules of taste, which have contributed to the artificial yet not displeasing jet-set flavour of the place. The introduction of non-native plants was prohibited, all electricity cables and water conduits had to be laid underground, no street advertising was allowed and buildings had to be in keeping with the surroundings. The whole was conceived as a kind of ideal Mediterranean village.

What began as something very exclusive indeed can scarcely be considered that any longer. By the late 1980s some 2500 villas had been built, and although it's been low-key, development has continued apace since then. Still, the Aga Khan's dream world remains strictly for the well-to-do and retains a distinctive aura of petrified perfection. Each summer Italian celebs are joined by the international jet set, and the Aga Khan himself still visits, although he no longer runs the place. Mere mortals make day trips to the beaches and wander into Porto Cervo to marvel at the luxury yachts and the cost of a Coke (€5, in case you were wondering).

Entertainment

The beautiful people hang around in several bars, but this is strictly a summer-only scene. The port-side Lord Nelson Pub attracts a yachty brigade for cocktails, and it's also one of the few places to stay open outside the high season. La Regata, also by the marina, keeps the drinks coming until about 2am.

The real action, however, happens a few kilometres south of Porto Cervo in a grouping of the Costa Smeralda's most exclusive clubs. **Sopravento** (☎ 0789 9 47 17; Località Abbiadori; ◷ 10.30pm-6am Jun–mid-Sep) and, across the road, **Sottovento** (☎ 0789 9 24 43; Località Abbiadori; ◷ 10.30pm-6am Jun–mid-Sep) are strictly for those with money or, at least, a moneyed look. The not-always-charming door people will decide whether you have what it takes.

Just before this pair and on the same road is the macro disco **Billionaire** (☎ 0789 9 41 92; www.billionaireclub.it; Località Alto Pevero; admission €50; ◷ Jul-Sep). This three-storey villa is a Moroccan fantasy of flickering candles and secluded, cushioned corners. Previous guests have included P Diddy and Paris Hilton, and the door code is strict (no jeans). You can also come here for dinner – a sure way of getting in. The restaurant

is run by Alberto Penati from Annabel's in London and features a special sushi corner.

Getting There & Away

ARST has up to five bus connections between the Costa Smeralda and Olbia (€2.58, one to 1½ hours). Otherwise, **Deluca** (☎ 0789 5 00 87) runs fast, direct buses from Porto Cervo to Olbia (30 minutes, two Monday to Saturday mid-June to mid-September). They leave Piazza Crispi in Olbia at 9am and 1pm.

BAIA SARDINIA

From Porto Cervo the coast road swings north then west 4.5km to Baia Sardinia, whose attraction is its main beach, **Cala Battistoni**. The shades of blue are remarkable and its popularity wholly understandable, but it is jammed solid in midsummer. The resort is aimed at the family market, with plenty of complexes overlooking the bay. Prices are a lot more reasonable here, but the development is rather heavy-handed and you may want to consider accommodation outside the town.

Nearby you'll find the chutes and slides of the **Aquadream** (☎ 0789 9 95 11; Località la Crucitta; ◷ 10am-7pm 12 Jun-12 Sep) water park.

Sleeping & Eating

Within the environs of Baia Sardinia lurk some very nice accommodation options with a bit more breathing space.

Hotel La Rocca (☎ 0789 93 31 31; www.hotella rocca.it; Località Pulicino; half board per person low/high season €75/160; ☑ Apr-Oct) A pastel-pink collection of villas make up this excellent hotel. Flowers froth around the balconies of the two-storey accommodation that sprawls throughout the gardens. The pool has a natural rocky fountain, and there's a free shuttle bus to Baia Sardinia and Porto Cervo.

Le Querce (☎ 0789 9 92 48; www.lequerce.com; Località Cala Bitta; 2-person cottage low/high season €70/145; ☑ Apr-Oct) Mere minutes from Baia Sardinia, on a high hill overlooking the sparkling bay, is the home of Claudio Fassi. He's a retired architect and has converted four stone *stazzi* into delightful self-catering cottages. The fantastical rust-red boulders form part of the architecture, protruding into the interiors. It's an utterly peaceful spot just a short distance from the coast.

Ristorante Grazia Deledda (☎ 0789 9 89 90; meals €30-35). Once the proud holder of a Michelin star, this place may have come down a little over the years, but you can still eat decent Sardinian fare here. You'll find it a few kilometres south of Baia Sardinia on the road to Cannigione.

L'Approdo (☎ 0789 9 90 60; meals €25-30) This cheery, glassed-in eatery is on the beach at Baia Sardinia. Offerings range from pizza to seafood.

Getting There & Away

From Olbia, the Deluca bus service to Porto Cervo continues on for 15 minutes to Baia Sardinia (see opposite).

SOUTH OF PORTO CERVO

Despite all its superficial fluff the coastline of the Costa Smeralda is stunning, the Gallura's bizarre granite mountains plunging into emerald waters in a series of dramatic fjord-like inlets. Each of these has its own marina stuffed with boats – a sight to behold in summer.

The first beach you come to travelling south of Porto Cervo is **Spiaggia del Principe** (or Portu Li Coggi). To find it, follow the signs for Hotel Romazzino but before reaching the hotel turn right at Via degli Asfodeli. You'll have to park your car and make a 10-minute descent to the beach, one of the most beautiful along the coast and little spoilt by development. **Spiaggia Romazzino**, easier to find, is also fine.

Next along is **Capriccioli**, another splendid choice of beach with crystalline water and a pleasant setting. Beyond that keep your eyes peeled for a turn-off to **Spiaggia Liscia Ruia**, shortly before reaching the grand Moorish fantasy that is the Hotel Cala di Volpe.

You finally reach the end of the Costa at the Golfo di Cugnana. The drive is nicely finished off by a spectacular view of **Porto Rotondo**, a second marina developed in 1963 following the success of Porto Cervo. To anyone coming from Sydney or San Francisco it might look like a miniature version of a posh harbourside suburb. Prime Minister Silvio Berlusconi has a huge villa, La Certosa, set in ample grounds around here.

Sleeping

As if in defiance of all the displays of wealth, you'll find a highly strategic camping ground here and one of the more reasonably priced hotels.

THE BIG THREE

It's one thing to describe the luxuries of Italy's most fashionable summer resort and another to experience it. Of all the Costa Smeralda's hotels, none is more stratospherically expensive than the three flagship architectural fantasies, **Hotel Pitrizza**, **Hotel Romazzino** and **Cala di Volpe**. The resort's biggest architects, Jacques Couelle and Michele Busiri, devised their neo-Mediterranean style. In the case of Cala di Volpe, which is reminiscent of a Moroccan kasbah, this teeters on the edge of theatre and good taste. Here big credit limits and egos – just check out those Ferraris in the car park – are the order of the day, and if you have the ready cash you'll want for nothing. But with room prices averaging €1500 per night and meals €150 per person (even for a salad!), you might need to win the lottery.

Hotel Capriccioli (☎ 0789 9 60 04; www.capriccioli .com; Località Capriccioli; half board per person low/high season €85/123; ☺ Apr-Sep) This family-run hotel has been owned by the Azanas since the 1960s, when the Ponza fishermen were the only people out here. Then it was a restaurant, now it is a 45-room hotel right next to the Capriccioli beach.

Villaggio Camping La Cugnana (☎ 0789 3 31 84; www.campingcugnana.it; Località Cugnana; camp sites per adult & tent €16.20, 2-person bungalow per week low/ high season €227/550; ☺ May-Sep) You'll find the camping ground on the road between Porto Rotondo and the north–south road leading to Porto Cervo. It has a supermarket and a swimming pool, backs onto the sea and, perhaps best of all, puts on a free shuttle bus to some of the better Costa Smeralda beaches, including Capriccioli, Liscia Ruia and Spiaggia del Principe. Book ahead for bungalows.

SAN PANTALEO

Another option you might consider is the cute-as-can-be village of San Pantaleo. It sits high up behind the Costa Smeralda (16km from Porto Cervo), cradled in a rocky embrace of granite. Each of the pointy peaks has a name, a typical conceit in San Pantaleo, which has now become something of an artists' haven. Unlike the *costa*, this place has bags of character and is one of the few Sardinian villages set around a picturesque piazza, a sturdy little church at one end. In summer you'll often find a bustling market here, and in spring the blossoms make it picture perfect. Narrow streets fan out from the piazza, lined by Lilliputian croft-like houses, draped artfully with vines, wisteria, climbing red hibiscus and unruly tufts of rosemary. Some even have tiny blue shutters.

This is also a good place for shopping, and you'll find soft-grey and chocolate-brown ceramics at **Petra Sarda** (Via Amalfi). You could also pop your head into **L'Antiquaire de San Pantaleo** (Via Caprera 10), and amuse yourself in the motley jumble of **Arte in Piazza** (Piazza Vittorio Emanuele).

Finished browsing? Then take at pew at chic little **Caffè Nina** (Piazza Vittorio Emanuele 3). In the early evening it's lovely to hang out here with a glass of Vermentino and enjoy some pecorino cheese and olives. Between 27 and 30 July San Pantaleo holds its annual

knees-up, a weekend of general jollity with traditional Sardinian dancing.

The town has its own boutique-style hotel, **Hotel Sant'Andrea** (☎ 0789 6 52 98; www .giagonigroup.com, in Italian; Via Zara 43; s low/high season €57/96, d €90/160; ☺ Apr-Oct; P X ⍥), full of warm, rustic furnishings. You can be sure of an excellent homemade breakfast here, as the same family manages the well -regarded **Ristorante Giagoni** (☎ 0789 6 52 05; Via Zara 36/44; meals €40; ☺ Tue-Sun Apr-Oct). Gourmet pasta, roasted meat and fresh fish daily are all presented exquisitely. Try the bream or bass baked with potatoes and Vernaccia.

Another hotel-restaurant is the more informal **Ca' La Somara** (0789 9 89 69; www.cala -somara.it; d low/high season €70/136; P ⍥), 1km along the road to Arzachena. It's a relaxed, ramshackle place with a cosy country dining room where you'll always find a dog or two lounging. Dinner is served on Monday, Tuesday, Thursday and Friday, although you're free to use the kitchen. Credit cards are not accepted.

ARST runs six daily buses to San Pantaleo from Olbia (€1.50, 35 minutes) and Arzachena (€0.88, 20 minutes).

ARZACHENA & AROUND

Arzachena sits well behind the front lines of coastal tourism and serves as a springboard to some inland treasures: a series of mysterious *nuraghe* (stone tower) ruins and two *tombe di giganti* (literally 'giants' tombs'; ancient mass graves) – the most impressive of such sites in Sardinia.

ARZACHENA

pop 11,100

Arzachena is the only real Sardinian town on the Costa Smeralda, previously a village of Corsican shepherds and farmers dedicated to producing the area's Vermentino wine. Since the 1960s and the development of the Costa Smeralda the population has trebled, and greater prosperity has brought an ugly modern veneer that's particularly noticeable on the roads in and out of town.

Still, **Piazza del Risorgimento** retains much charm, with its stone Chiesa di Santa Maria delle Neve. A quick stroll from here will bring you to the bizarre **Mont'Incappiddatu**, a mushroom-shaped granite rock at the end of Via Limbara. Archaeologists believe the overarching rock may have found use as a shelter for Neolithic tribespeople as long ago as 3500 BC.

Sleeping & Eating

There are four reasonable hotels in Arzachena itself, but far preferable are the excellent *agriturismi* in its environs. Most are housed in the characterful stone *stazzi* that dot the area. A useful website is www .arzachena.net.

B&B Lu Pastruccialeddu (☎ 0789 8 17 77; www .pastruccialeddu.com, in Italian; Località Lu Pastruccialeddu; d low/high season €50/90; P) A typical stone-built Gallurese farmstead in a tranquil rural setting, the B&B is run by Caterina Ruzittu, who grew up here and who prepares the un-believable breakfasts. Homemade biscuits, yogurt, freshly baked cakes with almonds and ricotta, salamis, cheese and cereals – let's just say you won't be needing lunch! There are seven charming bedrooms, which you'd be advised to book in advance. Dinner can be arranged at Agriturismo Rena, which is run by Caterina's brother.

Agriturismo Rena (☎ 0789 8 25 32; agriturismo .rena@virgilio.net; Località Rena; d low/high season €60/90; P) A bigger farm building than Lu Pastruccialeddu, this place overlooks fields of sheep. Inside, wooden chairs and tables and heavy beams are the signature of the place. You can expect to enjoy the farm's own cheese, honey, meat and wine. The restaurant is open to nonguests by reservation.

You'll find both farms if you drive north out of Arzachena and turn right just after the SISA supermarket.

In Arzachena itself you can check into the perfectly comfortable **Albatros Club Hotel** (☎ 0789 3 33 33; www.albatrosclubhotel.com; d low/high season €69/150; P ✖).

Getting There & Away

ARST runs regular buses to Porto Cervo via Baia Sardinia and intermediate stops. Eleven buses arrive from Olbia (€1.76, 45 minutes) and several come in from Santa Teresa di Gallura (€2.64, one hour, two daily) and Palau (€0.88, five daily) to the north.

Between 16 June and 14 September you can pick up the FdS (Ferrovie della Sardegna) **trenino verde** (☎ 0789 8 12 08; www.trenino verde.com, in Italian) train to Tempio Pausania (€9, one hour, two daily).

AROUND ARZACHENA

What makes Arzachena interesting lies in the countryside around it. Dozens of *nuraghi* and *tombe di giganti* litter the countryside. Five sites stand out. You can walk to some of them from central Arzachena, although you really need wheels to see them all in a day.

Information

Tickets and information on the sites can be obtained from **Lithos** (☎ 0789 8 15 37). You'll find the **information office** (☎ 0789 8 26 24; Viale Paolo Dettori 43; ☽ 8am-2pm & 2.30-6.30pm Mon-Fri, 8am-2pm Sat) on the road leading south out of town; you can purchase tickets there or on site.

Each site costs €2.50, or you can enter two/three/four/all five sites for €4.50/6.50/9/11. It's possible to join tours, sometimes with English-, Spanish- and French-speaking guides. The tours take place on the hour between 10am and 1pm and from 3pm to 7pm. The sites open from 9am to 7pm daily from June to September.

Sights

Just 3km east of Arzachena (just off the road to Olbia) you'll come to the first prehistoric site, the **Nuraghe di Albucciu**. It's unusual for several reasons, not least for its flat granite roof instead of the usual *tholos* (conical shape) and its warren of what appear to be emergency escape routes.

Two kilometres on is the **Tempio di Malchittu**, which dates back to 1500 BC. It is one of a few temples of its kind in Sardinia, but the experts can only guess at its true uses. It appears it had a timber roof and was closed with a wooden door, as was Nuraghe di Albucciu. From this relatively high point you have views over the surrounding territory.

Taking the Arzachena–Luogosanto road south, you can follow the signs to **Coddu Ecchju**, one of the most important *tombe di giganti* in Sardinia. The most visible part of it is the oval-shaped central stele (standing stone). Both slabs of granite, one balanced on top of the other, show an engraved frame that apparently symbolises a door to the hereafter, closed to the living. On either side of the stele stand further tall slabs of granite that form a kind of semicircular guard of honour around the tomb.

From the *tombe di giganti* return to the Arzachena–Luogosanto road and turn left (west) for Luogosanto. After about 3km you turn right (signposted) for Li Muri and Li Lolghi. After 2km (partly on a dirt trail) you reach a junction.

The left fork leads 2km uphill along another dirt track to the necropolis of **Li Muri**, a curious site made up of four interlocking megalithic burial grounds, possibly dating to 3500 BC. Archaeologists believe that VIPs were buried in the rectangular stone tombs. At the rim of each circle was a menhir or betyl, an erect stone upon which a divinity may have been represented.

Back down at the junction, the right fork (asphalt) takes you about 1km to the entrance to **Li Lolghi**, another *tomba di gigante*, similar to that of Coddu Ecchju. The central east-facing stele, part of which was snapped off and later restored, dominates the surrounding countryside from its hilltop location.

CANNIGIONE

Cannigione sits on the western side of the Golfo di Arzachena, the largest *ria* (inlet) along this coast. You may not be able to guess it, but it's an old fishing village, established in 1800 to supply the Maddalena islands with food. It grew bigger when coal and cattle ships began to dock at its harbour in the 1900s.

Nowadays tourism has made it prosperous, and the town bustles with shops, hotels, restaurants and a busy Monday market. It has a contented suburban air and its local animation is a refreshing change after the rather sterile environment of the Costa Smeralda. It's also a popular and reasonably priced base for families and lies within easy reach of rural Arzachena (5km), the seaside hot spots of Palau (15km) and the north coast, and the Maddalena archipelago.

The privately run **tourist office** (☎ 0789 8 85 10; Via Nazionale 47; ⏰ 9.30am-12.30pm & 6-7.30pm Mon-Sat) has helpful multilingual staff and bags of information on Cannigione and the surrounding area.

Down at the port you can arrange excursions to the Arcipelago di La Maddalena (€30). Diving and boat hire are available from **Anthias** (☎ 0789 8 63 11; www.anthiasdiving.com; Tanca Manna). You'll find the best beaches north of Cannigione at **Tanca Manna** and **L'Ulticeddu**.

Sleeping & Eating

Many view Cannigione as the poor relation to the Costa Smeralda, but it actually has a lot going for it and it certainly has its fair share of good hotels.

Li Capanni (☎ 0789 8 60 41; www.licapanni.com; Via Lungomare; half board per person low/high season €75/170; P) This place is about as far removed from the bloated extravagance of the Costa Smeralda as you can get. It's owned by the musician Peter Gabriel, who saved it from the developer's clutches. Amid its peaceful gardens sit six stone cottages linked by winding paths that lead to an open restaurant. Another path meanders downhill to a private beach, where you can snorkel and go kayaking.

Stelle Maris Hotel & Resort (☎ 0789 8 63 05; www.hotelstellemarine.com; Località Mannena; half board per person low/high season €70/152; ⏰ Apr-Sep; P ⚙ 🖥 📷) A family-friendly resort hotel with an appealing atmosphere of laid-back luxury, Stelle Maris is perched right on the edge of the long Mannena beach – perfect for kids.

Hotel del Porto (☎ 0789 8 80 11; www.hoteldel-porto.com, in Italian; Via Nazionale 94; d low/high season €80/158; ⏰ May-Sep; ⚙) For bright and breezy accommodation right in the centre of town, check into this place, which has rooms overlooking the marina.

Getting There & Away

Regular **ARST** (☎ 0789 2 11 97) buses make the run to Arzachena (€0.57, 10 minutes, four daily), Baia Sardinia (€0.88, 30 minutes, three Monday to Saturday), Palau (€0.88, 20 minutes, two Monday to Saturday) and Olbia (€2.64, one hour, three Monday to Saturday).

PALAU

pop 3600

Thanks to its strategic position within spitting distance of the Arcipelago di La Maddalena, Palau has become a prosperous and overgrown resort. The NATO presence on the Maddalena islands (see p184) has long provided Palau's bread and butter, and now a big spread of holiday complexes adds to the honey pot.

Away from the sprawl the pine-clad headlands of Capo d'Orso hide more-exclusive resorts in the same mould as those on the Costa Smeralda – gated communities of quiet villas and hidden coves patrolled by an alarming number of security personnel.

It's a beautiful stretch of coast famous for its bizarre weather-beaten rocks, like the Roccia dell'Orso, 6km east of Palau. If you have a car it's worth a drive up here for the fabulous views.

Information

If you need information on the town or the surrounding area, including the Arcipelago di La Maddalena, try the **tourist office** (☎ 0789 70 95 70; Via Nazionale 96; ☼ 8am-1pm Mon-Sat Jun-Aug, 9am-1pm Mon-Sat & 3-6pm Tue & Thu Sep-May). You can access the Internet at **Bar Frizzante** (Via Capo d'Orso 20; per hr €3.50; ☼ 8am-9pm).

Sights & Activities

Palau is a beach resort pure and simple, and its only sight is a wind-whipped fort, **Fortezza di Monte Altura** (☎ 329 224 43 78; admission €3; ☼ 9am-noon & 5-8pm Jun-Aug, 9am-noon & 3-6pm Apr-May, 9am-noon & 3-5pm Sep-Oct), 3km west of town. It was built to help defend the north coast and Arcipelago di La Maddalena from invasion – something it was never called on to do.

Other than that the main activities in Palau are the **boat excursions** (per person €30) around the Maddalena islands. A fleet of tour operators offer their services at the port. The trips usually take in several stops with time to swim on well-known beaches. The **Centro Ippico** (☎ 347 782 33 54; Cala di Lepre, Località Capo d'Orso) in the exclusive Cala di Lepre development up on Capo d'Orso runs two-hour riding treks around the scenic headlands with interludes for swimming. They're fully equipped for children and beginners.

After a hard day on the high seas it's also worth considering a drink at pretty **Porto Rafael**. It's another consortium of private villas, but its tiny piazzetta right on the bay is absolutely perfect.

Sleeping & Eating

With so much traffic heading through here, Palau has a big range of hotels and some of the best restaurants on the island.

Hotel La Roccia (☎ 0789 70 95 28; www.hotel -laroccia.com; Via dei Mille 15; s/d €80/125; ☼ Apr-Nov; P ☒) In a dominating position high up in the town, La Roccia has good views from most of its balconies. Inside, a blue-and-white boating theme makes for a cool Mediterranean atmosphere, and the service is friendly.

Camping Acapulco (☎ 0789 70 94 03; www.camping acapulco.com; camp sites per adult low/high season €8/17; ☼ Apr-Sep) An excellent camp site 500m west of the centre. It's situated right on the edge of a good beach, and the communal washing facilities have gorgeous sea views. There are also neat white bungalows with terracotta roofs and red doors, and there's a host of facilities including a restaurant, a diving centre and a dock for your boat.

La Gritta (☎ 0789 70 80 45; Località Porto Faro; meals €40-50; ☼ Thu-Tue Mar-Oct) In an incomparable setting, La Gritta is one of the island's most stylish restaurants. Floor-to-ceiling glass windows look out over a terrace to views of the sea. Gleaming crystal, white tablecloths and a quiet elegance set the scene for some delicious and inventive cuisine.

Ristorante Da Franco (☎ 0789 70 95 58; Via Capo d'Orso 1; meals €25-30) This longtime favourite with a hard-earned reputation has been going since 1962. Now Franco's grandson supervises the kitchen and the predominantly fishy fare. The décor is frilly and fussy, but the food is sublime. Try the prawns in ginger or the elaborate *zuppa dell'arcipelago*.

Getting There & Away

Palau is served by boats and buses and is also on the FdS train line.

BOAT

Several companies have regular car ferries to Isola di La Maddalena. **Enermar** (☎ 800 20 00 01, 0789 70 84 84; www.enermar.it) and **Saremar** (☎ 199 12 31 99, 0789 70 92 70; www.saremar.it, in Italian) operate regular services between 6am and midnight. The Enermar ferries run on the quarter-hour, while Saremar boats depart on the half-hour. The 20-minute crossing costs €2.30/2.60 weekday/weekend and a car costs €4.50. Ticket prices are similar on all vessels.

Enermar also runs a service to Genoa (€65, 12½ hours, four weekly), and between June and September **Linee Lauro** (☎ 081 551 33 52; www.medmargroup.it, in Italian) services Naples (€75, 13½ hours, once weekly).

BUS

There are **ARST** (☎ 0789 55 30 00) buses connecting Palau with destinations around the north and east coast, including Olbia (€2.58, six daily), Santa Teresa di Gallura

OLBIA & THE GALLURA

(€1.76, five daily) and Arzachena (€0.88, five daily).

Caramelli (☎ 0789 70 94 95) buses run frequently to nearby destinations like Isola dei Gabbiani and Capo d'Orso between May and September.

All buses leave from the port, and you can purchase tickets on board. Alternatively, you can buy tickets at **Stefy's Bar** (Via Razzoli 12), right at the top of town next to the SISA supermarket.

TRAIN

The **trenino verde** (☎ 079 24 57 40; www.treninoverde .com, in Italian) is an old-world train (sometimes of the steam variety) that runs from Palau to Tempio Pausania (€10.50, 1¾ hours, two daily) from 22 June to 11 September. It's a slow ride along a narrow-gauge line through some great countryside – bring some snacks because there's no onboard service. Trains leave from a station in the port.

PORTO POLLO & ISOLA DEI GABBIANI

Seven kilometres west of Palau, windsurfers converge on Porto Pollo (also known as Portu Puddu) for what are considered some of the best conditions for the sport on the island. You can also try kite surfing, canoeing, diving and sailing – it's a water sports paradise.

You can hire gear and get lessons at several places. You'll find **Paolo Silvestri** (☎ 0789 70 50 18; www.silvestri.it, in Italian) on the Isola dei Gabbiani, just across the causeway that separates Porto Pollo from the next bay, Porto Liscia. He hires out full kit for €16. A one-hour lesson costs €35, and a course of four lessons is €98. If sailing is more your thing, **Sporting Club Sardinia** (☎ 0789 70 40 01; www.portopollo.it) offers courses at various levels. A block of five 80-minute beginners' lessons costs €170.50.

The narrow isthmus separating Porto Pollo from Porto Liscia ends in a rounded promontory called Isola dei Gabbiani. It is largely occupied by **Camping Isola dei Gabbiani** (☎ 0789 70 40 19; www.isoladeigabbiani.it; camp sites per adult €17, 4-person bungalow low/high season €52/130), which also offers caravan and bungalow accommodation.

Buses on the Palau–Santa Teresa di Gallura route can stop off at the signposted road junction, from where you have to walk about 2km.

PARCO NAZIONALE DELL'ARCIPELAGO DI LA MADDALENA

Declared a park in 1996, the **Parco Nazionale dell'Arcipelago di La Maddalena** (www.lamaddalena park.it) consists of an archipelago of seven main islands and 40 islets, and several small islands to the south. The archipelago's seven main islands are the high points of a valley that once joined Sardinia and Corsica. When the two split into separate islands, waters filled the strait now called the Bocche di Bonifacio. Over the centuries the *maestrale* (northwesterly wind) that prevails here has helped to mould the granite into the bizarre natural sculptures that festoon the archipelago. Plans are well under way to merge the park with islands belonging to Corsica to create the Parco Marino Internazionale delle Bocche di Bonifacio (www .bocchedibonifacio.org, in Italian).

Nelson and Napoleon knew the straits well, as did that old warhorse Giuseppe Garibaldi, who bought Isola Caprera for his retirement. Now the US Navy has an atomic submarine base on Isola Santo Stefano. It's a controversial topic in a marine park, and critical public opinion blows as strongly as the *maestrale*. Up to 60 other islets, chips of granite, are sprinkled round about, the best of which are Isola Spargi, Isola Santa Maria, Isola Budelli and Isola Razzoli.

ISOLA MADDALENA

pop 11,500

The pink-granite island of Maddalena lies at the heart of the archipelago. As you approach on the ferry the place looks hot, dry and stony, the terracotta houses and apartments blurring into the severe rocky background.

But once you land in La Maddalena you'll be taken by the urbane character of the place, its cobbled piazzas and indoor market, and the perpetual holiday atmosphere that reigns due to boisterous crowds of service personnel on a night out from their dreary barracks. There are nearly 3000 of them at the NATO base on Isola Santo Stefano, and on the eastern side of Maddalena there's another base for the Italian Navy.

PARCO NAZIONALE DELL'ARCIPELAGO DI LA MADDALENA

Until the end of the 17th century the island's meagre population lived mainly in the interior, but the soil is poor and farming was obviously a lot of hard work. So when Baron des Geneys and the Sardo-Piedmontese navy arrived here in 1767 to take possession of the islands they gladly gave up the hilltops to settle in the growing village around Cala Gavetta, one of La Maddalena's bays.

Information

The **tourist office** (☎ 0789 73 63 21; www.la-madd alena.it, in Italian; Cala Gavetta; 🕑 8.30am-1pm & 4.30-7.30pm Jun-Sep, reduced hr Oct-May) has information on the entire archipelago. The **Banco di Sardegna** (Via Amendola) has an ATM and you can check your email at **Cart@tel** (☎ 0789 73 10

81; Largo Matteotti; per 30 min €2.50; 🕑 9.30am-12.30pm & 5-8pm Mon-Sat).

Sights

The best activity in La Maddalena is simply strolling around, taking a coffee along Via Vittorio Emanuele and a cold beer in Piazza Garibaldi. In the morning you can browse around the indoor food market on the piazza. In the evening the lively *passeggiata* takes place along Via Garibaldi.

Other than that you could inspect the religious bits and bobs in the **Museo Diocesano** (☎ 0789 73 74 00; Via Baron Manno; admission free; 🕑 10.30am-12.30pm Tue-Sun year-round & 3.30-8pm Tue-Sun May-Sep), at the back of the modern Chiesa di Santa Maria Maddalena.

OLBIA & THE GALLURA

TROUBLE IN PARADISE

The Mediterranean has always been considered one of the strategic keys to Europe, North Africa and the Middle East, and it's no surprise that the US Navy, under a NATO agreement ratified in 1972, continues to hold a base on Isola Santo Stefano in the Arcipelago di La Maddalena.

The base has long been a point of contention – after all, the Maddalena islands are supposed to be a national park and it is difficult to see how an atomic-submarine base is compatible with the environmental policies of such an area. Furthermore, local activists are enraged that the US/NATO agreement operates outside the control of the Sardinian parliament. Friends of the Earth representative Stefano Deliperi was quoted recently as saying 'it's simply scandalous'.

In 2003 there was a near-disastrous incident when atomic submarine *Hartford* became stranded on a sandbank. Fears of radioactive pollution are already a big issue, and this near miss has only added to the anxiety, despite the subsequent inquiry finding no such pollution. Other reports floating around suggest increased rates of all sorts of nasty diseases.

In 2005 more controversy hit the papers when it was discovered that the US wants to treble the size of its base in the Maddalena islands. Ambassador Mel Sembler was interviewed in *L'Unione Sarda* playing up the benefits, not least the €35 million that the naval presence brings to the island. Still, the Americans have few friends in the Soru government, which has ambitiously promised to make every effort to rid the island of its staggering 24 NATO bases.

A vaguely circular road system leads around the island, allowing easy access to several good beaches such as Giardinelli, Cala Spalmatore, Monti della Rena and Lo Strangolato. While touring around you could stop in at the **Museo Archeologico Navale** (admission €2.50; ☺ 10.30am-12.30pm Tue-Sun year-round & 3.30-7pm Tue-Sun May-Sep), a little over 1km out of La Maddalena on the road to Cala Spalmatore. The museum contains finds from ancient shipwrecks in its two modest rooms, presided over by an impressive reconstructed cross section of a Roman vessel containing more than 200amphorae.

You can arrange excursions around the islands with operators at Cala Mangiavolpe (east of the Cala Gavetta), as well as some excellent diving in the marine park. You will find **Sea World Scuba Centre** (☎ 0789 73 73 31; www.seaworldscuba.com; Piazza 23 Febbraio) at Cala Gavetta. A single dive costs €39.

Sleeping

Hotel Miralonga (☎ 0789 72 25 63; Strada Panoramica; d low/high season €90/140; P ⊠ ⓢ) One of the only hotels to stay open year-round is this big modern affair west of La Maddalena's centre. It goes for a minimalist look, which feels nice and cool in the baking-hot summer. It also has a very welcome pool.

Hotel Il Gabbiano (☎ 0789 72 25 07; Via Giulio Cesare 20; d low/high season €65/104; P) It could be tempting to dive into the waves from your balcony at this place. Situated at the edge of La Maddalena, the island's oldest hotel (and it looks it!) literally juts into the sea. The rooms are a little thrifty at this family-run place, but the downstairs bar has a welcoming home-hearth feel complete with dog basket and maritime memorabilia.

Camping Abbatoggia (☎ 0789 73 91 73; www.campingabbatoggia.it, in Italian; camp sites per adult €10.50; ⓢ Jun-Sep) The best of Isola Maddalena's handful of camping grounds is in the north of the island in Località Abbatoggia. It has access to a couple of good beaches, including Lo Strangolato, and can arrange the hire of canoes and windsurfing equipment.

Eating

There are lots of eating options in La Maddalena; elsewhere around the island there are slim pickings outside the big hotels.

Trattoria La Grotta (☎ 0789 73 72 28; www.lagrotta.it; Via Principe di Napoli 3; meals €25-50; ⓢ May-Sep) Tucked into a little side alley off Via Italia, this is not a place you want to rush. Elegant diners with tables laden with wine bottles spend most of the afternoon here gorging themselves on the refined fish dishes. The pasta is expensive (€16) but superb. Try it with a lip-smacking sauce of pesto and prawns.

Ristorante al Faone (☎ 0789 73 87 63; Via Ilvia 10; meals €25) This place is an old stalwart. Try the *gnocchetti sardi alla Campidanese* (little gnocchi in a sausage and tomato sauce) followed by a meat or seafood main.

Osteria Enoteca da Liò (☎ 0789 73 75 07; Corso Vittorio Emanuele 2-6; meals €10-20) A rare open-all-year choice, the *enoteca* is fronted by an earthy bar full of crusty locals. The menu is tummy filling (rather than wallet slimming), with a €10 lunch menu or à la carte options such as *carpaccio di salmone*.

Getting There & Away
See p181 for information on ferries to La Maddalena from the mainland. They arrive (and leave) at separate points along the waterfront.

Getting Around
Two local buses run from Via Amendola on the waterfront. One goes to the Compendio Garibaldi complex on Isola Caprera (see below), and the other heads around the island, passing the Museo Archeologico Navale and several beaches, including Cala Spalmatore and Spiaggia Bassa Trinità. Tickets cost €0.77.

You can hire mountain bikes (€10 a day) and scooters (around €30 a day; €200 deposit required) from **Noleggio Vacanze** (☎ 0789 73 52 00; Via Mazzini 1), just off the waterfront.

ISOLA CAPRERA
The road out of La Maddalena town towards the east takes you through desolate urban relics to the narrow causeway (first built towards the end of the 19th century) that spans the Passo della Moneta between Isola Maddalena and Isola Caprera. Unlike Maddalena, Caprera is covered in green pines, which look stunning against the ever-present seascape.

Sights
COMPENDIO GARIBALDI
Giuseppe Garibaldi, professional revolutionary and apotheosised in the folklore of Italian unification, bought half of Caprera in 1855 (he got the rest 10 years later). He made it his home and refuge, the place he would return to after yet another daring campaign in the pursuit of liberty. You can visit his home, the **Compendio Garibaldi** (admission €2; 🕑 9am-1.30pm & 4-6.30pm Tue-Sun Jun-Sep, 9am-1.30pm Tue-Sun Oct-May), an object of pilgrimage for many Italians. Entry is by guided visits (in Italian) only.

The red-shirted revolutionary first lived in a hut that still stands in the courtyard while building his main residence, the Casa Bianca. You enter the house proper by an atrium adorned with his portrait, a flag from the days of Peru's war of independence and a reclining wheelchair donated to him by the city of Milan when he became infirm a couple of years before his death. You then proceed through a series of bedrooms where he and family members slept. The kitchen had its own freshwater pump, a feat of high technology in such a place in the 1870s. In what was the main dining room are now displayed all sorts of odds and ends, from binoculars to the general's own red shirt. The last room contains his deathbed, facing the window and the sea, across which he would look longingly, dreaming until the end that he might return to his native Nice.

Outside in the gardens are his rough-hewn granite tomb and those of several family members (he had seven children by his three wives and one by a governess).

Activities
Green, shady Caprera is ideal for walking, and there are plenty of trails through the pine forests. There's a stairway right up to the top of the island (212m) where you'll find the **Teialone** lookout tower.

The island is also dotted with several tempting beaches. Many people head south for the **Due Mari** beaches. You could, however, head north of the Compendio Garibaldi for about 1.5km and look for the walking trail that drops down to the steep and secluded **Cala Coticcio** beach. Marginally easier is **Cala Brigantina** (signposted), southeast of the Garibaldi complex.

In the early evening you might consider a ride among the fragrant maquis with **Cavalla Marsala** (☎ 347 235 90 64; Isola di Caprera), or you could just lark around on water-skis in the calm waters of the Passo della Moneta with **Sci Club Saint Tropez** (☎ 0789 72 77 68, 335 654 52 14). Half an hour costs €70.

OTHER ISLANDS
The five other main islands can only be reached by boat. Numerous excursions leave from Isola Maddalena, Palau and Santa Teresa di Gallura and approach the islands in various combinations. Alternatively, you can hire motorised dinghies and do it yourself.

Isola Santo Stefano is partly occupied by the military and so is mostly inaccessible. **Isola Spargi**, west of Isola Maddalena, is surrounded by little beaches and inlets. One of the better-known ones is **Cala Corsara**. To the north lies a trio of islands, **Isola Budelli**, **Isola Razzoli** and **Isola Santa Maria**. With your boat and time to paddle about you could explore all sorts of little coves and beaches. On tours you are likely to be taken to see **Cala Rosa** (Pink Cove, so-called because of the sand's unique crimson tinge) on Isola Budelli (since 1999 swimming at the environmentally threatened Cala Rosa has been banned), **Cala Lunga** on Isola Razzoli and the often-crowded **Cala Santa Maria** on the island of the same name. The beautiful stretch of water between the three islets is known as the **Porto della Madonna** and is on most waterborne itineraries through the archipelago.

NORTH COAST

North of Palau the wind-whipped coast rises and falls like a rocky sculpture, culminating in the lunarlike headland of Capo Testa. Fine beaches stretch out towards Vignola in the west and sunny Santa Teresa di Gallura in the east, the fashionable heart of the summer scene. The windy waters are a magnet for wind- and kite-surfers, and the annual Kitesurfing World Cup is held here at the end of September. Many competitions also dash across the windy straits to Bonifacio in Corsica.

SANTA TERESA DI GALLURA
pop 4400

With its pretty seaside setting, quaint town centre and vibrant atmosphere, Santa Teresa is a fiendishly popular summer resort, with some 50,000 holidaymakers passing through here in July and August. Sitting on the brilliant white beach of Rena Bianca, watching the sails flit across the straits, you can see the attraction. The crowd is young and posey but also laid-back.

Unlike many Sardinian resorts, Santa Teresa has its own character. It was established by the Savoy rulers in 1808 to help combat smugglers, and it retains a debonair feeling. The neat grid of streets at its centre was designed by an army officer, but most of the town today is the result of the tourism boom since the early 1960s. Santa Teresa's history is caught up with Corsica as much as it is with Sardinia. Over the

centuries plenty of Corsicans have settled here, and the local dialect is similar to that of southern Corsica. You'll find the town fills up on Thursday, when Corsicans make the short trip over for market day.

Orientation
Santa Teresa is a straightforward grid-plan town, its centre resting on a rise. To the north, roads drop down to the Rena Bianca beach, while to the south they decline slowly towards the town exits.

Information
Banca di Sassari (Piazza Vittorio Emanuele) You can change money here.
Banco di Sardegna (Via Nazionale) You can also change money here.
Internet@phone (☎ 0789 75 54 48; Via Nazionale; per hr €5; ☽ 9am-1pm & 4.30-8.30pm Mon-Sat)
Libreria Roggero (☎ 0789 75 50 83; Piazza Vittorio Emanuele 30) A handy place with all sorts of guides and maps on Sardinia (mostly in Italian).
Post office (Via E d'Arborea; ☽ 8am-1pm Mon-Fri, 8am-12.30pm Sat)
Tourist office (☎ 0789 75 41 27; Piazza Vittorio Emanuele 24; ☽ 8.30am-1pm & 3.30-8pm Jun-Sep, 9am-1pm & 3.30-6.30pm Mon-Fri Oct-May) Has information on the town and surrounding area.

Sights & Activities
It's pleasant ambling around the town centre with its café-lined piazza and pastel-coloured houses, and there's some good shopping to be done here.

Otherwise, you can wander up to the 16th-century **Torre di Longonsardo** (admission €2; ☽ 10am-12.30pm & 4-7pm Jun-Sep). It's in a magnificent position, overlooking the natural deep port on one side and the entrance to the town's idyllic (but crowded) **Spiaggia Rena Bianca** on the other.

If you tire of navel gazing on the beach then head down to the tourist port, where you'll find the deep-sea fishing outlet **Bluefin Team** (☎ 392 388 25 11; www.bluefinteam.com, in Italian). A day's fishing for four people, including food and equipment, costs €650/450 in high/low season. Down here you'll also find the **Centro Benessere di Terme del Porto** (☎ 0789 74 10 78; www.termedelporto.com; ☽ 3-8.30pm Mon-Fri, 11am-8.30pm Sat & Sun), a wellbeing centre where you can check in for an evening of pampering in the spa or indulge in a Turkish hammam massage (€30).

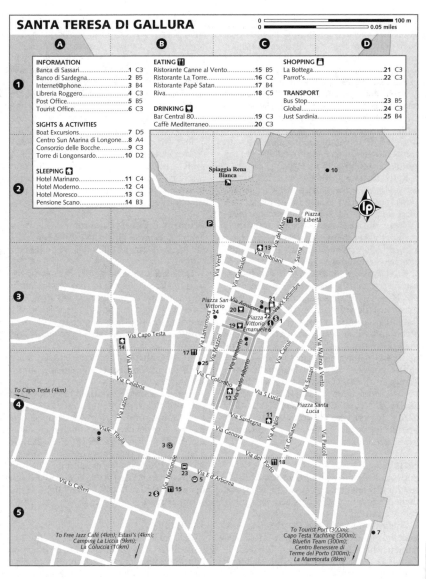

SANTA TERESA DI GALLURA

	0	100 m
	0	0.05 miles

INFORMATION
Banca di Sassari.....................**1** C3
Banco di Sardegna..................**2** B5
Internet@phone.....................**3** B4
Libreria Roggero.....................**4** C3
Post Office............................**5** B5
Tourist Office.........................**6** C3

SIGHTS & ACTIVITIES
Boat Excursions......................**7** D5
Centro Sun Marina di Longone...**8** A4
Consorzio delle Bocche............**9** C3
Torre di Longonsardo..............**10** D2

SLEEPING
Hotel Marinaro.....................**11** C4
Hotel Moderno......................**12** C4
Hotel Moresco.......................**13** C3
Pensione Scano.....................**14** B3

EATING
Ristorante Canne al Vento.......**15** B5
Ristorante La Torre.................**16** C2
Ristorante Papè Satan.............**17** B4
Riva....................................**18** C5

DRINKING
Bar Central 80......................**19** C3
Caffè Mediterraneo................**20** C3

SHOPPING
La Bottega............................**21** C3
Parrot's................................**22** C3

TRANSPORT
Bus Stop..............................**23** B5
Global.................................**24** C3
Just Sardinia.........................**25** B4

At the bottom of Via del Porto you'll find operators running excursions to the Maddalena archipelago. The biggest outfit is the **Consorzio delle Bocche** (☎ 0789 75 51 12; Piazza Vittorio Emanuele; ☺ 9am-1pm & 5pm-midnight), which also has an office in town. It runs two excursions, one to the Maddalena islands and the other down the Costa Smeralda

(summer only). Trips cost between €34 and €38 per person and include lunch (served on board).

The diving around Santa Teresa and the islands in the Bocche di Bonifacio is very good. **Centro Sun Marina di Longone** (☎ 0789 74 10 59; Viale Tibula 11) can help you organise dive trips and PADI courses.

Sleeping

There are plenty of hotels, although most open only from Easter to October. In August you'll probably have to pay *mezza pensione* (half board). Things get booked up months in advance, so it's best to plan ahead.

Hotel Moderno (☎ 0789 75 42 33; www.modernoweb.it, in Italian; Via Umberto 39; s/d incl breakfast €55/100; ☺ mid-Apr–Oct; ✂) This charming family-run B&B is in the heart of the *centro storico*. The 16 rooms are big and airy with shuttered windows and tiny balconies, and are decorated in a homy style.

Hotel Moresco (☎ 0789 75 41 88; www.morescohotel.it; Via Imbriani 16; d low/high season €92/132; ☺ mid-Apr–Oct; P) A rambling place with tiled floors and a splendid position overlooking the sea, the Moresco reserves a strip of the beach for its guests. Rooms have arched balconies and decent views, and the attached restaurant is good.

Hotel Marinaro (☎ 0789 75 41 12; www.hotelmarinaro.it; Via Angioi 48; s/d €85/120, half board per person €80; ✂ ▣) This elegant choice is in a leafy street just downhill from the centre. The tastefully decorated rooms, with their fresh green-and-white décor, have French doors that open onto balconies. Those on the upper floors have nice views.

The cheapest deal you'll find in Santa Teresa is at **Pensione Scano** (☎ /fax 0789 75 44 47; www.albergoscano.it, in Italian; Via Lazio 4; half/full board €60/72). You'll find **Camping La Liccia** (☎ / fax 0789 75 51 90; camp sites per adult/tent €11/15.70, 4-person bungalow €88; ☺ late Apr-Sep) 9km west of town, overlooking the sea.

Eating

Between May and September Santa Teresa's restaurants are open seven days a week and then close completely between December and March.

Ristorante Canne al Vento (☎ 0789 75 42 19; Via Nazionale 23; meals €30-35; ☺ Apr-Sep) A classic restaurant with a bamboo-covered terrace, the Canne al Vento has been serving Gallurese food here since 1957. It's still the best restaurant in town. Try the unusual local specialities, such as *suppa cuata* (cheese and bread broth) or pasta with *bottarga* (mullet roe). The management also has 22 rooms (single/double €30/50, half board per person €70).

Ristorante Papè Satan (☎ 0789 75 50 48; Via Lamarmora 20; pizzas up to €9; ☺ late Apr-Sep) With its wood-fired oven, this is one of the best pizza options in town and has earned the Vera Pizza recognition to prove it. The internal courtyard is a pleasant place to linger, and the service is smiley and quick.

Ristorante La Torre (☎ 0789 75 46 00; Via del Mare 36; meals €30; ☺ Thu-Tue Oct-Jun, daily summer) This place has seagull views from a vast picture window, and an outside terrace. Go for the robust portions of risotto or seafood dishes. Locals rate this place – always a good sign.

Riva (Via del Porto 29; meals €30; ☺ Thu-Tue Apr-Oct) An elegant, modern restaurant with big glass windows and chi-chi décor. The food is strictly fresh fish and includes fancy combinations such as mussels in saffron and rock lobster.

Drinking & Entertainment

Hanging around any of the three café-bars on Piazza Vittorio Emanuele is a pleasant option.

Caffè Mediterraneo (☎ 0789 75 90 14; Via Amsicora 7; cocktails €6.50, snacks €6-12; ☺ 7.30am-3.30am) The town's hottest spot is this gorgeous cafe, with its enormous arched windows and smooth, polished-wood bar. It's loaded with beautiful people sipping cocktails and listening to the music.

At **Bar Central 80** (Piazza Vittorio Emanuele) there are often musicians playing outside on the square.

Three kilometres south of town towards Palau you soon meet a turn-off to the right for Buoncammino. A quick jaunt down this road brings you to Santa Teresa's late-nightlife hub. **Free Jazz Café** (☎ 0789 75 58 11) is a late-night bar that happens to serve pizza. Right next door is the area's only club, the noisy, outdoor **Estasi's** (☎ 339 763 09 67), which opens on Friday and Saturday night in the summer season.

Shopping

Coral, some of it found locally, is the big item here, and you'll find no shortage of boutiques and jewellery shops. The pedestrianised Via Umberto and Via Carlo Alberto, leading south from Piazza Vittorio Emanuele, also host a nightly market from June to September.

Before jetting off you can stock up on delicious gourmet foodstuffs at **La Bottega** (☎ 0789 75 42 16; Via XX Settembre 5), and buy some attractive ceramic souvenirs from **Parrot's** (☎ 0789 75 61 19; Via Amsicora 17).

Getting There & Around

BOAT

Santa Teresa is the main jumping-off point for Corsica. Two companies run car ferries on this 50-minute crossing.

Saremar (☎ 0789 75 41 56; www.saremar.it, in Italian) has four to eight departures each day depending on the season. Adult one-way fares range up to €8.70. A small-car fare is up to €28. Those landing in Bonifacio pay a port tax of €4.10 per person and €2.70 per vehicle.

Mobyline (☎ 0789 75 14 49; www.moby.it) has 10 daily crossings in July and August and four during the rest of the year. Prices are virtually the same as for Saremar.

You don't need a licence to hire the smaller rubber speedboats. **Capo Testa Yachting** (☎ 0789 74 10 60; www.capotestayachting.com), down in the tourist port, has a four-seater for €150 per day in high season.

BUS

Most of the buses terminate at Via E d'Arborea, near the post office. ARST buses operate up to seven times a day between Olbia and Santa Teresa (€3.72, one hour 50 minutes). The same company services Sassari (€5.85, 2½ hours, five daily). These buses stop at numerous places (such as Castelsardo) en route. Get tickets from Bar Central 80, opposite.

Autobus Turmotravel (☎ 0789 2 14 87) makes a daily run from Cagliari (€17.30, six hours) at 5.30am (!), returning at 2.30pm. The same company runs a summer service between Olbia airport and Santa Teresa di Gallura (1½ hours, six daily June to September) via Arzachena and Palau.

From June to September Sardabus runs five circle-line buses connecting Baia Santa Reparata, Capo Testa, Santa Teresa and La Marmorata. The run takes half an hour.

CAR & MOTORCYCLE

You can rent a car from **Just Sardinia** (☎ 0789 75 43 43; Via Maria Teresa 26). Bicycles (€5 per day) and scooters (€30 per day) are available for hire from **Global** (☎ 0789 75 50 80; Piazza San Vittorio 7).

TAXI

If you're in a tearing hurry to get to Olbia airport you can get a special **airport taxi** (☎ 0789 74 10 35) for €65.

AROUND SANTA TERESA DI GALLURA

With the weight of people on pretty Rena Bianca in the summer you may want to head out of town to any number of long sandy beaches. East of Santa Teresa is the Conca Verde, a wild stretch of coastline covered with bushy umbrella pines. Along here you can try **La Marmorata** (8km) or (even better) **La Licciola** (11km), which is nearly completely devoid of beachside build-up.

Head 10km in the other direction (west) and you'll arrive at the long, sandy **Rena Maiore**, backed by appealing, soft dunes. A coastal walking track heads west to Vignola. ARST buses to Castelsardo can drop you at the turn-off. Further on are the beaches of **Spiaggia Montirussu**, **Spiaggia Lu Littaroni** and **Spiaggia Naracu Nieddu**, none of them very busy even in high summer. Finally, you'll come to the little seaside resort of **Vignola Mare**, the heart of kite-surfing territory.

La Coluccia (☎ 0789 75 80 04; www.mobygest .it; Località Conca Verde; half board per person low/high season €100/230; ☺ May-Sep; P ☒ ☒) is a hip hotel in every sense of the word. This serene retreat the setting is perfect – think manicured lawns sloping to azure seas and a bank of umbrella pines shading blissed-out guests. Inside, the design is sleek and contemporary, and the soothing natural tones and textures of wood, marble and limestone predominate. On offer are boat trips, hot-stone massages and a curvaceous pool – if you're looking for that honeymoon moment then this is it.

Capo Testa

Four kilometres from Santa Teresa, this extraordinary granite headland seems more like a sculptural garden. Nature has contrived to make this pocket of rock a unique scene – the undulating, curvaceous forms look as though they were squeezed and moulded by a master dessert maker. The Romans quarried granite here, as did the Pisans centuries later.

The place also has a couple of beaches. **Rena di Levante** and **Rena di Ponente** lie either side of the narrow isthmus that leads out to the headland itself.

Right on Rena di Ponente you can rent windsurfing gear at **Nautica Rena di Ponente** (☎ 348 033 31 66). Full kit costs €15.

OLBIA & THE GALLURA

THE INTERIOR

The Gallura isn't all about beaches and billionaires; there's a greener, quieter side to the province. In fact it was the Gallura's fertile hinterland that attracted the waves of Corsican migrants who settled here to farm the cork forests and plant the extensive Vermentino vineyards. Between the 17th and mid-19th centuries Tempio Pausania was the region 's capital, considered even more important than the port of Olbia.

TEMPIO PAUSANIA

pop 14,000

Elevated above the hot Gallurese plain and surrounded by dense cork woods, Tempio Pausania has the character of a mountain town. The old town's buildings are constructed almost exclusively from grey granite. They give Tempio a rather severe aspect, especially on rainy days, but they belie a thriving village community which comes out in force for the town's numerous festivities.

The surrounding countryside, dotted with rural towns, is perfect for touring, while the minor road leading south to the coast via Aglientu is one of the prettiest. Nearby Monte Limbara provides numerous trekking opportunities.

Information

Several banks with ATMs are scattered about.

Banco di Napoli (Piazza Gallura 2) On the central piazza.

Ospedale Civile (☎ 079 67 10 81; Via Grazia Deledda 19) Hospital.

Post office (Largo A de Gasperi; ☒ 8.15am-1.15pm Mon-Sat) In town.

Tourist office (☎ 079 639 00 80; www.comune .tempiopausania.ss.it, in Italian; Piazza Mercato 3; ☒ 9.30am-1.30pm & 3.30-7.30pm Mon-Sat) A privately run tourist office with excellent information and friendly multilingual staff.

Sights

The centrepiece of the town is the imposing granite **Cattedrale di San Pietro**. All that remains of the 15th-century original are the bell tower and main entrance. Across the square, the **Oratorio del Rosario** dates to the time of the Spanish domination of the island.

Behind the cathedral, the town's main square, **Piazza Gallura**, is fronted by the grave **Municipio** (town hall). A couple of cafés here make good spots for people-watching. The nearby Piazza del Purgatorio is presided over by the modest **Chiesa del Purgatorio**. The story goes that a member of the noble Misorro family was found guilty of carrying out a massacre on this very spot. To expiate his sins, the pope ordered the man to fund the building of this church, where to this day it is the custom of townspeople to come and pray after a funeral.

Tempio is replete with churches, and an indication of the town's former importance lies in the presence of the 17th-century former **Convento degli Scolopi** (Piazza Mazzini). It's now a college, but you can peer through the gates to the leafy cloister from Piazza del Carmine.

Since Roman days Tempio has been known for its springs; the **Fonti di Rinaggiu** is a pleasant 1km walk southwest from the centre (take the shady Via San Lorenzo and follow the 'Alle Terme' signs).

The local **Cantina Gallura** (☎ 079 63 12 41) produces the excellent Canayli wine, and you'd do well to try a bottle or two with a plate of fresh fish.

Festivals & Events

Tempio has a whole host of festivals and events, from music concerts to folklore parades and key religious festivals.

Carnevale is big here, as is **Easter**. On Good Friday members of *confraternita* (religious brotherhoods) dress up in sinister-looking robes and hoods for the **Via Crucis** night procession. The musical Festival d'Estate runs from July to mid-August.

Sleeping & Eating

Petit Hotel (☎ 079 63 11 34; www.petit-hotel.it, in Italian; Largo A de Gasperi 9/11; s/d €58/85; P ☒) Tempio's only central hotel is this modern affair. It's popular with visiting businesspeople, and some of the rooms have good views over the countryside. The tiled floors and French doors can make it a bit chilly out of season.

Agriturismo Muto di Gallura (☎ 079 62 05 59; www.mutodigallura.com; Località Fraiga; half board per person €70) This typical stone-built farmhouse is located between Tempio and Aggius. It has its own stables and offers horse treks

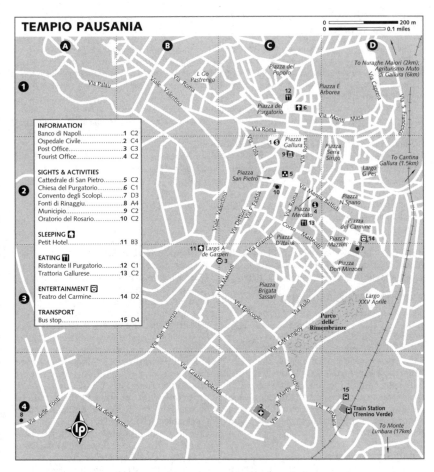

TEMPIO PAUSANIA

INFORMATION
Banco di Napoli.....................1 C2
Ospedale Civile.....................2 C4
Post Office.............................3 C3
Tourist Office........................4 C2

SIGHTS & ACTIVITIES
Cattedrale di San Pietro..........5 C2
Chiesa del Purgatorio.............6 C1
Convento degli Scolopi...........7 D3
Fonti di Rinaggiu...................8 A4
Municipio..............................9 C2
Oratorio del Rosario..............10 C2

SLEEPING 🏠
Petit Hotel...........................11 B3

EATING 🍴
Ristorante Il Purgatorio........12 C1
Trattoria Gallurese...............13 C2

ENTERTAINMENT 🎭
Teatro del Carmine...............14 D2

TRANSPORT
Bus stop..............................15 D4

---

in the countryside – a glorious experience. Expect to dine well on the farm's own produce. The proprietors speak English.

Ristorante Il Purgatorio (☎ 079 63 43 94; Piazza del Purgatorio; meals €30-35; ☷ Wed-Mon) One of the town's classiest restaurants, Il Purgatorio has soft lighting and bare stone walls. It's an intimate setting in which to try a variety of local and national dishes.

Trattoria Gallurese (☎ 079 67 10 48; Via Novara 2; meals €20-25; ☷ Sat-Thu & lunch Fri) Venture upstairs to the simple homespun dining area for a warm welcome and local food. The trattoria has a good-value set menu for €12. If you want something like *porceddu* (suckling pig) or *capretto* (kid meat), order a day in advance.

Entertainment

Teatro del Carmine (☎ 079 67 15 80; Piazza del Carmine) A variety of performances, from operetta to classical concerts, can be enjoyed here, especially during the summer Festival d'Estate.

Getting There & Away

ARST buses from Olbia (€2.89, 1½ hours, six Monday to Saturday, three Sunday) and Sassari (€2.64, 1½ hours, four daily), among others, arrive in the square in front of the train station.

The station itself, with its Biasi paintings, comes to life for the summertime **trenino verde** (☎ 079 639 31 13; www.treninoverde .com, in Italian) service to/from Arzachena (€9,

---

DETOUR: MONTE LIMBARA

The most interesting excursion from the town is to make for the summit of Monte Limbara (1359m), about 17km southeast. The most convenient way to do so is with your own vehicle, winding slowly along the ribbon of road that snakes up to the summit. From Tempio, drive south out of town past the train station and follow the SS392 road for Oschiri. After 8km you will hit the left turn-off for the mountain.

The initial stretch takes you through thick pine woods. As you emerge above the tree line, a couple of *punto panoramico* (viewing spots) are indicated, from where you have terrific views across all of northern Sardinia. One is marked by a statue of the Virgin Mary and child, near the simple little **Chiesa di Santa Maria della Neve** church.

The road then flattens out to reach the viewing point of Punta Balistreri (1359m), where the RAI national TV has stacked relay and communication towers. The air is cool and refreshing even on a midsummer's day, and the views west towards Sassari and beyond and north to Corsica are breathtaking.

Monte Limbara is also a popular trekking spot. The tourist office in Tempio can provide you with a list of guides.

---

one hour, two daily) and Palau (€10.50, 1¾ hours, two daily). There is also a regular link to Sassari (€12, 2½ hours, one daily).

AROUND TEMPIO PAUSANIA

Two kilometres north of town on the SS133 road to Palau is the **Nuraghe Maiori**, signposted off to the right and immersed in thick cork woods. As the name ('major') suggests, it is a good deal bigger than many of the simple ruined towers you will repeatedly spot around the countryside here. Off the entrance corridor is a chamber on each side, and a ramp leads you to a third, open room at the back. Stairs to the left allow you to walk to the top.

Calangianus & Luras

As it is a major centre of cork production, you can expect to find plenty of the stuff on sale in all imaginable forms in Calangianus, about 10km east of Tempio. If you get talking to some of the artisans, you may find them showing you how corks are made for your bottle of Vermentino. Three kilometres north at Luras, the main attraction is the **Dolmen de Ladas**.

Aggius & Luogosanto

Eight kilometres to the northwest of Tempio, Aggius is a quiet village set amid granite walls and cork woods. It's famous for its choral music and carpets, the latter tradition dating back to the 1900s, when 4000 looms were said to have been busy in the area. You can view some excellent work

at the local **tourist office** (☎ 079 62 02 06; www .aggius.net, in Italian; Largo Andrea Vasa; ☷ 10am-noon & 5-8pm) from mid-July to mid-September.

A few kilometres northwest of Aggius towards Trinità d'Agoltu, you come to the strange boulder-strewn landscape of the **Valle della Luna**. The valley is a fantastic place for a cycle ride, and the road through here down to the coast is tremendously scenic.

From Aggius it's possible to loop round northwest onto the SS133 towards remote **Luogosanto** (Holy Place). It's a pretty place peppered with churches, the grandest of which is the **Basilica di Nostra Signora di Luogosanto**, built in 1228. Pope Onorio III gave it the title of basilica when he sanctioned its Holy Door. Like the Holy Door at St Peter's in Rome, this door is walled up and only opened every seven years. The façade's austere rural character and silver-grey stonework has a simple, essential beauty. There's an even older church here, the **Chiesa di San Trano**, which was built to honour the 6th-century St Trano and is moulded into the granite rock.

From Luogosanto you can make your way round to Arzachena. In Aggius you can stay at the **Agriturismo Muto di Gallura** (see p190).

LAGO DI COGHINAS, OSCHIRI & BERCHIDDA

Those with wheels could make another excursion south of Monte Limbara. Once down from the mountain, turn left on the SS392 and head for Oschiri. The road skirts the western side of the Limbara massif, tops the Passo della Limbara (646m) and then begins its descent. After about 12km the green gives way to scorched straw-coloured fields and the blue mirror of the artificial Lago di Coghinas comes into view.

Just before the bridge over the lake, a narrow asphalted road breaks off east towards Berchidda around the northern flank of Monte Acuto (493m). Berchidda is a fairly nondescript farming town with a strong wine tradition. You can find out about local wine-making and taste some of the area's Vermentino at the **Museo del Vino** (☎ 079 70 45 87; admission €3; ⏰ 10am-2pm & 4-7pm).

The best time to visit is August, when Berchidda holds its big **Time in Jazz** (www.timeinjazz .it, in Italian) festival. It's a multi-ethnic event showcasing anything from string quartets to Moroccan *gnaoua* (sub-Saharan reed pipe and percussion) music.

Should you need to stay in Berchidda there are a couple of modest hotels with their own restaurants. **Sos Chelvos** (☎ 079 70 49 35; fax 079 70 49 21; Via Umberto 52; s/d €24/42) is a functional and friendly place.

Three or four buses a day pass through from Olbia and Ozieri. Berchidda is also on the Olbia–Chilivani train line, but the station is 2km out of town.

Nuoro & the East

If Sardinia is a world apart from the Italian mainland, Nuoro is an island within the island. Insulated by the great grey arena of the Gennargentu, the Nuoresi can appear brooding and introverted, yet they have a rough-diamond beauty. Like Calabria the region has a history of banditry and vendettas that continued right up until the 1980s. Other Sardinians will warn you to be circumspect with the village folk of Nuoro. While they can seem taciturn and guarded at first, on the whole they are a hospitable breed – you just have to break the ice first and not go charging in like a bull in a china shop.

The unruliness of the place is part of its charm. The dark majesty of the mountains and the resolutely rural character of inland Barbagia are matched by the oppressive breezeblock wildness of most of the province's towns and villages. Often downright ugly, they stand in stunning positions arranged like mountainside balconies, so steeply terraced that you wonder how they have any purchase on the soil they occupy.

Much of Sardinia's most rugged and spectacular scenery is concentrated in this province – the uncompromising territory provides the island's most exhilarating walking and climbing. Several fine prehistoric sites await discovery, and the province boasts some of Sardinia's most breathtaking coastline, particularly the Golfo di Orosei.

HIGHLIGHTS

- Be dazzled by the traditional island costumes on parade for Nuoro's August **Festa del Redentore** (p200)

- Marvel at the colours of Sardinia's festivals in the excellent **Museo della Vita e delle Tradizioni Sarde** (p198), in Nuoro

- Trek Europe's Grand Canyon, the **Gola Su Gorruppu** (p217), and explore the poignant prehistoric site of **Tiscali** (p204), hidden in its volcanic crater

- Find politics on the street in Orgosolo's dramatically executed **murals** (p205)

- Eat, drink and be merry on the terrace of **Hotel Su Gologone** (p203), where you'll feast like a king on traditional *porceddu* (suckling pig)

- Don't miss a speedboat trip to explore the stunning beauty of the **Golfo di Orosei's** beaches and coves (p218)

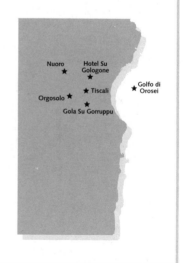

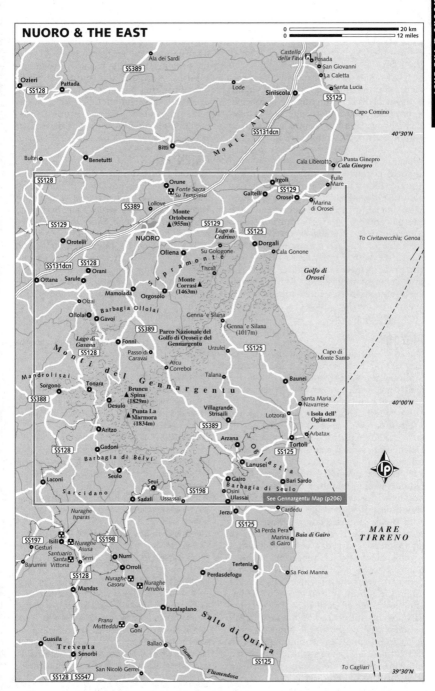

NUORO & THE EAST

0 — 20 km
0 — 12 miles

NUORO

pop 36,900

DH Lawrence was right about one thing: there's not much to see in Nuoro (Nugoro in the local dialect) other than Nuoro itself. It may be the provincial capital, but at heart it's really just another mountain village (elevation 554m), grown big with responsibility. Yet the town's rather shabby modern appearance disguises Nuoro's highly individual character and its ardent cultural heart. Famous as the birthplace of literary heroine Grazia Deledda, novelist Salvatore Satta and renowned poet Sebastiano Satta (see p37 and p37), the real drama of Nuoro comes from the Nuoresi themselves. They are some of Sardinia's most fervent traditionalists, with a great sense of integrity and pride in their local culture. You'll also find some of the island's most interesting museums here, which together form a showcase for the unique identity of this mountainous region.

HISTORY

Nuoro was settled as early as the 5th century AD but little is known of it before the Middle Ages, when it was passed from one feudal family to another under the Crown of Aragon and later Spain.

By the 18th century the town had grown to a self-important size of 3000 people, mostly farmers and shepherds – the folk that people Deledda's novels. If reports by the island's rulers of the time are true, Nuoro was also a violent nest of bandits and outlaws. Many Nuoresi were no doubt pushed to lawlessness by centuries of oppression and the precariousness of peasant life.

In 1820 a proposed law to privatise common land (effectively handing it to rich landowners) sparked a series of peasant revolts, during which rebels burnt down Nuoro's town hall. In 1859 Nuoro was demoted when the province was brought under the administration of Sassari, a situation not reversed until 1927. The decision was possibly influenced by the new Italian nation's view of the whole Nuoro district as a 'crime zone', an attitude reflected in its treatment of the area, which only served to further alienate the Nuoresi and cement their mistrust of authority.

After 1927 Nuoro quickly developed into a bustling administrative centre, attracting internal migrants from all over the province to its haphazardly expanding suburbs. Although the traditional problem of banditry has subsided and the town presents a cheerful enough visage, Nuoro remains troubled. Its population is falling as high unemployment is driving its people away.

ORIENTATION

The old centre of the town is bunched together in Nuoro's northeastern corner, on a high spur of land that juts eastward to become Monte Ortobene. Viale Francesco Ciusa and the Colle Sant'Onofrio afford pleasant views across the valley.

The heart of the town is contained in the warren of tidy streets and lanes around Piazza San Giovanni and Corso Garibaldi, the main street. Several restaurants dot the area. Apart from a couple of options near the centre and on Monte Ortobene, most of Nuoro's few hotels are oddly placed west of the centre near the hospital.

The train and main bus stations are also west of the city centre.

INFORMATION

Banco di Lavoro Nazionale (Via A Manzoni 26) You can change money here.

Banco di Sardegna (Corso Garibaldi 69) Another money-changing option.

CTS (☎ 0784 25 40 18; Via Attilio Deffenu 41-43) A branch of the national youth travel agent.

Libreria Mondadori (☎ 0784 3 41 61; Corso Garibaldi 147) A handy bookshop selling good maps, although there's little in English.

Main post office (Piazza F Crispi; ⏰ 8.15am-6.40pm Mon-Fri, 8.15am-1pm Sat) A Fascist showpiece in the centre of town.

Ospedale Civile San Francesco (☎ 0784 24 02 37; Via Mannironi) The city's main hospital, west of the centre.

Police station (☎ 0784 3 21 00; Viale Europa) Central and just north of the action.

Punto Informa (☎ 0784 3 87 77; Corso Garibaldi 155; ⏰ 9am-1pm & 3.30-7pm Mon-Sat) A private initiative run by FdS (Ferrovie della Sardegna) bus and train services. The most helpful and convenient information point.

Tourist office (☎ 0784 3 00 83; www.enteturismo .nuoro.it; Piazza Italia 19; ⏰ 9am-1pm & 4-7pm Mon-Sat) This tourist office is in the same building as the provincial tourist administration office. The website is a good reference point.

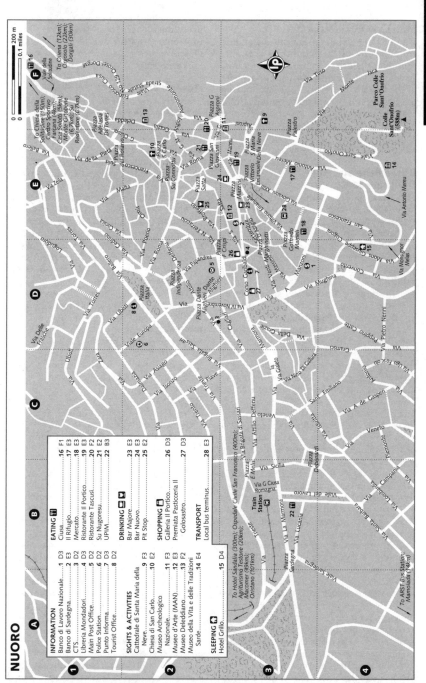

NUORO

0 ———— 200 m
0 ———— 0.1 miles

INFORMATION
Banco di Lavoro Nazionale.........1 D3
Banco di Sardegna.......................2 E3
CTS...3 D2
Libreria Mondadori.......................4 D3
Main Post Office...........................5 D2
Police Station................................6 D2
Punto Informa...............................7 D3
Tourist Office................................8 D2

SIGHTS & ACTIVITIES
Cattedrale di Santa Maria della
  Neve...9 F3
Chiesa di San Carlo.....................10 E2
Museo Archeologico
  Nazionale..................................11 F3
Museo d'Arte (MAN)..................12 E3
Museo Deleddiano......................13 F2
Museo della Vita e delle Tradizioni
  Sarde..14 E4

SLEEPING
Hotel Grillo.................................15 D4

EATING
Ciusa..16 F1
Il Rifugio....................................17 E3
Mercato.....................................18 E3
Ristorante Il Portico....................19 E3
Ristorante Tascusi.......................20 F2
Su Nugoresu...............................21 E2
UPIM..22 B3

DRINKING
Bar Majore..................................23 E3
Bar Nuovo...................................24 E3
Pit Stop......................................25 E2

SHOPPING
Galleria Il Portico........................26 D3
Premiata Pasticceria Il
  Golosastro.................................27 D3

TRANSPORT
Local bus terminus......................28 E3

SIGHTS & ACTIVITIES

Nuoro is not a pretty place, but the granite amphitheatre of the mountains that surround it provides an impressive panorama. The sober and slightly formal atmosphere of the town is especially noticeable during the *passeggiata* (traditional evening stroll). Make sure you go for a wander around Grazia Deledda's old house, as this knot of alleys gives an immediate insight into the village that Nuoro once was.

Museo della Vita e delle Tradizioni Sarde

This fascinating ethnographic **museum** (☎ 0784 25 70 35; Via Antonio Mereu 56; adult/child €3/1; ♥ 9am-8pm Tue-Sat, 9am-1pm Sun mid-Jun–Sep, 9am-1pm & 3-7pm Oct–mid-Jun) has a gorgeous collection of traditional Sardinian costumes and crafts. Exquisite examples of filigree jewellery fill the cabinets along with carpets, tapestries and rich embroideries. Other cabinets hold musical instruments, firearms and other curious household items, but it's the comprehensive display of costumes that catches the eye.

In the central hall mannequins crowd onto a podium like a throng of festivalgoers. The variety of styles, colours, patterns and materials speaks volumes about the people and their villages. The fiery red skirts belong to the fiercely independent mountain villages. Those of Orgosolo and Desulo have an Armenian flavour, their red wool aprons finished with a blue-and-yellow silk border. Is it coincidence that the headdress of the women of Orgosolo, Sardinia's most lawless town, includes a cloth to cover the face? Or that the bourgeois of Quartu Sant'Elena adorned themselves in velvets and lace, while the poor wives of the Iglesiente miners had to make do with a plain-Jane outfit of brown and black? And what of the burka-like headdresses of the ladies of Ittiri and Osilo?

Other rooms display life-size exhibits of figures in the region's more unusual festivals. These include Mamoiada's *mamuthones* (see p207), with their shaggy sheepskins and scowling masks, and Ottana's *boes* (see p207), with their tiny antelope-like masks, huge capes and furry boots. If they weren't kept on leashes by the *Issokadores* (revellers dressed as gendarmes) you'd feel they might run amok in the museum.

A short wander up from the museum will bring you to the quiet **Parco Colle Sant'Onofrio**.

From the highest point you can see across to Monte Ortobene and, further south, to Oliena and Orgosolo. There are swings for kids and benches for the pooped.

Museo d'Arte (MAN)

From past to present, the **MAN** (☎ 0784 25 21 10; www.museoman.it; Via S Satta 15; adult/child €3/2; ♥ 10am-1pm & 4.30-8.30pm Tue-Sat, 10am-1pm Sun) museum is the only serious contemporary art gallery in Sardinia. Its permanent collection is a wonderful sample of 20th-century Sardinian art, including big-name artists such as Antonio Ballero, Giovanni Ciusa-Romagna, Mario Delitalia and abstract artist Mauro Manca. Local sculptors Francesco Ciusa and Costantino Nivola are also represented. To see a bronze copy of Francesco Ciusa's *Madre dell'Ucciso* (Mother of the Killed), which won a prize at the Venice Biennale in 1907, you should visit the **Chiesa di San Carlo** (Piazza San Carlo).

This permanent show is usually accompanied by more wide-ranging temporary exhibits, usually held on the ground and top floors.

Feel inspired? Then head down the road to **Galleria Il Portico** (see p201), which sells the work of local artists, including some wonderful oils by Antonio Corriga.

Piazza Satta

A brief walk northwest up Via Satta will bring you to Piazza Satta, the square dedicated to the great poet Sebastiano Satta (1867–1914), who was born in a house here. In true Nuoro style the town felt that a cultural memorial was necessary and commissioned sculptor Costantino Nivola (1911–88) to come up with something. Nivola whitewashed the square to provide a blank background for a series of granite sculptures that rise up like menhirs. Each sculpture has a carved niche containing a small bronze figurine (a clear wink at the prehistoric *bronzetti*) depicting a character from Satta's poems. It was an unusual idea and must originally have been an impressive sight. However, graffiti and a general unkempt air now mar the piazza.

Museo Deleddiano

Piazza Satta verges on the oldest part of town, the small hill where Nobel prize–winner Grazia Deledda (1871–1936; see p37) lived the first 29 years of her life. Her house has now been transformed into a **museum** (☎ 0784 25 80 88; Via Grazia Deledda 53; adult/child €3/1; ☼ 9am-8pm Tue-Sat, 9am-1pm Sun mid-Jun–Sep, 9am-1pm & 3-7pm Oct–mid-Jun) which contains all sorts of memorabilia relating to the writer and her works – pens, letters, family snapshots and the like. What's really interesting, however, are the official pictures of the Nobel prize–giving ceremony. Just look at how tiny she was! The only woman in a room full of stiffly suited men, and barely shoulder high, she must have been a *tour de force*.

Other rooms in the house have been furnished to give an idea of what a traditional Nuoresi house was like, and it's really rather good – the kitchen crammed with pots and pans, and a coat on the hook by the back door, as if the occupants had all just popped out to the shops.

At the time of writing, the upstairs rooms and the basement housed a temporary photographic exhibition of the work of Donatello Tore (see the boxed text, below).

Although she lived 36 of her 65 years in Rome, Deledda's life was consumed by Nuoro and its essential dramas. Fittingly, she was brought home to be buried in the plain granite church of the **Chiesa della Solitudine** (Viale della Solitudine). You will find her granite sarcophagus to the right of the altar. On the eve of 28 August, the religious high point of Nuoro's Festa del Redentore, a solemn torchlight parade starts here at 9pm and concludes at the cathedral.

Museo Archeologico Nazionale

The only other museum of interest in Nuoro is the **archaeological museum** (☎ 0784 3 16 88; Via Mannu 1; admission free; ☼ 9am-1.30pm & 3-6pm Wed & Fri, 9am-1.30pm Tue, Thu & Sat). It is housed in the neoclassical Palazzo Asproni and displays a collection of artefacts excavated in Nuoro province. These range from ancient ceramics and fine *bronzetti* (bronze figurines) to a drilled skull from 1600 BC and Roman and early-medieval finds.

Cattedrale Santa Maria della Neve

All that can be said of the cinnamon-coloured neoclassical façade of Nuoro's 19th-century **cathedral** (Piazza Santa Maria Della Neve) is that it's big. Inside you can see a couple of mildly interesting works, including

---

BARBAGIA: PAST & PRESENT

The black-and-white pictures on the wall show a traditional Sardinian village. The small houses are made of stone and are in a ramshackle condition. In one a family crowds into a tiny courtyard; in others ancient couples sit amid the bare interior of their houses. You know the people are very poor from the deep lines on their faces, but they are proud – you can tell this from the poses they strike for their portraits. This is the village of Lollove, 12km from Nuoro, and one might think the pictures were taken in the 1950s or maybe even earlier. But this is Lollove in 1996. Photographer Donatello Tore spent two summers there in 1996 and 1997 recording the lives of the village's 60 or so inhabitants.

The temporary exhibition, held at the Museo Deleddiano, illustrates so much about Nuoro and its province. The people's pride, their living traditions, the palpable proximity of past and present, and all their simple passions – a bottle of beer after a hard day's work, rounds of creamy white ricotta (titled *The Treasure of Lollove*), a game of Jocu de Sa Murra (in which participants try to guess what numbers their opponents will form with their fingers) and big barrels of home-grown wine. In such a context Nuoro's history of lawlessness and banditry begins to make sense, as does the measured, taciturn nature of the people. Abandoned by the local council – which considered Lollove an uneconomic development prospect – the villagers struggled on alone.

With his reportage exhibition Tore joins a long Nuoresi tradition in extrapolating suffering into art. Here is the material that fills the tragic poetry of the Barbagia and forms the basis of its melancholy music – a hard life, heroically lived. But nowhere is this clash between past and present and traditional values and modernity given such passionate immediacy as in the murals of Orgosolo (see p205).

Some of the bookshops in Nuoro might stock Donatello Tore's video diary of his time in Lollove. Happily, the village is no longer so neglected and it now forms part of the Autunno in Barbagia festival. You can view Donatello's work on Lollove and Nuoro on his site, www.donatellotore.it.

Disputa de Gesù Fra i Dottori (Jesus Arguing with the Doctors), a canvas attributed to the school of Luca Giordano and located between the first and second chapels on the right as you enter. Half the panels of the Via Crucis (Stations of the Cross) are by Giovanni Ciusa-Romagna.

More exciting views are available behind the church from the small parking lot. Here the humdrum buildings give way to a magnificent view of the deep valley and Monte Ortobene in the distance.

Monte Ortobene

About 7km northeast of Nuoro is the granite peak of Monte Ortobene (955m), capped by its massive statue of the Redentore (Christ the Redeemer). It's a place of veneration, but it's also a favourite picnic spot for locals. On 29 August (starting bright and early at 6am) the brightly clothed faithful make a pilgrimage here from the cathedral. Afterwards Mass is celebrated in the nearby Chiesa di Nostra Signora del Monte, and there's another late-morning Mass at the feet of the statue.

After the spirit has been taken care of, the thoughts of the Nuoresi turn to more terrestrial needs. Many fan out in the woods (full of ilex, pine, fir and poplar) and open picnic hampers, while others crowd into a couple of bars or grab a restaurant table.

The statue was raised in 1901 in response to a call by Pope Leo XIII to raise 19 statues of Christ around Italy to represent the 19 centuries of Christianity. Grazia Deledda was behind the push by Nuoro to be one of the sites. Since then the statue, which shows Christ trampling the devil underfoot, has been the object of pilgrims who attribute to it all manner of cures and interventions.

The views across the valley to Oliena and Monte Corrasi are at their most breathtaking from the road to the left shortly before you reach the top of the mountain.

Local bus 8 runs up to the mountain seven times a day from Piazza Vittorio Emanuele. The last one back down leaves at 8.20pm.

Centro Sportivo Farcana

About 4km up Monte Ortobene from Nuoro, this **sports centre** (☎ 0784 3 23 57) is signposted off to the left. Its main attraction is the outdoor Olympic pool, a treat in summer if you haven't the energy to go to the seaside.

FESTIVALS

The **Festa del Redentore** (Feast of Christ the Redeemer) in the last week of August is the main event in Nuoro, and since its inception in 1901 it has become one of the most exuberant folkloric festivals in the island's calendar. Groups of towns and villages proudly display their festive dress, and there are dance and music performances in the evening. On the evening of 28 August a torch-lit procession winds its way through the city.

SLEEPING

Nuoro has a handful of decent but uninspiring hotels, many of them well out of the centre. A more interesting option might be one of the *agriturismi* (farm-holiday inns) in the surrounding countryside, but you will need your own car for these.

. **Hotel Grillo** (☎ 0784 3 86 78; www.grillohotel.it, in Italian; Via Monsignor Melas 14; s/d €55/75; 🖵) It's not especially exciting, but the Grillo is the most central hotel in town. The rooms are compact and squeeze in every mod con (including MTV on the telly); you pay an extra €10 for more space and a balcony. The restaurant is convenient if it's raining, but otherwise eat elsewhere.

Agriturismo Testone (☎ /fax 0784 23 05 39; Via Giuseppe Verdi; d incl breakfast €75, d half board €110; P) It might be inconveniently located about 20km from Nuoro, but this lovely old stone farmhouse has a simply gorgeous setting, completely isolated in a forest of cork trees. As is to be expected, the food is exceptional, and you dine in a characterful hall at long refectory tables.

Casa Solotti (☎ 0784 3 39 54; www.casasolotti.it; s/d €29/50) This charming house is set in a rambling garden on Monte Ortobene surrounded by woods and walking trails. The accommodation is suitably relaxed, and the place has a friendly family atmosphere and pets. Three of the five rooms have balconies with views, and you can use the kitchen. Call ahead to arrange a free pickup from town.

Hotel Sandalia (☎ /fax 0784 3 83 53; Via Einaudi 12/14; s/d €55/75; P 🖵) Right on the edge of town near the exit for the SS131dcn, this is only an option for motorists who don't want to get caught up in town. There are plenty of comfortable rooms with parquet floors, TV and en-suite bathroom.

EATING
Restaurants

Il Rifugio (☎ 0784 23 23 55; Via Antonio Mereu 28-36; set lunch €16, meals €25-30; ☽ Thu-Tue) Grab a table in front of the entertaining *pizzaioli* (pizza maker) if you can – this place is a favourite with locals. We recommend the pizzas, or try an inventive pasta dish such as *culurgiones, basilica e mandorlé* (culurgiones with fresh basil and pine nuts). Simple, elegant dinner tables and chairs, and old photos of Nuoro on the wall lend the place a welcome warmth.

Su Nugoresu (0784 25 80 17; Piazza San Giovanni 7; meals €20-30; ☽ Mon-Sat) This upmarket trattoria with outdoor seating is on the attractive Piazza San Giovanni. The clientele is young and modish, and the surroundings are subtly rustic. Pizzas come hot out of the oven, while other more refined dishes (including some very nice fish) are served with a flourish.

Ciusa (☎ 0784 25 70 52; Viale Francesco Ciusa 53; pizza €8, meals €24; ☽ Wed-Mon) Punters are drawn to Ciusa for its excellent pizzas, tempting pasta dishes, such as *maccarones de busa al ragù* (macaroni in a duck sauce), and lusciously rich risotto with melted cheese and wine.

Su Redentore (☎ 0784 3 15 38; meals €25-30; ☽ Tue-Sun) This cheerful and popular eatery is at the top of Monte Ortobene. It has a varied menu of seafood and more traditional local dishes, which are the better option.

Ristorante Tascusì (☎ 0784 3 72 87; Via Aspromonte 11; meals €25; ☽ Sun-Mon) In the heart of the old town, Tascusì offers a limited but reliable range of pastas and mains, including the region's famous roast pork.

Another longtime favourite, **Il Portico** (☎ 0784 25 50 62; Via Monsignor Bua 13; meals €30-35; ☽ Mon-Sat) was closed for renovations at the time of writing but it's worth checking out as well.

Self-catering

If you want to make your own meals, pick up fresh produce at the *mercato* on Piazza Goffredo Mameli and other goods at the **UPIM** (Viale del Lavoro) supermarket, near the train station.

DRINKING

Nuoro loves its café culture, and the cafés that line Corso Garibaldi are full nearly the whole day through.

Bar Majore (Corso Garibaldi 71) This is Nuoro's oldest café, and it's much loved by the locals. The interior is richly decorated with fancy gilded stucco, old fittings and an extraordinary frescoed ceiling.

Bar Nuovo (Piazza Mazzini) Strategically placed between two converging streets, Bar Nuovo makes optimum use of the position with a good people-watching terrace outside. It's as good for the morning paper as it is for an evening's beer.

Pit Stop (☎ 0784 25 70 30; Via Brofferio 19; meals & pizza €10; ☽ Mon-Sat) With its racing-car theme and cheap-as-chips fixed-price menus, this place is very popular with students and teenagers. You can eat here, too, but the main diversion is a drink in the square until around midnight.

SHOPPING

Galleria Il Portico (☎ 0784 3 05 11; Piazza del Popolo 3; ☽ 10am-1pm & 5-8pm Mon-Sat) This good art gallery exhibits a wide range of work by notable contemporary artists such as Antonio Corriga and Vittorio Calvi. Oils and watercolours predominate, and prices range from a few hundred euros to several thousand.

Premiata Pasticceria Il Golosastro (☎ 0784 3 79 55; Corso Garibaldi 173-5; ☽ 7.30am-3pm & 4-8pm Mon-Sat) A traditional pastry shop, Il Golosastro serves pastries so fine that they look as though they've been made out of lace.

GETTING THERE & AWAY
Bus

ARST (Azienda Regionale Sarda Trasporti; ☎ 0784 29 50 30) buses run from a station on Viale Sardegna all over the province and beyond. Runs to the coast are frequent, with up to seven daily trips to places like Dorgali (€2.68, 45 minutes), Orosei (€2.32, one hour), Cala Liberotto (€2.89, one hour 10 minutes), La Caletta (€4.91, one hour), Posada (€4.91, one hour 20 minutes) and San Teodoro (€6.30, one hour 50 minutes). The south coast is less well served, with only two or three daily runs to places such as Baunei (€4.91, two hours), Santa Maria Navarrese (€5.37, two hours 25 minutes) and Tortolì (€5.84, two hours 40 minutes). You can pick up buses for Olbia at Dorgali (see p217).

Deplano (☎ 0784 29 50 38) runs up to five daily buses to Olbia's airport (1¾ hours) from the Viale Sardegna bus station in

Nuoro via Budoni and San Teodoro. A few daily buses also run to Alghero and Fertilia airport (2½ hours).

Local operator PANI, which previously serviced Sassari and Cagliari, suspended all services in December 2005 due to government cost cutting. At the time of going to press, the best way to connect to these two towns was to take the train to Macomer (see p129) and make the relevant connections there.

To get into town from the bus station catch bus 8 from Viale Sardegna to the local bus terminus on Piazza Vittorio Emanuele.

Car & Motorcycle

The SS131dcn cross-country, dual-carriage highway between Olbia and Abbasanta (where it runs into the north–south SS131 Carlo Felice highway) skirts Nuoro to the north. Otherwise, the SS129 is the quickest road east to Orosei and Dorgali. Several roads head south for Oliena, Orgosolo and Mamoiada.

Train

The train station is west of the town centre on the corner of Via La Marmora and Via G Ciusa Romagna. FdS trains run from Nuoro to the interchange station of Macomer (€2.63, 1¼ hours), where mainline Trenitalia trains make it possible to link up with other destinations such as Cagliari (€10.80, 3½ hours).

GETTING AROUND

Local buses (€0.80 for 90 minutes) can be useful for the train station (2, 3 and 4), the ARST bus station (8) and heading up to Monte Ortobene (€1, also 8).

You can call for a taxi (☎ 0784 3 14 11) or try to grab one along Via La Marmora.

AROUND NUORO

FONTE SACRA SU TEMPIESU

Much ignored by visitors, owing to the lack of publicity and transport, this **well temple** (☎ 0784 27 67 16; adult/child €2/1; ☺ 9am-6pm), named after a farmer from Tempio who came across it in 1953, is set in dramatic hill country looking east to Monte Albo.

The temple displays a strange keyhole-shaped entrance with stairs leading down

to the well bottom, and it's oriented in such a way that on the day of the summer solstice sunlight shines directly down the well shaft. Water brims to the top of the stairs and trickles down a runnel to another small well, part of the original, more primitive temple that was built around 1600 BC. The newer temple, dating to about 1000 BC, is a (partially restored) masterpiece. Above the well and stairs rises an A-frame structure of carefully carved interlocking stones of basalt and trachyte (sealed watertight with lead). The stone was transported from as far away as Dorgali. No other such structure has been found in Sardinia, and this one, whose excavation began in 1981, was for centuries hidden by a landslide that had buried it back in the Iron Age.

Getting here is a problem if you don't have your own transport. Head for **Orune**, 18km northeast of Nuoro (turn off the SS131dcn highway at the Ponte Marreri exit for the 11km climb to the town). From Orune it is a 7km drive southeast down a narrow country route (signposted). Buses run only as far as Orune. From the ticket office you walk 800m downhill to the temple. You may be accompanied by a guide (in Italian).

SUPRAMONTE

Southeast of Nuoro rises the great limestone massif of the Supramonte, its sheer walls like an iron curtain just beyond Oliena. Despite its intimidating aspect, it's not that high – its peak, Monte Corrasi, only reaches 1463m – but it is impressively wild, the bare limestone plateau pitted with ravines and ragged defiles.

As much of the walking is over limestone there are often few discernible tracks to follow, and in spring and autumn you should check the weather conditions. Unless you are fully confident in your skills, engage a local guide at one of the cooperatives in Oliena or Dorgali.

OLIENA
pop 7590

From Nuoro you can see the fetching little town of Oliena across a deep valley to the south, especially when it's lit up like a Christmas tree at night. Behind it rises the magnificent spectacle of Monte Corrasi. The Jesuits who set up shop here in the 17th century helped to promote the local silk industry and taught the local farmers a thing or two about agriculture. Now Oliena is famous for both its beautiful silk embroidery – much on show during the peacock-coloured Easter parades – and its blood-red wine, Nepente di Oliena.

Orientation & Information

Follow the road up past the petrol station to the central Piazza Santa Maria, where buses stop and the town's 13th-century church of the same name is located.

On the square you will find **Servizi Turistici Corrasi** (☎ 0784 28 71 44; www.corrasi.com; Piazza Santa Maria 30), which has information on the town and mountains. It organises treks to Tiscali, the Gola Su Gorruppu and elsewhere.

Another source of information on Oliena is the private **Tourpass** (☎ 0784 28 60 78; Corso Deledda 32; ☺ 9am-1pm & 4-7pm) office, located just up from the main square on Corso Deledda.

Activities

There is not a great deal to do in Oliena unless you're lucky enough to be here during the Easter festivities, when the town bursts into life. If you plan ahead, however, you may be able to catch some of the cultural events held in September and October. They're part of the Barbagia-wide initiative **Autunno in Barbagia** (Autumn in Barbagia). See the boxed text, p208.

Oliena is also an excellent trekking base. Just 4km south of town in the woods of Maccione you'll find the track up to the highest peaks of the Supramonte. It's a hair-raising trail of vertigo-defying switchbacks called the **Scala 'e Pradu** (Steps of the Plateau) that culminates at the summit of **Punta sos Nidos** (Nests' Peak). The views are awesome! To reach the trail, head for the trekking centre **Cooperativa Enis** (www.coopenis .it), which can also arrange guided treks and 4WD excursions; see Hotel Monte Maccione, below.

Sleeping & Eating

Hotel Cikappa (☎ /fax 0784 28 87 33; Corso Martin Luther King; s/d €38/50; ✕) This cheerful hikers' hotel has tidy, functional rooms. Go for one in the front with a balcony, as the view overlooks the town and its mountain backdrop. There's a scruffy local bar downstairs, and a surprisingly good restaurant where dishes change according to what's in season.

Hotel Monte Maccione (☎ 0784 28 83 63; www .coopenis.it; s/d/tr €43.50/74/105, half board per person €60; P) Run by the Cooperativa Enis, this place is buried deep in the woods of Monte Maccione (700m), 4km south of Oliena and a good way uphill (21 hairpins, to be exact). The rustic rooms have leafy views, and the reasonably priced restaurant (€25 to €30) is packed with families at weekends.

Ristorante Masiloghi (☎ 0784 28 56 96; Via Galiani 68; meals €20-25) This is a good little spot at the eastern exit of town with tables out on the veranda. It specialises in lamb and young wild boar. You could also try the special gourmet menu (€38).

Getting There & Away

ARST runs frequent buses to Nuoro (€1.50, 20 minutes, up to 12 Monday to Saturday, six Sunday). They depart from the petrol station just below the central piazza.

AUTHOR'S CHOICE

Hotel Su Gologone (Map p206; ☎ 0784 28 75 12; www.sugologone.it; Località Su Gologone; s low/high season €105/180 d €160/230, half board per person €105-135; ☺ Mar-Sep & mid-Dec–mid-Jan; P ✕ ☻) Seven kilometres east of Oliena, perched on the edge of the Valle di Lanaittu, is one of the most gorgeous hotel-restaurant complexes on the island. Cobbled paths lead to a series of ivy-covered buildings whose small cottage-style rooms are decorated with the finest local handicrafts – embroidered pillows, heavy woven coverlets and antique headboards. Hidden in the grounds you'll find the pool on its own panoramic terrace, and there's a library, a huge wine cellar and an excellent shop. Massages? No problem. Excursions? Certainly. And there's also one of the best restaurants on the island. Even if you can't stay here you should definitely dine here (€40 to €50) and sample the succulent spin-roast *porceddu*, served on traditional cork plates.

DETOUR: SA SEDDA 'E SOS CARROS & TISCALI

Between Oliena and Dorgali lies the wide, green Valle di Lanaittu. It's a beautiful, unspoilt spot for trekking with dozens of prehistoric sites to explore, the two most interesting being the village of Sa Sedda 'e Sos Carros and the extraordinary site of Tiscali. A useful trekking map covering the area is the Balzano Edizioni *Barbagia* map (1:50,000).

The start of the walk is near the Hotel Su Gologone, signposted about 7km east of Oliena just off the Oliena–Dorgali road. Pass the hotel entrance and shortly afterwards turn right as signposted for the Valle di Lanaittu. The road climbs before rounding a rocky shoulder to reveal the valley crowned by imposing limestone peaks. Descend towards the Sa Oche River, and when the road splits in two keep to the left until you reach another fork.

Turn right here and you'll find the **Grotta Sa Oche** (Cave of the Voice), which is named after the water that gurgles in its secret underground caverns. You'll also find the Rifugio Lanaittu here (closed). Three hundred metres north of the *rifugio* is the five-hectare site of **Sa Sedda 'e Sos Carros** (Map p206; admission €5; ⊙ 9.30am-6.30pm). It's still being excavated, but you can ask the shepherd custodian to let you wander around the remains of some 150 *nuraghe* (stone tower) huts. The most interesting ruin, however, is the circular **Temple of the Sacred Well**, surrounded by stone spouts that would have fed spring water into a huge central basin, no doubt for some profound ancient ritual.

To continue to Tiscali you'll need a stout pair of boots and a bottle of water. Return to the fork and instead of turning right, turn left (southwest) up a steep dirt track. After about 20 minutes of hard climbing you'll come to a boulder with a painted arrow and a marker for Tiscali. Here you leave the dirt road and climb uphill to the left (east) into the forest, climbing the very steep slope until you come to the base of a rock face. To your left (north) is an impressive split in the mountain, which you climb into. After another short climb you'll come out of the fissure onto a wide ledge. The end of the ledge is high on the western edge of the enormous *dolina* (sinkhole) where you'll find the village of **Tiscali** (admission €5; ⊙ 8am-sunset), although you're unable to see the village at this point. To enter the *dolina* you need to go round to the east – head north and to the right – where you'll find a passage down through the rocks. It's an eerie sight, jumbled ruins huddled in the twilight of the mountain. The inhabitants of Sa Sedda 'e Sos Carros used it as a hiding place, and its inaccessibility ensured that the Sards were able to hold out here until well into the 2nd century BC. Nowhere on the island does the sense of a beleaguered indigenous people seem so overwhelmingly poignant.

You can arrange guided trips to Tiscali with trekking guides in Oliena and Dorgali. It usually costs between €30 and €45 for a group of four to six people. With a professional guide you can extend the trek through the valley to the Gola Su Gorruppu (see p217). This longer walk and others are described in detail in Lonely Planet's *Walking in Italy*.

ORGOSOLO
pop 4490

Orgosolo is to Sardinia what the Mafia town of Montelepre is to Sicily – between 1901 and 1950 the town was averaging a murder every two months. You'll find a graphic description of the village in Deledda's novel *Doves and Hawks,* in which she describes an effort in the early 1900s to defuse the enmities that saw the virtual extermination of the village's two most powerful families. In the postwar years sheep rustling gave way to more lucrative kidnapping, led by the village's most infamous son, Graziano Mesina, otherwise known as the Scarlet Rose. He spent much of the 1960s earning himself a Robin Hood reputation by stealing from the rich and giving to the poor. Although captured in 1968 and imprisoned on the mainland, he had to be flown back in 1992 to help negotiate the release of eight-year-old Saudi Farouk Kassam, who had been abducted from the Costa Smeralda and was being held on Monte Albo, near Siniscola.

Nowadays, Orgosolo's past is more colourful than its present, and it shows a rather battered and bruised appearance to the visitor. Still, the place has atmosphere, not least because of the murals that adorn the whole town. These political commentaries, on topics both domestic and international, make for a fascinating walking tour.

Sights & Activities

The majority of Orgosolo's **murals** line Corso Repubblica, so park at the entrance to the town and go for a wander. The murals were initiated by Professor Francesco del Casino as a school project to celebrate the 30th anniversary of the Resistance and Liberation.

There are now over 150 murals in the town, many of them executed by Casino himself, who was assisted by generations of Orgosolo students. Other notable artists include Pasquale Buesca and Vincenzo Floris. The styles vary wildly according to artist: some are naturalistic, others are like cartoons, and some, such as those on the Fotostudio Kikinu, are wonderfully reminiscent of Picasso. Like satirical caricatures, they depict all the big political events of the 20th century and vividly document the painful clash of traditional values with modern life and all its ills. Italy's own political failings are writ large, including the trial of Emilio Lussu (see p28), the shocking corruption of the Cassa del Mezzogiorno, and Prime Minister Giulio Andreotti's trial, where speech bubbles mock his court refrain of 'I don't remember'. WWII, the creation of the atomic bomb, the miner's strikes of the Iglesiente, the evils of capitalism, women's liberation – you can find it all here. Even more interesting are the murals depicting recent events. On the corner of the *corso* and Via Monni you'll find portrayals of the destruction of the two World Trade Center towers (dated 28 September 2001) and the fall of Baghdad (dated 17 April 2003). Further along there's an incredibly moving series of three images – made to look like photographic stills – depicting the murder of 12-year-old Palestinian Mohammed el Dura as he hid behind his father during a Gaza shoot-out that was televised around the world on 30 September 2000.

As you wander along you'll pass the **Cortile del Formaggio** (Corso Reppublica 214; ☉ 10am-1pm & 3-8pm Mon-Fri), a tiny courtyard house where you can buy locally made cheeses.

Five kilometres to the south of the town, the SP48 local road heads up to the Montes heights. Another 13km south is the **Funtana Bona** (Map p206), the spring at the source of the Cedrino river. On the way you pass through the tall oaks of the **Foresta de Montes** (Map p206).

Festivals

You should consider visiting Orgosolo during the **Festa dell'Assunta** (Feast of the Assumption) on 15 August, when folk from all around the Barbagia converge on the town for one of the region's most colourful processions.

Sleeping & Eating

Should you want or need to stay the night, you have two options.

Petit Hotel (☎ /fax 0784 40 20 09; Via Mannu; s/d €30/40; ☉ May-Oct) To find this place just follow the signs through the centre of town and turn right at Bar Candela. The rooms are clean but basic with balconies and flower-filled window boxes. It's a friendly, family-run place that's extra welcoming if you speak some Italian.

Hotel Sa 'e Jana (☎ /fax 0784 40 24 37; Via E Lussu; s/d €40/55) This place is slightly better than the Petit, but it's awkwardly located in a dead-end (and one might also be tempted to say deadbeat) lane at the western end of town.

Ristorante La Terrazza (Via Giovanni XXIII; snacks €2.50, pasta €4-7) The sunny 1st-floor terrace here is a popular place for a beer and a sandwich.

Getting There & Away

Regular buses make the run to/from Nuoro (€1.45, 35 minutes, eight Monday to Saturday, four Sunday).

LE BARBAGIE

The tough, uncompromising territory of Le Barbagie (a plural collective noun indicating the several distinct areas that make up the region) is at the geographical heart of Sardinia. This is perhaps fitting, since many would argue that it is the most truly Sardinian part of the island. Dialects of the Sardinian tongue are widely spoken in its villages, and people still cling to many local traditions, from Sardinian wrestling and ancient Carnevale rites to traditional costumes. It's still fairly common to see older women getting about in the vestments of another era.

At the region's heart are the bald, windswept heights of the Gennargentu massif, the highest points on the island. This also

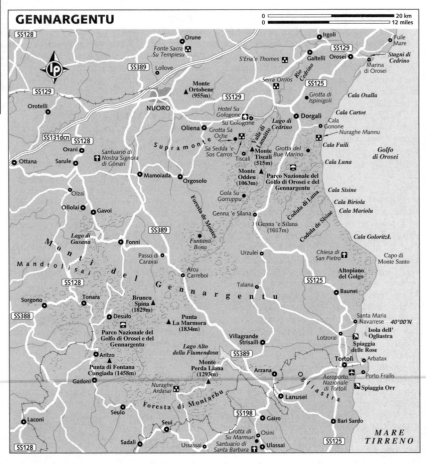

GENNARGENTU

0 — 20 km
0 — 12 miles

represents the centre of the **Parco Nazionale del Golfo di Orosei e del Gennargentu**, Sardinia's only national park, which takes in the Supramonte (p202) plateau and the Golfo di Orosei (p215).

Orientation & Information

Dozens of distinct village communities dot the Barbagia region, which is divided into districts that surround the peaks of the Gennargentu. To the north is Barbagia Ollolai, to the west Mandrolisai, and southwest and south are the Barbagia di Belvi and the Barbagia di Seulo, respectively.

Many villages are without a tourist office. The best sources of information are the tourist offices in Nuoro, Oliena and Dorgali. The most detailed trekking map of the region is Balzano Edizioni's *Barbagia* map (1:50,000), which can be found in the bookshops of Dorgali and Cala Gonone. It costs €6.20.

Getting There & Away

ARST (☎ 0784 29 50 30 in Nuoro) runs limited services between these mountain villages, usually only one or two per day and generally in the morning only. The most frequent services run to the larger towns of Mamoiada (€1.19, 20 minutes, 12 Monday to Saturday, five Sunday), Fonni (€2.01 to €3.15, 40 minutes to one hour depending on the route, seven Monday to Saturday, four Sunday), Gavoi (€2.58, 55 minutes, seven Monday to Saturday, four Sunday), Desulo (€3.72, one hour 20 minutes, one daily) and Aritzo (€4.44, two hours, two Monday to Saturday, one Sunday).

It's slow going around all the mountain roads, and it's certainly worth considering hiring a car if you want to tour the area with any freedom.

BARBAGIA OLLOLAI
Mamoiada
pop 2600

Just 14km south of Nuoro, this undistinguished town is the scene of a remarkable winter celebration for the **Festa di Sant'Antonio** on 17 January. According to myth, Sant'Antonio stole fire from hell to give to man, and the festival involves a huge bonfire and some serious drinking.

Much more bizarre, however, is Mamoiada's **Carnevale** (the week preceding Ash Wednesday), when up to 200 men don shaggy brown sheepskins and primitive wooden masks to parade the streets as *mamuthones*. Weighed down by up to 30kg of *campanacci* (cowbells), they make a frightening spectacle. Anthropologists believe that the *mamuthones* embodied all untold horrors that primitive humans feared, and the ritual is an attempt to exorcise nature's demons before the new spring. The *mamuthones* are paraded on a long leash held by the *Issokadores*, dressed in the guise of outmoded gendarmes, whose job it is to drive them out of town. The *Issokadores* also get an outing at the Festa di Sant'Antonio.

If you can't be here for Carnevale, you can get an idea of what it's all about at the **Museo delle Maschere** (☎ 0784 56 90 18; www .museodellemaschere.it; Piazza Europa 15; adult/child €4/2.60; 9am-1pm & 3-7pm Tue-Sun). The exhibit includes a multimedia presentation (in Italian) and garbed mannequins wearing their famous shaggy sheepskins.

The wooden masks worn by the *mamuthones* have become fairly uniform over the years, as only a few artisans make them. A couple of shops around the village sell them – don't expect to pay less than €100 for a good one.

For a bite to eat, try **La Campagnola** (Corso Vittorio Emanuele 59; meals €20; Tue-Sun). It does pizzas and a limited range of pasta and main courses.

Orani & Ottana

The main reason for visiting Orani is the **Museo Nivola** (☎ 0784 73 00 63; Via Gonare 2; adult/child €1.60/0.80; 9am-1pm & 4-9pm Jun-Sep, to 8pm Oct-May), just inside the southern entrance to the town. It celebrates the work of Costantino Nivola, the son of a local stonemason, who fled Fascist persecution in 1938 and spent most of his life working in America. He pioneered the technique of sandcasting, and most of his work is sculpted in marble, travertine and even cement, with some small *bronzetti*-style sculptures. The museum also houses sketches and models, and there's a good bookshop with lots of Nivola literature.

Five kilometres south of Orani, the town of Sarule doesn't warrant a stop but a narrow side road east leads to the 17th-century **Santuario di Nostra Signora di Gonare** (Map p206), a grey buttressed church and sanctuary atop a lone conical hill (1093m).

The road west of Sarule leads to lacklustre Ottana, said to be the dead centre of Sardinia. The place comes to life in February for **Carnevale**. As in Mamoiada, men dressed in the bizarre costumes of *boes* (men masked as cattle) and *merdules* (masked men symbolising our prehistoric ancestors) parade on Shrove Tuesday.

Gavoi
pop 2940

The pretty lakeside setting of Gavoi has made it the location of choice for the **Festival Letterario della Sardegna** (www.isoladellestorie.it, in Italian), aimed at celebrating the literature of Barbagia. It takes place in June or early July, and the village spends most of the year preparing for the throngs of authors and would-be writers who descend for the three-day event, which includes readings, workshops and interviews.

At other times of the year **Lago di Gusana** is popular for fishing, and the village boasts a modest late-Gothic church, the **Chiesa di San Gavino**, which has a red trachyte façade.

The comfortable, modern **Hotel Taloro** (☎ 0784 5 30 33; fax 0784 5 35 90; www.hoteltaloro.it; s/d €40/68, half board per person €55; P) has fine views of the lake.

When hunger strikes, head for **Ristorante Sante Rughe** (☎ 0784 5 37 74; Via Carlo Felice 2; meals €25-30; Mon-Sat), a charming place with bare stone walls close to the San Gavino church. In spring order the speciality *erbuzzu* soup, a heart-warming combination of bacon, sausage, cheese and beans flavoured with wild herbs.

Fonni & Desulo

At 1000m Fonni is the highest town in Sardinia and is a sizable rural community. It's also a popular base for hikers, who come to explore Sardinia's highest peaks – the Bruncu Spina (1829m) and the Punta La Marmora (1834m).

At the highest point of the village, just off Piazza Europa, is the imposing 17th-century **Basilica della Madonna dei Martiri**, surrounded by *cumbessias* (pilgrims' huts). It is one of the richest and most important baroque buildings in Sardinia, lavishly decorated with 1700 frescoes. Inside the church, on the right, a shrine contains a revered image of the Madonna that's said to be made from the crushed bones of martyrs. It's the focus of the town's two main feast days, the **Festa della Madonna dei Martiri** on the Monday after the first Sunday in June and the **Festa di San Giovanni** on 24 June.

Outside the church a couple of trees have been curiously transformed by sculptors into religious scenes, notably one showing Christ and the two thieves crucified.

Twenty-seven kilometres south of Fonni is Desulo, a long string of a town that was once three separate villages. There's nothing much to see there, but like Fonni it provides a good base for hikers, given its proximity to the peaks of the Gennargentu.

BRUNCU SPINA & PUNTA LA MARMORA

It's relatively easy to reach the island's two highest peaks from either Fonni or Desulo. You'll find the turn-off for the Bruncu Spina trailhead 5km along the Fonni–Desulo road. From here a 10km road winds through treeless territory to the base of Sardinia's one ski lift (non-operational at the time of research). One kilometre before the lift you'll see a steep dirt trail to the right, from where a 3km track leads right to the summit (1829m). From here you have broad, sweeping views across the island in all directions. For a view from 5m higher you need to march about 1½ hours south to Punta La Marmora (1834m). Although it looks easy enough from Bruncu Spina, you need a good walking map or a guide not to get into difficulty.

SLEEPING & EATING

There are two hotels in Fonni, the more cosy being the **Ristorante Albergo Il Cinghialetto** (☎ 0784 5 76 60; Via Grazia Deledda 115; s/d €35/70, half board per person €70; 🍴). It's primarily a very good restaurant, although it now has seven newly renovated rooms.

In Desulo there are a couple of hotels, but these are usually only open in summer. Try **Gennargentu** (☎ /fax 0784 61 92 70; Via Kennedy; s/d €35/50; ⏰ May-Oct), on the left as you enter the village from the north, or **Hotel Lamarmora** (☎ 0784 61 94 11; fax 0784 61 91 26; Via Lamarmora; s/d €40/65; ⏰ Dec-Mar & Jun-Sep), at the northern end of town by the hairpin bend that leads to Fonni.

BARBAGIA DI BELVI
Aritzo
pop 1435

Since the 19th century Aritzo has been the most popular mountain resort in Sardinia. The cool climate and alpine character (its elevation is 796m) recommended it to the Piedmontese nobility, who came here to hunt boar and mouflon in its forests.

Aritzo's little show of prosperity was due largely to its cleverly managed 'snow' industry. Snow farmers, known as *niargios*, collected the white stuff from **Punta di Funtana Cungiada** (1458m). It was then stored in ice houses in straw-lined wooden chests before being carted off to the high tables of Cagliari to be turned into lemon sorbet for noble lords and ladies.

You can see some of the chests in the **Museo Etnografico** (☎ 0784 62 96 21; admission €1.60; ⏰ 10.30am-1pm & 4.30-7pm Tue-Sun), down a side street just after the IP petrol station. The museum also has a motley collection of farm implements and household objects.

The same ticket gets you into **Sa Bovida Prigione Spagnola**, the 16th-century Spanish-era prison just off the main drag on the narrow Via Scale Carceri.

A few metres south, the originally Gothic (few traces remain) **Chiesa di San Michele Arcangelo** contains an 18th-century *Pietà* and a 17th-century portrait of *San Cristoforo*, in the second and last chapels, respectively, on the right-hand side. Across the road from the church is a viewpoint from where you can see the oddly box-shaped **Monte Texile**.

If you have a good map there are plenty of hiking trips around Aritzo that you can make unaccompanied. Alternatively, you can visit the snow mines and Monte Texile with **Centro Servizi Turistici** (☎ 0784 62 94 42; Via Monti 2). Costs vary between €22 and €45.

Aritzo also holds two good foodie festivals. In mid-August at the **Festa de San Carapigna** you can try Aritzo's ancient recipe of famous lemon sorbet. On the last Sunday of October the town fills up with people in search of chestnuts at the **Sagra delle Castagne**. Great piles of chestnuts are roasted in the streets and given away.

The town's hotels, each with its own restaurant, are clustered towards the southern exit. The chaotic **Hotel Castello** (☎ 0784 62 92 66; Corso Umberto; s/d €30/44), right at a bend in the road, is the cheapest place to stay. It's a grey hotel with awful interior décor – stuffed animals and sporting trophies – and mediocre cooking. But it's cosy and functional, and many rooms have rather nice views. **Hotel La Capannina** (☎ /fax 0784 62 91 21; Via A Maxia; s/d €46/58) is a slightly nicer option.

SARCIDANO

Southwest of Aritzo the mountains flatten out to the broad, bare Sarcidano plain, littered with *nuraghi* and other mysterious prehistoric sites.

Laconi
pop 2250

With its mountain air and bosky setting, Laconi is the largest community in the area. It's also one of the more attractive mountain towns, with a nice central piazza fronted by a neoclassical Municipio (Town Hall).

Behind the Municipio, down some stairs to the left, is the strange **Museo delle Statue Menhir** (☎ 0782 86 62 16; Via Amsicora; adult/child €3.50/2; ⏰ 9.30am-1pm & 4-7.30pm Apr-Sep, 9am-1pm & 4-6pm Oct-Mar, closed 1st Mon of month), exhibiting just some of the island's multitude of menhirs. The prehistoric anthropomorphic shapes are concentrated in this area and neighbouring La Marmilla (see, p112), and the museum presents a good selection of them over seven rooms. In the backlit gloom they appear even more mysterious, the shadows emphasising the faded sculptural relief that suggests whether they are 'male' or 'female'. Barrila I has particularly well defined detail. The

---

DETOUR: FORESTA DI MONTARBU & LAGO ALTO DELLA FLUMENDOSA

The road southeast from Aritzo winds pleasantly along through **Seulo** and **Seui**, the latter of which has a few traditional houses with wrought-iron balconies. Proceed another 9km towards Ussassai before taking a detour north. If you don't have the time for trekking, this drive takes you nicely off the beaten track.

Nine kilometres north of the turn-off you'll see Sardinia's largest *nuraghe*, the **Nuraghe Ardasai** (Map p206), on your left. Built on a rocky outcrop dominating the deep Flumendosa River valley to the north, it's worth a stop for the views. Six kilometres further is a turn-off for the dense **Foresta di Montarbu** (Map p206), towered over by the mountain of the same name (1304m). A few kilometres further is a turn-off that leads you to the more impressive **Monte Perda Liana** (Map p206), at 1293m. You are in deeply wooded country here, full of pines and firs.

If you continue you'll reach the southern bank of the **Lago Alto della Flumendosa** (Map p206), which the main road skirts eastward for about 10km before crossing over the scenic *trenino verde* train line a couple of times and reaching the main Nuoro–Lanusei road.

display is accompanied by well-presented explanations (in Italian). If you find this interesting you may want to detour to Pranu Mutteddu (right) further south, where you can see them *in situ*.

From the Municipio, cross the road and head down Via Sant'Ignazio to the **Casa Natale di Sant'Ignazio** (admission free), a simple two-roomed house where the town's St Ignatius is said to have been born (he died in 1781).

Once in Via Sant'Ignazio again, continue past the saint's house and take the first left. This brings you to the **Parco Laconi**, a rare retreat full of dense woods, exotic trees (such as an impressive cedar of Lebanon), springs, lakes, grottoes and the remains of the **Castello Aymerich**. Originally built in 1051, its most interesting elements are the Moorish-style windows in the now roofless upstairs hall. From here you have wonderful views across the park and the greenery surrounding Laconi.

Accommodation can be found at the new **Albergo Ristorante Sardegna** (☎ 0782 86 90 33; www .albergosardegna.it; s/d €32/60), where you can also enjoy a hearty plate of home-cooked pasta.

One bus connects Laconi with Isili, Aritzo, Barumini and other surrounding towns. The FdS *trenino verde* calls in here on its way north from Mandas. The station is about 1km west of the town centre.

Santuario Santa Vittoria

If you're at all interested in the island's ancient origins, the **Santuario Santa Vittoria** (adult/child €4/2; ☼ 9am-7pm) warrants some effort. It lies about 18km south of Laconi. On the way you can also visit the **Nuraghe Isparas** (admission free; ☼ 9am-1pm & 2-5pm), which sports the highest interior *tholos* (cone) of any *nuraghe* in Sardinia.

To reach the sanctuary, continue through Isili towards Serri for 8km and then follow signs 6km to the west.

Archaeologists first got to work on Santa Vittoria in 1907, and restoration work was carried out in the 1960s. Still, only four of about 22 hectares have been fully uncovered. The site is seen as a central point of worship in all Sardinia.

What you see today is divided roughly into three zones. The central area, the **Recinto delle Riunioni** (Meeting Area), is a unique enclave thought to have been the seat of civil power. A grand oval space is

ringed by a wall within which are towers and various rooms.

Beyond it is the religious area, which includes a **Tempietto a Pozzo** (Well Temple), a second temple, a structure thought to have been the **Capanna del Sacerdote** (Priest's Hut), defensive trenches, and a much later addition, the **Chiesa di Santa Vittoria**, a little country church after which the whole site is now named. Separated from both areas is the **Casa del Capo** (Chief's House), so-called perhaps because it is the most intact habitation, with walls still up to 3m high. Finally, a separate area, made up of several circular dwellings, is thought to have been the main residential quarter.

Nuraghe Arrubiu

Rising out of the Sarcidano plain, 5km south of Orroli, is the **Nuraghe Arrubiu** (adult/child €4/2, night guided visits €6; ☼ 9.30am-1pm & 3-8.30pm Apr-Oct, 9.30am-5pm Nov-Mar), which takes its Sardinian name (meaning red) from the curious colour lent it by the trachyte stone. It is an impressive structure. The central tower, about 16m high, is thought to have reached 30m. It is surrounded by the five-tower defensive perimeter and, beyond, the remains of an outer wall and nearby settlement. The artefacts found on the site indicate that the Romans made good use of it.

Pranu Mutteddu

Fans of all things ancient will be hard pressed to resist pursuing the road south from Nuraghe Arrubiu to reach this menhir-studded necropolis. Follow the road south 11.5km to Escalaplano and from there 8km towards Ballao. Take the first turn west to Goni (you are now just inside Cagliari province), which you hit after 9km. A few kilometres further on and you reach the site, just north of the road.

The site is dominated by a series of *domus de janas* (literally 'fairy houses'; tombs cut into rock) and some 50 menhirs, 20 of them lined up east to west, presumably in symbolic reflection of the sun's trajectory. The scene is reminiscent of similar sites in Corsica and is quite unique in Sardinia.

BARBAGIA DI SEULO

Right on the border of the national park and verging on the province of Ogliastra is the remote Barbagia di Seulo, with its little cluster of villages. You can reach it from Escalaplano.

Alternatively, take the SS198 from Seui or the SS125 direct from Muravera (see p88).

Jerzu & Gairo

The biggest of the region's towns is Jerzu, famous for its many varieties of Cannonau, produced at the **Vitivinicola di Jerzu** (☎ 0782 7 00 28; Via Umberto; ☺ 8.30am-1pm & 3-6pm Mon-Fri). It has a spectacular position, barely balanced on the side of the mountain facing the ruined remains of **Gairo Vecchio**, which slid down the mountain in a mudslide in the 1950s.

Ulassai

pop 1600

Heading north from Jerzu you're in for some scenic treats as the road licks a torturous path around the titanic mountains to Ulassai, dwarfed by the rocky pinnacles of Bruncu Pranedda and Bruncu Matzei. Trekkers and climbers take note: this is a fantastic place to hole up for a couple of days. The canyon that splits the Bruncu Pranedda provides 45 climbing opportunities, with 34 further climbs at the Lecori cliffs. Trekkers can walk the canyon or head 7km southwest to view the dramatic waterfall **Cascata Lequarci** before picnicking in the idyllic environs of the **Santuario di Santa Barbara** (Map p206). The www.ulassai.net site is a useful resource.

High above the village is another fascinating sight, the huge **Grotta di Su Marmuri** (Map p206; ☎ 0782 7 98 05; admission €7; tours ☺ 11am, 3pm, 5pm & 6.30pm Aug, 11am, 2pm, 4pm & 6pm May, Jun & Sep, 11am & 2.30pm Apr & Oct). The one-hour tour takes you on a magical 1km walk through an underground wonderland festooned with stalactites and stalagmites.

The lovely Tonino Lai and his wife run the **Hotel Su Marmuri** (☎ 0782 2 90 03; Corso Vittorio Emanuele 18/20; s/d/tr €25/40/55). It's a gathering place for all the old buffers in town, who come to play cards in their flat caps. The rooms are ever so neat and the views are stupendous. If there are a few of you Tonino is quite happy to act as a guide. You can certainly get all the information you need here.

Osini

Within spitting distance of Ulassai is the tiny village of Osini, another interesting spot for trekkers. Within its environs is the stunning narrow gully of **Scala di San Giorgio**, apparently walked by the bishop in 1117 during his proselytising. Also worth visiting are the extensive ruins of the **Complesso Nuragico di Serbissi**, a complex site with an unusual underground cave used to store foodstuffs.

OGLIASTRA

The southeastern sector of Nuoro province is known as the Ogliastra. From Dorgali the SS125 highway winds south through the mountainous terrain of the eastern end of the Parco Nazionale del Golfo di Orosei e del Gennargentu. The 18km stretch south to the **Genna 'e Silana** pass (1017m) is the most breathtaking. To the west your eyes sweep across a broad valley to a high chain of mountains, including the 1063m **Monte Oddeu** (Map p206) and, behind it, the impressive Supramonte. Various hiking maps of the area exist, but the best are the IGM's 1:25,000 sheets. Unfortunately, these are not easy to come by, but you could try in Dorgali (p216). A useful local website for this area is **Welcome in Ogliastra** (www.turinforma.it).

Ogliastra has its own port, Arbatax. You might consider taking a ferry here from Cagliari and picking up a hire car in Tortolì (Arbatax's parent town) to explore the Gennargentu.

TORTOLÌ & ARBATAX

pop 10,130

Tortolì is a busy little provincial capital with a well-organised tourist infrastructure. Along with its port, Arbatax, Tortolì is usually much maligned, but the truth is it's quite a cheerful place. After the heavy silences of the interior, its bustling, sunny atmosphere is a welcome change.

Ferries from Cagliari arrive at Arbatax port, and you can also arrange boat tours up the coast to the Golfo di Orosei from here. In summer you can catch the *trenino verde* from the station in Arbatax.

Orientation & Information

Tortolì and Arbatax are actually just one town joined by the long Viale Monsignor Virgilio. Roughly 4km separates the Tortolì town centre from the Arbatax port, and regular buses run between the two.

The **main tourist office** (☎ 0782 62 28 24; proloco .tortoli@tiscali.it; Via Mazzini 7; ☺ 9.30am-12.30pm Mon-Sat year-round & 6.30-9.30pm Mon-Sat Jun-Aug) is in the centre of Tortolì. It's full of information about the region and has helpful staff who can also give you details of all the car-hire outlets in town.

In summer another **tourist office** (☎ 0782 62 28 24; Via Lungomare; ☻ 9.30am-12.30pm & 5.30-8.30pm Mon-Sat Jun-Sep) opens at the *trenino verde* station in Arbatax. It sells tickets for the train between 7.30am and 8.30am. The *trenino verde* departs at 8am daily in summer.

You can book boat and plane tickets, and excursions from travel agent **Frailis Viaggi** (☎ 0782 62 00 21; Via Mazzini 3, Tortolì).

Sights & Activities

Tortolì and Arbatax are resort towns and have no real sights in themselves. The main curiosity in Arbatax lies just behind the train station. The **rocce rosse** or 'red rocks' are bizarre weather-beaten formations that have been sculpted by the wind and the sea.

At the port you can arrange **boat excursions** up the coast to the beaches and grottoes of the Golfo di Orosei (€25 to €30; see p215). Here you'll also find the terminus for the FdS **trenino verde**, the summer tourist train to Mandas. The route between Arbatax and Mandas is the most scenic on the island, taking an exhausting five hours to chug along a gravity-defying track amid some splendid mountain scenery. It stops at a multitude of towns in between, making it impossible to do the return journey in one day. Still, if you have some time it's a picturesque trip, and the ride in the steam locomotive is an experience in itself.

Other than that you can head out to the beaches on either side of Arbatax. You'll find the better beaches of **Spiaggia Orrì** (Map p206), **Spiaggia Musculedda** and **Spiaggia Is Scogliu Arrubius** about 4km south of Porto Frailis (the location of a number of hotels). If you're really determined you can continue even further south to the near-pristine beach of **Spiaggia Cala Francese** at the Marina di Gairo.

If you can't get to Jerzu but want to try some of the regional wine, you can taste the ruby-red Cannonau at **L'Enoteca del Cannonau** (☎ 0782 62 60 27; Via Monsignor Virgilio 74), in Tortolì.

Sleeping & Eating

Both Tortolì and Arbatax are well served with hotels. For beachside accommodation you should head for Porto Frailis, but if you're just thinking of overnighting it's more convenient to be based in Tortolì.

Hotel Victoria (☎ 0782 62 34 57; www.hotel-victoria .it; Via Monsignor Virgilio 72; s/d €79/118; P ✷ ▯ ▣) This medium-sized hotel is on Tortolì's main drag. You can't miss its big lemon-yellow façade. It's convenient, comfortable and well priced, and has the bonus of a little square pool and off-street parking.

La Bitta (☎ 0782 66 70 80; www.arbataxhotels .com; Porto Frailis; s/d €99/200; P ✷ ▯ ▣) For a touch of class, consider checking in here. The Bitta is right on the beach and has palatial rooms complete with columns, arches and seamless sea views. Even if you can't stay it's worth considering a meal in the very fine terrace restaurant (meals €30). The portions are simply huge and the views are delightful.

Da Lenin (☎ 0782 62 44 22; Via San Gemiliano 19; meals €30; ☻ Mon-Sat) This restaurant is sign-posted south of the main road connecting Tortolì with Arbatax. It's worth seeking out for the homemade pasta and good seafood. In summer the terrace fills quickly.

Getting There & Away

AIR

The tiny Arbatax-Tortolì **airstrip** (Map p206; ☎ 0782 62 49 00) is about 1.5km south of Tortolì. It's served by domestic airlines such as Meridiana and Air One, which fly in from Verona. No scheduled buses or taxis run here, but most arrivals come on a package with transport arranged.

Travel agent Frailis Viaggi (see left) should be able to advise on schedules and tickets.

BOAT

Tirrenia (☎ 0782 66 70 67; www.tirrenia.it; Via Venezia 10; ☻ 8.30am-1pm & 4-8pm Mon-Fri, 8.30am-1pm Sat) has an office along the *lungomare* in Arbatax. It serves both Genoa (€48, 20 hours, twice weekly) and Civitavecchia (€33, 10½ hours, twice weekly), and also has a ferry to Cagliari (€29.40, 5¼ hours, twice weekly).

For more information on the ferries arriving in Arbatax, see p241.

BUS

ARST (☎ 0782 62 22 14; Piazza Fraulocci) buses connect Tortolì with destinations along the coast, as well as Nuoro (€5.76, 2½ to three hours, four daily), Dorgali (€4.03,

1½ hours, one daily) and even Olbia (one daily via Nuoro). All of them pass through Lanusei.

Frequent local buses make the run to Santa Maria Navarrese (€0.88, 15 minutes, eight daily).

TRAIN
The FdS **trenino verde** (☎ 0782 66 72 85; www .treninoverde.com, in Italian) runs between Arbatax and Mandas (€16.50, 4¾ hours, one daily at 8am) between 19 June and 11 September. Stops include Lanusei, Arzana, Ussassai and Seui.

Getting Around
Local buses 1 and 2 connect Tortolì and Arbatax, and, in the case of the latter service, the beach and hotels at nearby Porto Frailis.

LOTZORAI
pop 2150
A few kilometres further north, Lotzorai is not of enormous interest in itself but it sits behind more glorious pine-backed beaches, such as **Spiaggia delle Rose**. To find it follow the signs to the three camping grounds that are clustered close to one another just behind the beach.

If while passing through here you are struck by hunger pangs, make for **L'Isolotto** (☎ 0782 6 69 43; Via Ariosto 4; meals €40-45; ☼ Tue-Sun), off Via Dante and not far from the centre (signposted). The place looks unprepossessing, but the homemade pasta and seafood mains make this money well spent.

SANTA MARIA NAVARRESE
Located at the southern end of the Golfo di Orosei, this delightful spot is a tempting alternative to Cala Gonone (p217). Shipwrecked Basque sailors built a small church here in 1052, dedicated to Santa Maria di Navarra, on the orders of the Princess of Navarre, who happened to be one of the survivors. The church was built in the shade of a grand olive tree that still thrives today – some say it's nearly 2000 years old.

Information
In the centre of town you'll find the helpful private **Tourpass** (☎ 0782 61 53 30; www.turinforma .it; Piazza Principessa di Navarra 19; ☼ 8.30am-1pm & 5-8pm year-round & 9-11.30pm summer) information office. Staff can advise on trekking and boat excursions.

You can find maps in the local bookshop **Punto E Virgola** (Viale Plammas 26).

Sights & Activities
The pleasant pine-backed beach (with more beaches stretching away further to the south) is lapped by transparent water, and the setting is a gem. Offshore are several islets, including the **Isola dell'Ogliastra**, and the leafy northern end of the beach is topped by a watchtower built to look out for raiding Saracens.

About 500m further north is the small pleasure port, where **Nautica Centro Sub** (☎ 0782 61 55 22; portosantamaria@tiscali.it) organises dives and diving courses, and hires out high-speed *gommoni* (dinghies). They range between €70 and €130 a day, depending on the season, and allow to you inspect some wonderful spots (see the boxed text, p218). Similar excursions to those from Cala Gonone (see p219) to some or all of these beauty spots also depart from here. Inquire at the kiosks in the port or at the Tourpass office in town.

In the last week of August is the **Sagra della Carne di Capra**, a goat roast and eating frenzy for all those who happen to be present at the right time (the meat is usually cooked by about 9pm).

Sleeping & Eating
Hotel Agugliastra (☎ 0782 61 50 05; www.hotel agugliastra.it, in Italian; half board per person low/high season €37/72; ❄) This is the most central hotel in town, convenient for the beach and the port. Right on the main piazza, it has comfortable modern rooms and a popular café.

Around the corner you'll find the rust-red **Hotel Nicoletta** (☎ 0782 61 40 45; www.hotelnicoletta .info; s/d €70/110; ❄). It has a more rustic feel, particularly in the beamed restaurant. The 28 rooms are quite small, but the frilly coverlets give them a homy feel and the French windows make them nice and light.

You'll find several eateries and a handful of bars dotted about within quick strolling distance of the centre. Bar L'Olivastro has tables and chairs set up on shady terraces below the weird and wonderful branches of a huge olive tree at the northern end of the beach.

Getting There & Around

Numerous ARST buses serve the town on the main Tortolì–Dorgali route.

You can hire scooters down at the port for around €35 per day.

BAUNEI & THE ALTOPIANO DEL GOLGO
pop 3830

About 9km north of Santa Maria is the shepherds' town of Baunei, surrounded by airy mountain views, which you can enjoy from Café Belvedere.

There's little to recommend the town itself, but from here you can take a 10km detour up to the mountain plateau known as the **Altopiano del Golgo** (Map p206), signposted from the middle of town. A 2km set of switchbacks on a steep (10-degree) incline gets you up to the plateau and sailing north through a sea of fragrant *macchia* (scrub). After 8km you see a sign to your right to Su Sterru (also known as Il Golgo), a 270m abyss that proves a big hit with cavers who like abseiling. To the untrained eye the overgrown opening may just look like a big, dark hole!

Opposite the turn-off for Su Sterru is a signpost for the **Ristorante Golgo** (☎ 0782 61 06 75; Località Golgo; meals €25; ⏲ Apr-Sep), a quaint stone-built place serving a delicious array of carnivorous treats cooked on a spit in the traditional way.

Another good spot for a hearty lunch – right at the end of the track – is the **Locanda Il Rifugio** (☎ 0782 61 05 99 in Baunei, mobile 368 702 89 80; www.coopgoloritze.com, in Italian; s/d €45/60, d half board €105; ⏲ Apr-Oct), which is run by the Cooperativa Goloritzè. It is a serious trekking base and offers basic rooms in the converted farmstead. You'll want to consider the half-board option given the remote location. Excursions include anything from trekking (€16 to €30) and horse riding (€15 per hour) to 4WD adventures (€25 to €50). Many treks involve a descent from the plateau through dramatic *codula* (canyons), such as the Codula di Luna (Map p206) and the Codula de Sisine (Map p206), to the beautiful beaches of the Golfo di Orosei

---

DEADLY SERIOUS JOCU DE SA MURRA

The scene is tense. Two pairs of men lean in towards one another in deadly earnest competition. Tempers can be short as they each launch hands at one another and scream out numbers in Sardinian in what appears for all the world like an excitable version of the rock, paper or scissors game.

The rules of the game, a pastime with centuries of colourful history in central Sardinia and especially in the Barbagia region of Nuoro, are not that complicated. Two or four men can participate – in the latter case it works a little like a tag-team match. One on each side stretches out a hand and shows some of his fingers. They both scream out numbers in an attempt to guess the total number of fingers shown by both players. The operation is repeated in rapid-fire manner until one side guesses correctly and so wins a point. At each successful guess (where four are playing) the winner of the round then continues with the loser's partner. The side to reach 16 points (sometimes 21) first with a two-point advantage wins. Where both teams are neck and neck at 16 (or 21), they pass to a sudden-death round, in which the first to five points wins.

The game is played with extraordinary passion and speed, and at the increasingly popular organised competitions the passions grow as wine bottles empty. The numbers are cried out amid oaths and taunts. Men with heart conditions are advised not to participate.

Traditionally, the game was an impromptu affair played on street corners or wherever idle men came together. The problem was that no-one liked to lose, and accusations of cheating often flew. Frequently the game ended with knives drawn and used, so much so that for long periods the *murra* was banned. Since the late 1990s championships have been organised, especially in Urzulei and Gavoi, but also on the Montiferru outside Seneghe in Oristano province. The competition takes place in the morning, followed by a long and boozy lunch, and impromptu bouts are held in the afternoon. To the outsider these postprandial bouts can seem more inflamed than the official morning sessions!

If you can't make the 'championships' you can nearly always see the game played at any of the island's big festivals.

(see below). The trek down the Codula di Luna starts from the nearby **Chiesa di San Pietro** (Map p206), a humble 16th-century church with dedicated *cumbessias* (pilgrims' huts).

A huge variety of exciting itineraries, involving overnight camps, are possible with planning. If you're interested in something like this, plan about a month in advance. The *locanda* can also help climbers with information and transfers to Pedra Lungo, the start of the demanding Selvaggio Blu trek. Staff can pick you up in Baunei if you don't have your own transport.

GOLFO DI OROSEI

This spectacular gulf forms the seaward section of the Parco Nazionale del Golfo di Orosei e del Gennargentu. It's Sardinia's most memorable stretch of coastline, although you wouldn't think it, what with all the hype about the Costa Smeralda.

Here the high mountains of the Gennargentu abruptly meet the sea, forming a crescent of dramatic cliffs riven by false inlets and huge sea grottoes, and lapped by crystalline waters. Italian tourists flock to its picturesque beaches in summer, but even if you arrive in August you won't regret having made the effort to see the gulf's mighty cliffs and coves.

OROSEI
pop 6050

At the most northerly point of the gulf you'll find the prosperous town of Orosei. It was once a relatively poor area, frequently flooded by the Rio Cedrino. Damming and tourism have significantly changed its fortunes, and now Orosei sits amidst thriving citrus orchards and olive groves, providing one of the busier tourist centres along the coast.

Follow the Centro signs to wind up in **Piazza del Popolo**, with its pretty tree-lined garden surrounded by churches. You'll find the local **tourist office** (☎ 0784 99 83 67; Piazza del Popolo 13; ☯ 9.30am-noon & 4.30-7pm Mon-Sat, 9am-noon Sun) here.

The piazza is ringed by imposing buildings, not least the **Cattedrale di San Giacomo**. It presents an unusual picture; its blank neoclassical façade flanked by a set of tiled domes is strangely reminiscent of churches

in Valencia (Spain). Across the square is the more modest 17th-century **Chiesa del Rosario**, which has a baroque façade. The lane leading up from its left-hand side takes you to Piazza Sas Animas and the **church** of the same name, a pleasant stone building with a vaguely Iberian feel about it. Opposite rises the empty hulk of the **Prigione Vecchia**, also known as the Castello, a tower left over from a medieval castle.

Another lane leading from the right-hand side of the Chiesa del Rosario passes out of the old town and down into Piazza Sant'Antonio, a shady square off which lies the modest **Chiesa di Sant'Antonio**, dating largely from the 15th century. The broad, uneven courtyard surrounding the church is lined with squat *cumbessias* and has a solitary Pisan watchtower.

Hotel options are not abundant. The best option is the modern, three-star **Su Barchile** (☎ 0784 9 88 79; www.subarchile.it; Via Mannu 5; s/d €50/80; ☯), which is housed in a converted dairy. It only has 10 rooms, so it's better to book ahead. It also has a very good restaurant specialising in seafood.

Otherwise, for food you might head to **La Taverna** (☎ 0784 99 83 30; Piazza G Marconi 6; meals €25), with tables spilling out onto the pleasant leafy square (just off Piazza Sas Animas). Try its *gnocchetti sardi al ragù d'asino* (small gnocchi in donkey-meat sauce). It sometimes has a few rooms to rent as well – it's a pleasant, central location and worth a try.

Several daily buses run to Orosei from Nuoro (€2.32, about one hour, seven daily) and Dorgali (€1.19, 25 minutes, four daily).

Marina di Orosei

This beach marks the northern end of the gulf, which from here you can see arched in all its magnificence to the south. A broad sandy strip runs 5km south and undergoes several name changes along the way: **Spiaggia Su Barone**, **Spiaggia Isporoddai** and **Spiaggia Osalla**. All are equally tempting and are mostly backed by pine stands, giving you the option of retreating to the shade for a picnic or even a BBQ (facilities are scattered about the pines). Even in August you can find plenty of space to stretch out – most of the punters tend not to wander too far from where they park their cars. The water is a cool, clear emerald green.

Narrow roads run from Orosei and Marina di Orosei along the coast here, giving you several access points along the way. The Marina di Orosei beach is closed off to the north by the Rio Cedrino and behind the beaches stretch the **Stagni di Cedrino** lagoons.

Past a big breakwater you can wander from Spiaggia Osalla around to **Caletta di Osalla** (Map p206), the second stretch of sand after the main beach. It's cute, with the Rio di Osalla, a small river, running into the beach down the valley behind it. A couple of bars and an *agriturismo* cater for the lunch and snack needs of punters, who can be numerous in August.

AROUND OROSEI
Galtellì

If you take the inland SS129 route from Orosei to Nuoro, which you might wish to do in order to visit the site of Serra Orrios and S'Ena 'e Thomes (see opposite) on the way to Dorgali, you will pass through this unremarkable farming town. A short way into the town, a road left leads to the cemetery and what little remains of the Romanesque **Chiesa di San Pietro**, cited in Grazia Deledda's *Canne al Vento*. The house of the Nieddu sisters, characters in the same book, is signposted 20m off as the **Casa delle Dame Pintor** (☎ 0784 9 00 05; ☼ 9am-noon & 4-8pm May-Sep). The 18th-century building has been restored to re-create a typical house of the period, with ethnographic bits and bobs all in their relevant places.

Occasional buses run between Galtellì, Orosei and Cala Liberotto.

Grotta di Ispinigoli

Mexico is home to the world's tallest stalagmite (40m), but you shouldn't worry about settling for second best here – the natural spectacle of its slightly shorter counterpart in the **Grotta di Ispinigoli** (Map p206; adult/child €7/4.50; ☼ tours on the hr 9am-5pm Mar-Nov, to 6pm in Aug) is every bit as awe-inspiring.

Unlike most caves of this type, which you enter from the side, here you descend 60m inside a giant 'well', at whose centre stands the magnificent 38m-high stalagmite.

Exploration of the caves began in earnest in the 1960s. In all, a deep network of 15km of caves with eight subterranean rivers has been found. Cavers can book tours of up to 8km through one of the various tour organ-

isers in Dorgali or Cala Gonone. *Nuraghe* artefacts were discovered on the floor of the main well, and Phoenician jewellery on the floor of the second main 'well', another 40m below. On the standard tour you can just peer into the hole that leads into this second cavity, known also as the **Abbisso delle Vergini** (Abyss of the Virgins). The ancient jewellery found has led some to believe that the Phoenicians launched young girls into the pit in rites of human sacrifice. The artefacts found are now on display at Dorgali's archaeological museum.

Hotel Ispinigoli (☎ 0784 9 52 68; www.hotelispinigoli.com; s/d €72/98, half board per person €67) is a reasonable hotel located just below the entrance to the cave. It's also home to a well-known restaurant. You can eat à la carte or choose from a series of set menus (€23).

DORGALI
pop 8250

Dorgali is a bustling provincial town at the crossroads between Nuoro and the coast, and Arbatax and Orosei. It's also the base for a number of trekking companies, given that it is within easy reach of Nuoro, the Supramonte, Cala Gonone and the Gola Su Gorruppu.

Information

The local **tourist office** (☎ 0784 9 62 43; www.dorgali.it, in Italian; Via La Marmora 108/b; ☼ 9am-1pm Mon-Fri year-round, 4-8pm Mon-Fri Jul-Oct & 3.30-7pm Mon-Fri Jan-Jun) can book rooms in hotels and B&Bs in Dorgali and Cala Gonone – a handy service when things fill up in summer. You can change money at the **Banca di Sassari** (Corso Umberto 48). The **Cartolibreria La Scolastica** (Via La Marmora 75) sometimes has IGM hiking maps.

Sights & Activities

The **Museo Archeologico** (☎ 0784 9 61 13; Via Vittorio Emanuele; adult/child €3/2; ☼ 9am-1pm & 4-7pm Tue-Sun) holds a modest collection of local archaeological finds, including those dug up in the nearby Grotta di Ispinigoli.

The local **Cooperative Ghivine** (☎ /fax 0784 9 67 21, 338 834 16 18; www.ghivine.com; Via La Marmora 69/e) offers a huge range of 4WD excursions, guided hikes and canyoning, climbing and caving expeditions. Similar excursions are offered by **Gennargentu Escursioni** (☎ 0784 9 43 85; www.gennargentu.com; Via La Marmora 197).

Sleeping & Eating

The town has some B&Bs and two reasonable hotels should you have no luck on (or inclination for) the coast at Cala Gonone.

Hotel S'Adde (☎ 0784 9 44 12; hotelsadde -sardegna@libero.it; Via Concordia 38; s/d €60/108; P ❷) This is the more attractive option, sitting at the northeastern end of town next to a small park with kids' rides. It's a big, modern place in the style of an alpine chalet. Rooms are appropriately pine-clad with terraces and green views. The restaurant-pizzeria opens onto a 1st-floor terrace.

Hotel Il Querceto (☎ 0784 9 65 09; www.ilquer ceto.com; Via La Marmora; s/d €60/120; ❷ Apr-Oct) Another attractive alpine-style option, Il Querceto lies about half a kilometre outside the southwestern end of town. It has a pretty garden setting and even boasts tennis courts. The rooms are light and spacious, and are decorated in a homy style. All have balconies and woodland views.

Ristorante Colibrì (☎ 0784 9 60 54; Via Gramsci 14; meals €27-30; ❷ Mon-Sat) Tucked away in a residential area off the main drag (follow the signs) is this over-lit haven for carnivores. Speciality dishes include *cinghiale al romarino* (wild boar with rosemary) and goat roasted with thyme, as well as the more typical *porcetto* (suckling pig). The pasta is also excellent – try the *culurgiones*, a kind of ravioli.

Getting There & Away

ARST buses serve Nuoro (€2.68, 45 minutes, seven Monday to Friday, three Saturday and Sunday) and Olbia (€6.77, one to 1½ hours, four daily). Up to eight shuttle back and forth between Dorgali and Cala Gonone (€0.67, 20 minutes). You can pick up buses at several stops along Via La Marmora. Buy tickets at the bar at the junction of Via La Marmora and Corso Umberto.

GOLA SU GORRUPPU

When you reach the Genna 'e Silana pass (hard to miss, as a hotel and restaurant mark the spot on the eastern side of the SS125 at kilometre 183), you could stop for a morning's hike down the mighty Gola Su Gorruppu gorge. The trail is signposted to the right (east) side of the road and is easy to follow. You reach the gorge, with its claustrophobically high walls, after two hours' hiking. There's nothing to stop you

wandering a little way along the Rio Flumineddu river bed, but don't be tempted to go too far without being properly equipped and, preferably, accompanied by a guide. This magnificent gorge offers myriad possibilities and in autumn, when the river is fuller, it becomes a serious challenge.

Although some people go it on their own, you will be safer going on longer walks with a guide. You could do worse than approach the **Cooperativa Gorropu** (☎ 0782 64 92 82, 333 850 71 57; www.gorropu.com; Via Sa Preda Lada 2, Urzulei), but you can also arrange guides in Dorgali and Cala Gonone. These guides (English and German speaking) organise treks of varying duration in and to the gorge, as well as all over the inland territory of the Golfo di Orosei and the Supramonte. They also organise meals with shepherds in the countryside and might be able to swing rooms in private houses for you.

For more tips on hiking in this area, see Lonely Planet's *Walking in Italy*.

SERRA ORRIOS & S'ENA 'E THOMES

Eleven kilometres northwest of Dorgali (and 3km off the Dorgali–Oliena road) you'll find the ruins of **Serra Orrios** (Map p206; adult/child €5/2; ❷ hourly visits 9am-1pm & 4-6pm), a *nuraghe* village occupied between 1500 and 250 BC. The remains outline a cluster of 70 or so houses grouped around two temples: Tempietto A, thought to be used by visiting pilgrims, and Tempietto B, for the villagers. Recently a third temple was discovered, which has led experts to believe that this may have been a significant religious centre. There's a diagram near the entrance, which helps you to understand the site, as the guided tours are in Italian.

From here you could continue north to see a fine example of a *tomba di gigante* (literally 'giant's tomb'; ancient mass grave). Continue 3km north of the crossroads with the Nuoro–Orosei route and **S'Ena 'e Thomes** (Map p206; ❷ dawn-dusk) is signposted to the right. Just open the gate and walk on about 200m. The stone monument is dominated by a central, oval-shaped stone stele (standing stone) that closed off an ancient burial chamber.

CALA GONONE

Surrounded by the imposing grey peaks of **Monte Tului** (917m), **Monte Bardia** (882m) and **Monte Irveri** (616m), Cala Gonone enjoys an impressive setting. Back in the 1930s Italian aristocrats and well-placed Fascists rather liked it and used it as a privileged summer meeting place. In those days it was still a tiny fishing port. It only began to see the first trickle of real tourists in the mid-1950s, when the Grotta del Bue Marino first opened.

Since then things have come a long way, although development has been sensitive enough to ensure that Cala Gonone retains its village atmosphere. Most importantly, its pleasure-craft port is a starting point for boat excursions to the magical coves and cliffs of the Golfo di Orosei's coastline.

Information

At the roundabout before you enter Cala Gonone you'll find the **Atlantika** (☎ 328 972 97 19; info@atlantika.it; Località Iscrittiorè; ✆ 9am-12.30pm & 5-8.30pm) information point. It's the new company face for several local cooperatives such as Ghivine in Dorgali and Gorropu in Urzulei, and can fix you up with all their excursions, plus any number of canoeing,

biking, caving, diving and canyoning activities. The staff also speak excellent English. They can also arrange English-speaking guides for treks through the Gola Su Gorruppu (€30) and to Tiscali (€35).

Otherwise you can find information at the local **tourist office** (☎ 0784 9 36 96; www.cala gonone.com; Viale Bue Marino 1/a; ✆ 9am-6pm Apr-Oct, to 11pm Jul & Aug). The English-speaking staff members are enthusiastic and have plenty of info on the area.

There's an ATM down at the port, and you can buy trekking maps from **Cartolibreria Edicola Namaste** (Via C Colombo 25). On the same street you'll find an **Internet point** (Via C Colombo 5; per 30 min €5; ✆ 10am-1pm & 5-8pm Mon-Sat).

Sights & Activities

Cala Gonone is arranged around the cute **Spiaggia Centrale**, a little arc of sand that does very well for a quick dip. South along the waterfront, **Spiaggia Palmasera** is a sequence of extremely narrow patches of sand interrupted by rocky stretches. For something

---

THE BLUE CRESCENT

If you do nothing else in Sardinia, you should try to make an excursion along the 20km southern stretch of the Golfo di Orosei by boat. Intimidating limestone cliffs plunge headlong into the sea, interrupted periodically by pretty beaches, coves and grottoes. With an ever-changing palette of sand, rocks, pebbles, seashells and crystal-clear water, the unfathomable forces of nature have conspired to create sublime tastes of paradise. The colours are at their best until about 3pm, when the sun starts to drop behind the higher cliffs.

From the port of Cala Gonone you head south to the **Grotta del Bue Marino** (Map p206), the last island refuge of the monk seal, although none have been seen around for a long time. The watery gallery is certainly impressive, with shimmering light playing on the strange shapes within the cave. Guided visits (in Italian and English) take place up to seven times a day. In peak season you may need to book in advance in Cala Gonone or Santa Maria Navarrese.

The first beach after the cave is **Cala Luna** (Map p206), a crescent-shaped strand closed off by high cliffs to the south. Thick vegetation covers the mountains that stretch back from the beach. The strand (part sand, part pebble) is lapped by rich turquoise and deep emerald-green waters close in, changing to a deep, dark blue further out. Some enterprising individuals run a restaurant behind the beach.

Cala Sisine (Map p206) is the next beach of any size, also a mix of sand and pebbles and backed by a deep, verdant valley. **Cala Biriola** (Map p206) quickly follows, and then several enchanting spots where you can bob below the soaring cliffs – look out for the patches of celestial blue.

Cala Mariolu (Map p206) is arguably one of the most sublime spots on the coast. Split in two by a cluster of bright limestone rocks, there is virtually no sand here. Don't let the smooth, white pebbles put you off, though. The water that laps these beaches ranges from a kind of transparent white at water's edge through every shade of light and sky blue and on to a deep purplish hue.

The last beachette of the gulf, **Cala Goloritzè** (Map p206), rivals the best. At the southern end bizarre granite figures soar away from the cliffside. Among them is **Monte Caroddi**, a 100m-high pinnacle loved by climbers. Beyond the beach you can proceed in the shadow of the coast's stone walls towards **Capo di Monte Santo**, the cape that marks the end of the gulf.

better, walk 1km south to **Spiaggia Sos Dorroles**, backed by a striking yellow-orange rock wall.

The last easily accessible beach south of Cala Gonone is the smaller, rockier **Cala Fuili**, a couple of kilometres south at the end of the road (follow Via Bue Marino out of Cala Gonone). It's backed by a deep green valley and is a taste of what lies further south. From here it's possible to take a walking trail inland and up into the cliff tops to reach Cala Luna, about two hours' hike to the south.

A worthwhile excursion takes you north of Cala Gonone to the beautiful and wild-feeling beach of **Cala Cartoe**. In August it's predictably busy, but come out of season and it will probably be all yours. You need a vehicle to get there. Take Via Marco Polo from behind the port and follow it to a T-junction; the cove is signposted to the right (north). Follow this narrow road, in itself worth the effort as it ascends rapidly, affording breathtaking views across the Golfo di Orosei. Over the pass you descend to another T-junction, where you turn right. One kilometre on brings you to the turn-off (right) for Cala Cartoe, 4km on. A kiosk sells drinks, ice cream and snacks in summer. The beach, its fine white sand lapped by emerald waters, is backed by a small stream and a swath of dense woodland. No wonder it was chosen as a set for Madonna's ill-fated film *Swept Away* (2002).

To get an eagle's eye view over the whole coast, take the short detour from Cala Gonone to the **Nuraghe Mannu** (adult/child €4/2; 9am-7pm Jun-Sep, to 5pm Mar-May). You'll find the signposted turn-off (to the south) on the Cala Gonone–Dorgali road. After 3km the rocky track peters out at a wild headland where you can see nearly the entire curve of the gulf. The *nuraghe* itself is a modest ruin, but its location is terribly romantic, the silver-grey blocks strewn beneath the olive trees.

The main activity in Cala Gonone is undoubtedly the plethora of boat trips that you can take along this gorgeous coast (see right). Diving and snorkelling are other options. **Argonauta** (☎ 0784 9 30 46, 347 530 40 97; www.argonauta .it; Via dei Lecci 10) runs snorkelling tours and diving courses (for children, too), and Graziano Frontéddu at **Sardinia Adventure** (☎ 0784 92 00 77, 340 336 01 87; www.sardiniaadventure) provides assistance to climbers, among other things. You'll find Graziano at the southern end of

Spiaggia Palmasera, where he supervises a climbing wall. On Monday, Wednesday and Friday there's a dedicated mini-climb for children between 5pm and 7pm.

Tours

A huge fleet of boats, from large high-speed dinghies to small cruisers and graceful sailing vessels, is on hand at Cala Gonone port to whisk you south along the beautiful coastline. The most basic option would see you joining a band of punters to be transported to one of the beaches along the coast.

Such trips start at €15 for the return journey to Cala Luna. For a minicruise of the entire coastline you're looking at around €20 (€10 for children), with a further €7 for entry into the Grotta del Bue Marino.

Much nicer is the day-long trip on a sailing boat, costing €67 a head (€33 for children). If you want lunch on board (instead of taking you own), add €18. Contact **Cala Gonone Charter** (☎ 0784 9 37 37; Via S'Abba Irde 3) or **Dovesesto** (☎ 0784 9 37 37; www.dovesesto.com; Piazzale del Porto). A minimum of four people can hire the *Dovesesto* for a week or weekend for €150 per person all inclusive.

The final option is to hire a *gommone* (motorised dinghy). They start at €150 (this drops to around €80 out of season) with an extra €10 to €15 for petrol. Nothing quite beats the freedom this offers, and if you're a beginner, don't worry, so were we! The only minus is that you can't get into the Grotta del Bue Marino this way.

Boats operate from March until about November – dates depend a lot on demand. Prices vary according to season, of which there are four. 'Very high season' is around 11 to 25 August. You can get information at agencies around town or at a series of booths at the port.

Several excursion and hiking outfits will put you onto the trail (on foot or in a 4WD) for the Supramonte, including descents of the Gola Su Gorruppu gorge and visits to Tiscali. Try **Dolmen** (☎ 0784 9 32 60; www.sardegnadascoprire.it; Via Vasco da Gama 18).

Sleeping

Cala Gonone is well served with hotels. Still, in July and August you will need to book ahead.

Hotel Costa Dorada (☎ 0784 9 33 32; www.hotel costadorada.it; Lungomare Palmasera; s/d €90/180;

(Y Apr-Oct; P X) This lovely low-key hotel is situated at the southern end of the *lungomare* amid a profusion of flowers. You can't miss its vine-draped terrace. Inside it's decorated in a Spanish-Sardinian style with terracotta-tiled floors and local handicrafts. Family run, the hotel has its own boat, which ferries guests to some of the few hidden spots along the coast.

Hotel Cala Luna (☎ 0784 9 31 33; www.hotelcala luna.com; Lungomare Palmasera 6; s/d €60/85; Y Mar-Nov; X ▣) The sleek, modern Cala Luna is next to the Miramare, and its minimalist décor and sharp, straight lines offer something a little different. The all-white rooms are light and bright with little splashes of colour, and the rooftop terrace is a romantic setting for dinner.

Hotel Miramare (☎ 0784 9 31 40; www.htlmira mare.it; Piazza Giardini; s/d €67/120; Y Apr-Oct; P X) The first hotel to be built here in 1955, the Miramare has a charming, if faded appeal. It has the best location, right in the centre of town, and many rooms have sea-view balconies. The restaurant serves reliably tasty Sardinian dishes.

Piccolo Hotel (☎ 0784 9 32 32; fax 0784 9 32 35; Viale Colombo; s/d €31/51; Y year-round) This is the cheapest place in town, and it looks it, with its institutional-looking grey exterior. The rooms are predictably no-frills basic, but the location is quite convenient, only a short schlep from the port.

Camping Cala Gonone (☎ 0784 9 31 65; fax 0784 9 32 56; camp site per adult €16; bungalows up to €134; Y Apr-Oct) This camp site is a little way back from the waterfront along the main road from Dorgali. The facilities are excellent and include tennis court, playground, bar, restaurant, pizzeria and barbecue grills.

Eating

There are plenty of restaurants on or near the waterfront, but you'll definitely need to make a reservation in July and August. Most close in winter.

Ristorante Acquarius (☎ 0784 9 34 28; Lungomare Palmasera 34; pizza €6-8, meals €30; Y Apr-Sep) A big, popular restaurant on the *lungomare*, Acquarius serves pizzas from its wood-fired oven at lunchtime. It's also an ice-cream bar. You can sit on the front terrace and choose from a mix of Sardinian and standard Italian dishes. Try the *anzelottos* (ricotta-filled ravioli) or the *cozze alla marinara* (mussels).

Il Pescatore (☎ 0784 9 31 74; Via Acqua Dolce 7; meals €25-30; Y Apr-Sep) This serious fish restaurant is on the northern side of the port. The big, bare space lacks any discernible atmosphere, but once you have a plate of fresh fried fish and a glass of chilled white wine things definitely take on a rosy glow.

Next to Il Pescatore is the tatty **Due Chiacchiere** (☎ 0784 9 33 86; Via Acqua Dolce 13; meals €15-20), where you can get an excellent bowl of pasta. You should also consider a meal at the 4th-floor terrace restaurant of the **Hotel Bue Marino** (☎ 0784 92 00 78; www.hotelbue marino.it; Via Vespucci 8; meals €25), which serves surprisingly good food and has views over the port. It also has a popular cocktail bar street-side.

Entertainment

A lot of dance punters head for the disco tents set up at the southern end of Spiaggia Palmasera – you can hear the music all over Cala Gonone!

Lo Skrittiore (☎ 339 330 37 08; www.skrittiore.com; Località Iscrittiore) This big summer disco rocks the Centro Sportivo, a couple of kilometres uphill off the Dorgali road. Music ranges from Latin American to house hits.

Getting There & Away

Frequent ARST buses run from Dorgali (€0.67, 20 minutes, eight daily), 10km away, and pull up at Via Marco Polo near the port in summer. Seven of these come from Nuoro (€2.58, one hour 10 minutes). Buy tickets from **Bar La Pineta** (Viale C Colombo).

Directory

CONTENTS

PRACTICALITIES

- Sardinia uses the metric system for weights and measures.
- Buy or watch videos on the PAL system.
- Plugs have two round pins; the current is 230V, 50Hz.
- The island has two regional papers, the Cagliari-based *L'Unione Sarda* and Sassari's *La Nuova Sardegna*. They focus on island affairs with scant attention to national and international news. Italy's leading daily, the *Corriere della Sera*, is also available. The *International Herald Tribune* is available from Monday to Saturday. It has a daily four-page supplement, *Italy Daily*, covering specifically Italian news.
- Popular local stations include Radio Sardegna and Radiolina (frequencies change depending on where you are on the island). Otherwise you can tune in to RAI-1 (1332AM or 89.7FM), RAI-2 (846AM or 91.7FM) and RAI-3 (93.7FM), which combine music with news broadcasts and discussion programmes. The BBC World Service is on medium wave at 648kHz; short wave at 6195kHz, 9410kHz, 12095kHz and 15575kHz; and on long wave at 198kHz.
- Sardinia has three very amateur TV stations, Sardegna 1 and 2 and Videolina. You can also watch Italy's commercial stations Canale 5, Italia 1, Rete 4 and La7, as well as the state-run RAI-1, RAI-2 and RAI-3.

ACCOMMODATION

Accommodation in Sardinia ranges from the sublime to the ridiculous, with prices to match. The Costa Smeralda and Santa Margherita di Pula resorts have such a constellation of star ratings and sky-high prices that mere mortals will never cross their hallowed thresholds. However, many more reasonably priced resorts, a range of modest hotels and a growing number of B&Bs and *agriturismi* (farm-holiday inns) are slowly addressing this imbalance. You will also be pleasantly surprised by the drop in rates outside the July and August high season and the Easter peak – in some cases by as much as half.

In this book we've used a two-tier pricing system to cover these wildly varying prices.

In Cagliari, Sassari and Olbia prices are very reasonable. A budget double room will cost up to €60, a midrange double €61 to €120 and a top-end double over €121. In seaside resorts and hot spots like Alghero the price of a double room races up, with budget accommodation just under €80, midrange €81 to €180 and the top end often well over €200. During the high, high season (August, or part of August) many places only offer half board (room, breakfast and dinner) and in this case we have listed low- and high-season prices per person. High-season prices have been quoted throughout; depending on when you plan to visit, you should reconfirm rates as they may be considerably cheaper.

It is essential to book in advance during peak periods. Prices rise 5% to 10% annually and drop between 30% and 40% in low season.

In winter (November to Easter) many places, particularly on the coast, almost completely shut down. In the cities and larger towns accommodation tends to remain open all year. The relative lack of visitors to the island in these down periods means you should have little trouble getting a room in the places that stay open.

Unlike in the rest of Italy, you will seldom be asked for a letter or fax to confirm a reservation in a regular hotel. For popular resort hotels, however, you will need to confirm your booking by fax or email. In many cases you'll also be required to pay a deposit.

Agriturismo & B&Bs

An *agriturismo* is a holiday on a working farm. Traditionally, families rented out rooms in their farmhouses, and it's still possible to find this type of accommodation, although many *agriturismi* have now evolved into quite sophisticated accommodation. All *agriturismi* are operating farms, and you will usually be able to sample the local produce. For detailed information on all *agriturismo* facilities in Sardinia, order a list from **Agriturismo in Sardegna** (www.sardinia.net/agritur). Another excellent web resource is www.agriturismisardi .it (in Italian).

Another increasingly popular option (especially in Cagliari, Sassari and Alghero) is the B&B. There is no island-wide umbrella group for these, but a couple of more localised organisations are emerging. The most comprehensive are www.bbsardegna.it and www.bed-and-breakfast.it.

In Cagliari **Domus Karalitanae** (www.domuska ralitanae.com) offers a comprehensive listing of the city's B&Bs, while in Oristano **La Mia Casa** (www.lamiacasa.sardegna.it) and **Sardinian Way** (www.sardinianway.it) cover most of the B&Bs and apartments in the province. On average they cost €20 to €30 per person a night.

Camping

Most camping facilities in Sardinia are serious complexes with swimming pools, restaurants and supermarkets. They tend to offer camping space as well as a variety of other accommodation options, such as bungalows. With hotels at a premium and expensive in many parts of the island in July and August, camping grounds can be an important option, especially given that quite a few have enviable seaside locations.

Prices at even the most basic camping grounds can be surprisingly expensive during the peak months and especially in August. That said, given what many hotels charge in the same period, camping or even a bungalow may be an attractive option. Prices range from around €10 to €18 per adult. Tent space is often (but not always) free, but there are usually extra charges for parking, showers and electricity.

At most grounds there is no need to book for camping space or to park a caravan. If you want a bungalow, treat them like hotel rooms and book in advance in July and August. A two-person bungalow generally works out between €80 and €100 per night.

Most camping grounds operate only in season, which means roughly April to October (in some cases June to September only).

Independent camping is generally not permitted, but, out of the main summer tourist season, independent campers who try to be inconspicuous and don't light fires shouldn't have too much trouble. Always get permission from the landowner if you want to camp on private property.

Full lists of camp sites are available from local tourist offices or can be looked up on www.touringclub.it, the website of Touring Club Italiano (TCI). Membership costs €25 per annum.

TCI publishes an annual book listing all camp sites in Italy, *Campeggi in Italia,* and the Istituto Geografico de Agostini publishes the annual *Guida ai Campeggi in Europa,* sold with *Guida ai Campeggi in Italia.* Otherwise, log on to www.camping.it (not in English).

Hostels

Ostelli per la gioventù (youth hostels), of which there are only a handful on Sardinia, are run by the **Associazione Italiana Alberghi per la Gioventù** (AIG; www.ostellionline.org), which is af-

filiated with **Hostelling International** (HI; www.hihos
tels.com). You need to have an HI card to stay
at these hostels, but, given that there are only
three on the island, it's not worth becoming a
member just for a trip to Sardinia.

Nightly rates vary from €15 to €25, including breakfast. A meal usually costs
around €8. Accommodation is in segre-
gated dormitories, although two of the
three hostels in Sardinia offer family rooms
(at a higher price per person).

Hostels usually have a lock-out period between 10am and 3.30pm. Check-in is from
6pm to 10.30pm, although some hostels will
allow you a morning check-in before they
close for the day (confirm beforehand). It is
usually necessary to pay before 9am on the
day of your departure, otherwise you could
be charged for another night.

Hotels & Guesthouses

There is often no difference between a *pensione* (guesthouse) and an *albergo* (hotel).
However, a *pensione* will generally be of
one- to three-star standard, while an *albergo* can be awarded up to five stars.

While the quality of accommodation can
vary a great deal, a one-star *pensione* will
tend to be very basic and will usually have
communal bathroom facilities. Standards
at two-star places are often only slightly
better, but rooms will generally have a private bathroom. Once you arrive at three
stars you can assume that standards will be
reasonable. Four- and five-star hotels offer
facilities such as room service, laundry,
parking and Internet.

For guaranteed character and comfort
look out for the Charme e Relax sign.
This Italian association specialises in small
to mid-sized hotels, usually in unique
buildings (monasteries, castles, old inns
and so on) or special locations, and it offers
an excellent standard of accommodation
combined with professional service.

Hotels in Sardinia are generally unexciting. Until the 1960s there were not too
many around, so the chances of staying in a
charming old hotel are few and far between.
The majority are unimaginative modern
buildings, whose main attributes are based
on position (near the sea) and facilities such
as swimming pools. As a rule, most places
are kept clean and tidy. Serious dives are as
rare as the glittering jewels.

Tourist offices have booklets listing all
local accommodation, including prices.

Rental Accommodation

About the only way to locate *affittacamere*
(local rooms for rent) is through tourist
offices, although a handful are listed in provincial hotel guides. They are more common in the north than elsewhere.

Tourist offices can provide lists of apartments and villas for rent in popular centres
like Santa Teresa di Gallura, Stintino and
Alghero. **Karel Bed & Breakfast** (www.karel-bed
andbreakfast.it, in Italian) now also offers apartment rental in Cagliari. **GULP** (☎ 0789 75 56 89;
www.gulpimmobiliare.it, in Italian; Via Nazionale 58, Santa
Teresa di Gallura) deals with apartments and villas for rent in the northeast of the island.

Resorts

The best spots on Sardinia's coastline are
dominated by resort-style hotels, usually in
the four- to five-star category. These places
can be huge – the Forte Village resort on the
southwest coast takes up 25,000 hectares –
and they usually include several restaurants, pools, shopping malls and, on the
Costa Smeralda, marinas.

Prices are as stunning as the facilities. Forte
Village and Is Morus on the southwest coast
and the big Starwood hotels on the Costa
Smeralda can charge up to €1500 for a standard double room! The Starwood platinum
members' forum reveals that even the most
well-heeled clientele find the €150-a-head
charge for a meal difficult to swallow.

Interspersed between these bastions of
luxury are other more affordable resorts, particularly around Villasimius on the southeast
coast, Cannigione and Baia Sardinia on the
northeast coast, and Pula and Chia on the
southwest coast. With all the activities on
offer and an impressive array of facilities,
they are particularly well suited to families.

ACTIVITIES

For detailed information on the island's activities, turn to p46. If you're planning an
activity holiday have a look at **SardegnaNet**
(www.sardegna.net) for some ideas.

BUSINESS HOURS

Shops open from 9am to 1pm and 4pm to
8pm (or 5pm to 9pm) Monday to Saturday.
In summer, in many of the more touristy

areas (such as Alghero, Bosa, Olbia, the Costa Smeralda, Santa Teresa di Gallura and many of the southern resorts), shops tend to open until 11pm. The length of the midday break can range from three hours to as many as five.

Big department stores, which you will only find in Cagliari and Sassari, and some supermarkets have continuous opening from 9am to 8.30pm Monday to Saturday. A few open on Sunday, too.

Banks tend to open from 8.30am to 1.30pm and 3pm to 4.30pm Monday to Friday. They close at weekends, when in most places you will have difficulty changing money. Most banks have ATMs that accept foreign credit and debit cards.

Major post offices open from 8.15am to 5pm or 6pm Monday to Friday, and also from 8.30am to noon or 1pm on Saturday. Smaller post offices generally open from 8.15am to 1.15pm Monday to Friday, and 8.30am to noon on Saturday. All post offices close at least two hours earlier than normal on the last business day of each month (not including Saturday).

Farmacie (pharmacies) open 9am to 12.30pm and 3.30pm to 7.30pm. Most close on Sunday and Saturday afternoon. In any given area there will be at least one pharmacy rostered on to do extra hours, usually until 10pm. When closed, pharmacies are required to display a list of nearby pharmacies rostered on.

Bars (in the Italian sense; that is, coffee-and-sandwich places) and cafés generally open from 7.30am to 8pm. Those with a nocturnal vocation open until about 1am during the week but as late as 3am on Friday and Saturday. Clubs and discos open from around 10pm to 5am, but there'll be no-one there until after midnight.

Restaurants open from about noon to 3pm and 7.30pm to 11pm. In summer (June to September) most restaurants open seven days for lunch and dinner. In the coastal resorts many restaurants shut for several months in the off-season. Those that stay open all year usually close one day a week (although most open daily from June to September).

The opening hours of museums, galleries and archaeological sites vary enormously. As a rule museums close on Monday, but from June to September many are open daily. Outside the high season, hours tend to reduce drastically, and more out-of-the-way sights frequently close altogether.

CHILDREN

Sardinians love children and at coastal resorts they are usually well catered for. However, in less touristy spots like the major cities and inland in the Gennargentu you will find few special amenities, and travel in these parts of the island will require some planning.

Practicalities

Discounts are available for children (usually aged under 12) on public transport and for admission to sights. Although Sardinian trains are seldom very busy it's always advisable to book seats. You'll also need to book car seats if you're planning to hire a car.

You can buy baby formula in powder or liquid form, as well as sterilising solutions such as Milton, at *farmacie*. Disposable nappies (diapers) are widely available at supermarkets and at *farmacie* (where they are also more expensive). Fresh cow's milk is sold in cartons in some bars and in supermarkets. If it is essential that you have milk, you should carry an emergency carton of UHT, since most bars close at 8pm.

For additional information, see Lonely Planet's *Travel with Children* or consult the websites www.travelwithyourkids.com and www.familytravelnetwork.com.

Sights & Activities

Successful travel with children usually requires special effort. Don't try to overdo things, and plan activities that include the kids – older children could help you here. Try to think of things that will capture their imagination, such as staying at one of the *agriturismi* around Oristano province that offer horse-riding excursions (see p128 and p122) or coastal resorts offering child-friendly water sports and boating trips. With so many beautiful beaches in Sardinia, swimming and sandcastle-building are bound to feature in any family holiday.

The water-sports centre of Porto Pollo (p182) and the family-orientated resorts of Cannigione (p180) and Cala Gonone (p217) are good places to start. Many resort-style hotels have excellent facilities for children, including kids' clubs and babysitting so you can get out in the evening.

Remember to factor in time for the kids to play; taking a toddler to a playground for an hour or so can make an amazing difference to their tolerance for sightseeing in the afternoon.

CLIMATE CHARTS

Sardinia has a mild Mediterranean climate, defined by hot, dry summers followed by mild winters with light rainfall. However, climatic conditions vary across the island. The finest weather is usually found around the coast. The southern and western coasts are hotter due to their exposed aspect and proximity to North Africa. The eastern coast is shielded by the Gennargentu mountains and the weather there can be changeable.

Sardinia's interior presents a different story. Summer days are dry and hot, although at altitude the air is surprisingly fresh and it's even cold in the evenings. On the highest mountains there is substan-

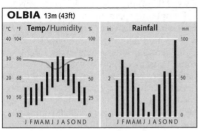

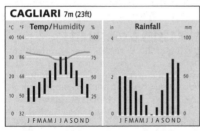

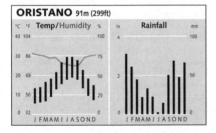

tial snowfall, usually in January. Rain falls mainly in spring and autumn.

See p13 for information on the best times to visit Sardinia.

CUSTOMS

Duty-free sales within the EU no longer exist. Under the rules of the single market, goods bought in and exported within the EU incur no additional taxes, provided duty has been paid somewhere within the EU and the goods are for personal consumption.

Travellers entering Italy from outside the EU are allowed to import, duty free, 200 cigarettes, 1L of spirits, 2L of wine, 60mL of perfume, 250mL of eau de toilette and other goods up to a total value of €175. Anything over this limit must be declared on arrival and the appropriate duty paid (it is advisable to carry all your receipts with you).

DANGERS & ANNOYANCES

Sardinia is a relatively peaceful island and long may it remain so. You will seldom, if ever, be subject to the more unsavoury cons or petty crime that are prevalent in so much of Italy. Muggings, moped-assisted bag snatching and overcharging in hotels are unheard of, and your stay should be trouble-free.

Theft

Theft is not a big problem in Sardinia. Still, you should use common sense. Wear a money belt under your clothing and keep important items, such as money, passport and tickets, there at all times. If you are carrying a bag, wear the strap across your body and have the bag on the side away from the road. Don't leave valuables lying around your hotel room.

Never leave valuables in your car – in fact, try not to leave anything in the car and certainly not overnight. It's worth paying extra to leave your car in supervised car parks.

In case of theft or loss, always report the incident at the *questura* (municipal police station) within 24 hours and ask for a statement, otherwise your travel insurance company won't pay out. Emergency numbers are listed throughout this book.

Traffic

In July and August traffic on Sardinia's many minor roads can be a pain, as can parking. In the bigger towns you need to keep a keen eye on what's going on around you. Driving, however, isn't nearly as intimidating as it is in the rest of Italy, and Sardinians generally observe the road rules. However, you should still be alert at pedestrian crossings.

DISABLED TRAVELLERS

Sardinia has almost no infrastructure to ease the way for disabled travellers, and few museums, with the exception of the national museum in Cagliari, have wheelchair access.

Alitalia operates a courtesy wheelchair service on departure and arrival and also in Milan, Verona and Rome where transfers are required – useful, as you have to change planes in Rome or Milan. This service needs to be reserved when you book your ticket and should be reconfirmed the day before you travel.

The Italian State Tourist Office in your country may be able to provide advice on Italian associations for the disabled and information on what help is available in the country. **Disability World** (www.disabilityworld.com) is another useful website with hotel listings. So far it lists three hotels in Sardinia.

Organisations

Accessible Italy (☎ 378 0549 94 11 00 Italy, 39-3486 91 30 64 outside Italy; www.accessibleitaly.com) A Turin-based company that specialises in holiday services for the disabled, including tours and the hiring of adapted transport.
Associazione Italiana Assistenza Spastici (☎ 070 379 10 10; www.aiasnazionale.it, in Italian; Viale Poetto 312, Cagliari) Operates an information service for disabled travellers called the Sportello Vacanze Disabili.
Holiday Care Service (☎ 0845 124 9971; www .holidaycare.org.uk) Produces an information pack on Italy for the physically disabled and others with special needs. The website also has lots of useful resources.
La Viaggeria (☎ 06 7158 29 45; Via Lemonia 161, 00174 Rome) The Roman branch of Accessible Italy.
Royal Association for Disability & Rehabilitation (RADAR; ☎ 020-7250 3222; www.radar.org.uk) A UK-based charity that publishes *Holidays & Travel Abroad: A Guide for Disabled People*, which provides a useful overview of the facilities available for disabled travellers throughout Europe.

DISCOUNT CARDS
Senior Cards

Senior citizens will find that they are not entitled to many discounts around Sardinia, although admission to some of the sites is reduced for those aged 65 (sometimes 60) and over.

Contact senior citizens' organisations and travel agents in your own country for information on travel packages and discounts for senior travellers.

Student & Youth Cards

Discounts (usually half the normal fee) are available to EU citizens aged between 18 and 25 (you may need to produce proof of age) at some of Sardinia's sights. An International Student Identity Card (ISIC) is usually sufficient proof of age. If you're under 26 but not a student you can apply for a **Euro<26** (www.euro26.org). Similar cards (ITIC) are available to teachers. For nonstudents under 25, there's the **International Youth Travel Card** (IYTC; www.istc.org), which offers the same benefits.

Student cards are issued by student unions, hostelling organisations and some youth travel agencies. **Centro Turistico Studentesco e Giovanile** (CTS; ☎ 06 44 11 11; www.cts.it, in Italian) youth and travel organisation can issue ISIC, ITIC and Euro<26 cards. You have to join the CTS first, however, which costs €28.

EMBASSIES & CONSULATES

It's important to realise what your own embassy – the embassy of the country of which you are a citizen – can and can't do to help you if you get into trouble. Generally speaking, it won't be much help in emergencies if the trouble you're in is remotely your own fault. Remember that you are bound by the laws of the country you are in. Your embassy will not be sympathetic if you end up in jail after committing a crime locally, even if such actions are legal in your own country.

In genuine emergencies you might get some assistance, but only if other channels have been exhausted. For example, if you need to get home urgently, a free ticket is exceedingly unlikely – the embassy would expect you to have insurance. If all your money and documents have been stolen, it might assist with getting a new passport but a loan for onward travel is out of the question.

Italian Embassies & Consulates

Following is a selection of Italian diplomatic missions abroad. As a rule, you should approach the consulate rather than the embassy (where both are present) on visa matters.
Australia Embassy (☎ 02-6273 3333; www.ambitalia .org.au; 12 Grey St, Deakin, Canberra ACT 2600); Consulate (☎ 03-9867 5744; itconmel@netlink.com.au; 509 St Kilda

Rd, Melbourne VIC 3004); Consulate (☎ 02-9392 7900; itconsydn@itconsyd.org; Level 43, The Gateway, 1 Macquarie Pl, Sydney NSW 2000)

Austria (☎ 01-712 5121; ambitalviepress@via.at; Metternichgasse 13, Vienna 1030)

Canada Embassy (☎ 613-232 2401; www.italyincanada .com; 21st fl, 275 Slater St, Ottawa, Ontario K1P 5H9); Consulate (☎ 514-849 8351; www.italconsul.montreal .qc.ca; 3489 Drummond St, Montreal, Quebec H3G 1X6); Consulate (☎ 416-977 1566; www.toronto.italconsulate .org; 136 Beverley St, Toronto, Ontario M5T 1Y5)

France Embassy (☎ 01 49 54 03 00; ambasciata@amb -italie.fr; 47 Rue de Varenne, Paris 75007); Consulate (☎ 01 44 30 47 00; fax 01 45 25 87 50; 5 Blvd Emile Augier, Paris 75016)

Germany Berlin (☎ 030-25 44 00; www.botschaft -italien.de; Hiroshimastr 1, 10785 Berlin); Frankfurt (069-753 10; www.consolati-italiani.de/francoforte; Beethovenstrasse 17, D60326 Frankfurt-am-Main)

Ireland (☎ 01-660 1744; info@italianembassy.ie; 63-65 Northumberland Rd, Dublin 4)

Netherlands (☎ 070-302 1030; www.italy.nl; Alex anderstraat12, The Hague 2514 JL)

New Zealand (☎ 04-473 53 39; www.italy-embassy .org.nz; 34 Grant Rd, Thorndon, Wellington)

Spain Barcelona (93 467 7305; cgbarconsolare@infone gocio.com; Calle Majorca 270, Barcelona 08037); Madrid (☎ 91 423 3300; ambitalsp@cempresarial.com; Calle de Lagasca 98, Madrid 28006)

UK Embassy (☎ 020-7312 2200; www.embitaly.org .uk; 14 Three Kings Yard, London, W1K 4EH); Consulate (☎ 020-7235 9371; www.itconlond.org.uk; 38 Eaton Pl, London SW1X 8AN)

USA New York (☎ 212-737 9100; www.italconsulnyc .org; 690 Park Ave, New York, NY 10021-5044); Washington (☎ 202-612 4400; www.italyemb.org; 1601 Fuller St, NW Washington, DC 20009)

Embassies & Consulates in Rome & Cagliari

Most countries have an embassy in Rome, and several also maintain an honorary consul in Cagliari. Passport inquiries should be addressed to the Rome-based offices. Most missions open from 8.30am or 9am to 5pm Monday to Friday. However, the immigration section is usually only open in the mornings, from around 8.30am to 11.30am.

Australia (☎ 06 85 27 22 93; www.italy.embassy.gov .au; Via Antonio Bosio 5, 00161 Rome)

Canada (☎ 06 44 59 81; www.dfait-maeci.gc.ca/canada europa/italy; Via G B de Rossi 27, 00161 Rome)

France Cagliari (☎ 070 66 42 72; Piazza Deffenu 9); Rome (☎ 06 68 60 11; www.france-italia.it; Piazza Farnese 67, 00186)

Germany Cagliari (☎ 070 30 72 29; Via Rafa Garzia 9); Rome (☎ 06 49 21 31; www.ambgermania.it; Via San Martino della Battaglia 4, 00185)

Ireland (☎ 06 697 91 21; fax 06 679 23 54; Piazza Campitelli 3, 00186, Rome)

Netherlands Cagliari (☎ 070 30 38 73; Viale Diaz 76); Rome (☎ 06 36 76 71; www.olanda.it; Via della Camilluccia 701-3, 00135)

New Zealand (☎ 06 441 71 71; www.nzembassy.com; Via Zara 28, 00198, Rome)

Spain Cagliari (☎ 070 66 82 08; Via Roma 121); Rome (☎ 06 684 04 01; www.amba-spagna.com; Palazzo Borghese, Largo Fontanella Borghese 19, 00186)

UK Cagliari (☎ 070 82 86 28; Viale Colombo 160, Quartu Sant'Elena); Rome (☎ 06 4220 00 01; www.fco.gov.uk; Via XX Settembre 80/a, 00187)

USA (☎ 06 4 67 41; www.usembassy.it; Via Vittorio Veneto 119/a-121, 00187, Rome)

FESTIVALS & EVENTS

Since time immemorial Sardinians have marked the turning of the seasons with traditional festivals. The most important predate Christianity and are linked to the farming calendar. As elsewhere in the Christian world, these feast days were often 'Christianised' and so appropriated by the Church simply by attaching the celebration of one saint or another to the original pagan ritual.

In the wake of WWII and the economic boom years of the 1960s, many of these traditions began to die off. Sardinians have remained doggedly faithful to some of their most important dates, though, and since the 1980s they have resurrected others.

January

Festa di Sant'Antonio Abate (16 January; all over Sardinia) With the winter solstice passed, many villages in Nuoro province celebrate the arrival of spring with great bonfires. The places you can be sure of seeing a good bonfire include Orosei, Orgosolo, Sedilo and Paulilatino.

Mamuthones (16–17 January and Carnevale; Mamoiada) A bizarre pre-Christian festival celebrated in Mamoiada. A dozen townspeople don hairy costumes and masks with a half-human, half-animal allure. Ritually chasing them are eight *Issokadores*, in the guise of outmoded gendarmes.

Festa di San Sebastiano (19 January; all over Sardinia) Similar to the festival of Sant'Antonio. Many towns set up their winter bonfires for San Sebastiano.

February

Carnevale (Carnival) During the period running up to Ash Wednesday many towns stage carnivals preceding the 40 days of Lent. In Alghero the effigy of a French soldier is

DIRECTORY

tried and condemned to burn at the stake. Similar 'executions' take place at other towns, including Cagliari. In Mamoiada the *mamuthones* come out again, while Orotelli and Ottana have similarly bizarre processions involving masked men clothed in heavy sheepskins.

Sa Sartiglia (Sunday and Tuesday before Lent; Oristano) Oristano's carnival involves a medieval tournament of horsemen in masquerade. Processions of locals in traditional costume precede the knightly challenge. Horse races of a less disciplined and fancy nature take place at Santu Lussurgiu, Scano Montiferro and Sedilo.

March/April

Pasqua (Easter) Holy Week in Sardinia is a very big deal and is marked by solemn processions and Passion plays all over the island. Some are more striking than others. The celebrations in Alghero, Castelsardo, Cagliari, Iglesias and Tempio Pausania are particularly evocative.

May

Festa di Sant'Efisio (1–4 May; Cagliari) One of the island's most colourful festivals takes place to honour the memory of Sardinia's patron saint. On 1 May the saint's image is paraded around the city on a baroque bullock-drawn carriage amid a colourful costume procession. Then the statue is taken to Nora, from where it returns on 4 May at nightfall to be greeted by still more street celebrations.

Festa di Santa Giusta (14–18 May; Santa Giusta) Held in the town of the same name just south of Oristano, the festival involves parades and music over four days.

Cavalcata Sarda (Sardinian Parade; second-last Sunday in May; Sassari) Hundreds of Sardinians wearing colourful traditional costume gather at Sassari to mark a victory over the Saracens in AD 1000. They are followed by horsemen who make a spirited charge through the streets at the end of the parade.

June

Festa della Madonna dei Martiri (Monday after the first Sunday of June; Fonni) The people of Fonni dress in traditional costume and stage a procession with a revered image of the Virgin Mary, starting at the town's grand basilica.

July

S'Ardia (6–7 July; Sedilo) More dangerous than Siena's famed Il Palio, this impressive and chaotic horse race celebrates the victory of Roman Emperor Constantine over Maxentius in AD 312. An unruly pack of skilled horsemen race around the chapel erected in Constantine's name.

Festa della Madonna del Naufrago (Second Sunday of July; Villasimius) This striking seaborne procession takes place off the coast of Villasimius, where a statue of the Virgin Mary lies on the seabed in honour of shipwrecked sailors.

August

Estate Musicale Internazionale di Alghero (International Summer of Music; July and August; Alghero) This festival features classical-music concerts.

Festa di Santa Maria del Mare (First Sunday of August; Bosa) Bosa's fishermen celebrate their devotion to the Virgin Mary with a river parade of boats bearing her image. Town celebrations continue for four days.

I Candelieri (The Candlesticks; 14 August; Sassari) Sassari's big traditional feast. In the 16th century the city's *gremi* (trade guilds) organised a thanksgiving parade to the Virgin Mary for ending one of Sassari's many bouts of plague. On the big day the traditional high point is the Faradda, when the nine guilds, accompanied by drummers and pipers, parade giant timber 'candles' through the streets.

Festa dell'Assunta (15 August; Orgosolo) This is one of the most important festivals in the Barbargia. The event is marked by processions of religious fraternities and the colourful local costumes worn by the women.

Estate Medioevale Iglesiente (Mid-August; Iglesias) Since the mid-1990s Iglesias has hosted an increasingly popular 'medieval summer', whose high point is the Corteo Storico Medioevale (Historic Medieval Parade), a grand costumed affair.

Festa del Redentore (Second-last or last Sunday of August; Nuoro) Possibly the grandest parade of traditional Sardinian costume, accompanied by horsemen and dance groups. A torch-lit procession winds through the city on the evening of 28 August and an early-morning pilgrimage to the statue of Christ the Redeemer on Monte Ortobene takes place the following day.

September

Festa di San Salvatore (First Sunday of September; San Salvatore) Several hundred young fellows clothed in white set off from Cabras on the Corsa degli Scalzi (Barefoot Race), an 8km run to the hamlet and sanctuary of San Salvatore.

Festa di Nostra Signora di Regnos Altos (Mid-September; Bosa) The people of the old town of Bosa decorate their streets with huge palm fronds, flowers and *altarittos* (votive altars) in honour of the Virgin Mary.

October

Sagra delle Castagne (Feast of Chestnuts; last Sunday of October; Aritzo) The streets of Aritzo fill with the smoky perfume of roasting chestnuts, which thousands of people from all around come to munch on.

December

Natale (Christmas) During the weeks preceding Christmas there are numerous processions and religious events. Many churches set up elaborate cribs or nativity scenes, known as *presepi*. The day itself is a quiet family affair.

FOOD

In this book we have used the term 'budget' to describe places where you can get a meal for less than €15. For a full, midrange restaurant meal you should reckon on €25 to €35 per person with wine. The most expensive meal will set you back around €40 to €50 per person.

In very touristy places like the northeast coast, Alghero and the Golfo di Orosei, a number of establishments may offer a three-course tourist menu for around €15, although this is not common in Sardinia. Top-end restaurants also offer set menus, which include all courses but no wine. These usually hover around €40 to €50 a head.

Within each section, restaurants are listed in order of preference.

For more on what to eat in Sardinia, turn to p51.

GAY & LESBIAN TRAVELLERS

There is practically no open gay scene in Sardinia, despite the fact that homosexuality is legal and the age of consent is 16. Sardinian culture is very conservative and macho, and overt displays of affection by homosexual couples could attract consternation and unpleasant responses in many towns. The only places where views on homosexuality are really changing are the island's two largest cities, Sassari and Cagliari.

The official organisation dedicated to changing local attitudes is the Sassari-based **Movimento Omosessuale Sardo** (079 21 90 24; www .movimentomosessualesardo.org, in Italian; Via Rockfeller 16/c). In Cagliari the main organisation is **Kaleidos** (Associazione di Cultura Omosessuale; ☎ 349 263 9791; fax 178 223 96 00; aco.kaeidos@tiscalinet.it; Via Leopardi 3, c/o Sinistra Giovanile).

Gay-friendly bars, clubs and hotels can be tracked down through the very useful site http://it.gay.com. You may also find limited information on Sardinia through the national Italian organisation **ARCI-GAY** (☎ 051 649 30 55; www.arcigay.it; Via Don Minzoni 18, 40121 Bologna), with which ARCI-Lesbica is affiliated.

HOLIDAYS

Most Italians take their annual holiday in July or August, deserting the cities for the cooler coastal or mountain resorts. Thus a good deal of Italy's vacation populace heads *for* Sardinia, along with a healthy contingent of foreigners. But the Sardin-

ians have to go on holiday, too – many leave the big towns for holiday apartments, and quite a few businesses and shops close in midsummer, particularly during the week around Ferragosto (Feast of the Assumption) on 15 August. Settimana Santa (Easter Week) is another busy holiday time for Italians.

Public Holidays

Individual towns have public holidays to celebrate the feasts of their patron saints (see p227). National public holidays in Sardinia include the following:

Anno Nuovo (New Year's Day) Celebrations take place on Capodanno (New Year's Eve)
Befana (Epiphany) 6 January
Venerdì Santo (Good Friday) March/April
Pasquetta (Easter Monday) March/April. Also called Giorno dopo Pasqua.
Giorno della Liberazione (Liberation Day) 25 April. Marks the Allied victory in Italy.
Giorno del Lavoro (Labour Day) 1 May
Giorno del Repubblica (Republic Day) 2 June
Ferragosto 15 August
Ognissanti (All Saints' Day) 1 November
Concezione Immaculata (Feast of the Immaculate Conception) 8 December
Natale (Christmas Day) 25 December
Festa di Santo Stefano (Feast of Santo Stefano; Boxing Day) 26 December

INSURANCE

A travel-insurance policy to cover theft, loss and medical problems is a good idea. It may also cover you for cancellation of and delays in your travel arrangements. Paying for your ticket with a credit card can often provide limited travel accident insurance, and you may be able to reclaim the payment if the operator doesn't deliver.

Some insurance policies offer lower and higher medical-expense options; the higher ones are chiefly for countries such as the USA, which have extremely high medical costs. See p249 for more details.

Some policies specifically exclude 'dangerous activities', which can include scuba diving, climbing and even trekking.

You may prefer a policy that pays doctors or hospitals directly, so you don't have to pay on the spot and claim later. If you have to claim later make sure you keep all documentation. Some policies ask you to call a centre in your home country (reverse charges), where an immediate assessment of your problem is made. Check that the policy covers ambulances and an emergency flight home.

For information on car and motorcycle insurance, see p246.

INTERNET ACCESS

Major Internet service providers have dial-in nodes throughout Europe; it's best to download a list of the dial-in numbers before you leave home. If you access your Internet account at home through a smaller ISP or your office or school network, your best options are either to open an account with a global ISP or to rely on cybercafés to collect your mail. For more detailed information on Internet roaming, see www.kropla.com.

If you intend to rely on cybercafés, you'll need to carry three pieces of information to access your Internet mail account: your incoming (POP or IMAP) mail server name, your account name and your password. Your ISP or network supervisor will be able to give you these.

You'll find cybercafés in most of Sardinia's main cities, and some of them are listed throughout this book. In smaller towns and villages Internet cafés are unheard of. Access is expensive, frequently costing €4 to €5 an hour.

For advice on travelling with a portable computer, see www.teleadapt.com.

LEGAL MATTERS
Drink & Drugs

Sardinia's drug laws are relatively lenient on drug users and heavy on pushers. If you're caught with drugs that the police determine are for your personal use, you'll be let off with a warning. If it is determined that you intend to sell the drugs in your possession, you could find yourself in prison. The police decide whether you're a pusher, since the law is not specific about quantities.

The legal blood-alcohol limit is 0.05%, and random breath tests do occur.

Police

If you run into trouble in Italy, you're likely to end up dealing with the *polizia statale* (state police) or the *carabinieri* (military police). The former are a civil force and take their orders from the Ministry of the

Interior, while the *carabinieri* fall under the Ministry of Defence. There is considerable duplication of their roles, despite a 1981 reform of the police forces. Both are responsible for public order and security, which means that you can visit either in the event of robbery or attack.

The *carabinieri* wear a black uniform with a red stripe and drive dark-blue cars with a red stripe. They are well trained and tend to be helpful. Their police station is called a *caserma* (barracks), a reflection of their military status.

The *polizia* wear powder-blue trousers with a fuchsia stripe and a navy-blue jacket, and drive light-blue cars with a white stripe. Their headquarters is the *questura*.

Vigili urbani are the local traffic police. You will have to deal with them if you get a parking ticket or your car is towed away.

Your Rights

Italy has antiterrorism laws that could make life difficult if you are detained by the police. A suspected terrorist can be held for 48 hours without a magistrate being informed and can be interrogated without the presence of a lawyer. It is difficult to obtain bail, and you can be held legally for up to three years without being brought to trial.

MAPS

For detailed information on specialist trekking maps, see p46.

City Maps

The city maps in this book, combined with tourist-office maps, are generally adequate. More detailed maps are available in Sardinia in big-city bookshops (the best places being Cagliari, Olbia and Alghero). The best large-scale maps are produced by Litografia Artistica Cartografica (LAC) at a scale of 1:3500 or 1:5000. Otherwise Belletti Editore produces maps at a scale of 1:5000 and 1:9000.

Island Maps

The best maps of Sardinia are the Michelin island map (series number 566) at a scale of 1:350,000, and the Istituto Geografico de Agostini map at 1:200,000. Touring Club Italiano publishes a map on the same scale. These maps are more than sufficient to find your way around the island.

MONEY

Sardinia's unit of currency is the euro (€), which is divided into 100 cents. Coin denominations are one, two, five, 10, 20 and 50 cents, €1 and €2. The notes are €5, €10, €20, €50, €100, €200 and €500. All euro notes of each denomination are identical on both sides in all EU countries, and the coins are identical on the side showing their value, but there are 12 different obverses, each representing one of the 12 euro-zone countries. For more information on the euro, see www.europa.eu.int/euro.

Quick Reference on the front-cover flap has a handy table to help you calculate the exchange rate; alternatively, log on to www.oanda.com. See p15 for information on costs.

Money can be exchanged in banks, post offices and exchange offices. Banks generally offer the best rates, but shop around, as rates fluctuate considerably.

ATMs

Credit cards can be used in *bancomats* (ATMs) displaying the appropriate sign or (if you have no PIN number) to obtain cash advances over the counter in many banks – Visa and MasterCard are among the most widely recognised. Check what charges you will incur with your bank.

You'll find ATMs throughout Sardinia, and this is undoubtedly the simplest (and safest) way to handle your money while travelling. However, there is a limit of €250 on withdrawals.

Cash

You will need cash for many day-to-day transactions, as credit cards are not universally accepted in hotels and restaurants.

Credit & Debit Cards

Carrying plastic is the simplest way to organise your holiday funds. You don't have large amounts of cash to lose, you can get money after hours and the exchange rate is often better.

Major cards such as Visa, MasterCard, Eurocard, Cirrus and Eurocheque are accepted in Sardinia. Check charges with your bank but, as a rule, there is no charge for purchases on major cards.

You should check the procedure on what to do if you experience problems or if your card is stolen. Most card suppliers will give you an emergency number you can call free of charge for help and advice.

Tipping

You are not expected to tip on top of restaurant service charges, but it is common to leave a small amount, perhaps €1 per person. If there is no service charge, the customer might consider leaving a 10% tip, but this is by no means obligatory. In bars, Italians often leave small change as a tip. Tipping taxi drivers is not common practice, but you should tip the porter at top-end hotels.

Travellers Cheques

Travellers cheques can be cashed at most banks and exchange offices. American Express (AmEx), Thomas Cook and Visa are the most widely accepted brands.

It may be preferable to buy travellers cheques in euros rather than another currency, as they are less likely to incur commission on exchange. Get most of the cheques in largish denominations to save on per-cheque exchange rates.

It's vital to keep your initial receipt, and a record of your cheque numbers and the ones you have used separate from the cheques themselves. If your travellers cheques get stolen, you'll need these documents to get them replaced. You must take your passport with you when cashing cheques.

POST

Italy's, and by association Sardinia's, postal system is notoriously slow, and the island's distance from the mainland doesn't help matters.

Francobolli (stamps) are available at post offices and authorised tobacconists (look for the official *tabacchi* sign, a big T, usually white on black). Since letters often need to be weighed, what you get at the tobacconist's for international airmail will occasionally be an approximation of the proper rate.

Postcards and letters up to 20g sent *via aerea* (by airmail) cost €0.62 to Australia, Japan, New Zealand, the US, Africa and Asia, and €0.45 within Europe. It can take up to two weeks for mail to arrive in the UK or USA, and a letter to Australia will take between two and three weeks. Postcards take even longer – put them in an envelope and send them as letters.

You can also send letters express, using *posta prioritaria*, which guarantees to deliver letters within Europe in three days and to the rest of the world within four to eight days. For more important items, use *raccomandato* (registered mail), or *assicurato* (insured mail), the cost of which depends on the value of the object being sent.

Information about postal services and rates can be obtained at www.poste.it.

SHOPPING

Although Sardinia has a rich craft heritage, shopping on the island isn't terribly exciting. The most interesting craft shops and delis cluster around the tourist resorts, but these can be very expensive.

To be sure of reasonable prices and quality, head for the local Istituto Sardo Organizzazione Lavoro Artigiano (Isola) shop. As the official promoter of traditional crafts, it authenticates all the pieces it sells. It has shops in several cities and towns, and some are indicated in the course of the guide.

Particular regions are known for different craft traditions. For example, in the north of the island – particularly in Castelsardo – women still make baskets from asphodel, rush, willow and dwarf palm leaves. Aggius and Tempio Pausania have a strong cottage industry in wool carpets, decorated with the traditional geometric designs.

Sardinia has a strong history of ceramics, which tend to use simple patterns and colour combinations (often just blue and white, giving the pots a Greek flavour). As most tourists frequent the northwest and northeast of the island, you'll find the better shops along the Costa Smeralda and in towns such as Santa Teresa di Gallura and Alghero.

Alghero and Santa Teresa di Gallura both have a long tradition of coral jewellery. The best-quality coral is harvested off Alghero's Riviera del Corallo (Coral Riviera) and is tightly controlled. In many cases coral is combined with exquisite *filigrana* (filigree work), for which the whole island is justifiably famous. If you catch a local festival you will see Sardinian women decked out in some extraordinary pieces. The best places to purchase *filigrana* are Cagliari and Alghero.

A Sardinian man will undoubtedly say that the island's greatest craft is the hand-made pocket knife, notably produced in Pattada and Arbus. The knives are real works of art, and these days only a few master craftsmen continue to produce them. For more information, see the boxed text, p146.

SOLO TRAVELLERS

Women will find it more difficult to travel alone than men, especially in the villages of the interior. This isn't due to any particular dangers but is largely a result of old-fashioned local attitudes. In rural areas it is not considered respectable for a woman to travel alone, although at most this will earn you uncomfortable stares rather than unpleasant comments.

Other than this the greatest problem facing solo travellers is the dearth of single rooms in popular tourist spots like the northeast coast, along the Golfo di Orosei, and in and around Alghero. In these places you will probably find yourself paying pretty much a double-room rate, and in high summer the single supplement can be very expensive. If you are on a budget you should seek out B&Bs and *agriturismi*, where the rates are much more reasonable and many places charge per person rather than per room, although in high summer this can be a problem in smaller places.

Backpacking is virtually unheard of, and visiting bars and restaurants on your own will earn you a few incredulous stares. Sardinia culture is also quite tight-knit, so you may find yourself feeling a little lonely at times, although contrary to the stereotype Sardinians are actually very friendly and helpful.

Other than that, normal common-sense rules apply. Avoid unlit streets and parks in Cagliari and Sassari at night, and ensure your valuables are safely stored.

TELEPHONE
Mobile Phones

Italy uses GSM 900/1800, which is compatible with the rest of Europe and Australia but not with the North American GSM 1900 or the totally different system in Japan (although some North American GSM 1900/900 phones do work here). If you have a GSM phone, check with your service provider about using it in Sardinia and beware of calls routed internationally (very expensive for a 'local' call).

You can buy SIM cards in Italy for your own national mobile phone (provided you own a GSM, dual- or tri-band cellular phone) and buy prepaid time. This only works if your national phone hasn't been blocked, something you might want to find out before leaving home. If you buy a SIM card and find your phone *is* blocked you won't be able to take it back to the shop.

Both Telecom Italia Mobile (TIM) and Vodaphone-Omnitel offer *prepagato* (prepaid) accounts for GSM phones (frequency 900mHz). The card costs €50 to €60, which includes prepaid phone time. You can top it up in the telcos' shops or by buying cards in tobacconists and newsstands. You need your passport to open a mobile-phone account, prepaid or otherwise.

TIM and Vodaphone-Omnitel retail outlets operate in most Sardinian cities. Call rates vary according to an infinite variety of call plans.

Payphones & Phonecards

The partly privatised Telecom Italia is the largest phone company in the country, and its orange payphones are scattered all over the island. The most common accept only *carte/schede telefoniche* (telephone cards), although you will still find some that accept both cards and coins. Some card phones now also accept special Telecom credit cards and even commercial credit cards.

You can buy phonecards (usually at a fixed euro rate of €2.50, €5 or €10) at post offices, tobacconists and newsstands. Remember to snap off the perforated corner before using them. For directory inquiries within Italy, dial ☎ 12.

Phone Codes

The international country code for Italy is ☎ 39. You must always include the initial 0 in area codes.

Direct international calls from Sardinia can easily be made from public telephones using a phonecard. Dial ☎ 00 to get out of Italy, then the relevant country and area codes, followed by the telephone number.

Area codes are an integral part of all telephone numbers in Italy, even if you are calling within a single zone. If you are in Cagliari and are calling another fixed line in Cagliari the first three digits of the phone number will be ☎ 070.

Mobile-phone numbers begin with a three-digit prefix such as ☎ 330, 335, 347 or 368. Free-phone or toll-free numbers are known as *numeri verdi* and start with ☎ 800. The national-rate phone numbers start with ☎ 848 and ☎ 199.

TIME

Sardinia operates on a 24-hour clock. It is one hour ahead of GMT/UTC. Daylight-saving time starts on the last Sunday in March, when clocks are put forward one hour. Clocks are put back an hour on the last Sunday in October.

TOURIST INFORMATION

The quality of tourist offices in Sardinia varies dramatically. One office might have enthusiastic staff (Alghero, Cala Gonone and Sassari), while others are largely indifferent and devoid of any useful information. As a result of this Sardinia has a plethora of privately run tourist offices, many of which are excellent (Cannigione and Tempio Pausania). We have included a number of these in this guide where they provide a better alternative source of information.

At the time of research all of Sardinia's tourist offices were undergoing a major reorganisation, which should see them administered from a local rather than national level. In theory this is going to make them more responsive to local needs with better information, but in practice much will depend on regional vision and available funds. These changes should be in place by 2006.

Sardinia's regional **tourist office** (☎ 070 60 62 80; Viale Trieste 105) has its headquarters in Cagliari. You can also find information on the website of the **Italian State Tourist Office** (ENIT; www.enit.it).

Throughout the island, three tiers of tourist office exist: regional, provincial and local. They have different names but offer roughly the same services, with the exception of the regional offices, which are generally concerned with promotion, planning and budgeting. Throughout this book offices are referred to as 'tourist office' rather than by their elaborate and confusing titles. Most offices will respond to written and telephone requests for information.

Azienda Autonoma di Soggiorno e Turismo

(AAST) Otherwise known as Informazioni e Assistenza ai Turisti, this is the local tourist office. These offices have

DIRECTORY

town-specific information and should also know about bus routes and museum opening times.

Azienda di Promozione Turistica (APT) The provincial – read: main – tourist office should have information on the town you're in and the surrounding province.

Pro Loco This is the local office in small towns and villages, and is similar to the AAST office.

Tourist offices are generally open 9am to 12.30pm or 1pm and 4pm to 6pm Monday to Friday. Hours are usually extended in summer, when some offices also open on Saturday or Sunday.

As you would expect, offices in popular destinations along the Costa Smeralda and the southwest coast, as well as tourist centres such as Alghero, Cala Gonone and Villasimius, are usually well stocked and staffed by employees with a working knowledge of English and often German.

TOURS

Options for organised travel to Sardinia are increasing all the time. The **Italian State Tourist Office** (www.enit.it) has a list of operators, noting what each specialises in. Tours can save you a lot of hassle, but you'll find they don't come cheap – prices range from €1200 to €2000 per person for a one- to two-week trip.

Two established specialists are **Magic of Italy** (☎ 0870 888 0228; www.magicofitaly.co.uk) and Alitalia's subsidiary, **Italiatour** (www.italiatour .com). Between them they offer a wide range of tours, city breaks and resort-based holidays covering most of the island.

Specialist Operators

Two UK tour operators specialising in a plethora of activity-based holidays in Sardinia are **Just Sardinia** (☎ 01202-484858; www .justsardinia.co.uk) and **Location Sardinia** (☎ 01494-601012; www.scuba-tours.co.uk). They can set you up with almost any holiday you can imagine, including sailing, scuba diving, kayaking, golf, horse riding, fishing and trekking.

An Australian company with specialist knowledge of Italy (and Sardinia) is **ATI Tours** (☎ 02-9798 0588; www.atitours.com.au).

WALKING & CYCLING TOURS

Several companies offer organised walking tours. One of the largest operators in the UK is **ATG** (☎ 01865-315678; www.atg-oxford.co.uk), whose eight-day itinerary covers the stunning Golfo di Orosei, the Gola Su Gorruppu

and Tiscali. A similar but shorter five-day trek is run by the bespoke walking specialists **Tabona & Walford** (☎ 020-8870 6015; www.tabonaand walford.com), but the itinerary also covers the Monte Sette Fratelli near Cagliari.

For something combining a bit of seaside fun with some serious days of trekking, check out the **Headwater** (☎ 0870 066 2650; www.headwater.com) itinerary. This week-long walking and boat-trip holiday takes in the Maddalena islands, the Golfo di Orosei coast and other parts of Sardinia. Headwater also offers the choice of guided or independent walking.

In the US, **Breakaway Adventures** (☎ 1-800-567 6286; www.breakaway-adventures.com) offers a week-long walking tour of the Maddalena islands in a private boat, and it has also just added a new cycling tour to its dossier. Another specialist cycling operator is **Saddle Skedaddle** (☎ 0191-265 1110; www.skedaddle.co.uk), which offers short breaks and week-long cycles across the island on and off road.

CULTURAL TOURS

Andante Travels (☎ 01722-713800; www.andan tetravels.co.uk), a UK company, specialises in historical and archaeological tours. One itinerary is focused on ancient Sardinia, scrutinising the era of the *nuraghe* (stone tower) and the Phoenician traders who supplanted that culture.

A similar American organisation is **Archaeological Tours Inc** (☎ 866-740-5130; www.ar chaeologicaltrs.com). Its 20-day itinerary around Malta, Corsica and Sardinia puts the island in a wider context. Tours are guided by expert scholars.

VISAS

Italy is one of 15 countries that have signed the Schengen Convention, an agreement whereby all EU member countries (except the UK and Ireland) plus Iceland and Norway have abolished checks at common borders. EU, Norwegian and Icelandic nationals do not need a visa, regardless of the length or purpose of their visit in Italy. Citizens of the UK and Ireland are also exempt from visa requirements. In addition, nationals of a number of other countries, including Australia, Canada, Japan, New Zealand, Switzerland and the USA, do not require visas for tourist visits of up to 90 days to any Schengen country.

All non-EU nationals entering Italy for any reason other than tourism (such as study or work) should contact an Italian consulate as they may need a specific visa. They should also insist on having their passport stamped on entry as, without a stamp, they could encounter problems when trying to obtain a *permesso di soggiorno* (residence permit; see right). If you are a citizen of a country not mentioned in this section, you should check with an Italian consulate whether you need a visa.

The standard tourist visa issued by Italian consulates is the Schengen visa, valid for up to 90 days. However, individual Schengen countries may impose additional restrictions on certain nationalities. It is therefore worth checking visa regulations with the consulate of each Schengen country you plan to visit.

It is mandatory that you apply for a visa in your country of residence. You can apply for no more than two Schengen visas in any 12-month period, and they are not renewable inside Italy. It's a good idea to apply early for your visa, especially in the busy summer months.

Study Visas

Non-EU citizens can obtain a study visa at their nearest Italian embassy or consulate. You will normally require confirmation of enrolment, proof of payment of fees and adequate funds to support yourself before a visa is issued.

Permits

EU citizens do not require permits to live, work or start a business in Sardinia. They are, however, advised to register with a *questura* if they take up residence. Failure to do so carries no consequences, although some landlords may be unwilling to rent a flat to you if you cannot produce proof of registration. Those considering long-term residence will eventually want to consider getting a work permit (see below).

WORK PERMITS

Non-EU citizens wishing to work in Sardinia need to obtain a *permesso di lavoro* (work permit). If you intend to work for an Italian company, that company must organise the *permesso* and forward it to the Italian consulate in your country – only then will you be issued an appropriate visa. In other cases, you must organise the permit through the Italian consulate in your country of residence.

RESIDENCE PERMITS

Visitors are technically obliged to report to the *questura* and receive a *permesso di soggiorno* if they plan to stay at the same address for more than a week. Tourists who are staying in hotels and the like need not bother, as hotel owners register guests with the police.

A *permesso di soggiorno* only becomes necessary if you plan to study, work (legally) or live in Sardinia. For details, approach the nearest *questura*.

WOMEN TRAVELLERS

Sardinians are almost universally polite to women, and it is very unlikely that you will be subjected to the catcalls you may encounter on the mainland. If you do find yourself the recipient of unwanted male attention it's best to ignore it. If that doesn't work, tell your would-be companion that you are waiting for your *marito* (husband) or *fidanzato* (boyfriend) and, if necessary, walk away. Avoid becoming aggressive, as this almost always results in an unpleasant confrontation. If all else fails, approach the nearest member of the police or *carabinieri*.

Women travelling on their own should use their common sense. Avoid walking alone in deserted and dark streets, and look for hotels that are central and within easy walking distance of places where you can eat at night. Women should also avoid hitchhiking alone.

It is wise – and polite – to dress modestly in the towns of inland Sardinia. Communities here are very conservative, and you will still see older women wearing the traditional long, pleated skirts and shawls. Skimpy clothing in such a context is both shocking and inconsiderate. Take your cue from Sardinian women on this one.

Transport

CONTENTS

THINGS CHANGE

The information in this chapter is particularly vulnerable to change. Check directly with the airline or a travel agent to make sure you understand how a fare (and ticket you may buy) works, and be aware of the security requirements for international travel. Shop carefully. The details given in this chapter should be regarded as pointers and are not a substitute for your own careful, up-to-date research.

GETTING THERE & AWAY

Sardinia is not the easiest place in Europe to get to. The best (and fastest) way to get there is by air – it is undoubtedly cheaper than the overland route, which will involve a lengthy ferry crossing. If you're coming from outside Europe, competition between airlines on intercontinental routes means you should be able to pick up a reasonably priced fare to Rome or Milan, from where you can pick up an onward connecting flight. If you live in Europe there are a limited number of direct flights as well as some very cheap charter options. Another alternative is to arrive by boat from Genoa, Livorno or Civitavecchia.

ENTERING THE COUNTRY

If you're coming from outside Italy you'll have to pick up a connecting flight (and change airlines) in Rome or Milan. All airport formalities will take place there and the Sardinian leg of your journey will be considered an internal flight. This makes entering Sardinia a pretty painless procedure.

Boarding a ferry to Sardinia is almost as easy as getting on a bus, although you will need to book your passage if you are travelling in the high season, especially if you have a vehicle. You don't need to show your passport on these internal routes, but it is a good idea to keep some ID handy.

Citizens of European Union (EU) member states can travel to Italy with their national identity cards. People from countries that do not issue ID cards, such as the UK, must carry a valid passport. All non-EU nationals must have a full valid passport.

You're likely to have your passport stamped when you arrive by air, but not if you're coming from another Schengen country (see p234). If you're staying for an extended time, be sure to get the entry stamp. Without it you could encounter problems when trying to get a *permesso di soggiorno* – permission to remain in the country for a nominated time – which is essential for everything from enrolling at a language school to applying for residency in Italy (see p235).

AIR

High season in Sardinia is June to September, and prices are at their highest during this period. Holidays such as Easter also see a huge jump in prices.

A return fare to Rome costs about £70/375 in the low/high season from the UK (low-cost airlines offer much better deals); US$700/900 from the eastern coast of North America and about US$900/1200 from Los Angeles; C$1000/1800 from the Canadian east and C$1400/2000 from the Canadian west coast; and A$1800/2600 from Australia.

For the internal leg of the journey you are looking at €70 to €130 from Rome to Olbia or Cagliari. Ryanair offers a flight from Rome Ciampino that severely undercuts these prices. Flights cost as little as €30, and some during the winter months are free (the passenger only paying the airport taxes)!

Prices are slightly more from Milan (€100 to €170 to Olbia and Cagliari). Local airlines Alitalia, Meridiana and Air One also offer flights from other Italian cities such as Bologna, Pisa and Verona.

Airports & Airlines

Sardinia is served by three airports: **Aeroporto Elmas** (www.aeroportodicagliari.com) at the capital, Cagliari, in the south of the island; **Aeroporto Internazionale di Olbia Costa Smeralda** (☎ 0789 6 90 00; www.geasar.com) in Olbia in the northeast; and Alghero's **Fertilia** (☎ 079 93 50 39; www .aeroportodialghero.it) in the northwest.

The island is not served by intercontinental flights, and only a limited number of airlines fly into Sardinia. Meridiana is the main carrier from the Italian mainland. Alitalia has been largely knocked out of the game, preserving only a regular series of flights to Cagliari. Traffic to Alghero's Fertilia airport is dominated by Air One.

Otherwise Easyjet has daily charters from London's Luton Airport to Cagliari, and from London Gatwick and Berlin to Olbia. The latter is also served by the German charter Hapag-Lloyd Flug, while charter flights to Alghero are run by Ryanair from London Stansted, Frankfurt and Girona (Spain). Other local airlines are Air Dolomiti and Alpi Eagles.

The tiny Arbatax-Tortolì airstrip, 1.5km south of Tortolì on the southern Nuoro coast, opens in summer only for specialist charter flights from the Italian mainland.

International and national airlines in Sardinia:

Air Alps (A6; ☎ 06 474 03 40 Rome; www.airalps.it; hub Innsbruck Airport, Innsbruck)

Air Dolomiti (EN; ☎ 045 288 61 40; www.airdolomiti.it; hub Munich International Airport, Munich)

Air One (AP; ☎ 199 20 70 80 Italy call centre; www .flyairone.it; hub Leonardo da Vinci Airport, Rome)

Alitalia (AZ; ☎ 022 314181; www.alitalia.it, in Italian; hub Leonardo da Vinci Airport, Rome)

Alpi Eagles (E8; ☎ 022 314181; www.alpieagles.com; hub Marco Polo Airport, Venice)

Easyjet (U2; ☎ 848 88 77 66 Rome; www.easyjet.com; hub Gatwick Airport, London)

THE TROUBLE WITH AIR TRAVEL

Low-cost airlines were introduced to Italy in 1998 as the first step in liberalising the heavily regulated air-transport sector. But the partial opening up of the domestic flight market and growing competition by high-speed trains plunged the state-controlled national carrier, Alitalia, into financial crisis, and by September 2004 it was on the brink of insolvency. During 2004, other domestic airlines were also forced to suspend their services, including Minerva Airlines, which previously served Sardinia.

On 5 October 2004 Alitalia and the Italian government signed an agreement on the rescue and relaunch of the national airline. A bridging loan of €400 million was obtained to prop up the company while it restructures over the next three years. By 2008, following 4000 redundancies, the company should be a streamlined private venture.

Today low-cost airlines provide the model of service delivery in the Italian market, operating 2500 flights out of 26 airports. In April 2005 Ryanair launched three new routes, one of which is from Rome Ciampino to Alghero in Sardinia. However, full-blown competition on domestic routes is still restricted by regulation barriers. This applies in particular to Sardinia, where according to public service obligations the government maintains subsidised routes – at a constant frequency and fixed tariff – throughout the year, even in the unprofitable winter months. According to these rules the Italian civil aviation authority, ENAC, granted Ryanair the Rome–Alghero route, but Ryanair maintains that these restrictions aren't necessary and inhibit free competition. It's now involved in a dispute with ENAC.

It's a difficult problem in a country with an intense tourist season that's usually followed by very quiet winter months. Over the next couple of years, as the air-transport service continues to liberalise, we are likely to see the demise of more local carriers unless they can rise to the challenge presented by low-cost airlines such as Easyjet, Hapag-Lloyd Flug and Ryanair. As their presence increases in the Italian market it will further heighten competition and on some routes may trigger a bidding war for target custom. In theory this is great news for Sardinia, which has long suffered a high degree of isolation due to the prohibitive costs and lengthy journeys required to reach the island.

Hapag-Lloyd Flug (X; ☎ 01805 09 35 09; www.hlx
.com; hub Köln Bonn Airport, Cologne)
Iberia (IB; ☎ 199 10 11 91 Italy call centre; www.iberia
.com; hub Barajas International Airport, Madrid)
Meridiana (IG; ☎ 199 11 13 33 Italy call centre; www
.meridiana.it; hub Aeroporto Internazionale di Olbia Costa
Smeralda, Sardinia)
Ryanair (FR; ☎ 899 89 98 44; www.ryanair.com; hub
Prestwick Airport, Glasgow)

Tickets

The best place to buy airline tickets for Sardinia is on the web with one of the low-cost airlines listed above. If you book early you can buy a ticket for as little as €15 (one way), although if you leave it to the last minute in high season this can rise to around €80.

Students and people aged under 26 years (under 30 in some countries) coming from outside Europe have access to discounted fares with valid ID such as an International Student Identity Card (ISIC). Discounted tickets are also released to selected travel agents and specialist discount agencies.

The alternative to booking direct with a low-cost airline on the Internet is to surf online agents such as www.travelocity.co.uk, www.cheaptickets.com, www.travelcuts.com and www.expedia.com.

Australia

Cheap flights from Australia to Europe generally go via Southeast Asian capitals. Qantas and Alitalia offer the only direct flights from Melbourne and Sydney to Rome, but if you're looking for a bargain fare you will probably end up on either Thai Airways or Malaysia Airlines. Flights from Perth are generally a few hundred dollars cheaper.

Quite a few travel offices specialise in discount air tickets. Some travel agencies, particularly smaller ones, advertise cheap air fares in the travel sections of weekend newspapers, such as the *Age* in Melbourne and the *Sydney Morning Herald*.

STA Travel (☎ 1300 733 035; www.statravel.com.au) is a reliable travel agency with branches around Australia and on many university campuses. **Flight Centre** (☎ 133 133; www.flightcentre.com.au) has dozens of offices throughout Australia.

Canada

Alitalia has direct flights to Rome and Milan from Toronto and Montreal. Scan the budget travel agencies' advertisements in the *Toronto Globe & Mail*, the *Toronto Star* and the *Vancouver Province*.

Air Canada flies daily from Toronto to Rome direct and via Montreal. British Airways, Air France, KLM and Lufthansa all fly to Italy via their respective home countries. Given Lufthansa's partnership with Air One, this may be the most cost-effective way to go.

Travel CUTS (☎ 800 667 2887; www.travelcuts.com) is Canada's national student travel agency and has offices in all major cities.

Continental Europe

All national European carriers fly to Italy. The largest of these, Air France, Iberia, Lufthansa and KLM, have representatives in all major European cities. Alitalia has a huge range of offers on all European destinations.

Local Italian airlines Meridiana, Air One, Alpi Eagles and Air Dolomiti fly from Cagliari, Olbia and Alghero to a few European destinations, including Barcelona, Berlin, Frankfurt, Madrid, Paris and Zurich, but these require a change in Rome or Milan.

In France student travel agency **OTU Voyages** (☎ 0820 817 817; www.otu.fr, in French) is a safe bet for cut-price travel. **Voyageurs du Monde** (☎ 01 40 15 11 15; www.vdm.com, in French) and **Nouvelles Frontières** (☎ 0825 000 747; www.nouvelles-frontieres .fr, in French) are also recommended, as are www .lastminute.fr and www.travelprice.fr.

In Germany the low-cost **Hapag-Lloyd Flug** (☎ 01805 09 35 09; www.hlx.com) operates direct flights from many German cities to Olbia. Lufthansa has recently partnered with Air One and during summer it has numerous flights connecting with German destinations. Otherwise, Munich is a haven of bucket travel outlets such as **STA Travel** (☎ 1805-45 64 22; www.statravel.de, in German). Germany also has a number of online travel agents that are worth checking out, like www.lastminute.de and www.expedia.de (both in German).

Kilroy Travel Group (www.kilroygroups.com, not in English) offers discounted travel to people aged between 16 and 33, and has representative offices in Denmark, Sweden, Norway, Finland and the Netherlands. Online, log on to www.airfair.nl (in Dutch).

Getting cheap flights between Spain and Italy is difficult. The best option is Ryanair's flight from Girona to Alghero. **Iberia** (www .iberia.com) has a flight from Madrid to Cagliari. On other airlines the best-value flights may be routed through another European city such as Munich. In Madrid the most reliable budget travel agencies are **Viajes Zeppelin** (☎ 91 542 51 54; www.viajeszeppelin.com, in Spanish), **Barcelo Viajes** (☎ 902 11 62 26; www.barceloviajes.com, in Spanish) or **TIVE** (☎ 91 543 74 12; tive.juventud@madrid.org), the student and youth organisation.

In addition to this **Virgin Express** (www.virgin-express.com) has a host of cheap flights out of Brussels to Rome. Details of its offices in Belgium, Denmark, France, Germany and Greece can be found on the website.

New Zealand

In New Zealand, as in Australia, **STA Travel** (☎ 0508 782 872; www.statravel.co.nz) and **Flight Centre** (☎ 0800 24 35 44; www.flightcentre.co.nz) are popular travel agents. Ads for other agencies can be found in the travel section of the *New Zealand Herald.*

Air New Zealand flies direct from Auckland to Rome and Milan; otherwise Qantas or Alitalia flights from Australia are the most direct way to get to Italy and then Sardinia.

UK & Ireland

Discount air travel is big business in London. Advertisements for many travel agencies appear in the travel pages of the weekend broadsheet newspapers, such as the *Independent* and the *Guardian* on Saturday and the *Sunday Times,* as well as in publications such as *Time Out* and the *Evening Standard.*

A couple of major airlines now operate direct routes to Cagliari, Olbia and Alghero. **Ryanair** (www.ryanair.com) flies twice daily from Stansted to Alghero (once daily in winter), and **Easyjet** (www.easyjet.com) operates daily flights to Cagliari from London's Luton Airport and to Olbia from Gatwick Airport.

STA Travel (☎ 0870 160 0599; www.statravel.co.uk) and **Trailfinders** (☎ 020-7292 1888; www.trailfinders.co.uk) both have offices throughout the UK selling discounted and student tickets. Other good sources of discounted fares are www.ebookers.com, www.opodo.co.uk and www.flynow.com.

There are no direct scheduled flights to Sardinia from Ireland, so you will need to pick up a connection in Milan or Rome. It is worth comparing the cost of flying to Italy directly from Dublin with the cost of flying to London first and then on to Italy.

Both Alitalia and **Aer Lingus** (☎ 0818 365 000; www.aerlingus.com) have regular daily flights to Rome from Dublin.

USA

The North Atlantic is the world's busiest long-haul air corridor and the flight options are bewildering. There are no direct flights from the USA to Sardinia. Depending on which airline you choose, you will have to make a change in Rome or Milan and possibly another European city en route, too.

Both the enormous **American Airlines** (www.aa.com) and **Delta Airlines** (www.delta.com) have regular flights from New York to Milan and Rome, while **United Airlines** (www.united.com) has a service from Washington to Rome. Standard fares can be expensive, but you can usually find something cheaper if you shop around.

Reliable travel agencies include **STA** (☎ 1-800-781 4040; www.statravel.com) and **Council Travel** (☎ 1-800-226 8624; www.counciltravel.com). Both have offices in major cities. Discount travel agencies, known as consolidators, can be found in the weekly travel sections of the *New York Times, Los Angeles Times, Chicago Tribune* and *San Francisco Examiner.*

Stand-by fares are often sold at 60% of the normal price for one-way tickets. **Airhitch** (www.airhitch.org) is an online specialist. You give a general idea of where and when you need to go, and a few days before your departure you will be presented with a choice of two or three flights. A one-way flight from the USA to Europe costs from US$180 (east coast) to US$250 (west coast), plus taxes. This won't necessarily get you to Sardinia, but it could get you a cheap flight to somewhere close.

Courier Travel (☎ 303 570 7586; www.couriertravel.org) is a comprehensive search engine for courier and stand-by flights. You can also check out the **International Association of Air Travel Couriers** (IAATC; ☎ 308 632 3273; www.courier.org).

Online travel agencies www.expedia.com and www.travelocity.com are useful and reliable North American online booking agencies, but there are plenty of others.

If you can't find a good deal, consider a cheap transatlantic hop to London and stalk the bucket shops there.

LAND

Sardinia is the most isolated island in the Mediterranean, some 200km from the nearest land mass. This makes getting to it overland an arduous process involving in most cases a 10- to 20-hour ferry crossing. The quickest route is the five-hour fast ferry from Civitavecchia, north of Rome. The two

TRANSPORT

other main points of departure are Genoa and Livorno, and in summer there are a couple of ferries from Marseille in France.

Travelling to Sardinia this way can be either an enormous drain on your time and money (ferry tickets are not cheap) or, if you have plenty of time to spare, a bit of a European adventure.

If you are travelling by bus, train or car to Italy it will be necessary to check whether you require visas to the countries you intend to pass through.

Border Crossings

The Mt Blanc tunnel from France at Chamonix connects with the A5 for Turin and Milan, and the Grand St Bernard tunnel from Switzerland (SS27) also connects with the A5. The Brenner Pass from Austria (A13) connects with the A22 to Bologna. Mountain passes in the Alps are often closed in winter and sometimes in autumn and spring, making the tunnels a less scenic but more reliable way to arrive in Italy. Make sure you have snow chains in winter.

Regular trains on two lines connect Italy with main cities in Austria and on into Germany, France or Eastern Europe. Those crossing the frontier at the Brenner Pass go to Innsbruck, Stuttgart and Munich. Those crossing at Tarvisio proceed to Vienna, Salzburg and Prague. Trains from Milan head for Switzerland and on into France and the Netherlands. The main international train line to Slovenia crosses near Trieste.

Continental Europe
BUS

Eurolines (www.eurolines.com), in conjunction with local bus companies across Europe, is the main international carrier. You can contact it in your own country or in Italy, and its multilingual website gives comprehensive details of prices, passes and travel agencies where you can book tickets.

CAR & MOTORCYCLE

Those choosing to travel overland to Sardinia are most likely to be taking their own wheels. This is a perfectly sensible idea, as the island's public-transport network leaves a little to be desired and car hire is relatively expensive.

As with bus or train, you need to make your way to the most convenient port. For many this will be Genoa, although you could add a few hours' driving time and continue down as far as Livorno, from where the sea crossing is shorter. Drivers coming from the UK, Spain or France may prefer to time their trip with vessels leaving from Marseille.

Motorcycle fever has not migrated from the mainland to Sardinia, although there is a strong contingent constantly racing around the hairpin bends of the Gennargentu. Still, with a bike you rarely have to book for ferries and can enter restricted traffic areas in cities. Crash helmets are compulsory. Unless you're touring it's probably easier to rent a bike once you have reached Sardinia.

An interesting website loaded with advice for people planning to drive in Europe is at www.ideamerge.com. If you want help with route planning, try www.euroshell.com.

TRAIN

Although more expensive than the bus, travel by rail is infinitely more comfortable and can be quicker, too. As with the bus, your options will be determined by your choice of embarkation point, which for most will mean Genoa.

You can book a couchette for around €18 to €25 on most international trains. In 1st class there are four bunks per cabin and in 2nd class there are six bunks. It is advisable, and sometimes compulsory, to book seats on international trains to and from Italy. Some of the main international services include transport for private cars – an option that'll save wear and tear on your vehicle before it arrives in Italy.

The *Thomas Cook European Timetable* is the trainophile's bible, giving a complete listing of train schedules. It is updated monthly and is available from Thomas Cook offices and agents worldwide.

UK
CAR & MOTORCYCLE

From the UK you can take your car across to France by ferry or the Channel Tunnel car train, **Eurotunnel** (☎ 0870 535 3535; www.euro tunnel.com). The latter runs 24 hours, with up to four crossings (35 minutes) each hour between Folkestone and Calais in the high season. You pay for the vehicle only, and fares vary according to the time of day and season, but a standard return fare could be as much as £300 (valid for one year).

UK drivers holding the old-style green driving licence will need to obtain an International Driving Permit (IDP) before they can drive on the continent. For breakdown assistance both the **AA** (☎ 0870 600 03 71; www .theaa.co.uk) and the **RAC** (☎ 0870 010 63 82; www.rac .co.uk) offer comprehensive cover in Europe.

TRAIN

Eurostar (☎ 0870 518 6186; www.eurostar.com) travels from London to Paris and Lille. Alternatively, you can get a train ticket that includes the Channel crossing by ferry, SeaCat or hovercraft. To get to Marseille for summer-only ferries to Porto Torres in Sardinia, it is best to take the Eurostar to Lille and then change for the overnight **TGV** (www.sncf-voyages.com) service to Marseille. An alternative would be to take the Eurostar to Paris and the overnight *Train Bleu* to Toulon, from where you can pick up ferries to Corsica and then on to Porto Torres in Sardinia. Fares from London to Marseille or Toulon are around £120 to £160.

For Genoa and Livorno, take the Eurostar to Paris and then travel overnight to Milan. From Milan you will need to pick up a local intercity train to Genoa, from where you can pick up ferries to Olbia, Arbatax and Porto Torres. The cheapest adult return fare to Genoa (changing in Paris and Milan) is £220 (including couchette for the Paris–Milan run). People under 26 pay £195.

For the latest fare information on journeys to Italy, including Eurostar, contact the **Rail Europe Travel Centre** (☎ 0870 584 8848; www .raileurope.co.uk) or **Rail Choice** (www.railchoice.com).

Alternatively, log on to the website www .seat61.com – this man has surely been on every train in the world!

SEA

Daily car/passenger ferries depart from Genoa, Livorno and Civitavecchia on the Italian mainland for Sardinian ports. Numerous ferry companies ply these routes (see the boxed text, p242) and services are most

FERRY FARES TO SARDINIA

From	To	Company	Fare (€)	Car Fare (€)	Duration (hr)
Civitavecchia	Arbatax	Tirrenia	36	82	10½
Civitavecchia	Cagliari	Tirrenia	42	87	14½
Civitavecchia	Olbia	Moby	63	116	4¾
Civitavecchia	Olbia	Tirrenia	36	82	8
Civitavecchia	G. Aranci	Sardinia F	42	82	6¾
Civitavecchia	G. Aranci+	Sardinia F	52	115	3½
Civitavecchia	Olbia*+	Tirrenia	46.50	92	4
Fiumicino	Arbatax*+	Tirrenia	50	73	4½
Fiumicino	G. Aranci*+	Tirrenia	48.50	95	4
Genoa	Arbatax	Tirrenia	49	93.50	19
Genoa	Olbia*	GNV	82	133	8-10
Genoa	Olbia*	Moby	66	112	9½
Genoa	Olbia	Tirrenia	48	93.50	13¼
Genoa	Olbia*+	Tirrenia	67	103	6
Genoa	Palau	Enermar	65	89	11
Genoa	P. Torres	GNV	79	133	11
Genoa	P. Torres	Tirrenia	68	104	10
Livorno	G. Aranci	Sardinia F	48	115	10
Livorno	G. Aranci+	Sardinia F	63	109	6
Livorno	Olbia	Moby	59	112	7-11
Naples	Cagliari	Tirrenia	43	80	16¼
Naples	Palau*	L. Lauro	75	125	14
Palermo	Cagliari	Tirrenia	40	80.50	13½
Piombino	Olbia*	Linea Golfi	39	80	8
Trapani	Cagliari	Tirrenia	39	79	11

* indicates the service runs in summer only (Jun-Sep); + indicates a high-speed service

TRANSPORT

frequent from mid-June to mid-September, when it is advisable to book well ahead.

Ferry prices are determined by the season and are at their highest between June and September. You can book tickets at travel agents throughout Italy or directly on the Internet. Offices and telephone numbers for the ferry companies are listed in the Getting There & Away sections for the relevant cities. The search engine **Traghetti Online** (☎ 010 58 20 80; www.traghettionline.net) covers all the ferry companies in the Mediterranean. You can also book online.

Corsica

There are regular links between Santa Teresa di Gallura and Bonifacio, in Corsica. **Saremar** (☎ 199 12 31 99; www.saremar.it), run by Tirrenia, has three daily departures each way depending on the season. A one-way fare in high season is €8.70. A small car costs up to €28. Those landing in Bonifacio pay a €4.10 port tax per person and €2.70 per vehicle. The trip takes 50 minutes. **Moby Lines** (☎ 199 30 30 40; www.moby.it) has 10 daily crossings in July and August, and four during the rest of the year. Prices are virtually the same.

Linee Lauro (☎ 081 551 33 52; www.medmargroup.it, in Italian), which runs a summer ferry from Naples to Palau in Sardinia, also sails to Porto Vecchio in Corsica. The Palau–Porto Vecchio ride costs €10 per person and €20 per car, and the crossing takes 1½ to two hours. The ferry leaves twice a week.

FINDING A FERRY FROM ITALY

The following is a rundown of Italian ports from which there are departures to Sardinia, with a list of company details and destinations.

Civitavecchia

Moby Lines (☎ 199 30 30 40; www.mobylines.it) Services to Olbia.
Sardinia Ferries (☎ 495 32 95 95 Corsica; www.sardiniaferries.com) Runs ferries to Golfo Aranci.
Tirrenia (☎ 199 12 31 99; www.tirrenia.it) Has ferries to Olbia, Arbatax and Cagliari; fast boats also run to Olbia in summer only.

Fiumicino

Tirrenia (☎ 199 12 31 99) Has fast ferries to Golfo Aranci, and a few times a week to Arbatax, in summer only.

Genoa

Enermar (☎ 800 20 00 01; www.enermar.it, Italian only) Ferries and high-speed boats to Palau. Enermar was previously called Tris.
Grandi Navi Veloci (Grimaldi Group; ☎ 899 19 90 69; www.gnv.it) Luxury ferries to Porto Torres and Olbia.
Moby Lines (☎ 199 30 30 40) Has ferries year-round to/from Olbia (and Bastia in Corsica).
Tirrenia (☎ 199 12 31 99) Ferries and high-speed boats to Porto Torres, Olbia and Arbatax.

Livorno

Moby Lines (☎ 0586 82 68 23/4/5) Services to Olbia.
Sardinia Ferries (☎ 019 21 55 11) Regular services to Golfo Aranci.

Naples

Linee Lauro (☎ 081 551 33 52; www.medmargroup.it, in Italian) Has services once or twice a week to Palau (en route to Porto Vecchio in Corsica) from mid-June to mid-September.
Tirrenia (☎ 199 12 31 99) Once- or twice-weekly run to Cagliari.

Palermo

Tirrenia (☎ 199 12 31 99) Operates a service to Cagliari (at least once a week).

Piombino

Linea dei Golfi (☎ 0565 22 23 00; www.lineadeigolfi.it) Has ferries to Olbia from April to September.

Trapani

Tirrenia (☎ 199 12 31 99) Operates a weekly service to Cagliari (en route from Tunisia).

SNCM (☎ 825 88 80 88 France; www.sncm.fr) ferries between Porto Torres and the French mainland call at Propriano or, less frequently, Ajaccio on the way to Marseille and Toulon. The adult one-way fare in either case is €20 and €49 for a small car. Special return fares apply (eg, €93 for a car and two adults).

France
SNCM (☎ 825 88 80 88 France; www.sncm.fr) and **CMN La Méridionale** (☎ 04 919 9 45 00 Marseille; www.cmn .fr) together operate ferries from Marseille to Porto Torres (via Corsica) from April to October. There are nine to 16 sailings each month, but in July and August some leave from Toulon instead. Crossing time is 15 to 17 hours (12½ hours from Toulon). A seat costs €72 in high season (July to August) and a small car €104. A basic cabin for two costs €175. Ask about special return-trip offers.

For tickets and information in Porto Torres, go to **Agenzia Paglietti** (☎ 079 51 44 77; fax 079 51 40 63; Corso Vittorio Emanuele 19).

Italy
Several companies run ferries of varying types and speeds from a number of Italian ports to Sardinia. For company contact details, see the boxed text, opposite. The table, p241, gives standard high-season one-way fares in a *poltrona* (reclining seat) for adults – children aged four to 12 generally pay around half; those under four go free – and small cars. Depending on the service you take, you can also get cabins, the price of which varies according to the number of occupants (generally one to four) and location (with or without window). Most companies offer discounts on return trips and other deals – it's always worth asking. You might want to consider taking a sleeping berth for overnight trips, which will cost as much as double.

Only Grandi Navi Veloci, Moby Lines and Tirrenia have year-round services. The rest operate from March/April to October.

Tunisia
Once a week a Tirrenia vessel from Tunis arrives in Cagliari (via Trapani, Sicily). The trip takes around 36 hours, and you have to change in Trapani. The Cagliari–Trapani part of the journey takes 10 hours and costs €39 in an armchair. The onward journey to Tunisia takes 11 hours and costs €52.

GETTING AROUND

You can reach all of the major – and most of the minor – destinations in Sardinia by bus. Services are generally cheap and relatively efficient. In most cases buses are preferable to trains, which are nearly always slower and often involve time-consuming changes.

If at all possible it is preferable to have your own car in Sardinia. Unlike in the rest of Italy, driving on the island is stress free and parking isn't a problem outside July and August.

Regular ferries and fast boats link the mainland with the offshore islands of the Arcipelago di La Maddalena in the northeast and Isola di San Pietro in the southwest. Services drop off considerably outside high season (mid-June to mid-September), when many of the islands close down for winter.

AIR
Sardinia is so small that you don't really need internal flights. However, Meridiana (see p238) operates a couple of daily flights between Cagliari and Olbia – which is, admittedly, a long grind overland. The flight takes 40 minutes and generally costs €60, although return trips can cost €75 to €85 if you book in advance.

BICYCLE
If you plan to fly your own bike into Sardinia, check with the airline about hidden costs. It will have to be disassembled and packed for the journey.

There are no special road rules for cyclists. Helmets and lights are not obligatory, but you would be wise to equip yourself with both. You cannot cycle on the highway. Make sure you include a few tools, spare parts and a very solid bike lock.

Cycle touring across Sardinia is certainly possible, although the hilly (and in some cases mountainous) terrain makes it quite a challenge. In summer the heat can be exhausting. You should be fit and also prudent, as roads are frequently narrow and local drivers are not greatly accustomed to cyclists.

Bikes can be taken on almost all trains in Sardinia. They are put in a separate wagon and the cost (€5) is the same regardless of the destination. Bikes can also be transported for free on ferries to Sardinia.

In the UK **Cyclists' Touring Club** (☎ 0870 873 0060; www.ctc.org.uk) can help you plan your own bike tour or organise guided tours. Membership costs £32.

Hire

Bikes are available for hire in Alghero, Santa Teresa di Gallura, La Maddalena, Palau and Olbia. Rates range from around €8 per day to as much as €25 for mountain bikes. See Getting Around under the relevant cities in this guide for more information.

BOAT

Local ferries **Enermar** (☎ 800 20 00 01, 0789 70 84 84; www.enermar.it) and **Saremar** (☎ 199 12 31 99, 0789 70 92 70; www.saremar.it) connect Palau with the Isola di La Maddalena. In summer services run every 15 minutes and cost €2.30/2.60 weekdays/weekend for the 20-minute crossing. A car fare is €4.50.

In the southwest Saremar has up to 15 sailings per day from Portovesme to Carloforte on Isola di San Pietro. The trip takes about 30 minutes and costs €2.60/7.60 per person/car. Saremar and **Delcomar** (☎ 0781 85 71 23) boats connect San Pietro with Sant'Antioco. In summer half-hourly services run from early morning to midnight. Tickets for the 30-minute crossing cost €2.50 per person.

Although services are frequent in summer, car drivers should turn up a while before their intended departure as boats fill up quickly.

BUS

Bus services within Sardinia are provided by a variety of private companies and vary from local routes linking small villages to intercity connections. By utilising the local services, it is possible to get to just about any location on the island. Buses are usually a more reliable and faster way to get around, as the rail network is limited. However, services to out-of-the-way places can be slow and very infrequent (often only one service per day).

Each of the provincial capitals has an ARST (Azienda Regionale Sarda Trasporti) bus station, which is centrally located except in Nuoro. Other companies also sometimes use these bus stations, but by no means always. Generally, bus companies merely have a stop (and sometimes a ticket office) elsewhere around town. Often you have to buy tickets from a nearby bar.

In smaller towns and villages there will simply be a *fermata* for interurban buses, not always in an immediately apparent location.

ARST and FdS (Ferrovie della Sardegna) tickets must be bought prior to boarding at stations or designated bars, *tabacchi* (tobacconists) or newspaper stands near the stop. With other companies you generally buy the ticket on board. Timetables are sometimes posted, but don't hold your breath. Tourist offices in bigger towns occasionally have timetable information for their area. In smaller locations you would do well to ask wherever you buy tickets. As services are often infrequent in out-of-the-way locations, you need

SAMPLE BUS FARES

The following table of sample one-way trips provides an idea of the cost and time involved in making bus journeys around Sardinia. Frequencies given are for weekdays in summer. Further information appears in the individual destination chapters.

From	To	Frequency (daily)	Fare (€)	Duration (hr)
Alghero	Olbia	1	7.64	2
Cagliari	Olbia	1	15	4
Cagliari	Oristano	up to 7	5.84	1½
Nuoro	Sassari	6	7	2½
Nuoro	Olbia	7	6.30	2½
Olbia	Sassari	2	5.84	1½
Porto Torres	Castelsardo	3-5	2.01	40-50 min
Santa Teresa di Gallura	Olbia	7	3.72	1hr 50 min
Sassari	Castelsardo	up to 11	2.01	1
Sassari	Alghero	24	2.58	1

to plan ahead. In the light of government cost-cutting in 2005, local bus operator PANI suspended all services. At the time of writing it wasn't clear whether it might start up again or whether further operators or unprofitable routes might be affected.

Services can be frequent on weekdays but reduce considerably on Sundays and holidays – runs between smaller towns often fall to one or none. Keep this in mind if you depend on buses, as it is easy to get stuck in smaller places, especially at weekends.

Bus Operators
The main bus company on the island is **ARST** (Azienda Regionale Sarda Trasporti; ☎ 800 86 50 42; www.arst.sardegna.it, in Italian), which runs the majority of local and long-distance services.

The other major bus companies are **FdS** (Ferrovie della Sardegna; ☎ 079 24 13 01, 079 25 26 01; www.ferroviesardegna.it) and **FMS** (Ferrovie Meridionali della Sardegna; ☎ 800 04 45 53; www.ferroviemeridionalisarde.it, in Italian). FdS also operates a limited network of private narrow-gauge railways, most notably the *trenino verde* (see p248). FMS also used to operate trains, but these have now been taken over by Trenitalia.

Otherwise, smaller companies operate limited services, frequently in summer only. **Turmo Travel** (☎ 078 92 14 87; www.turmotravel.it, in Italian) runs express buses from Cagliari up the east coast to Olbia (airport and port) and on to Santa Teresa di Gallura. Others you may come across include the Nuoro-based **Deplano** (☎ 0784 29 50 30), **Nuragica Tour** (☎ 079 51 04 94) and **Logudoro Tours** (☎ 079 28 17 28).

CAR & MOTORCYCLE
Unlike their mainland cousins, Sardinians are pretty responsible drivers. Main roads are generally good throughout the island and traffic is light, except in the height of summer in tourist hot spots.

To really explore the island, travellers will need to use the system of provincial roads, *strade provinciali,* represented as P or SP on maps. These are sometimes little more than country lanes, but they provide access to some of the more beautiful scenery and the many small towns and villages.

Automobile Associations
The **Automobile Club Italiano** (ACI; 24-hr info line ☎ 80 31 16, 06 49 11 15; www.aci.it) no longer offers free roadside assistance to tourists. Residents of the UK and Germany should organise assistance through their own national organisations, which will entitle them to use ACI's emergency assistance number (☎ 116) for a small fee. Without this entitlement, you'll pay a fee of €80 if you call ☎ 116.

If you are hiring a car from a reputable company they will usually give you an emergency number of their own to call in the case of breakdown.

Bring Your Own Vehicle
Every vehicle travelling across an international border should display the nationality plate of its country of registration. You should also carry proof of ownership of a private vehicle. A warning triangle (to be used in the event of a breakdown) is compulsory throughout Europe. A first-aid kit, a spare-bulb kit and a fire extinguisher are also recommended.

Driving Licence
EU member states' driving licences are recognised in Sardinia. If you hold a licence from other countries, you should obtain an International Driving Permit (IDP), too. Your national automobile association can issue this and it is valid for 12 months.

Fuel
The cost of fuel in Sardinia is very high. You'll pay around €1.12 to €1.13 per litre for *benzina senza piombo* (unleaded fuel) and €0.91 to €0.98 for *gasolio* (diesel). There are plenty of fuel stations in and around towns and on the main road networks.

Hire
With the advent of budget airlines flying into all of Sardinia's airports, the rise of the fly/drive package now provides some reasonably priced car rental. It is *always* better to arrange car hire before you arrive. All the major car-hire outlets have offices at the airports, where you usually pick up your car and deposit it at the end of your stay. The most competitive multinational and national agencies:

Auto Europe (☎ 1 888 223 5555 toll free; www.autoeurope.com)

Autos Abroad (☎ 44 8700 66 77 88; www.autosabroad.com)

Avis (☎ 02 754 197 61; www.avis.com)

Budget (☎ 1 800 472 33 25; www.budget.com)

Europcar (☎ 06 481 71 62; www.europcar.com)

Hertz (☎ 199 11 22 11; www.hertz.com)

Road Distances (km)

	Alghero	Bosa	Cagliari	Iglesias	Nuoro	Olbia	Oristano	Porto Torres	Santa Teresa di Gallura	Sant'Antioco	Sassari
Bosa	45										
Cagliari	207	148									
Iglesias	210	152	58								
Nuoro	128	86	180	183							
Olbia	138	143	265	269	105						
Oristano	109	56	94	97	90	173					
Porto Torres	39	82	230	233	137	120	122				
Santa Teresa di Gallura	139	208	300	304	162	62	210	101			
Sant'Antioco	243	191	84	38	219	302	132	268	340		
Sassari	37	82	217	220	123	106	126	20	100	256	
Tempio Pausania	110	150	256	260	146	46	164	87	58	299	68

If you only want to hire a car for a couple of days, or decide to hire one after you have arrived, you will find car-hire outfits in most of the coastal resorts, although the big international companies only have offices in a handful of big cities. In Sardinia you have to be aged 21 or more (23 for some companies) to hire a car and you must have a credit card. Price-wise you will generally be looking at between €45 and €55 for a Fiat Panda, depending on season and demand.

No matter where you hire your car, make sure you understand what is included in the price (unlimited kilometres, tax, insurance, collision damage waiver and so on) and what your liabilities are. It is also a very good idea to get fully comprehensive insurance to cover any untoward bumps or scrapes.

In some popular tourist centres (like Santa Teresa di Gallura and Alghero) you will find a few rental outlets offering motorcycles and scooters. The former can easily cost €60 to €75 a day for, say, a Honda 600. Scooters cost around €25 to €35 per day.

Most agencies will not hire out motorcycles to people under 18. Note that many places require a sizable deposit and that you could be responsible for reimbursing part of the cost of the bike if it is stolen.

Insurance

Third-party motor insurance is a minimum requirement in Italy. The Green Card, an internationally recognised proof of insurance obtainable from your insurer, is mandatory. Ask your insurer for a European Accident Statement form, which can simplify matters in the event of an accident. A European breakdown-assistance policy is a good investment (see Automobile Associations, p245).

Road Conditions

Ask Sardinians what their biggest gripes are, and roads will be close to the top of the list. The mostly dual-carriageway SS131 Carlo Felice highway from Cagliari to Sassari (and on to Porto Torres) and a similar stretch (SS131dcn) from Olbia via Nuoro to Abbasanta (where it links with the Carlo Felice) are the main motorway-style highways on the island. Another strip (the SS130) runs west from the Carlo Felice to Iglesias, and new dual-carriageway stretches reach from Sassari part of the way to Alghero and from Porto Torres to that Sassari–Alghero road.

Other minor concessions to speedy motoring include improved runs like the *via di scorrimento veloce* (inland road) to bypass Castelsardo between Santa Teresa di Gallura and Sassari/Porto Torres.

If you move around the island a lot you will come to know other key arteries. One of the most important is the SS125, or Orientale Sarda, which runs down the eastern side of the island from Palau in the north to Cagliari in the south.

These and many roads in the more touristed coastal areas are well maintained but are narrow and curvy. In summer, when the island fills with visitors, it is virtually impossible not to get caught in tailbacks along many of them. The area between Olbia and Santa Teresa di Gallura is particularly bad. You may find your patience wears thin in the midsummer heat, and you won't be the only one executing dodgy overtaking manoeuvres. Further inland, the quality of roads is uneven. Main arteries are mostly good but narrow and winding, while many secondary routes are potholed and in pretty poor shape.

Getting into and out of the cities, notably Cagliari and Sassari, can be a test of nerves as traffic chokes approaches and exits.

You will also be surprised by the number of unpaved roads on the island – a cause of worry as you bounce down mountain terrain in that expensive rental car. Still, you'll find many a good *agriturismo* (farm-holiday inn), prehistoric site or fine country restaurant at the end of a dirt track.

Road Rules

In Sardinia, as in the rest of continental Europe, drive on the right-hand side of the road and overtake on the left. Unless otherwise indicated, you must always give way to cars entering an intersection from the right. It is compulsory to wear seat belts if they are fitted to the car. If you are caught not wearing a seat belt you will be required to pay an on-the-spot fine.

Random breath tests occasionally take place. If you're involved in an accident while under the influence of alcohol, the penalties can be severe. The blood-alcohol limit is 0.05%.

Speed limits on main highways (there are no *autostrade* in Sardinia) are 110km/h, on secondary highways 90km/h and in built-up areas 50km/h. Speeding fines are proportionate with the number of kilometres that you are caught driving over the speed limit. Fines can reach €260. Since 2002 drivers are obliged to keep headlights switched on day and night on all dual carriageways.

You don't need a licence to ride a moped under 50cc, but you should be aged 14 or over. You can't carry passengers or ride on highways. The speed limit for a moped is 40km/h. To ride a motorcycle or scooter up to 125cc, you must be aged 16 or over and have a licence (a car licence will do). Helmets are compulsory for everyone riding a motorcycle bigger than 50cc. For motorcycles over 125cc you will need a motorcycle licence.

On a motorcycle you will be able to enter restricted traffic areas in cities and towns without any problems, and traffic police generally turn a blind eye to motorcycles or scooters parked on footpaths. There is no lights-on requirement for motorcycles during the day.

HITCHING

Hitching is never entirely safe in any country, and we don't recommend it. Travellers who decide to hitch are taking a small but potentially serious risk. However, many people choose to hitch, and the advice that follows should help to make their journeys as fast and safe as possible.

Sardinians don't really hitchhike and can be wary of picking up strangers, which can make getting around this way a frustrating business. Never hitch where drivers can't stop in good time or without causing an obstruction. Look presentable, carry as little luggage as possible and hold a sign in Italian indicating your destination.

LOCAL TRANSPORT
Boat Tours

In summer it is possible to join boat tours from various points around the coast. This is an excellent way to see Sardinia's more inaccessible highlights. The most popular tours include trips out of Cala Gonone and Santa Maria Navarrese along the majestic Golfo di Orosei. Close behind is a trip around the islands of the Maddalena archipelago. Boats frequently head out of Porto San Paolo, south of Olbia, for trips around Isola Tavolara and the nearby coast. Others do trips out of Alghero and from the Sinis Peninsula. Most trips are done by motorboats or small tour ferries, but a handful of sailing vessels are also on hand. For more information, see the relevant destination chapters.

Bus

All the major cities and towns have a reasonable local bus service. Generally, you won't need to use them, as the towns are compact, with sights, hotels, restaurants and long-distance transport stations within walking distance of each other. Tickets (between €0.67 and €0.88 per ride) must be purchased from newspaper stands or *tabacchi* outlets and stamped on the bus.

All three airports are linked by local bus services to their respective town centres.

TRANSPORT

SAMPLE TRAIN FARES				
From	To	Frequency (daily)	Fare (€)	Duration (hr)
Cagliari	Olbia	4	13	4
Cagliari	Oristano	up to 17	4.75	1½-2
Cagliari	Porto Torres	2	13.60	4½
Cagliari	Sassari	5	12.10	4¼
Cagliari	Nuoro	2	10.80	3½
Olbia	Golfo Aranci	up to 7	1.85	½
Olbia	Oristano	up to 5	9.25	2hr 50 min
Olbia	Sassari	3	5.90	1hr 50 min
Sassari	Oristano	4	7.75	2½
Sassari	Porto Torres	up to 10	1.20	15-20 min

TRAIN

Travelling by train in Sardinia may be slow, but it is simple and cheap. **Trenitalia** (☎ 89 20 21; www.trenitalia.it), previously the Ferrovie dello Stato (FS; State Railway Service), is the partially privatised state train system that runs the bulk of the limited network in Sardinia. You will find the *orario* (timetable) posted on station notice boards. *Partenze* (departures) and *arrivi* (arrivals) are clearly indicated.

A full timetable, *In Treno Sardegna* (€1), is published every six months (winter and summer) and is intermittently available at some newsagents and stations. The timetable includes the limited FdS lines (see below). Note that there are all sorts of permutations on schedules. Some handy indicators are *feriale* (Monday to Saturday) and *festivo* (Sunday and holidays only).

Private railway **FdS** (☎ 070 34 31 12; www .ferroviesardegna.it) offers limited services. The trains are not the most recent models and often consist of a mere handful of clunky carriages. The lines are Sassari–Alghero, Sassari–Nulvi, Sassari–Sorso, Macomer–Nuoro and Cagliari–Isili (via Mandas).

In summer FdS puts on a scenic service known as the **trenino verde** (www.treninoverde.com, in Italian). These lines are for tourists (although Sardinian residents sometimes use them and pay reduced fares) and some are particularly pretty, especially that between Arbatax and Mandas. The others are Palau–Tempio Pausania, Tempio Pausania–Nulvi (from where you can connect with a regular service to Sassari), Bosa–Macomer (which links with the Macomer–Nuoro line), Isili–Sorgono and the already mentioned Arbatax–Mandas line (which connects with the Mandas–Cagliari regular service). This service only runs from mid-June to mid-September.

For more detailed information on prices and frequency, see the Getting There & Away sections in the relevant destination chapters.

Costs & Classes

There is only one class of service in Sardinia, the basic *regionale*. Most of these trains are all-stops jobs and you won't find any fancy high-speed variations.

Some trains offer 1st and 2nd class, although the essential difference between them is the fact that few people opt to pay extra for the former.

Sample one-way, 2nd-class fares and times are shown on the table, above. Those travelling from Cagliari to Olbia have only one direct train; otherwise, they have to wait for a connection at Chilivani. The same can be said for those travelling between Cagliari and Sassari or Porto Torres, with only two direct trains. To increase your options you have to change at Oristano or Chilivani. Macomer is also a busy stop, as you can pick up FdS trains from there for Nuoro and Bosa.

Train Passes & Discounts

It is not worth buying a Eurail or Inter-Rail pass if you are going to travel only in Sardinia. However, one local pass that just might be worth a thought if you intend to move around a lot is the week-long tourist card Treno e Sardegna (€50), valid for all trains and buses run by Trenitalia and FdS.

Health

CONTENTS

BEFORE YOU GO

While Italy has excellent health care, prevention is the key to staying healthy while abroad. A little planning before departure, particularly for pre-existing illnesses, will save trouble later. Bring medications in their original, clearly labelled containers. A signed and dated letter from your physician describing your medical conditions and medications, including their generic names, is also a good idea. If carrying syringes or needles, be sure to have a physician's letter documenting their medical necessity. If you are embarking on a long trip, make sure your teeth are OK (dental treatment is expensive in Italy) and take your optical prescription with you.

INSURANCE

If you're an EU citizen, a European Health Insurance Card (EHIC), available from health centres or, in the UK, post offices, covers you for most medical care. It will not cover you for nonemergencies or emergency repatriation.

Citizens from other countries should find out if there is a reciprocal arrangement for free medical care between their country and Italy; Australia, for instance, has such an agreement. If you do need health insurance, make sure you get a policy that covers you for the worst possible scenario, such as an accident requiring an emergency flight home. Find out in advance if your insurance plan will make payments directly to providers or reimburse you later for overseas health expenditures.

RECOMMENDED VACCINATIONS

No jabs are required to travel to Italy. The World Health Organization (WHO), however, recommends that all travellers should be covered for diphtheria, tetanus, measles, mumps, rubella and polio, as well as hepatitis B.

INTERNET RESOURCES

The WHO's publication *International Travel and Health* is revised annually and is available online at www.who.int/ith. Other useful websites include www.mdtravelhealth.com (travel-health recommendations for every country; updated daily), www.fitfortravel .scot.nhs.uk (general travel advice for the layman), www.ageconcern.org.uk (advice on travel for the elderly) and www.marie stopes.org.uk (information on women's health and contraception).

IN TRANSIT

DEEP VEIN THROMBOSIS (DVT)

Blood clots may form in the legs during plane flights, chiefly because of prolonged immobility (the longer the flight, the greater the risk). The chief symptom of DVT is swelling or pain of the foot, ankle or calf, usually but not always on just one side. When a blood clot travels to the lungs, it may cause chest pain and breathing difficulties. Travellers with any of these symptoms should immediately seek medical attention. To prevent the development of DVT on long flights you should walk about the cabin of the plane, contract the leg muscles while sitting down, drink plenty of fluids, and avoid alcohol and tobacco.

HEALTH

JET LAG

To avoid jet lag try drinking plenty of nonalcoholic fluids and eating light meals. Upon arrival, get exposure to natural sunlight and readjust your schedule (for meals, sleep etc) as soon as possible.

IN ITALY

AVAILABILITY & COST OF HEALTH CARE

If you need an ambulance anywhere in Italy call ☎ 118. For emergency treatment, go straight to the *pronto soccorso* (casualty) section of a public hospital, where you can also get emergency dental treatment.

Excellent health care is readily available throughout Italy, but standards can vary. Pharmacists can give valuable advice and sell over-the-counter medication for minor illnesses. They can also advise when more specialised help is required and point you in the right direction. In major cities you are likely to find English-speaking doctors or a translator service available.

TRAVELLERS' DIARRHOEA

If you develop diarrhoea, be sure to drink plenty of fluids, preferably in the form of an oral rehydration solution such as Dioralyte. If diarrhoea is bloody, persists for more than 72 hours or is accompanied by fever, shaking, chills or severe abdominal pain you should seek medical attention.

ENVIRONMENTAL HAZARDS

Heatstroke

Heatstroke occurs following excessive fluid loss with inadequate replacement of fluids and salt. Symptoms include headache, dizziness and tiredness. Dehydration is already happening by the time you feel thirsty – aim to drink sufficient water to produce pale, diluted urine. To treat heatstroke drink water and/or fruit juice, and cool the body with cold water and fans.

Hypothermia

Hypothermia occurs when the body loses heat faster than it can produce it. As ever, proper preparation will reduce the risks of getting it. Even on a hot day in the mountains the weather can change rapidly, so carry waterproof garments, warm layers and a hat, and inform others of your route. Hypothermia starts with shivering, loss of judgment and clumsiness. Unless rewarming occurs, the sufferer deteriorates into apathy, confusion and coma. Prevent further heat loss by seeking shelter, warm dry clothing, hot sweet drinks and shared bodily warmth.

Bites, Stings & Insect-Borne Diseases

Throughout the centuries Sardinia was devastated by malaria, with nearly 60% of the population affected in 1945. After the war, however, the malarial mosquito was eradicated by an American health programme, which cleared the island in 1952.

Mosquitoes are still a real problem around low-lying marshy areas such as Cabras and Olbia; you should be particularly wary if you are considering camping. If travelling in summer you should pack mosquito repellent as a matter of course.

Italian beaches are occasionally inundated with jellyfish. Their stings are painful but not dangerous. Dousing in vinegar will deactivate any stingers that have not fired. Calamine lotion, antihistamines and analgesics may reduce the reaction and relieve pain. On dry land, you'll be much safer as Sardinia has absolutely no poisonous snakes.

Always check all over your body if you have been walking through a potentially tick-infested area as ticks can cause skin infections and other more serious diseases such as Lyme disease and tick-borne encephalitis. If a tick is found attached, press down around the tick's head with tweezers, grab the head and gently pull upwards. Avoid pulling the rear of the body as this may squeeze the tick's gut contents through the attached mouth parts into the skin, increasing the risk of infection and disease. Lyme disease begins with the spreading of a rash at the site of the bite, accompanied by fever, headache, extreme fatigue, aching joints and muscles, and severe neck stiffness. If untreated, symptoms usually disappear but disorders of the nervous system, heart and joints can develop later. Treatment works best early in the illness – medical help should be sought. Symptoms of tick-borne encephalitis include blotches around the bite, which is sometimes pale in the middle, and headaches, stiffness and other flu-like symptoms (as well as extreme

HEALTH

tiredness) appearing a week or two after the bite. Again, medical help must be sought.

Leishmaniasis is a group of parasitic diseases transmitted by sandflies and found in coastal parts of Italy. Cutaneous leishmaniasis affects the skin tissue and causes ulceration and disfigurement; visceral leishmaniasis affects the internal organs. Avoiding sandfly bites by covering up and using repellent is the best precaution against this disease.

TRAVELLING WITH CHILDREN

Make sure children are up to date with routine vaccinations and discuss possible travel vaccines well before departure as some vaccines are not suitable for children aged under a year. Lonely Planet's *Travel with Children* includes travel-health advice for younger children.

WOMEN'S HEALTH

Emotional stress, exhaustion and travelling through different time zones can all contribute to an upset in the menstrual pattern.

If using oral contraceptives, remember that some antibiotics, diarrhoea and vomiting can stop the pill from working. Time zones, gastrointestinal upsets and antibiotics do not affect injectable contraception.

Travelling during pregnancy is usually possible but always consult your doctor before planning your trip. The most risky times for travel are during the first 12 weeks of pregnancy and after 30 weeks.

SEXUAL HEALTH

Condoms are readily available, but emergency contraception is not, so take the necessary precautions.

HEALTH

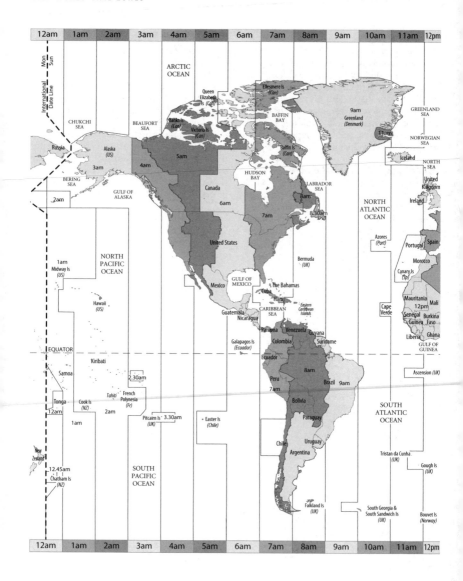

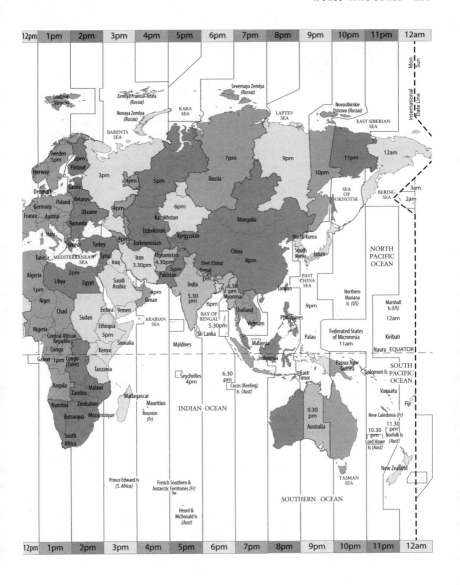

Language

CONTENTS

Sardinians with a fluent command of foreign languages are not all that thick on the ground, but this is perhaps to be expected on an island with a long history of introspection.

Many Sardinians are bilingual, speaking Sardinian and Italian with equal ease, although a growing proportion of people, especially those in the cities and bigger towns, are losing command of the island tongue (which itself divides into several dialects). A 16th century version of Catalan is still spoken in Alghero, although locals differ in opinion on how widely it is used.

Tourism to the island has been, at least until recently, predominantly Italian (more than 80% even now), so locals haven't felt a pressing need to devote too much time to other tongues. This will no doubt change with time, but if you bother to learn a little Italian, you'll find it both useful (especially in the interior) and culturally rewarding.

ITALIAN

Italian is a Romance language related to French, Spanish, Portuguese and Romanian. The Romance languages belong to the Indo-European group of languages, which includes English. Indeed, as English and Italian share common roots in Latin, you will recognise many Italian words.

Although it's commonly accepted that modern standard Italian developed from the Tuscan dialect, history shows that Tuscany's status as the political, cultural and financial power base of the nation ensured that the region's dialect would ultimately be installed as the national tongue.

The Italian of today is something of a composite. What you hear on the radio and TV, in educated discourse and indeed in the everyday language of many people is the result of centuries of cross-fertilisation between the dialects, greatly accelerated in the postwar decades by the modern media.

If you have more than the most fundamental grasp of the Italian language, you need to be aware that many Sardinians still expect to be addressed in the third person formal (*lei* instead of *tu*). Also, it isn't polite to use the greeting *ciao* when addressing strangers unless they use it first; it's better to say *buongiorno* (or *buona sera*, as the case may be) and *arrivederci* (or the more polite form, *arrivederla*). This is the case in most parts of Italy, but in Sardinia use of the informal can be considered gravely impolite – and in some cases downright insulting – especially when talking to an older person.

We've used the formal mode of address for most of the phrases in this guide. Use of the informal address is indicated by 'inf' in brackets. Italian also has both masculine and feminine forms (usually ending in 'o' and 'a' respectively). Where both forms are given in this guide, they are separated by a slash, the masculine form first.

If you'd like a more comprehensive guide to the language, pick up a copy of Lonely Planet's *Italian Phrasebook*.

PRONUNCIATION

Sardinian's pronunciation of standard Italian is refreshingly clear and easy to understand, even if you have only a limited command of the language.

Italian pronunciation isn't very difficult to master once you learn a few easy rules. Although some of the more clipped vowels

SARDINIAN – A LATIN LANGUAGE & ITS DIALECTS

Speakers of Italian will not be long in noticing the oddness of Sardinian. Signs, family and place names and traditional menus will soon have you wondering about all the 'uddus' and other strange sounds and suffixes. Another giveaway are the definite articles, *su, sa, sus, sos, sas* etc, in place of the Italian *il, lo, la, i, gli* and *le*.

Sardinia has seen colonists, occupiers, pirates, foreign viceroys and kings come and go since Rome managed to occupy the island more than 2000 years ago. Many Sardinians reacted by retreating into themselves and their island and it is probably largely due to this passive defiance that they've managed to preserve a key to their own identity – their language.

Sardinians will tell you with a sort of contrary pride that their language is much closer to its mother tongue, Latin, than any of its other offshoots, Italian and all its dialects included. Simple words confirm the claim – while in Italian the word for house is *casa*, the Sardinians have stuck with the Latin *domus* (the Italian equivalent, *duomo* has come to mean 'cathedral').

The 'purest' form of Sardinian is supposedly Logudorese, the dialect of the Logudoro area in the north of the island, although it is probably more a question of quantity (of speakers) than quality. Also considered important is the southern Campidanese. Other dialectal variants thrive across the island.

Nowadays, Sardinian (*sardo*) is experiencing the same problems other minority regional languages face in the fight for survival against imposed national tongues. Since Italian unity in the 19th century, the erosion of Sardinian in the cities and towns has accelerated. While many Sardinians still understand the language, city folk tend not to speak it. You're more likely to hear it in the small towns and villages of the interior.

No language is impermeable and the centuries of Catalan and Spanish rule inevitably had an effect on Sardinian. In particular, Catalan words managed to slip through. In Catalonia and Sardinia a river is generally called a *riu* (often rendered in the Spanish *rio* in Sardinia now), while glasses are *ulleres* in the former and *oglieras* in the latter. The spelling may be different but the pronunciation is virtually the same.

On the subject of Catalan, some residents of Alghero, long an independent Catalan settlement, even today speak a dated version of Catalan, snubbing both Sardinian and Italian.

and stress on double letters require careful practice for English speakers, it's easy enough to make yourself understood.

Vowels

Vowels sounds are generally shorter than English equivalents:

a as in 'art', eg *caro* (dear); sometimes short, eg *amico/a* (friend)

e short, as in 'let', eg *mettere* (to put); long, as in 'there', eg *mela* (apple)

i short, as in 'it', eg *inizio* (start); long, as in 'marine', eg *vino* (wine)

o short, as in 'dot', eg *donna* (woman); long, as in 'port', eg *ora* (hour)

u as the 'oo' in 'book', eg *puro* (pure)

Consonants

The pronunciation of most Italian consonants is similar to that of their English counterparts. Pronunciation of some consonants depends on certain rules:

c as the 'k' in 'kit' before **a**, **o** and **u**; as the 'ch' in 'choose' before **e** and **i**

ch as the 'k' in 'kit'

g as the 'g' in 'get' before **a**, **o**, **u** and **h**; as the 'j' in 'jet' before **e** and **i**

gli as the 'lli' in 'million'

gn as the 'ny' in 'canyon'

h always silent

r a rolled 'rr' sound

sc as the 'sh' in 'sheep' before **e** and **i**; as 'sk' before **a**, **o**, **u** and **h**

z at the beginning of a word, as the 'dz' in 'adze'; elsewhere as the 'ts' in 'its'

Note that when **ci**, **gi** and **sci** are followed by **a**, **o** or **u**, the 'i' is not pronounced unless the accent falls on the 'i'. Thus the name 'Giovanni' is pronounced jo-*va*-nee.

A double consonant is pronounced as a longer, more forceful sound than a single consonant. This can directly affect the meaning of a word, eg *sono* (I am), *sonno* (sleep), but the context of a sentence will usually get the message across.

Word Stress

Stress is indicated in our pronunciation guide by italics. Word stress generally falls on the second-last syllable, as in spa-*ghet*-ti, but when a word has an accent, the stress falls on that syllable, as in cit-*tà* (city).

ACCOMMODATION

I'm looking for a ...	*Cerco ...*	*cher*·ko ...
guesthouse	*una pensione*	oo·na pen·*syo*·ne
hotel	*un albergo*	oon al·*ber*·go
youth hostel	*un ostello per la gioventù*	oon os·*te*·lo per la jo·ven·*too*

Where is a cheap hotel?
Dov'è un albergo   do·*ve* oon al·*ber*·go
a buon prezzo?   a bwon *pre*·tso
What is the address?
Qual'è l'indirizzo?   kwa·*le* leen·dee·*ree*·tso
Could you write the address, please?
Può scrivere l'indirizzo,   pwo *skree*·ve·re leen·dee·*ree*·tso
per favore?   per fa·*vo*·re
Do you have any rooms available?
Avete camere libere?   a·*ve*·te *ka*·me·re *lee*·be·re

MAKING A RESERVATION

(for inclusion in letters, faxes and emails)

To ...	*A ...*
From ...	*Da ...*
Date	*Data*
I'd like to book ...	*Vorrei prenotare ...* (see the list on this page for bed/room options)
in the name of ...	*nel nome di ...*
for the night/s of ...	*per la notte/le notti di ...*
credit card ...	*carta di credito ...*
number	*numero*
expiry date	*data di scadenza*
Please confirm availability and price.	*Vi prego di confirmare disponibilità e prezzo.*

I'd like (a) ...	*Vorrei ...*	vo·*ray* ...
bed	*un letto*	oon *le*·to
single room	*una camera singola*	oo·na *ka*·me·ra *seen*·go·la
double room	*una camera matrimoniale*	oo·na *ka*·me·ra ma·tree·mo·*nya*·le
room with two beds	*una camera doppia*	oo·na *ka*·me·ra *do*·pya
room with a bathroom	*una camera con bagno*	oo·na *ka*·me·ra kon *ba*·nyo
to share a dorm	*un letto in dormitorio*	oon *le*·to een dor·mee·*to*·ryo

How much is it ...?   *Quanto costa ...?*   *kwan*·to *ko*·sta ...
per night   *per la notte*   per la *no*·te
per person   *per persona*   per per·*so*·na

May I see it?
Posso vederla?   *po*·so ve·*der*·la
Where is the bathroom?
Dov'è il bagno?   do·*ve* eel *ba*·nyo
I'm/We're leaving today.
Parto/Partiamo oggi.   *par*·to/par·*tya*·mo o·jee

CONVERSATION & ESSENTIALS

Hello.	*Buon giorno.*	bwon *jor*·no
	Ciao. (inf)	chow
Goodbye.	*Arrivederci.*	a·ree·ve·*der*·chee
	Ciao. (inf)	chow
Yes.	*Sì.*	see
No.	*No.*	no
Please.	*Per favore/*	per fa·*vo*·re/
	Per piacere.	per pya·*chay*·re
Thank you (very much).	*Grazie (mille).*	*gra*·tsye (*mee*·le)
You're welcome.	*Prego.*	*pre*·go
Excuse me. (for attention)	*Mi scusi.*	mee *skoo*·zee
Excuse me. (when going past)	*Permesso.*	per *me*·so
I'm sorry.	*Mi dispiace/*	mee dees·*pya*·che/
	Mi perdoni.	mee per·*do*·nee

What's your name?
Come si chiama?   *ko*·me see *kya*·ma
Come ti chiami? (inf)   *ko*·me tee *kya*·mee
My name is ...
Mi chiamo ...   mee *kya*·mo ...
Where are you from?
Da dove viene?   da *do*·ve *vye*·ne
Di dove sei? (inf)   dee *do*·ve *se*·ee
I'm from ...
Vengo da ...   *ven*·go da ...
Do you like ...?
Ti piace ...?   tee *pya*·che ...
I (don't) like ...
(Non) Mi piace ...   (non) mee *pya*·che ...
Just a minute.
Un momento.   oon mo·*men*·to

LANGUAGE

DIRECTIONS

Where is ...?
Dov'è ...? do·ve ...
Go straight ahead.
Si va sempre diritto. see va sem·pre dee·ree·to
Vai sempre diritto. (inf) va·ee sem·pre dee·ree·to
Turn left.
Giri a sinistra. jee·ree a see·nee·stra
Turn right.
Giri a destra. jee·ree a de·stra
at the next corner
al prossimo angolo al pro·see·mo an·go·lo
at the traffic lights
al semaforo al se·ma·fo·ro

SIGNS

Ingresso/Entrata	Entrance
Uscita	Exit
Informazione	Information
Aperto	Open
Chiuso	Closed
Proibito/Vietato	Prohibited
Camere Libere	Rooms Available
Completo	Full/No Vacancies
Polizia/Carabinieri	Police
Questura	Police Station
Gabinetti/Bagni	Toilets
Uomini	Men
Donne	Women

---

behind	*dietro*	dye·tro
in front of	*davanti*	da·van·tee
far (from)	*lontano (da)*	lon·ta·no (da)
near (to)	*vicino (di)*	vee·chee·no (dee)
opposite	*di fronte a*	dee fron·te a

beach	*la spiaggia*	la spya·ja
bridge	*il ponte*	eel pon·te
castle	*il castello*	eel kas·te·lo
cathedral	*il duomo*	eel dwo·mo
island	*l'isola*	lee·so·la
(main) square	*la piazza (principale)*	la pya·tsa (preen·chee·pa·le)
market	*il mercato*	eel mer·ka·to
old city	*il centro storico*	eel chen·tro sto·ree·ko
palace	*il palazzo*	eel pa·la·tso
ruins	*le rovine*	le ro·vee·ne
sea	*il mare*	eel ma·re
tower	*la torre*	la to·re

EMERGENCIES

Help!
Aiuto! a·yoo·to
There's been an accident!
C'è stato un incidente! che sta·to oon een·chee·den·te
I'm lost.
Mi sono perso/a. mee so·no per·so/a
Go away!
Lasciami in pace! la·sha·mi een pa·che
Vai via! (inf) va·ee vee·a

Call ...! *Chiami ...!* kee·ya·mee ...
a doctor *un dottore/* oon do·to·re/
un medico oon me·dee·ko
the police *la polizia* la po·lee·tsee·ya

HEALTH

I'm ill. *Mi sento male.* mee sen·to ma·le
It hurts here. *Mi fa male qui.* mee fa ma·le kwee

I'm ... *Sono ...* so·no ...
asthmatic *asmatico/a* az·ma·tee·ko/a
diabetic *diabetico/a* dee·a·be·tee·ko/a
epileptic *epilettico/a* e·pee·le·tee·ko/a

I'm allergic ... *Sono allergico/a ...* so·no a·ler·jee·ko/a ...
to antibiotics *agli antibiotici* a·lyee an·tee·bee·o·tee·chee
to aspirin *all'aspirina* a·la·spe·ree·na
to penicillin *alla penicillina* a·la pe·nee·see·lee·na
to nuts *ai noci* a·ee no·chee

antiseptic *antisettico* an·tee·se·tee·ko
aspirin *aspirina* as·pee·ree·na
condoms *preservativi* pre·zer·va·tee·vee
contraceptive *contraccetivo* kon·tra·che·tee·vo
diarrhoea *diarrea* dee·a·re·a
medicine *medicina* me·dee·chee·na
sunblock cream *crema solare* kre·ma so·la·re
tampons *tamponi* tam·po·nee

LANGUAGE DIFFICULTIES

Do you speak English?
Parla inglese? par·la een·gle·ze
Does anyone here speak English?
C'è qualcuno che parla inglese? che kwal·koo·no ke par·la een·gle·ze
How do you say ... in Italian?
Come si dice ... in italiano? ko·me see dee·che ... een ee·ta·lya·no

What does ... mean?
Che vuol dire ...? ke vwol *dee*·re ...
I (don't) understand.
(Non) capisco. (non) ka·*pee*·sko
Please write it down.
Può scriverlo, per favore? pwo *skree*·ver·lo per fa·*vo*·re
Can you show me (on the map)?
Può mostrarmelo pwo mos·*trar*·me·lo
(sulla pianta)? (soo·la *pyan*·ta)

NUMBERS

0	*zero*	*dze*·ro
1	*uno*	*oo*·no
2	*due*	*doo*·e
3	*tre*	tre
4	*quattro*	*kwa*·tro
5	*cinque*	*cheen*·kwe
6	*sei*	say
7	*sette*	*se*·te
8	*otto*	*o*·to
9	*nove*	*no*·ve
10	*dieci*	*dye*·chee
11	*undici*	oon·*dee*·chee
12	*dodici*	do·*dee*·chee
13	*tredici*	tre·*dee*·chee
14	*quattordici*	kwa·*tor*·dee·chee
15	*quindici*	*kween*·dee·chee
16	*sedici*	*se*·dee·chee
17	*diciassette*	dee·cha·*se*·te
18	*diciotto*	dee·*cho*·to
19	*diciannove*	dee·cha·*no*·ve
20	*venti*	*ven*·tee
21	*ventuno*	ven·*too*·no
22	*ventidue*	ven·tee·*doo*·e
30	*trenta*	*tren*·ta
40	*quaranta*	kwa·*ran*·ta
50	*cinquanta*	cheen·*kwan*·ta
60	*sessanta*	se·*san*·ta
70	*settanta*	se·*tan*·ta
80	*ottanta*	o·*tan*·ta
90	*novanta*	no·*van*·ta
100	*cento*	*chen*·to
1000	*mille*	*mee*·le
2000	*due mila*	*doo*·e *mee*·la

PAPERWORK

name	*nome*	*no*·me
nationality	*nazionalità*	na·tsyo·na·lee·*ta*
date/place of	*data/luogo di*	*da*·ta/*lwo*·go dee
birth	*nascita*	*na*·shee·ta
sex (gender)	*sesso*	*se*·so
passport	*passaporto*	pa·sa·*por*·to
visa	*visto*	*vee*·sto

QUESTION WORDS

Who?	*Chi?*	kee
What?	*Che?*	ke
When?	*Quando?*	*kwan*·do
Where?	*Dove?*	*do*·ve
How?	*Come?*	*ko*·me

SHOPPING & SERVICES

I'd like to buy ...
Vorrei comprare ... vo·*ray* kom·*pra*·re ...
How much is it?
Quanto costa? *kwan*·to *ko*·sta
I don't like it.
Non mi piace. non mee *pya*·che
May I look at it?
Posso dare *po*·so *da*·re
un'occhiata? oo·no·*kya*·ta
I'm just looking.
Sto solo guardando. sto *so*·lo gwar·*dan*·do
It's cheap.
Non è caro/cara. non e *ka*·ro/*ka*·ra
It's too expensive.
È troppo caro/a. e *tro*·po *ka*·ro/*ka*·ra
I'll take it.
Lo/La compro. lo/la *kom*·pro

Do you accept	*Accettate carte*	a·che·*ta*·te *kar*·te
credit cards?	*di credito?*	dee *kre*·dee·to

I want to	*Voglio*	*vo*·lyo
change ...	*cambiare ...*	kam·*bya*·re ...
money	*del denaro*	del de·*na*·ro
travellers	*assegni di*	a·*se*·nyee dee
cheques	*viaggio*	vee·*a*·jo

more	*più*	pyoo
less	*meno*	*me*·no
smaller	*più piccolo/a*	pyoo *pee*·ko·lo/la
bigger	*più grande*	pyoo *gran*·de

I'm looking for ...	*Cerco ...*	*cher*·ko ...
a bank	*un banco*	oon *ban*·ko
the church	*la chiesa*	la *kye*·za
the city centre	*il centro*	eel *chen*·tro
the ... embassy	*l'ambasciata*	lam·ba·*sha*·ta
	di ...	dee ...
the market	*il mercato*	eel mer·*ka*·to
the museum	*il museo*	eel moo·*ze*·o
the post office	*la posta*	la *po*·sta
a public toilet	*un gabinetto*	oon ga·bee·*ne*·to
the telephone	*il centro*	eel *chen*·tro
centre	*telefonico*	te·le·fo·*nee*·ko
the tourist	*l'ufficio*	loo·*fee*·cho
office	*di turismo*	dee too·*reez*·mo

TIME & DATES

What time is it?	*Che ore sono?*	ke *o*·re *so*·no
It's (8 o'clock).	*Sono (le otto).*	*so*·no (le *o*·to)
in the morning	*di mattina*	dee ma·*tee*·na
in the afternoon	*di pomeriggio*	dee po·me·*ree*·jo
in the evening	*di sera*	dee *se*·ra
When?	*Quando?*	*kwan*·do
today	*oggi*	*o*·jee
tomorrow	*domani*	do·*ma*·nee
yesterday	*ieri*	*ye*·ree
Monday	*lunedì*	loo·ne·*dee*
Tuesday	*martedì*	mar·te·*dee*
Wednesday	*mercoledì*	mer·ko·le·*dee*
Thursday	*giovedì*	jo·ve·*dee*
Friday	*venerdì*	ve·ner·*dee*
Saturday	*sabato*	*sa*·ba·to
Sunday	*domenica*	do·*me*·nee·ka
January	*gennaio*	je·*na*·yo
February	*febbraio*	fe·*bra*·yo
March	*marzo*	*mar*·tso
April	*aprile*	a·*pree*·le
May	*maggio*	*ma*·jo
June	*giugno*	*joo*·nyo
July	*luglio*	*loo*·lyo
August	*agosto*	a·*gos*·to
September	*settembre*	se·*tem*·bre
October	*ottobre*	o·*to*·bre
November	*novembre*	no·*vem*·bre
December	*dicembre*	dee·*chem*·bre

TRANSPORT
Public Transport

When does the	*A che ora parte/*	a ke *o*·ra *par*·te/
... leave/arrive?	*arriva ...?*	a·*ree*·va ...
boat	*la nave*	la *na*·ve
(city) bus	*l'autobus*	*low*·to·boos
(intercity) bus	*il pullman*	eel *pool*·man
plane	*l'aereo*	la·*e*·re·o
train	*il treno*	eel *tre*·no
I'd like a ...	*Vorrei un*	vo·*ray* oon
ticket.	*biglietto ...*	bee·*lye*·to ...
one way	*di solo andata*	dee *so*·lo an·*da*·ta
return	*di andata e*	dee an·*da*·ta e
	ritorno	ree·*toor*·no
1st class	*di prima classe*	dee *pree*·ma *kla*·se
2nd class	*di seconda*	dee se·*kon*·da
	classe	*kla*·se

I want to go to ...		
	Voglio andare a ...	*vo*·lyo an·*da*·re a ...

The train has been cancelled/delayed.

	Il treno è soppresso/	eel *tre*·no e so·*pre*·so/
	in ritardo.	een ree·*tar*·do

the first	*il primo*	eel *pree*·mo
the last	*l'ultimo*	*lool*·tee·mo
platform (two)	*binario (due)*	bee·*na*·ryo (*doo*·e)
ticket office	*biglietteria*	bee·lye·te·*ree*·a
timetable	*orario*	o·*ra*·ryo
train station	*stazione*	sta·*tsyo*·ne

Private Transport

I'd like to hire	*Vorrei*	vo·*ray*
a/an ...	*noleggiare ...*	no·le·*ja*·re ...
car	*una macchina*	oo·na *ma*·kee·na
4WD	*un fuoristrada*	oon fwo·ree·*stra*·da
motorbike	*una moto*	oo·na *mo*·to
bicycle	*una bici(cletta)*	oo·na bee·chee·(*kle*·ta)

ROAD SIGNS

Dare la Precedenza	Give Way
Deviazione	Detour
Divieto di Accesso	No Entry
Divieto di Sorpasso	No Overtaking
Divieto di Sosta	No Parking
Entrata	Entrance
Passo Carrabile	Keep Clear
Pericolo	Danger
Rallentare	Slow Down
Senso Unico	One Way
Uscita	Exit

Is this the road to ...?

	Questa strada porta	*kwe*·sta *stra*·da *por*·ta
	a ...?	a ...
Where's a service station?		
	Dov'è una stazione	do·*ve* oo·na sta·*tsyo*·ne
	di servizio?	dee ser·*vee*·tsyo
Please fill it up.		
	Il pieno, per favore.	eel *pye*·no per fa·*vo*·re
I'd like (30) litres.		
	Vorrei (trenta) litri.	vo·*ray* (*tren*·ta) *lee*·tree

diesel	*gasolio/diesel*	ga·zo·lyo/*dee*·zel
leaded petrol	*benzina con*	ben·*dzee*·na kon
	piombo	*pyom*·bo
unleaded petrol	*benzina senza*	ben·*dzee*·na
	piombo	*sen*·dza *pyom*·bo

(How long) Can I park here?

	(Per quanto tempo)	(per *kwan*·to *tem*·po)
	Posso parcheggiare qui?	*po*·so par·ke·*ja*·re kwee

Where do I pay?
Dove si paga?   *do·ve see pa·ga*

I need a mechanic.
Ho bisogno di un   *o bee·zo·nyo dee oon*
meccanico.   *me·ka·nee·ko*

The car/motorbike has broken down (at ...).
La macchina/moto   *la ma·kee·na/mo·to*
si è guastata (a ...).   *see e gwas·ta·ta (a ...)*

The car/motorbike won't start.
La macchina/moto   *la ma·kee·na/mo·to*
non parte.   *non par·te*

I have a flat tyre.
Ho una gomma bucata.   *o oo·na go·ma boo·ka·ta*

I've run out of petrol.
Ho esaurito la benzina.   *o e·zo·ree·to la ben·dzee·na*

I've had an accident.
Ho avuto un incidente.   *o a·voo·to oon een·chee·den·te*

TRAVEL WITH CHILDREN

Is there a/an ...? *C'è ...?*   *che ...*
I need a/an ... *Ho bisogno di ...*   *o bee·zo·nyo dee ...*
  baby change *un bagno con*   *oon ba·nyo kon*
    room *fasciatoio*   *fa·sha·to·yo*

car baby seat *un seggiolino*   *oon se·jo·lee·no*
    per bambini   *per bam·bee·nee*
child-minding *un servizio*   *oon ser·vee·tsyo*
  service *di babysitter*   *dee be·bee·*
    see·ter
children's menu *un menù per*   *oon me·noo per*
    bambini   *bam·bee·nee*
(disposable) *pannolini*   *pa·no·lee·nee*
  nappies/diapers *(usa e getta)*   *(oo·sa e je·ta)*
formula (milk) *latte in polvere*   *la·te in pol·ve·re*
(English- *un/una*   *oon/oo·na*
  speaking) *babysitter (che*   *be·bee·see·ter*
  babysitter *parli inglese)*   *(ke par·lee*
    een·gle·ze)
highchair *un seggiolone*   *oon se·jo·lo·ne*
potty *un vasino*   *oon va·zee·no*
stroller *un passeggino*   *oon pa·se·jee·no*

Do you mind if I breastfeed here?
Le dispiace se allatto il/la bimbo/a qui?
le dees·pya·che se a·la·to eel/la beem·bo/a kwee

Are children allowed?
I bambini sono ammessi?
ee bam·bee·nee so·no a·me·see

Also available from Lonely Planet:
Italian Phrasebook

Glossary

AAST – Azienda Autonoma di Soggiorno e Turismo (tourist office)
ACI – Automobile Club Italiano, the Italian automobile club
agriturismo – tourist accommodation on farms
AIG – Associazione Italiana Alberghi per la Gioventù, Italy's youth-hostel association
albergo – hotel (up to five stars)
alto – high
ambulanza – ambulance
anfiteatro – amphitheatre
apse – domed or arched semicircular recess at the altar end of a church
arco – arch
assicurato/a – insured
atrium – forecourt of a Roman house or a Christian basilica
autobus – local bus
autostazione – bus station/terminal

bancomat – ATM
basilica – in ancient Rome, a rectangular administrative building with an *apse* at the end; later, a Christian church built in the same style
benzina – petrol
benzina senza piombo – unleaded petrol
biglietteria – ticket office
biglietto – ticket
binario – platform
borgo – ancient town or village

camera – room
camera doppia – double room with twin beds
camera matrimoniale – double room with a double bed
camera singola – single room
campanile – bell tower
cappella – chapel
carabinieri – military police (see *polizia*)
Carnevale – carnival period between Epiphany and Lent
carta – menu
carta telefonica – phonecard
cartolina (postale) – postcard
castello – castle
cattedrale – cathedral
cena – evening meal
centro – centre
centro storico – literally 'historical centre'; old town
chiesa – church
chiostro – cloister; covered walkway, enclosed by columns, around a quadrangle
CIT – Compagnia Italiana di Turismo, the Italian national tourist/travel agency

colazione – breakfast
comune – equivalent to a municipality or county; town or city council
coperto – cover charge
corso – main street, avenue
cortile – courtyard
CTS – Centro Turistico Studentesco e Giovanile, the student/youth travel agency
cumbessias – pilgrims' lodgings found in courtyards around country churches traditionally the scene of annual religious festivities (of up to nine days' duration) in honour of a particular saint
cupola – dome

deposito bagagli – left luggage
digestivo – after-dinner liqueur
distributore di benzina – petrol pump (see *stazione di servizio*)
domus de janas – literally 'fairy house'; ancient tomb cut into rock
duomo – cathedral

ENIT – Ente Nazionale Italiano per il Turismo, the Italian state tourist office
enoteca – wine bar or wine shop

farmacia – pharmacy
farmacia di turno – late-night pharmacy
fassois – traditional rush fishing vessels from Oristano province
ferrovia – railway
festa – festival
fiume – (main) river
fontana – fountain
foro – forum
francobollo – postage stamp
fregola – a large couscous-like grain

golfo – gulf
grotta – cave
guardia medica – emergency doctor service

isola – island

lago – lake
largo – (small) square
lavanderia – laundrette
lido – managed section of beach
lettera – letter
lettera raccomandata – registered letter

loggia – porch; lodge
lungomare – seafront road; promenade

macchia – Mediterranean scrub
mare – sea
mattanza – literally 'slaughter'; the annual tuna catch in southwest Sardinia
mezza pensione – half board
monte – mountain, mount
municipio – town hall
muristenes – see *cumbessias*
murra – a popular game in the Barbagia region, in which participants try to guess what numbers their opponents will form with their fingers

navata centrale – nave; central part of a church
navata laterale – aisle of a church
nave – large ferry, ship
necropolis – (ancient) cemetery, burial site
nuraghe – Bronze Age stone towers and fortified settlements

oggetti smarriti – lost property
oratorio – oratory
ospedale – hospital
ostello per la gioventù – youth hostel
osteria – snack bar/cheap restaurant

palazzo – palace; a large building of any type, including an apartment block
parco – park
Pasqua – Easter
passeggiata – traditional evening stroll
pasticceria – shop selling cakes, pastries and biscuits
pensione – small hotel, often with board
pensione completa – full board
piazza – square
piazzale – (large) open square
pietà – literally 'pity or compassion'; sculpture, drawing or painting of the dead Christ supported by the Madonna
pinacoteca – art gallery
polizia – police
poltrona – literally 'armchair'; airline-type chair on a ferry
polyptych – artwork consisting of more than three panels (see *triptych*)
ponte – bridge
portico – covered walkway, usually attached to the outside of buildings
porto – port
posta aerea – air mail
pronto soccorso – first aid, casualty ward
Punic – adjective often used to mean Carthaginian (ie, the Punic Wars were those fought between Rome and Carthage)

questura – police station

rio – secondary river
riserva naturale – nature reserve
rocca – fortress

sagra – festival (usually dedicated to one culinary item, such as *funghi* (mushrooms), wine etc)
saline – saltpans
salumeria – delicatessen that sells mainly cheeses and sausage meats
santuario – sanctuary, often with a country chapel
scalette – 'little stairs' (as in Scalette di Santa Chiara, a steep stairway up into Cagliari's Il Castello district)
scavi – excavations
scheda telefonica – see *carta telefonica*
servizio – service fee
S'Istrumpa – Sardinian wrestling
spiaggia – beach
stagno – lagoon
stazione marittima – ferry terminal
stazzo/u – farmstead in the Gallura region
strada – street, road
superstrada – expressway; highway with divided lanes (but no tolls)

teatro – theatre
telegramma – telegram
tempio – temple
terme – thermal baths
tesoro – treasury
tetrastyle – four columns forming a square
tholos – name used to describe the conical shape of many *nuraghe*
tomba di gigante – literally 'giant's tomb'; ancient mass grave
tonnara – tuna-processing plant
tophet – sacred Phoenician or Carthaginian burial ground for children and babies
torre – tower
traghetto – ferry
tramezzini – sandwiches
treno – train
triptych – artwork on three panels, hinged so that the outer panels fold over the middle one (see *polyptych*)
trompe l'oeil – image designed to 'deceive the eye', creating the impression that the image is real

ufficio postale – post office
ufficio stranieri – (police) foreigners' bureau

via – street, road
via aerea – air mail
viale – avenue
vicolo – alley, alleyway

Behind the Scenes

THIS BOOK
This 2nd edition of *Sardinia* was written by Paula Hardy. The 1st edition was written by Damien Simonis. The Health chapter was adapted from material written by Dr Caroline Evans.

THANKS
PAULA HARDY
Despite all that stuff about Sardinian reserve, I met with nothing other than helpfulness and hospitality throughout my research trip. Firstly, thank you to Emma Bird from Weaveaweb, who put me in touch with a network of people around the island, and thanks also to Valeria Pintus, Sabina Morreale, Valeria Brandano and Diletta Pia, for allowing us to quote them. Thank you to David Loy and Francesca Pugno Vanoni for opening my eyes to so many gems in Oristano province. Giulia Fonnesu, thank you for all your diving tips and for being the most enthusiastic guide to Cagliari. In Cagliari thank you also to Valentino Sanna, and the crazy Andrea and Franco. In Sassari thank you to Anne Janot for being one of the island's most efficient tourist-office representatives and to Domenica Lissia in Tempio Pausania. For honey and great hospitality, thank you to Rita Denza in Olbia and Claudio Fassi in Baia Sardinia. For specialist knowledge a huge thank you to musical maestros Barnaby Brown and Gianluca Dessi, food gurus Roberto Marongiu and the ladies of Durke, and coral expert Sara Marogna.

Last, but never least, thank you to all LP readers who take the time to write in with new suggestions. A big thank you also to commissioning editors Michala Green and Tasmin McNaughtan for lots of hand-holding, and to all the production people in Melbourne who worked so hard in whipping this 2nd edition into shape.

CREDITS
This book was commissioned in Lonely Planet's London office and produced by the following:
Commissioning Editors Michala Green, Tasmin McNaughtan
Coordinating Editor Sarah Bailey
Coordinating Cartographer Csanad Csutoros
Coordinating Layout Designer Gary Newman
Managing Cartographer Mark Griffiths
Assisting Editor Liz Heynes
Proofreader Janet Austin
Cover Designer James Hardy
Project Managers Nancy Ianni, John Shippick
Language Content Coordinator Quentin Frayne
Thanks to Sally Darmody, Heather Dickson, Mark Germanchis, Korina Miller, Wayne Murphy, Wibowo Rusli, Jacqui Saunders, Celia Wood

OUR READERS
Many thanks to the travellers who used the last edition and wrote to us with helpful hints, useful advice and interesting anecdotes:
Janette Ackroyd, P Bokanowski, Joan Brown, Leigh Campbell, Marion Dunn, Elena Frazzoni, Guido & Chiara Gossi, Diedre Riordan Holmberg, Noora Kainulainen, Kai Klinge, Karen Lakeman, Ugo Masala, Goerge McKenna, Tim Meddings, Sarah Nortcliffe, Brigida Paulucci, Ute Ramseger, Mary Richards, Victor Ruskin, Romana Salaris, Hanna Schwarz, Andrew Skinner, Lynda Smith, Andrew Szusterman, Paul Twarog, Urs Wiss

---

THE LONELY PLANET STORY

The story begins with a classic travel adventure: Tony and Maureen Wheeler's 1972 journey across Europe and Asia to Australia. There was no useful information about the overland trail then, so Tony and Maureen published the first Lonely Planet guidebook to meet a growing need.

From a kitchen table, Lonely Planet has grown to become the largest independent travel publisher in the world, with offices in Melbourne (Australia), Oakland (USA) and London (UK). Today Lonely Planet guidebooks cover the globe. There is an ever-growing list of books and information in a variety of media. Some things haven't changed. The main aim is still to make it possible for adventurous travellers to get out there – to explore and better understand the world.

At Lonely Planet we believe travellers can make a positive contribution to the countries they visit – if they respect their host communities and spend their money wisely. Every year 5% of company profit is donated to charities around the world.

SEND US YOUR FEEDBACK

We love to hear from travellers – your comments keep us on our toes and help make our books better. Our well-travelled team reads every word on what you loved or loathed about this book. Although we cannot reply individually to postal submissions, we always guarantee that your feedback goes straight to the appropriate authors, in time for the next edition. Each person who sends us information is thanked in the next edition – and the most useful submissions are rewarded with a free book. See the Behind the Scenes section.

To send us your updates – and find out about Lonely Planet events, newsletters and travel news – visit our award-winning website: **www.lonelyplanet.com/feedback**.

Note: We may edit, reproduce and incorporate your comments in Lonely Planet products such as guidebooks, websites and digital products, so let us know if you don't want your comments reproduced or your name acknowledged. For a copy of our privacy policy, go to www.lonelyplanet .com/privacy.

Index

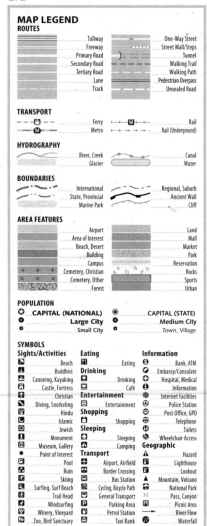

MAP LEGEND
ROUTES

Tollway	One-Way Street
Freeway	Street Mall/Steps
Primary Road	Tunnel
Secondary Road	Walking Trail
Tertiary Road	Walking Path
Lane	Pedestrian Overpass
Track	Unsealed Road

TRANSPORT

Ferry	Rail
Metro	Rail (Underground)

HYDROGRAPHY

River, Creek	Canal
Glacier	Water

BOUNDARIES

International	Regional, Suburb
State, Provincial	Ancient Wall
Marine Park	Cliff

AREA FEATURES

Airport	Land
Area of Interest	Mall
Beach, Desert	Market
Building	Park
Campus	Reservation
Cemetery, Christian	Rocks
Cemetery, Other	Sports
Forest	Urban

POPULATION

CAPITAL (NATIONAL)	CAPITAL (STATE)
Large City	Medium City
Small City	Town, Village

SYMBOLS

Sights/Activities
- Beach
- Buddhist
- Canoeing, Kayaking
- Castle, Fortress
- Christian
- Diving, Snorkeling
- Hindu
- Islamic
- Jewish
- Monument
- Museum, Gallery
- Point of Interest
- Pool
- Ruin
- Skiing
- Surfing, Surf Beach
- Trail Head
- Windsurfing
- Winery, Vineyard
- Zoo, Bird Sanctuary

Eating
- Eating

Drinking
- Drinking
- Café

Entertainment
- Entertainment

Shopping
- Shopping

Sleeping
- Sleeping
- Camping

Transport
- Airport, Airfield
- Border Crossing
- Bus Station
- Cycling, Bicycle Path
- General Transport
- Parking Area
- Petrol Station
- Taxi Rank

Information
- Bank, ATM
- Embassy/Consulate
- Hospital, Medical
- Information
- Internet Facilities
- Police Station
- Post Office, GPO
- Telephone
- Toilets
- Wheelchair Access

Geographic
- Hazard
- Lighthouse
- Lookout
- Mountain, Volcano
- National Park
- Pass, Canyon
- Picnic Area
- River Flow
- Waterfall

LONELY PLANET OFFICES

Australia
Head Office
Locked Bag 1, Footscray, Victoria 3011
☎ 03 8379 8000, fax 03 8379 8111
talk2us@lonelyplanet.com.au

USA
150 Linden St, Oakland, CA 94607
☎ 510 893 8555, toll free 800 275 8555
fax 510 893 8572
info@lonelyplanet.com

UK
72–82 Rosebery Ave,
Clerkenwell, London EC1R 4RW
☎ 020 7841 9000, fax 020 7841 9001
go@lonelyplanet.co.uk

Published by Lonely Planet Publications Pty Ltd
ABN 36 005 607 983

2nd Edition – May 2006

First Published – June 2003

© Lonely Planet Publications Pty Ltd 2006

© photographers as indicated 2006

Cover photographs: Man diving from rocks, Look GMBH/eStock Photo (front); Boat in waters of Cala de Mariolu, Golfo di Orosei, Damien Simonis/Lonely Planet Images (back). Many of the images in this guide are available for licensing from Lonely Planet Images: www .lonelyplanetimages.com.

Printed through Colorcraft Ltd, Hong Kong.
Printed in China.